高 橋 和 希

I BELIEVE THAT EVERYONE HAS AN "OTHER SELF" INSIDE THEM.
IT MAY BE YOUR IDEAL SELF, SOMEONE WHO IT'S YOUR GOAL TO
BECOME. BUT WHEN YOU'RE PRESSURED TO BE A CERTAIN WAY
BY THE EXPECTATIONS OF YOUR PARENTS OR THE WORLD, THE
BURDEN MAY BE TOO MUCH TO BEAR, AND YOU MAY LOSE SIGHT
OF YOURSELF. IN OTHER WORDS, YOUR "OTHER SELF" IS SOME-
THING YOU YOURSELF HAVE TO CREATE, NOT THAT OTHER PEO-
PLE CAN FORCE UPON YOU. I THINK IT'S BEST TO TAKE IT EASY,
KEEP AN EYE ON YOUR "OTHER SELF," AND AIM FOR THAT
GOAL...BUT DON'T STRESS OUT ABOUT REACHING IT RIGHT AWAY.

—KAZUKI TAKAHASHI, 1998

Artist/author Kazuki Takahashi first tried to break into
the manga business in 1982, but success eluded him
until **Yu-Gi-Oh!** debuted in the Japanese **Weekly
Shonen Jump** magazine in 1996. **Yu-Gi-Oh!**'s themes
of friendship and fighting, together with Takahashi's
weird and wonderful art, soon became enormously
successful, spawning a real-world card game, video
games, and two anime series. A lifelong gamer,
Takahashi enjoys Shogi (Japanese chess), Mahjong,
card games, and tabletop RPGs, among other games.

YU-GI-OH!: DUELIST VOL. 2
The SHONEN JUMP Graphic Novel Edition

STORY AND ART BY
KAZUKI TAKAHASHI

Translation & English Adaptation/Joe Yamazaki
Touch-up Art & Lettering/Rina Mapa
Design/Sean Lee
Editor/Jason Thompson

Managing Editor/Elizabeth Kawasaki
Director of Production/Noboru Watanabe
Editorial Director/Alvin Lu
Executive Vice President & Editor in Chief/Hyoe Narita
Sr. Director of Acquisitions/Rika Inouye
Vice President of Sales & Marketing/Liza Coppola
Vice President of Strategic Development/Yumi Hoashi
Publisher/Seiji Horibuchi

YU-GI-OH! © 1996 by KAZUKI TAKAHASHI. All rights reserved. First published in Japan in 1996 by SHUEISHA Inc., Tokyo. English translation rights in the United States of America and Canada arranged by SHUEISHA Inc. The stories, characters and incidents mentioned in this publication are entirely fictional.

In the original J~~apanese edition, YU-GI-OH! and YU-G~~I-OH!: DUELIST are known collect~~ively as YU-GI-OH! YU-GI-~~OH!: DUELIST was origin~~ally volumes 8-31 of the original~~ Y-GI-OH!.

Printed in the U.S.A.

Published by VIZ, LLC
P.O. Box 77010
San Francisco, CA 94107

SHONEN JUMP Graphic Novel Edition
10 9 8 7 6 5 4 3 2 1
First printing, February 2005

PARENTAL ADVISORY
YU-GI-OH! is rated T for Teen. It contains fantasy violence. It is recommended for ages 13 and up.

THE WORLD'S
MOST POPULAR MANGA
SHONEN JUMP
GRAPHIC NOVEL
www.shonenjump.com

www.viz.com

SHONEN JUMP GRAPHIC NOVEL

Vol. 2
THE PUPPET MASTER

STORY AND ART BY
KAZUKI TAKAHASHI

《MAIN CAST》

THE STORY SO FAR...

When 10th grader Yugi solved the Millennium Puzzle, he became Yu-Gi-Oh, the King of Games, a dark avenger who challenged evildoers to "Shadow Games" of life and death. But Yugi isn't the only gamer with a strange powers. Maximillion Pegasus, creator of the world's No. 1 collectible card game, challenged Yugi to enter a "Duel Monsters" tournament on his private island, Duelist Kingdom. Can Yugi and Jonouchi fight their way through dozens of duelists to win the grand prize...and discover the secret of the Millennium Items?

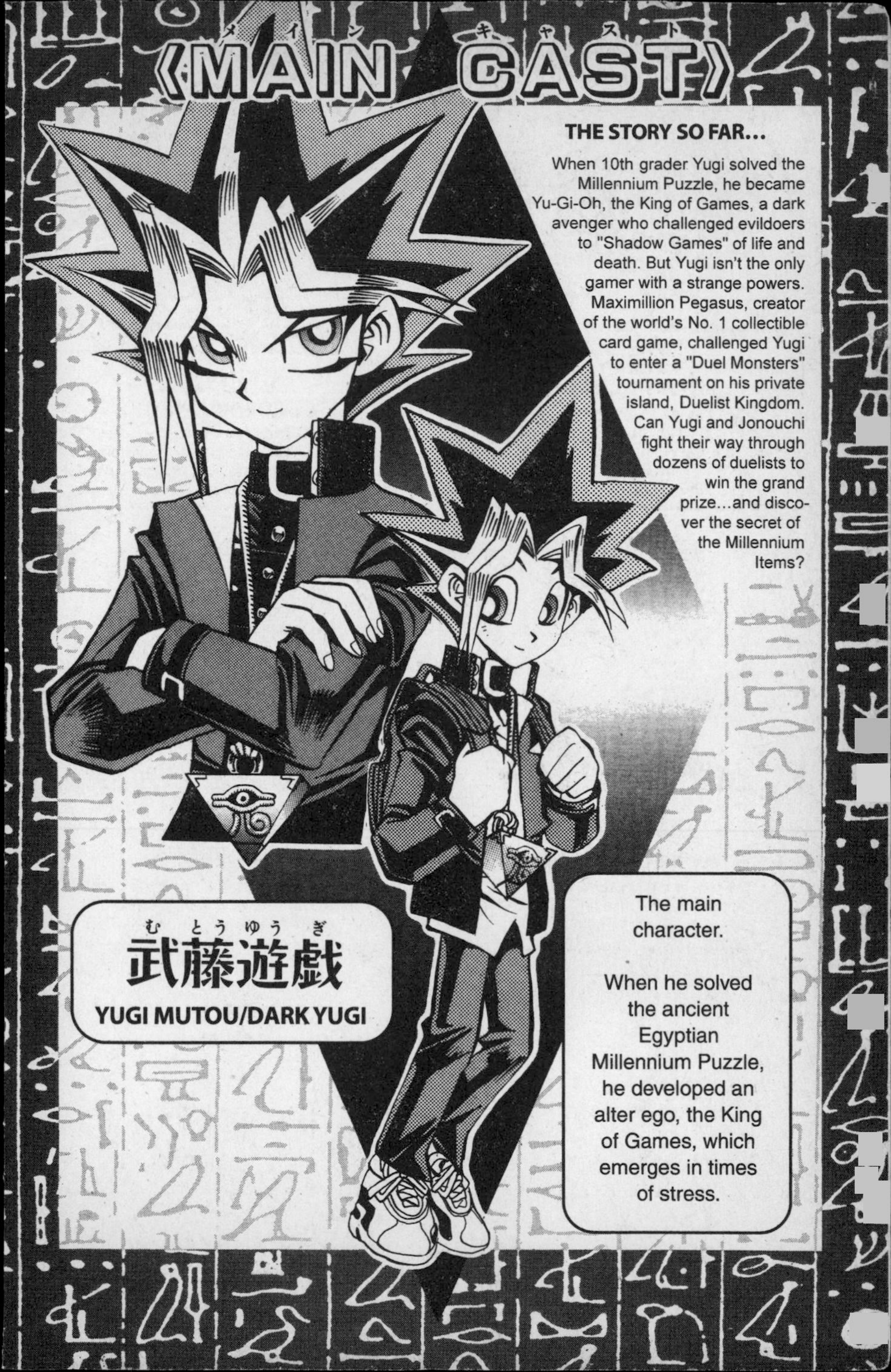

武藤遊戯

YUGI MUTOU/DARK YUGI

The main character.

When he solved the ancient Egyptian Millennium Puzzle, he developed an alter ego, the King of Games, which emerges in times of stress.

武藤双六 (むとうすごろく)

SUGOROKU MUTOU

Yugi's grandfather, the owner of the Kame ("Turtle") game store. To force Yugi to enter his tournament, Pegasus imprisoned Sugoroku's soul inside a videotape, leaving his body in a coma.

城之内克也 (じょうのうちかつや)

KATSUYA JONOUCHI

Yugi's classmate, a tough guy who's still a novice at "Duel Monsters." He wants to use the tournament prize money to pay for his sister's eye surgery. In the English anime he's known as "Joey Wheeler."

真崎杏子 (まざきあんず)

ANZU MAZAKI

Yugi's classmate and childhood friend. Her first name means "Peach." In the English anime she's known as "Téa Gardner."

本田ヒロト (ほんだ)

HIROTO HONDA

Yugi's classmate, a friend of Jonouchi. In the English anime he's known as "Tristan Taylor."

ペガサス・J・クロフォード (ジェイ)

MAXIMILLION J. PEGASUS

The American game designer who created "Duel Monsters." His Millennium Eye gives him the power to read people's minds. In the original Japanese manga he's called "Pegasus J. Crawford."

獏良 了 (ばくら りょう)

RYO BAKURA

Like Yugi and Pegasus, Bakura owns a Millennium Item: the Millennium Ring. Unfortunately for him, it's possessed by an evil spirit.

Yu-Gi-Oh! Duelist

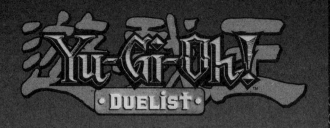

Vol. 2

CONTENTS

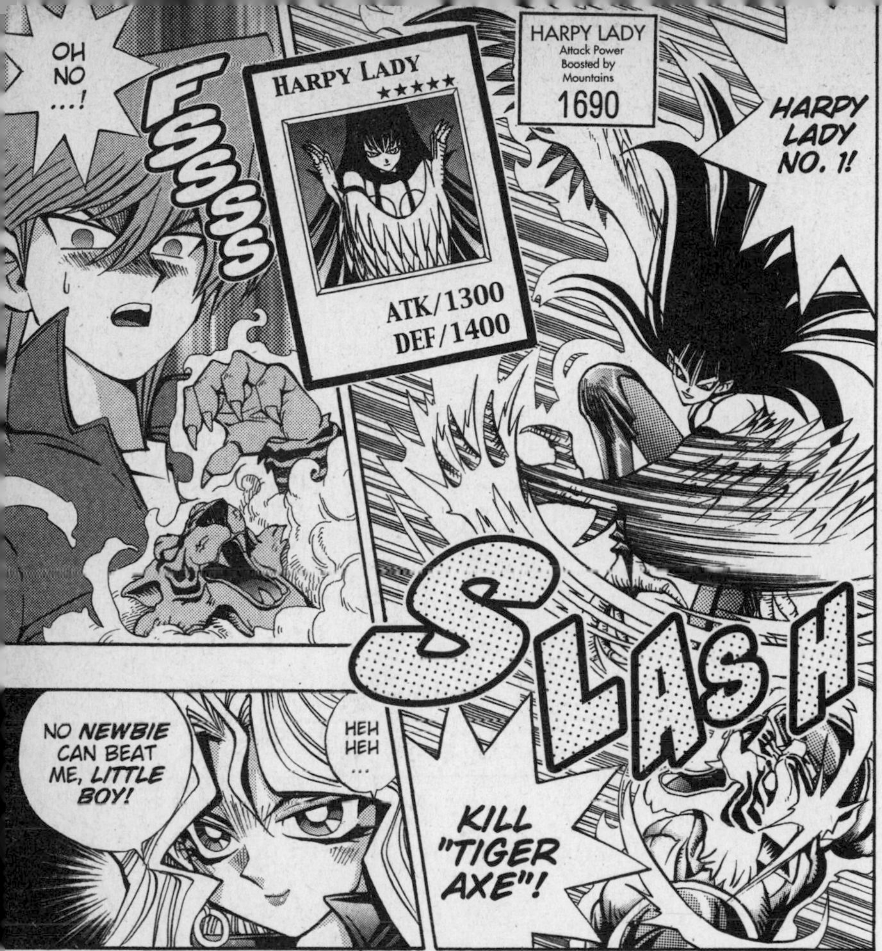
HARPY LADY
Attack Power Boosted by Mountains
1690
HARPY LADY NO. 1!
SLASH
KILL "TIGER AXE"!
OH NO ...!
FSSSS
HARPY LADY ★★★★★
ATK/1300
DEF/1400
HEH HEH ...
NO NEWBIE CAN BEAT ME, LITTLE BOY!

DUEL 11: THINGS THAT DON'T CHANGE

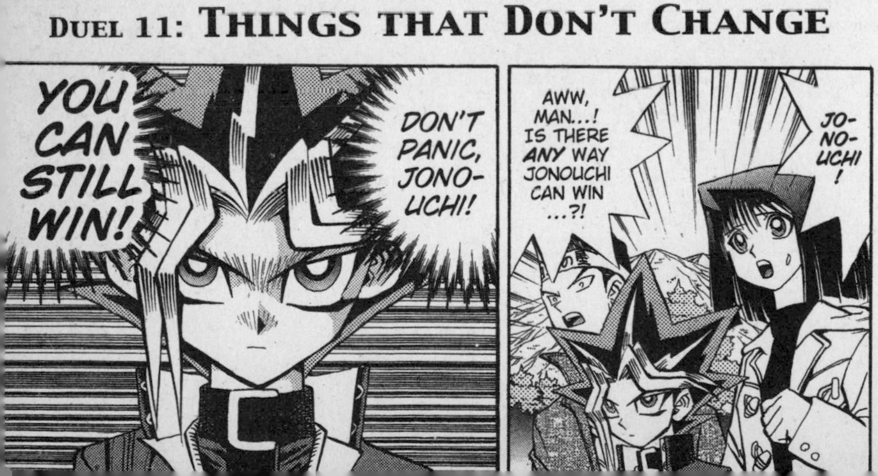
JONOUCHI!
AWW, MAN...! IS THERE ANY WAY JONOUCHI CAN WIN ...?!
DON'T PANIC, JONOUCHI!
YOU CAN STILL WIN!

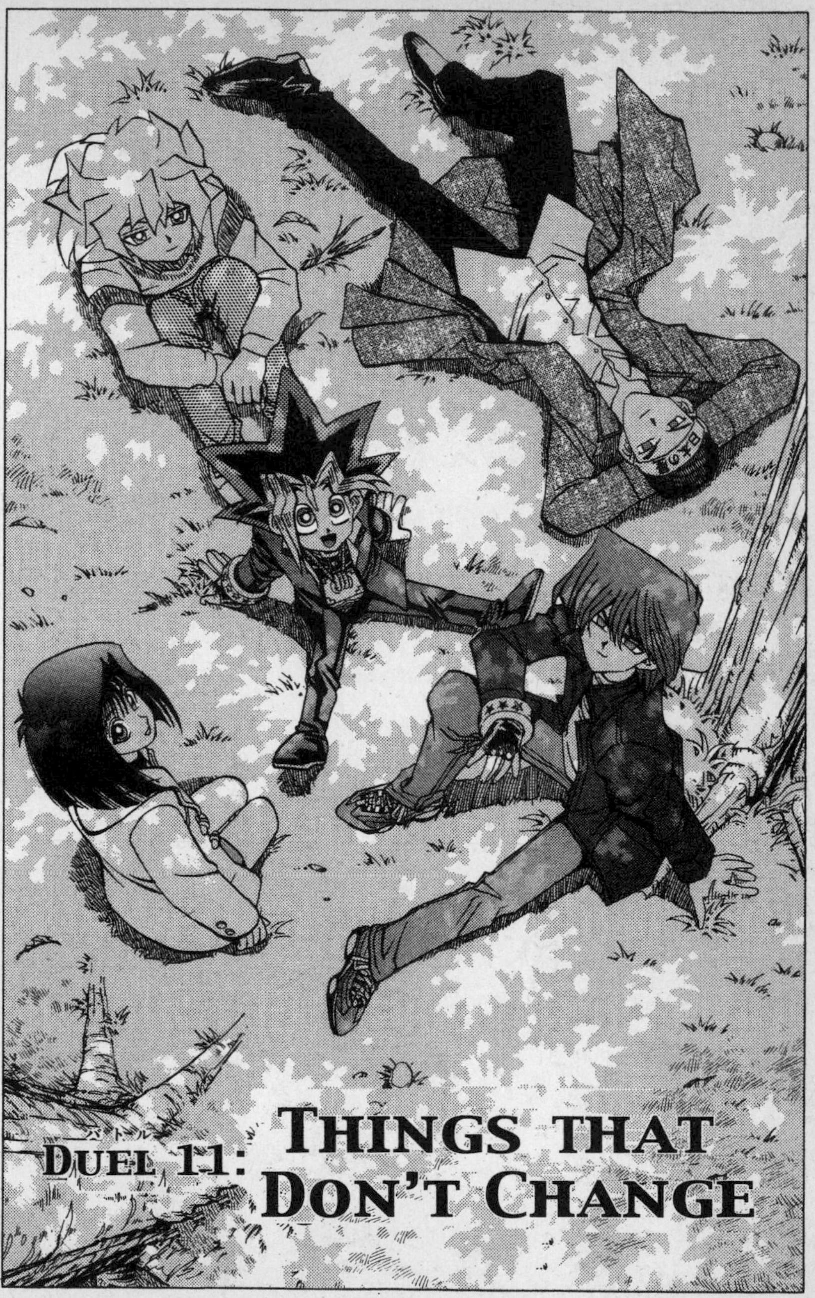
バトル
Duel 11: Things that Don't Change

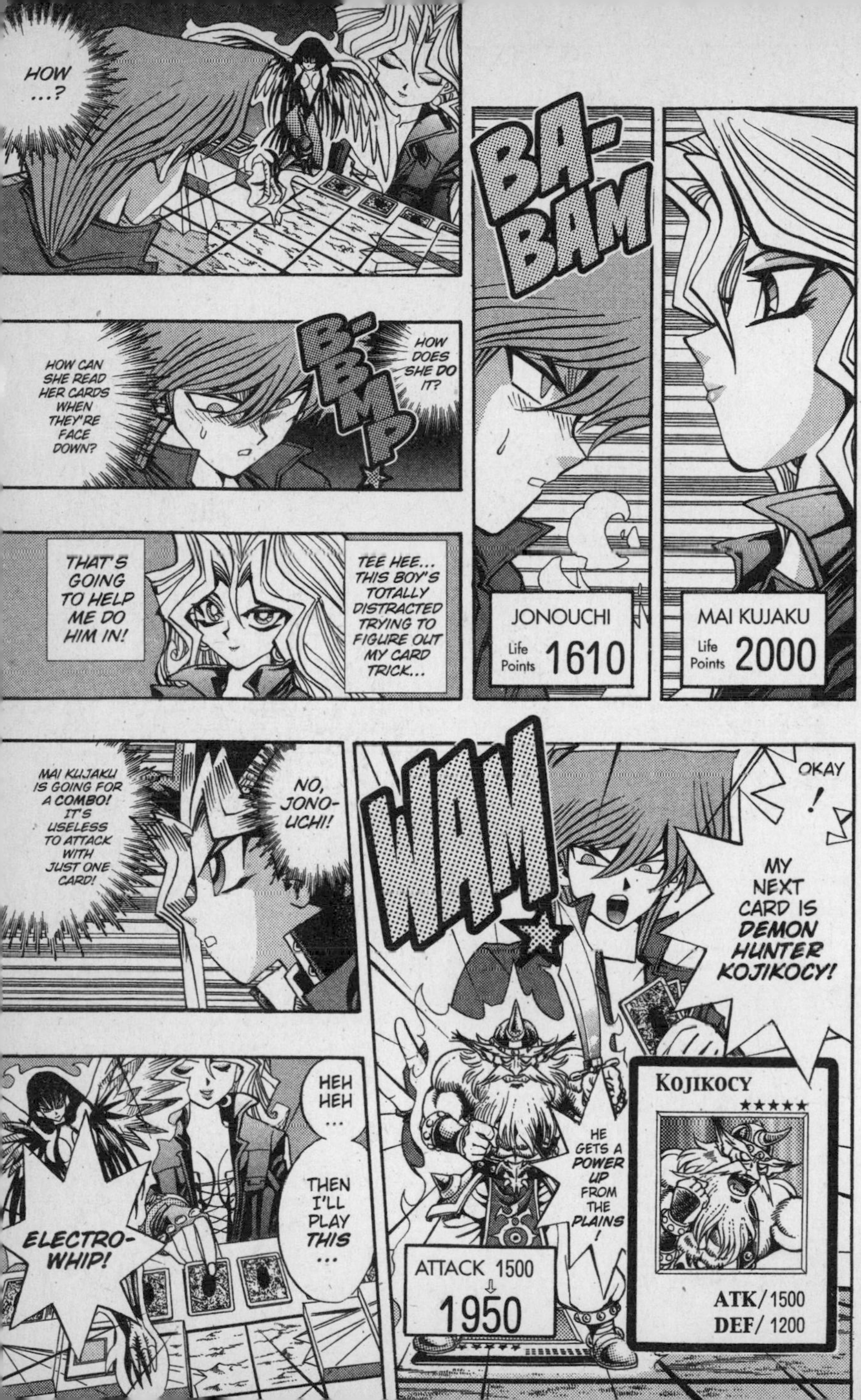
MAI KUJAKU
Life Points 2000
BA-BAM
JONOUCHI
Life Points 1610
HOW ...?
HOW DOES SHE DO IT?
B-BUMP
HOW CAN SHE READ HER CARDS WHEN THEY'RE FACE DOWN?
TEE HEE... THIS BOY'S TOTALLY DISTRACTED TRYING TO FIGURE OUT MY CARD TRICK...
THAT'S GOING TO HELP ME DO HIM IN!
OKAY!
MY NEXT CARD IS DEMON HUNTER KOJIKOCY!
WAM
KOJIKOCY
ATK/1500
DEF/1200
HE GETS A POWER UP FROM THE PLAINS!
ATTACK 1500
↓
1950
NO, JONOUCHI!
MAI KUJAKU IS GOING FOR A COMBO! IT'S USELESS TO ATTACK WITH JUST ONE CARD!
HEH HEH ...
THEN I'LL PLAY THIS ...
ELECTRO-WHIP!

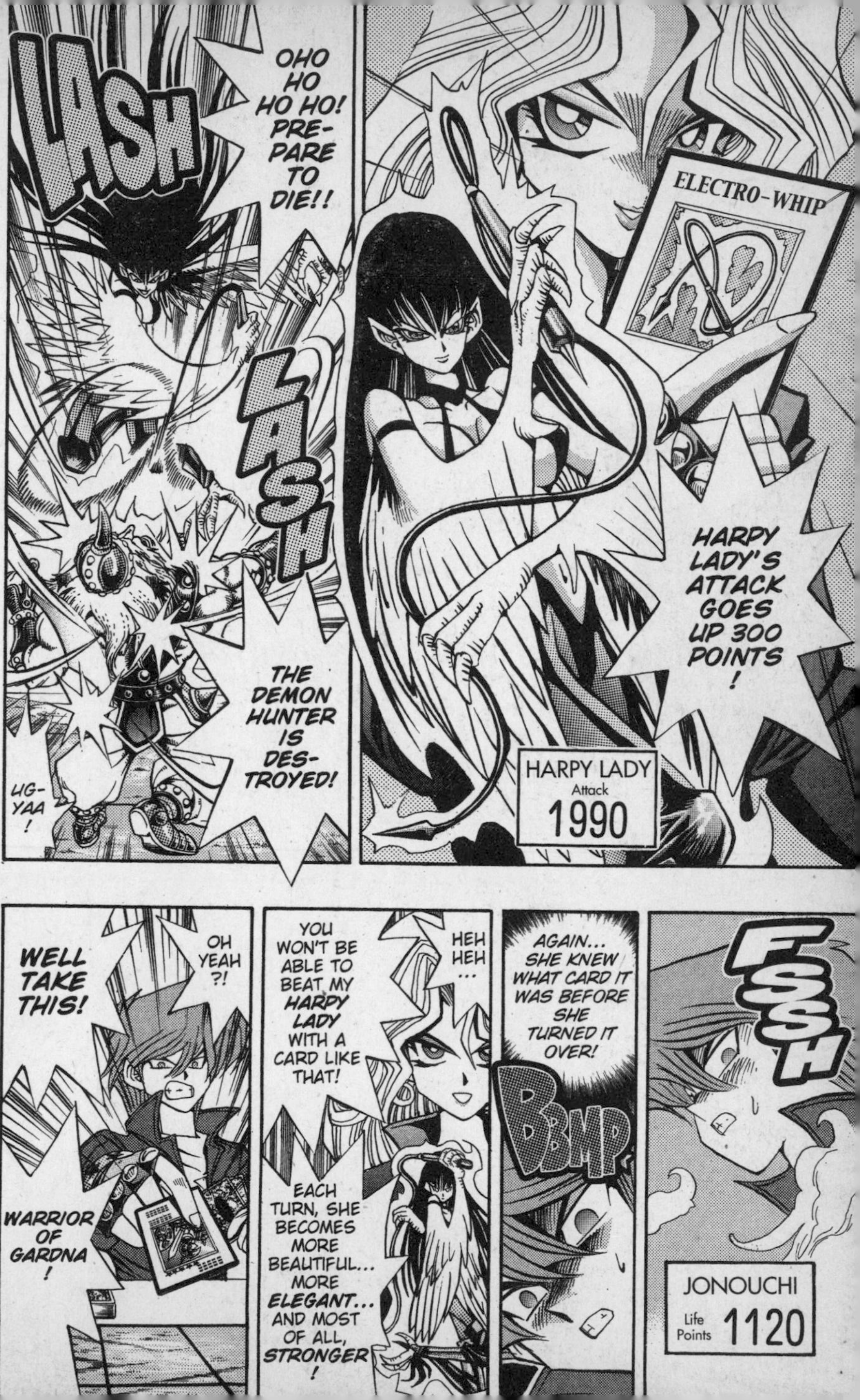
ELECTRO-WHIP
HARPY LADY'S ATTACK GOES UP 300 POINTS!
HARPY LADY Attack 1990
OHO HO HO HO! PRE-PARE TO DIE!!
LASH
LASH
THE DEMON HUNTER IS DES-TROYED!
UG-YAA!
FSSH
JONOUCHI Life Points 1120
AGAIN... SHE KNEW WHAT CARD IT WAS BEFORE SHE TURNED IT OVER!
BBMP
HEH HEH ...
YOU WON'T BE ABLE TO BEAT MY *HARPY LADY* WITH A CARD LIKE THAT!
EACH TURN, SHE BECOMES MORE BEAUTIFUL... MORE *ELEGANT*... AND MOST OF ALL, *STRONGER*!
OH YEAH ?!
WELL TAKE THIS!
WARRIOR OF GARDNA!

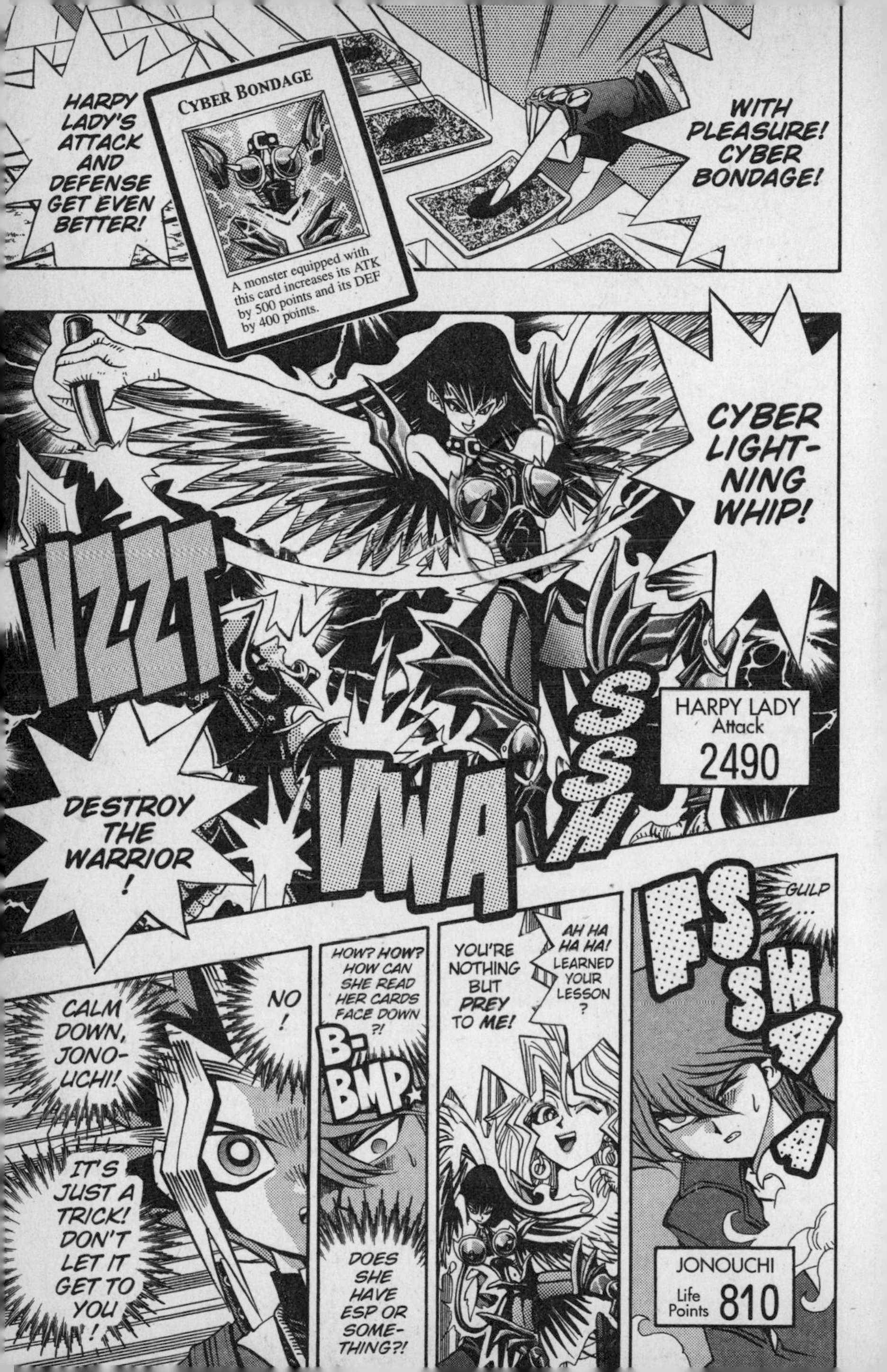
WITH PLEASURE! CYBER BONDAGE!
CYBER BONDAGE
A monster equipped with this card increases its ATK by 500 points and its DEF by 400 points.
HARPY LADY'S ATTACK AND DEFENSE GET EVEN BETTER!
CYBER LIGHTNING WHIP!
VZZT
HARPY LADY Attack 2490
SSH
VWA
DESTROY THE WARRIOR!
GULP...
FSSH
JONOUCHI Life Points 810
AH HA HA HA! LEARNED YOUR LESSON?
YOU'RE NOTHING BUT PREY TO ME!
HOW? HOW? HOW CAN SHE READ HER CARDS FACE DOWN?!
B-BMP
DOES SHE HAVE ESP OR SOMETHING?!
NO!
CALM DOWN, JONOUCHI!
IT'S JUST A TRICK! DON'T LET IT GET TO YOU!

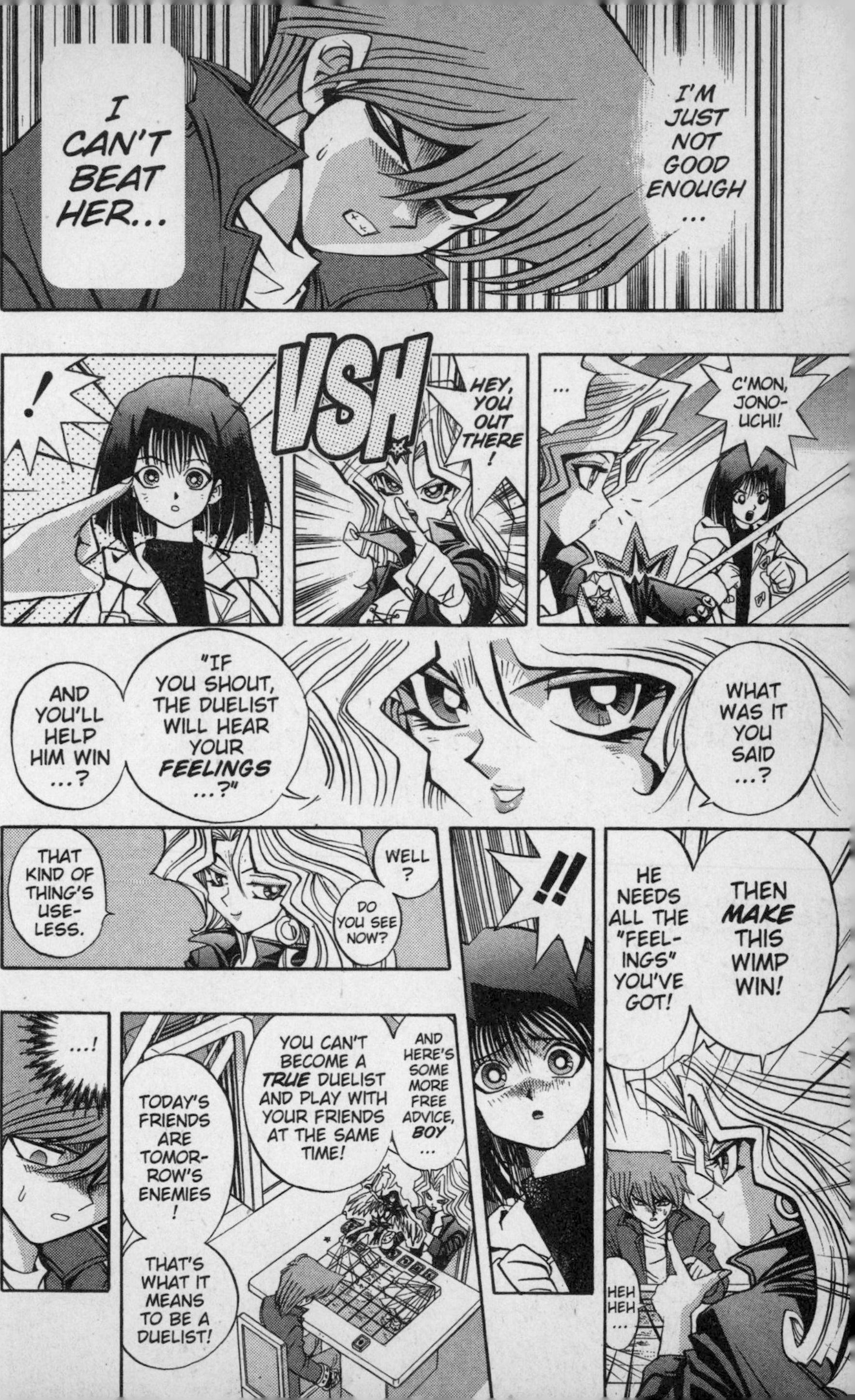
I'M JUST NOT GOOD ENOUGH ...
I CAN'T BEAT HER...
C'MON, JONO-UCHI!
...
HEY, YOU OUT THERE!
VSH
!
WHAT WAS IT YOU SAID ...?
"IF YOU SHOUT, THE DUELIST WILL HEAR YOUR FEELINGS ...?"
AND YOU'LL HELP HIM WIN ...?
THEN MAKE THIS WIMP WIN!
HE NEEDS ALL THE "FEEL-INGS" YOU'VE GOT!
HEH HEH ...
!!
WELL?
DO YOU SEE NOW?
THAT KIND OF THING'S USE-LESS.
AND HERE'S SOME MORE FREE ADVICE, BOY ...
YOU CAN'T BECOME A TRUE DUELIST AND PLAY WITH YOUR FRIENDS AT THE SAME TIME!
TODAY'S FRIENDS ARE TOMOR-ROW'S ENEMIES!
THAT'S WHAT IT MEANS TO BE A DUELIST!
...!

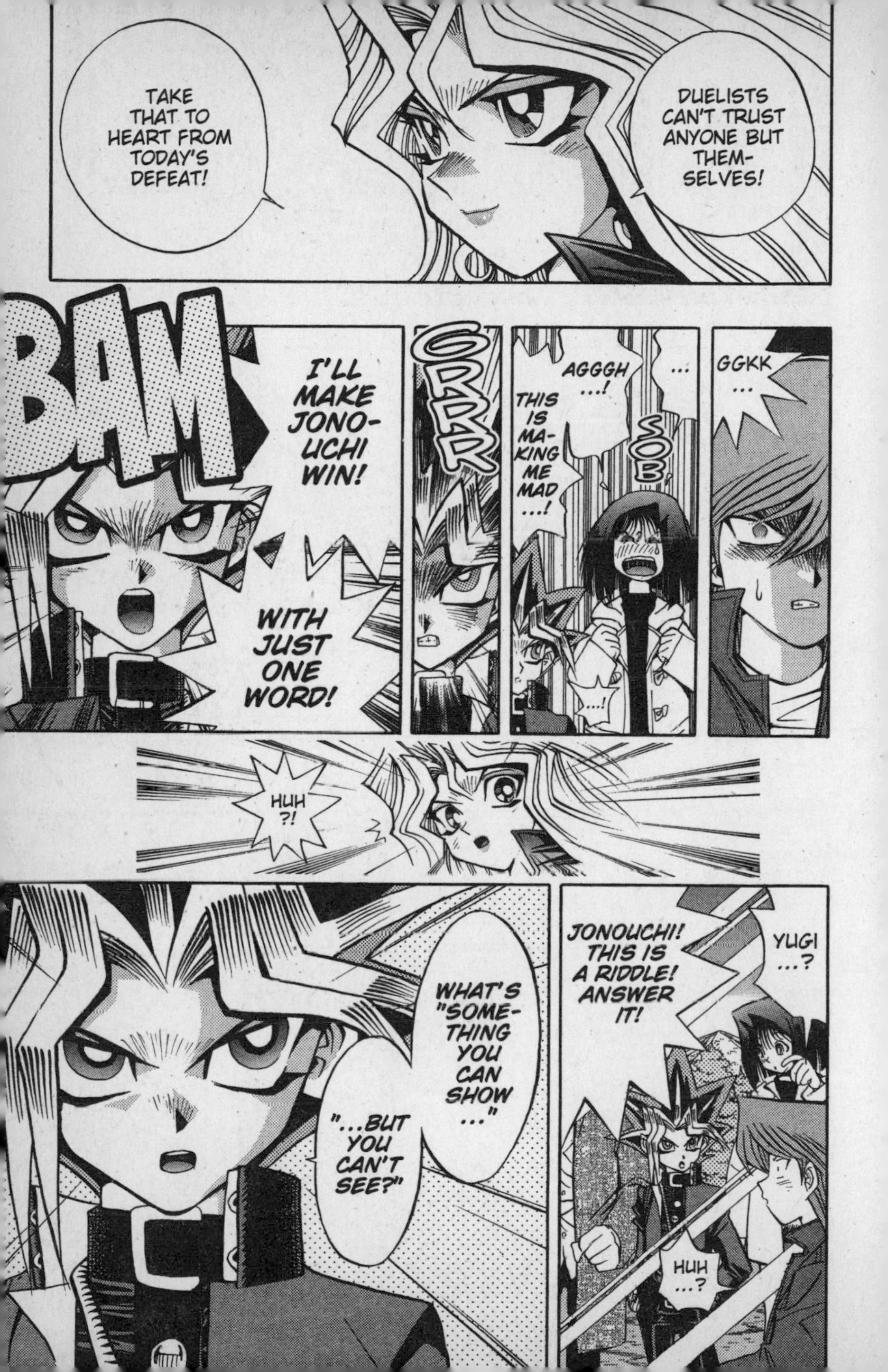
DUELISTS CAN'T TRUST ANYONE BUT THEM-SELVES!
TAKE THAT TO HEART FROM TODAY'S DEFEAT!
GGKK ...
...
AGGGH ...!
THIS IS MA-KING ME MAD ...!
SOB
...!
GRRR
BAM
I'LL MAKE JONO-UCHI WIN!
WITH JUST ONE WORD!
HUH ?!
YUGI ...?
JONOUCHI! THIS IS A RIDDLE! ANSWER IT!
HUH ...?
WHAT'S "SOME-THING YOU CAN SHOW ..."
"...BUT YOU CAN'T SEE?"

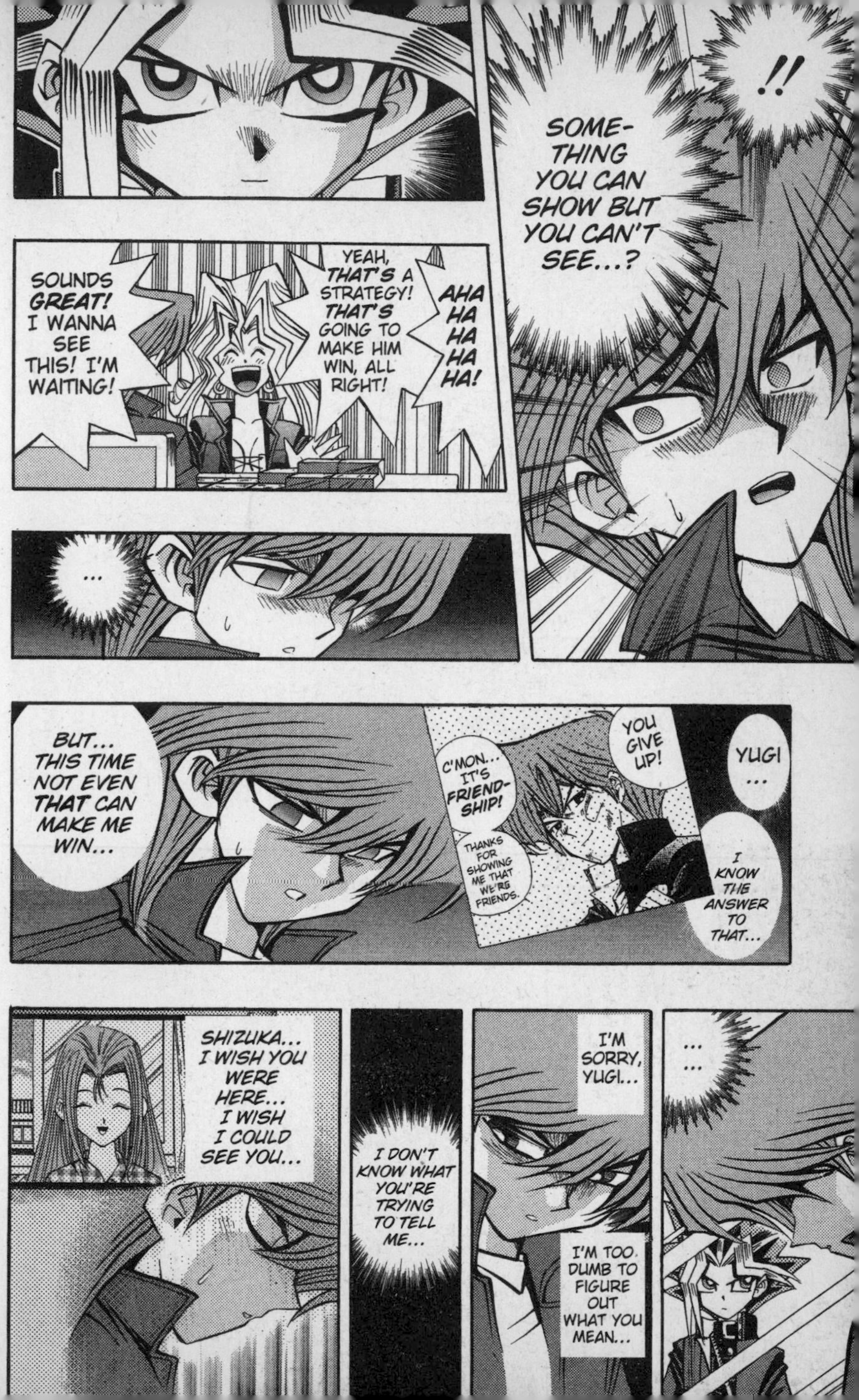
!!
SOME-THING YOU CAN SHOW BUT YOU CAN'T SEE...?
AHA HA HA HA HA!
YEAH, THAT'S A STRATEGY! THAT'S GOING TO MAKE HIM WIN, ALL RIGHT!
SOUNDS GREAT! I WANNA SEE THIS! I'M WAITING!
...
YUGI...
I KNOW THE ANSWER TO THAT...
YOU GIVE UP!
C'MON... IT'S FRIENDSHIP!
THANKS FOR SHOWING ME THAT WE'RE FRIENDS.
BUT... THIS TIME NOT EVEN THAT CAN MAKE ME WIN...
... ...
I'M SORRY, YUGI...
I'M TOO DUMB TO FIGURE OUT WHAT YOU MEAN...
I DON'T KNOW WHAT YOU'RE TRYING TO TELL ME...
SHIZUKA... I WISH YOU WERE HERE... I WISH I COULD SEE YOU...

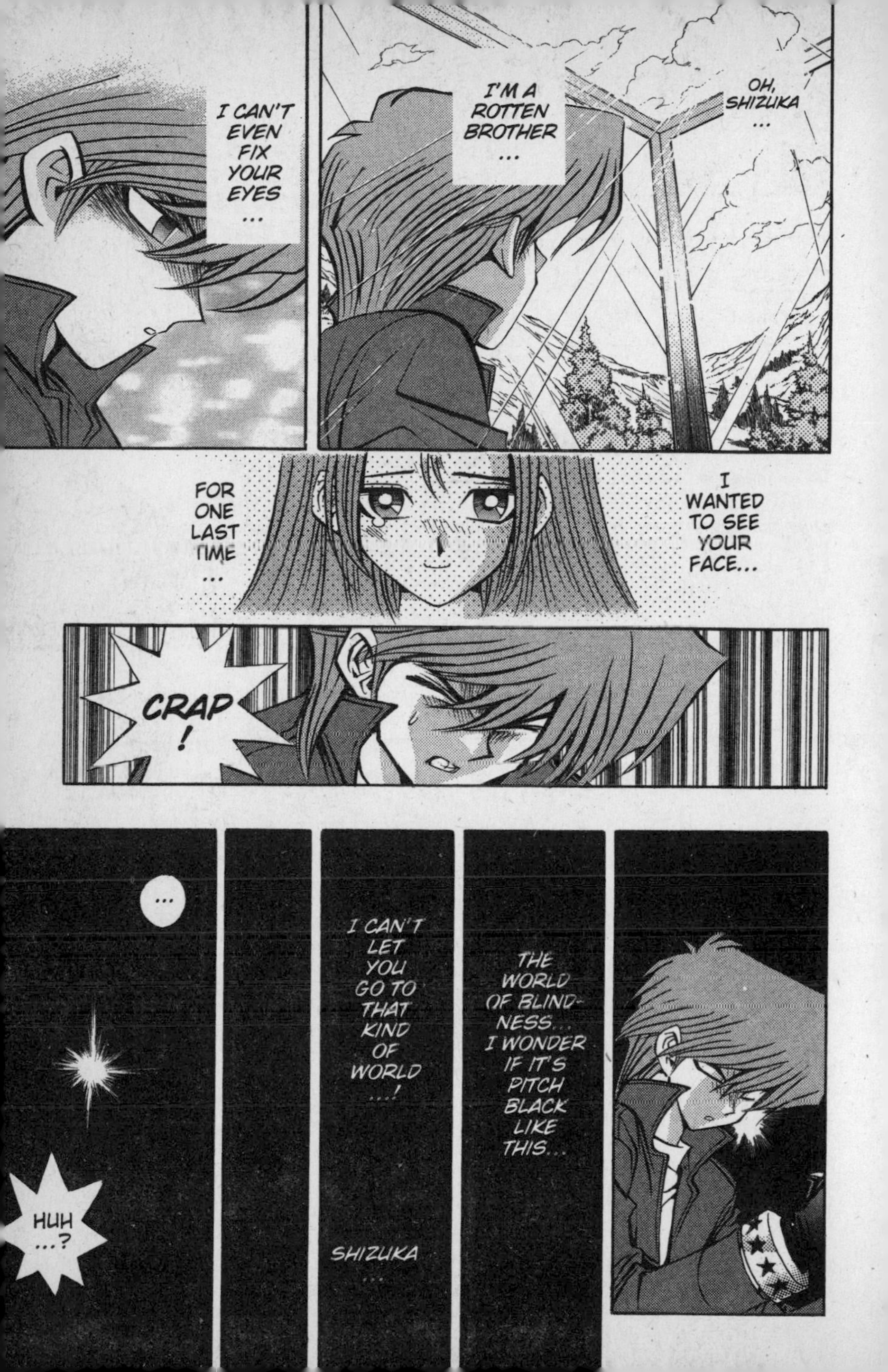
OH, SHIZUKA ...
I'M A ROTTEN BROTHER ...
I CAN'T EVEN FIX YOUR EYES ...
I WANTED TO SEE YOUR FACE...
FOR ONE LAST TIME ...
CRAP!
THE WORLD OF BLINDNESS... I WONDER IF IT'S PITCH BLACK LIKE THIS...
I CAN'T LET YOU GO TO THAT KIND OF WORLD ...!
SHIZUKA ...
...
HUH ...?

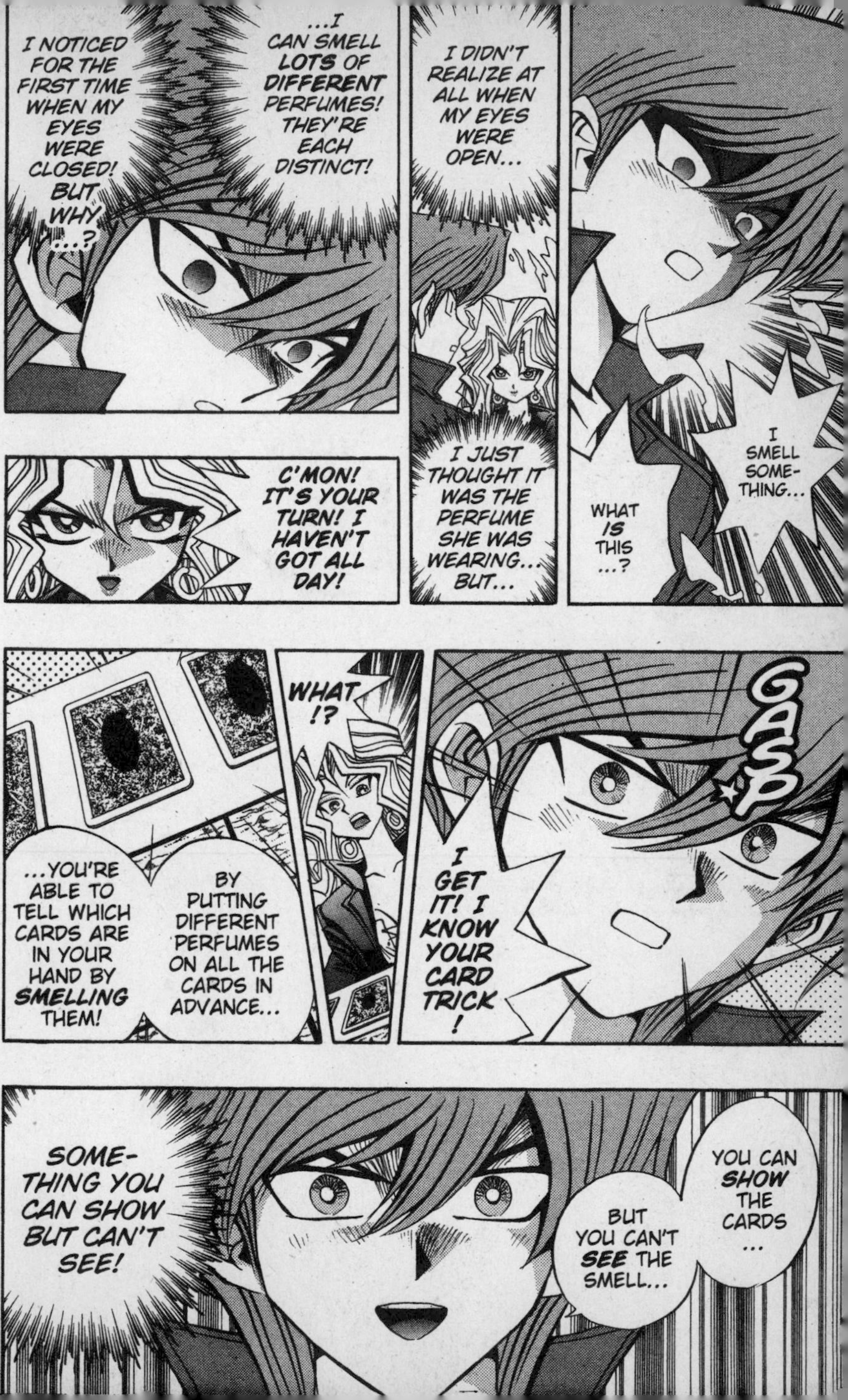
I SMELL SOMETHING...
WHAT IS THIS ...?
I DIDN'T REALIZE AT ALL WHEN MY EYES WERE OPEN...
I JUST THOUGHT IT WAS THE PERFUME SHE WAS WEARING... BUT...
...I CAN SMELL LOTS OF DIFFERENT PERFUMES! THEY'RE EACH DISTINCT!
I NOTICED FOR THE FIRST TIME WHEN MY EYES WERE CLOSED! BUT WHY...?
C'MON! IT'S YOUR TURN! I HAVEN'T GOT ALL DAY!
GASP
I GET IT! I KNOW YOUR CARD TRICK!
WHAT!?
BY PUTTING DIFFERENT PERFUMES ON ALL THE CARDS IN ADVANCE...
...YOU'RE ABLE TO TELL WHICH CARDS ARE IN YOUR HAND BY SMELLING THEM!
YOU CAN SHOW THE CARDS...
BUT YOU CAN'T SEE THE SMELL...
SOMETHING YOU CAN SHOW BUT CAN'T SEE!

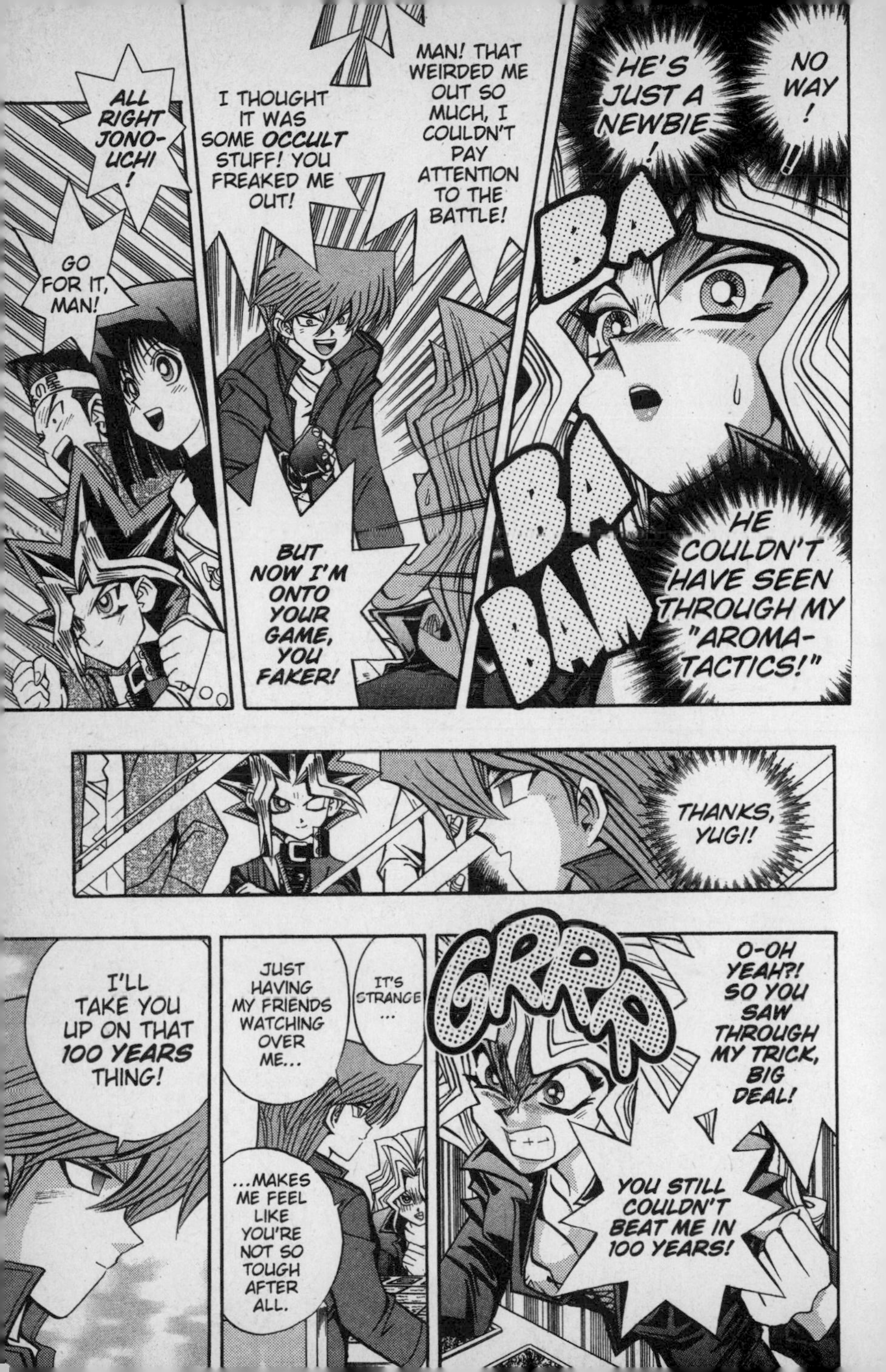
NO WAY!
HE'S JUST A NEWBIE!
BA BA BAM
HE COULDN'T HAVE SEEN THROUGH MY "AROMA-TACTICS!"
MAN! THAT WEIRDED ME OUT SO MUCH, I COULDN'T PAY ATTENTION TO THE BATTLE!
I THOUGHT IT WAS SOME OCCULT STUFF! YOU FREAKED ME OUT!
BUT NOW I'M ONTO YOUR GAME, YOU FAKER!
ALL RIGHT JONO-UCHI!
GO FOR IT, MAN!
THANKS, YUGI!
GRRR
O-OH YEAH?! SO YOU SAW THROUGH MY TRICK, BIG DEAL!
YOU STILL COULDN'T BEAT ME IN 100 YEARS!
IT'S STRANGE...
JUST HAVING MY FRIENDS WATCHING OVER ME...
...MAKES ME FEEL LIKE YOU'RE NOT SO TOUGH AFTER ALL.
I'LL TAKE YOU UP ON THAT 100 YEARS THING!

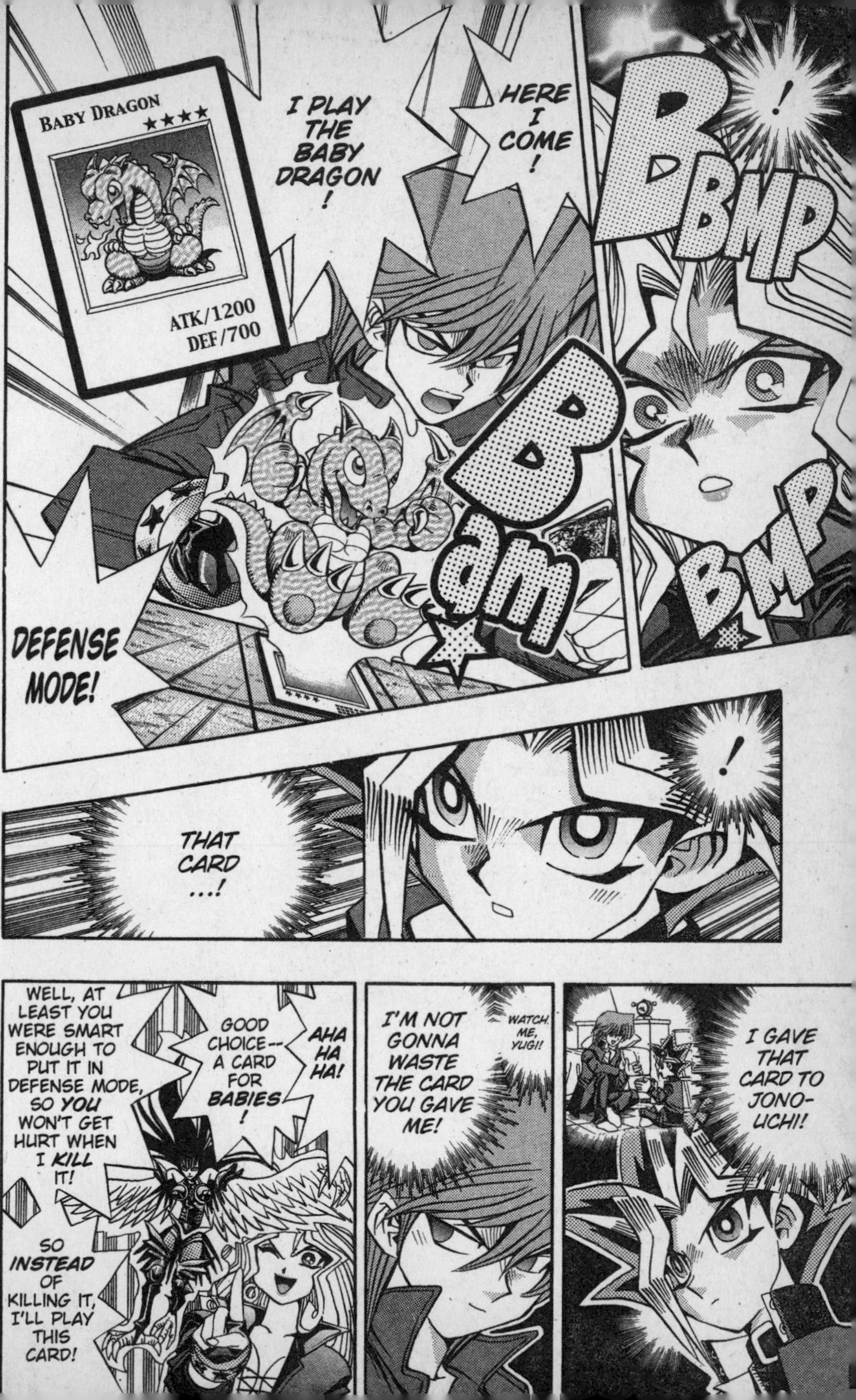

BBMP
!
HERE I COME!
I PLAY THE BABY DRAGON!
BABY DRAGON ★★★★
ATK/1200 DEF/700
BMP BMP
Bam
DEFENSE MODE!
!
THAT CARD ...!
WATCH ME, YUGI!
I GAVE THAT CARD TO JONO-UCHI!
I'M NOT GONNA WASTE THE CARD YOU GAVE ME!
AHA HA HA!
GOOD CHOICE-- A CARD FOR BABIES!
WELL, AT LEAST YOU WERE SMART ENOUGH TO PUT IT IN DEFENSE MODE, SO YOU WON'T GET HURT WHEN I KILL IT!
SO INSTEAD OF KILLING IT, I'LL PLAY THIS CARD!

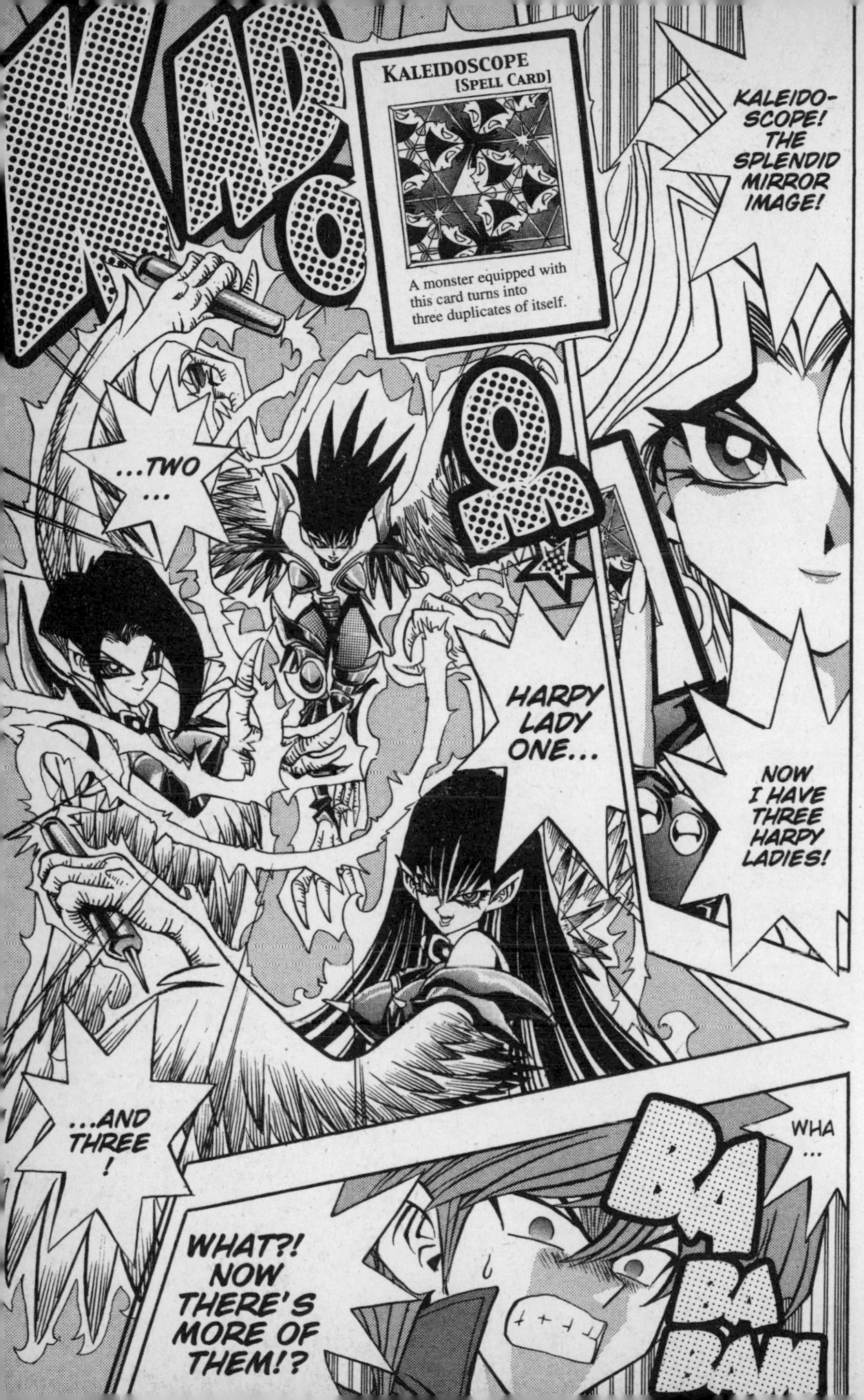
KALEIDO-SCOPE! THE SPLENDID MIRROR IMAGE!
KALEIDOSCOPE
[SPELL CARD]
A monster equipped with this card turns into three duplicates of itself.
NOW I HAVE THREE HARPY LADIES!
HARPY LADY ONE...
...TWO ...
...AND THREE !
WHA ...
BA BA BAM
WHAT?! NOW THERE'S MORE OF THEM!?

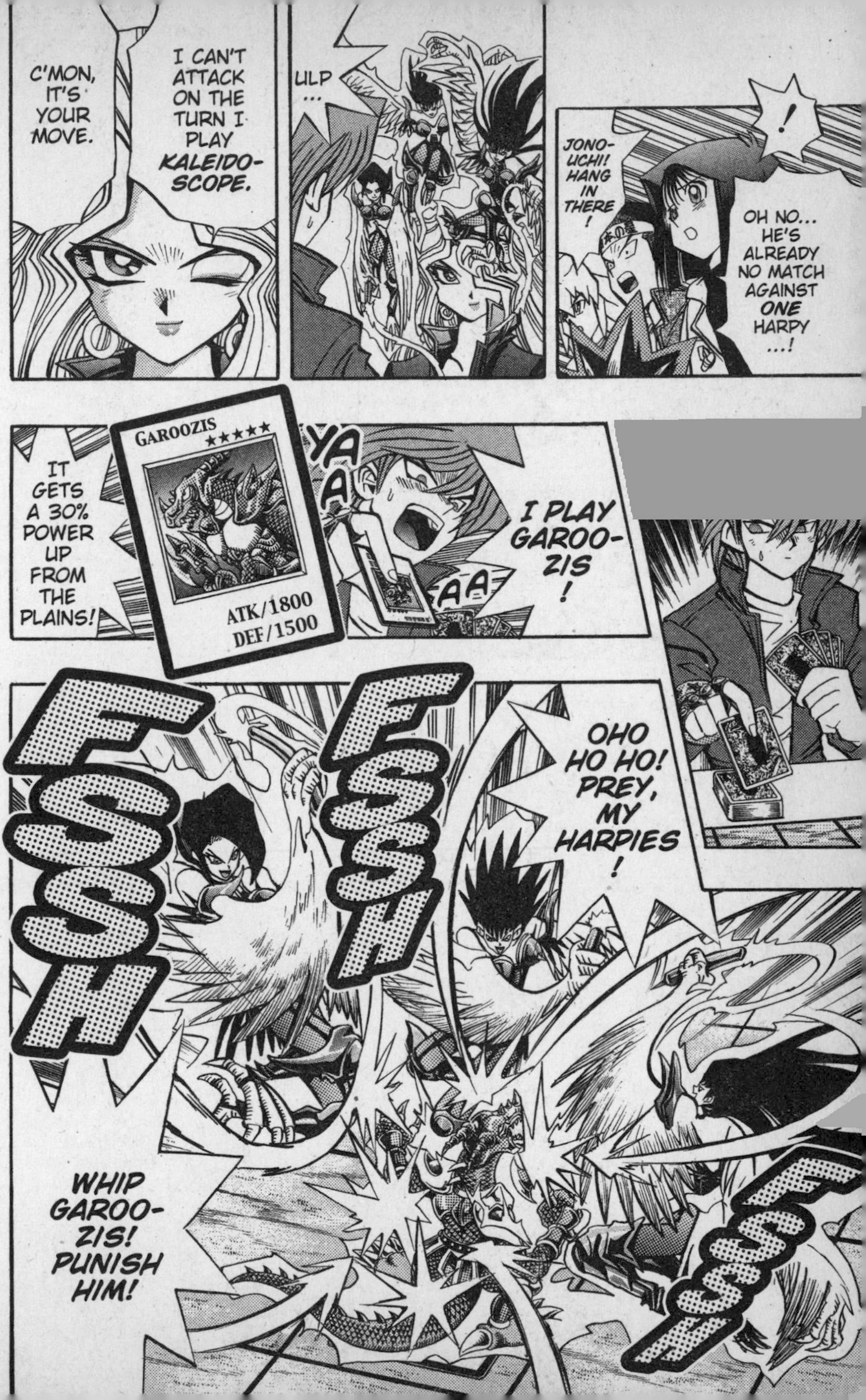
!
OH NO... HE'S ALREADY NO MATCH AGAINST ONE HARPY ...!
JONO-UCHI! HANG IN THERE!
ULP ...
I CAN'T ATTACK ON THE TURN I PLAY KALEIDO-SCOPE.
C'MON, IT'S YOUR MOVE.
I PLAY GAROO-ZIS!
YAAAA
GAROOZIS ★★★★★
ATK/1800
DEF/1500
IT GETS A 30% POWER UP FROM THE PLAINS!
OHO HO HO! PREY, MY HARPIES!
FSSH
FSSH
WHIP GAROO-ZIS! PUNISH HIM!

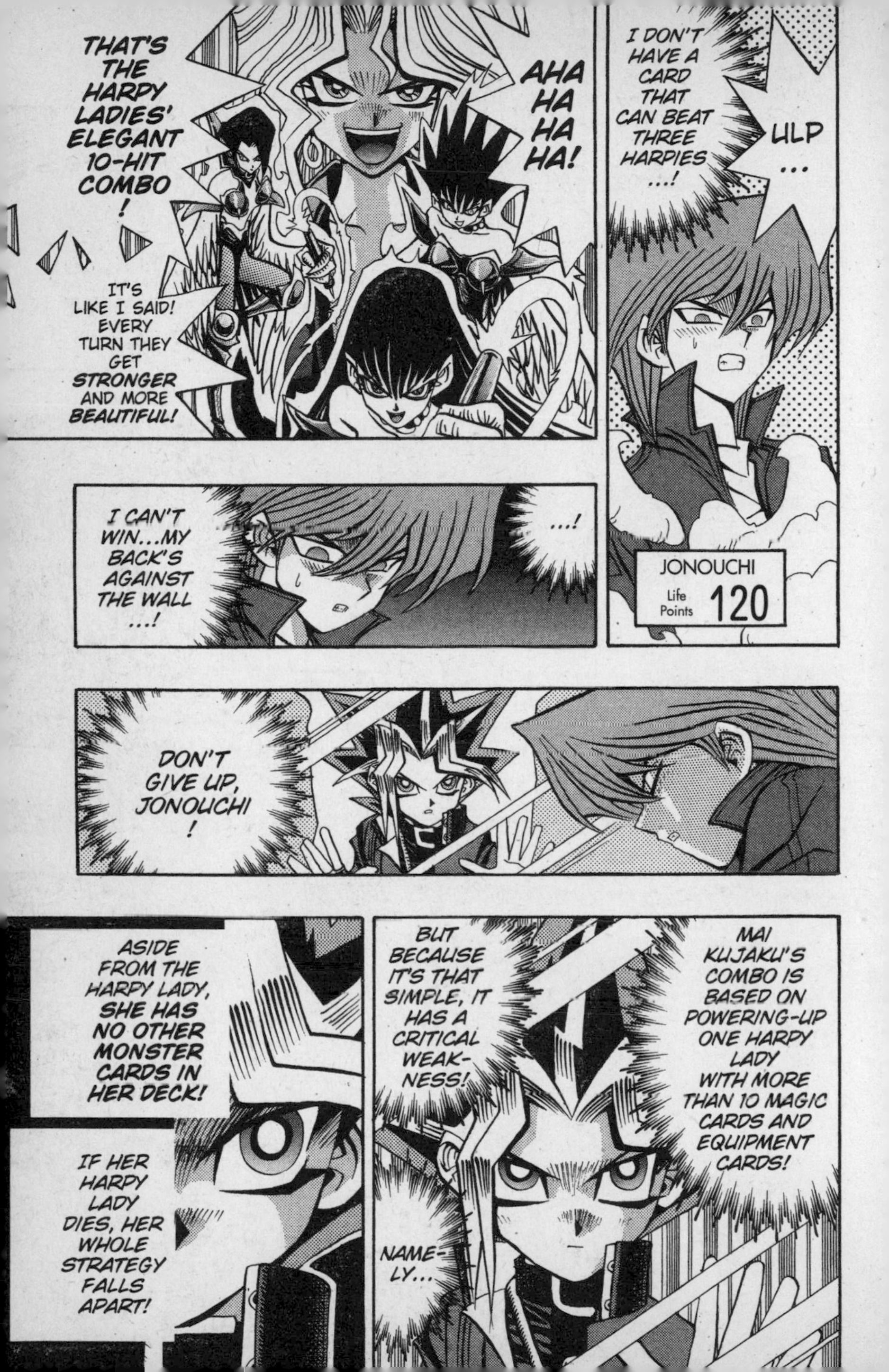
I DON'T HAVE A CARD THAT CAN BEAT THREE HARPIES ...!
ULP ...
JONOUCHI Life Points 120
AHA HA HA HA!
THAT'S THE HARPY LADIES' ELEGANT 10-HIT COMBO!
IT'S LIKE I SAID! EVERY TURN THEY GET STRONGER AND MORE BEAUTIFUL!
...!
I CAN'T WIN...MY BACK'S AGAINST THE WALL ...!
DON'T GIVE UP, JONOUCHI!
MAI KUJAKU'S COMBO IS BASED ON POWERING-UP ONE HARPY LADY WITH MORE THAN 10 MAGIC CARDS AND EQUIPMENT CARDS!
BUT BECAUSE IT'S THAT SIMPLE, IT HAS A CRITICAL WEAK-NESS!
NAME-LY...
ASIDE FROM THE HARPY LADY, SHE HAS NO OTHER MONSTER CARDS IN HER DECK!
IF HER HARPY LADY DIES, HER WHOLE STRATEGY FALLS APART!

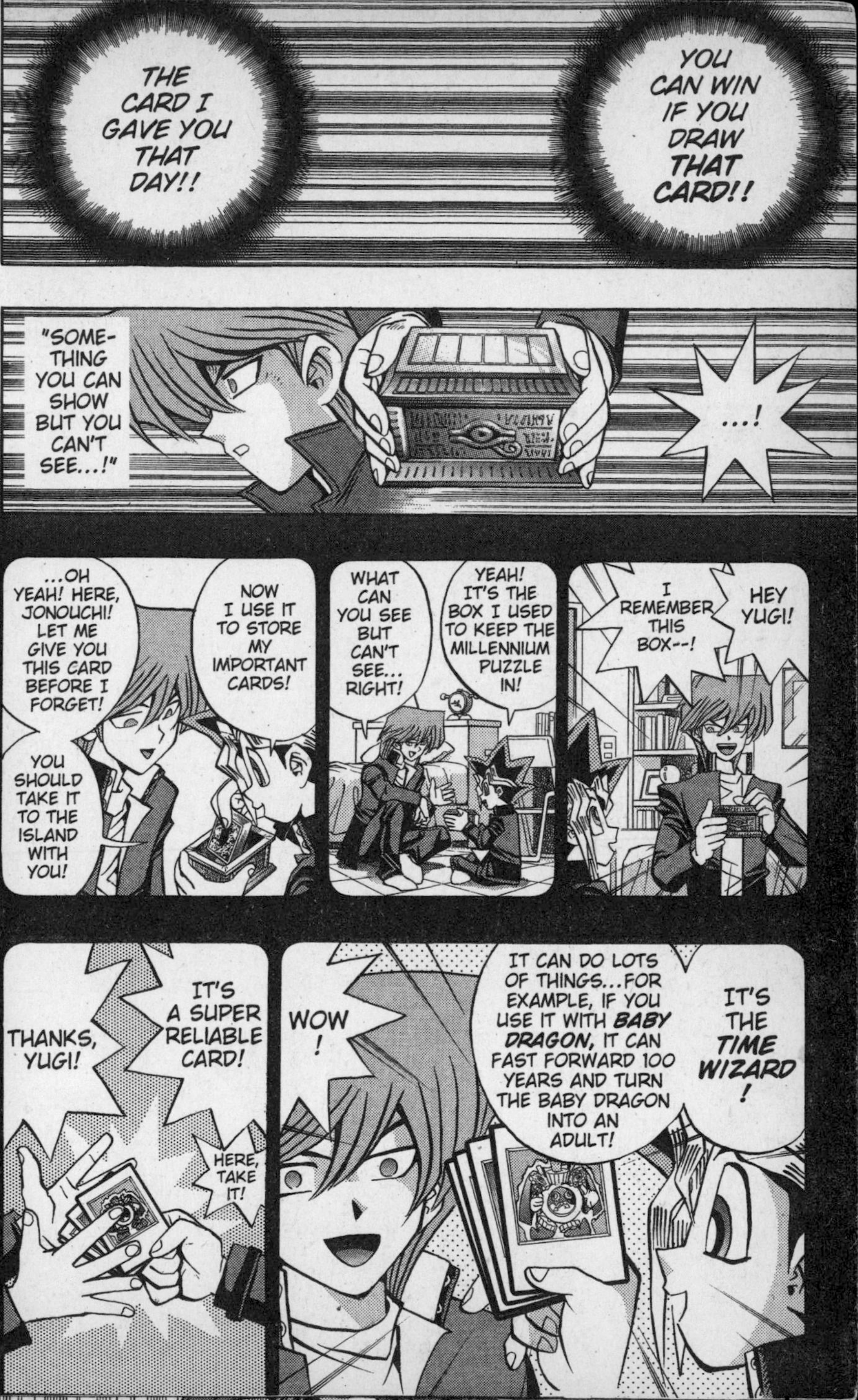
YOU CAN WIN IF YOU DRAW THAT CARD!!
THE CARD I GAVE YOU THAT DAY!!
...!
"SOMETHING YOU CAN SHOW BUT YOU CAN'T SEE...!"
HEY YUGI!
I REMEMBER THIS BOX--!
YEAH! IT'S THE BOX I USED TO KEEP THE MILLENNIUM PUZZLE IN!
WHAT CAN YOU SEE BUT CAN'T SEE... RIGHT!
NOW I USE IT TO STORE MY IMPORTANT CARDS!
...OH YEAH! HERE, JONOUCHI! LET ME GIVE YOU THIS CARD BEFORE I FORGET!
YOU SHOULD TAKE IT TO THE ISLAND WITH YOU!
IT'S THE TIME WIZARD!
IT CAN DO LOTS OF THINGS...FOR EXAMPLE, IF YOU USE IT WITH BABY DRAGON, IT CAN FAST FORWARD 100 YEARS AND TURN THE BABY DRAGON INTO AN ADULT!
WOW!
IT'S A SUPER RELIABLE CARD!
THANKS, YUGI!
HERE, TAKE IT!

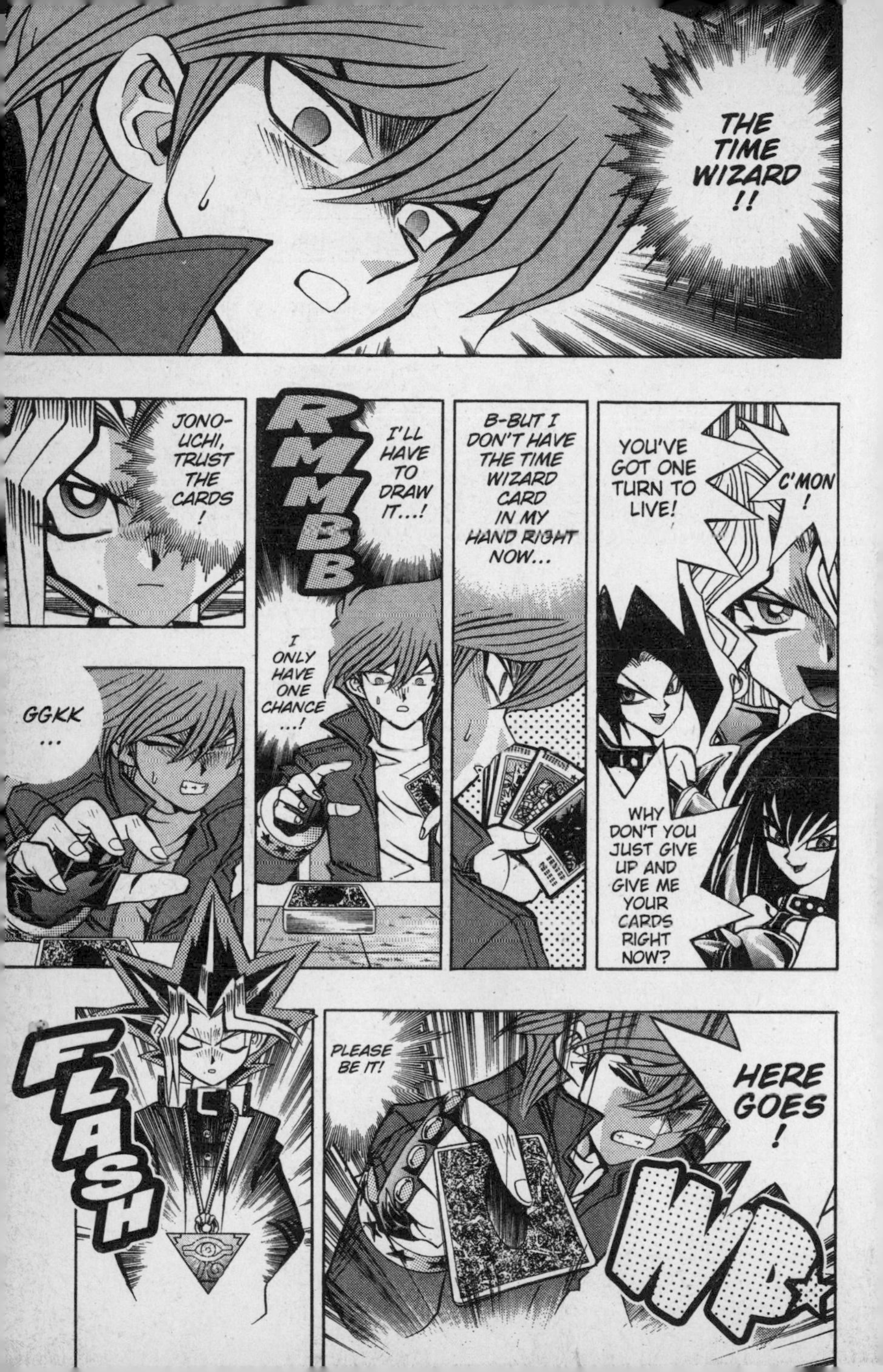
THE TIME WIZARD !!
C'MON!
YOU'VE GOT ONE TURN TO LIVE!
WHY DON'T YOU JUST GIVE UP AND GIVE ME YOUR CARDS RIGHT NOW?
B-BUT I DON'T HAVE THE TIME WIZARD CARD IN MY HAND RIGHT NOW...
RMMBB
I'LL HAVE TO DRAW IT...!
I ONLY HAVE ONE CHANCE...!
JONO-UCHI, TRUST THE CARDS!
GGKK...
HERE GOES!
PLEASE BE IT!
WHP
FLASH

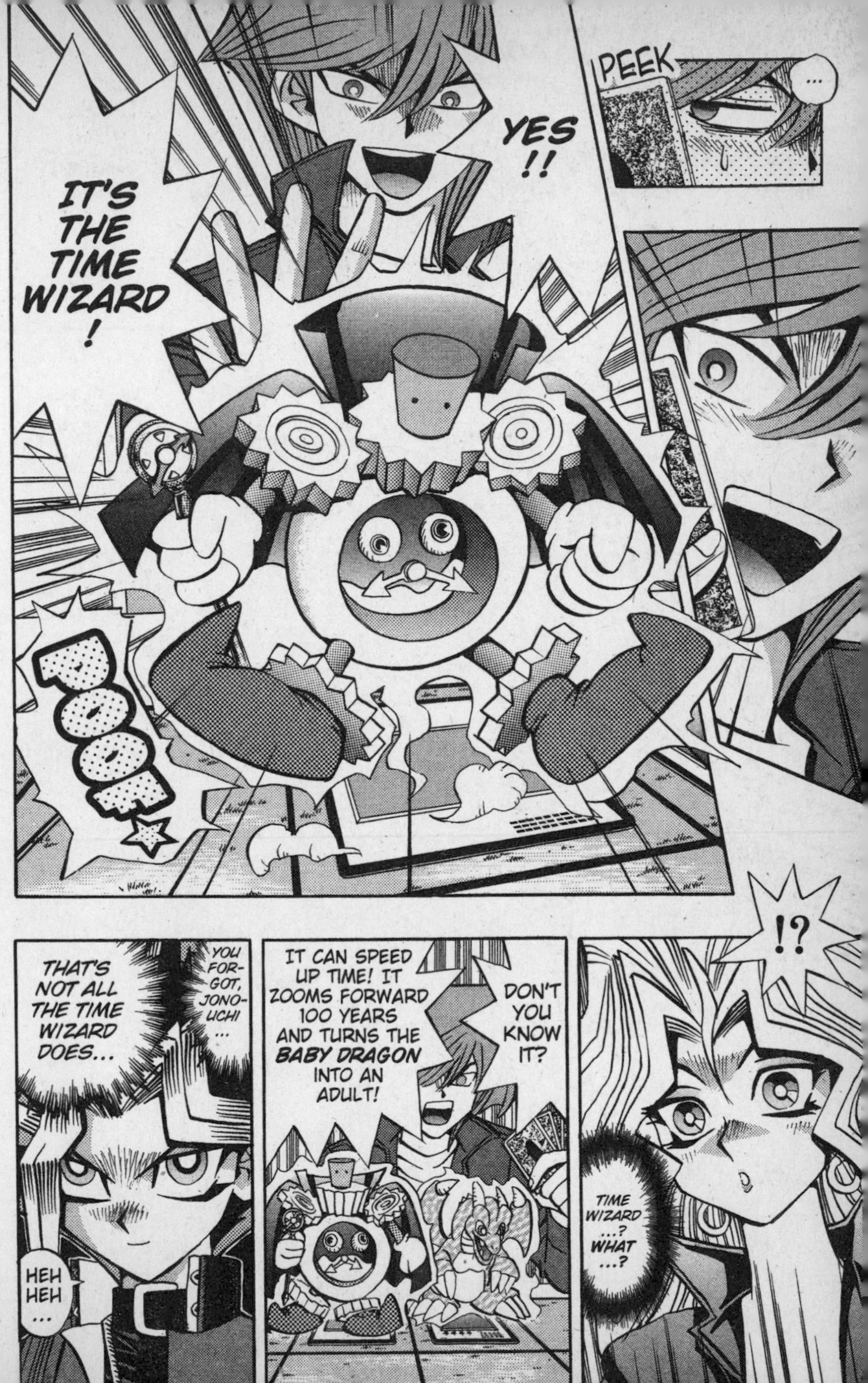
PEEK
...
YES!!
IT'S THE TIME WIZARD!
POOF
!?
TIME WIZARD ...? WHAT ...?
DON'T YOU KNOW IT?
IT CAN SPEED UP TIME! IT ZOOMS FORWARD 100 YEARS AND TURNS THE BABY DRAGON INTO AN ADULT!
YOU FORGOT, JONOUCHI ...
THAT'S NOT ALL THE TIME WIZARD DOES...
HEH HEH ...

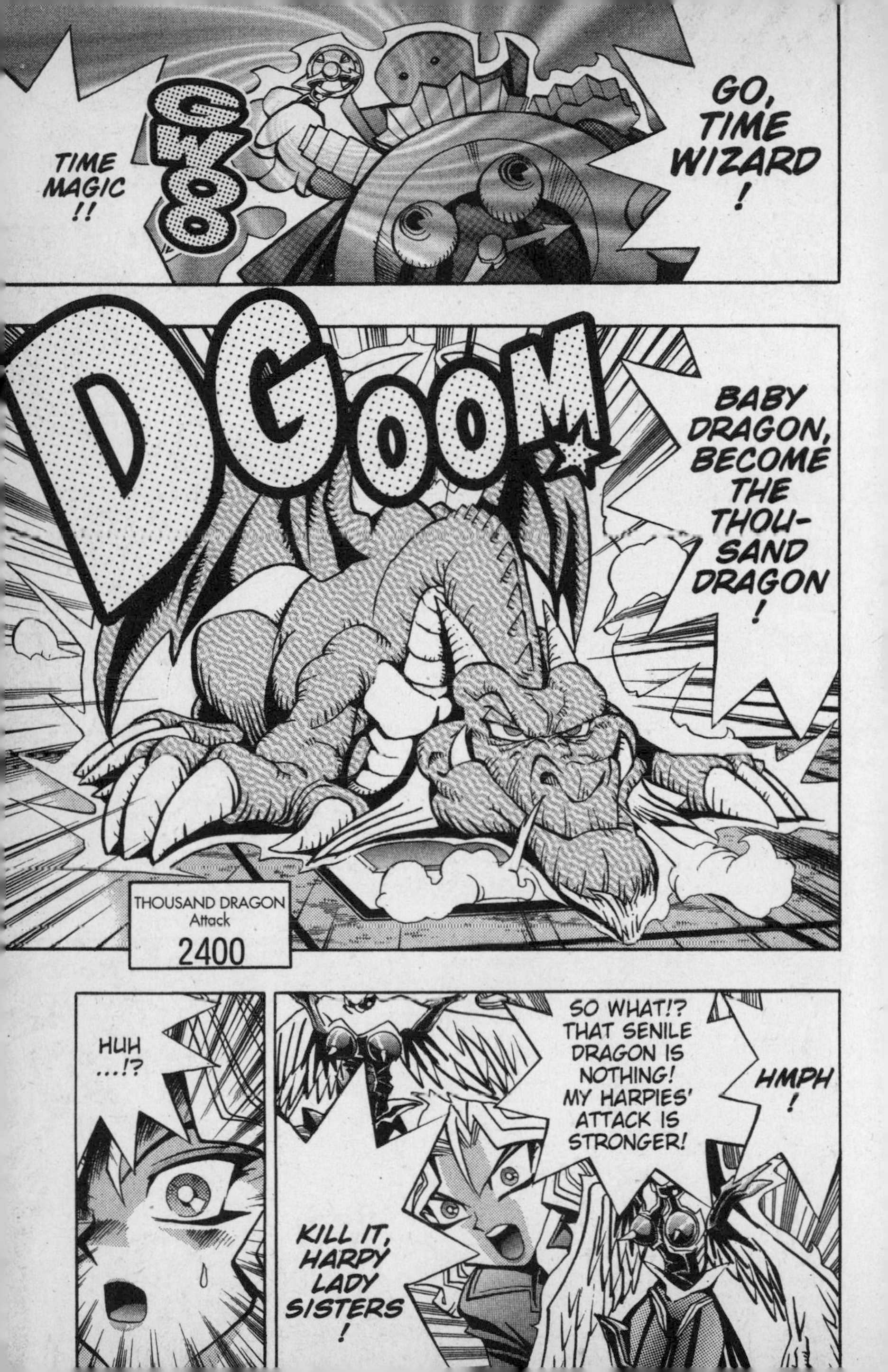
GO, TIME WIZARD!
GWOO
TIME MAGIC!!
BABY DRAGON, BECOME THE THOU-SAND DRAGON!
DGOOM
THOUSAND DRAGON Attack 2400
HMPH!
SO WHAT!? THAT SENILE DRAGON IS NOTHING! MY HARPIES' ATTACK IS STRONGER!
KILL IT, HARPY LADY SISTERS!
HUH ...!?

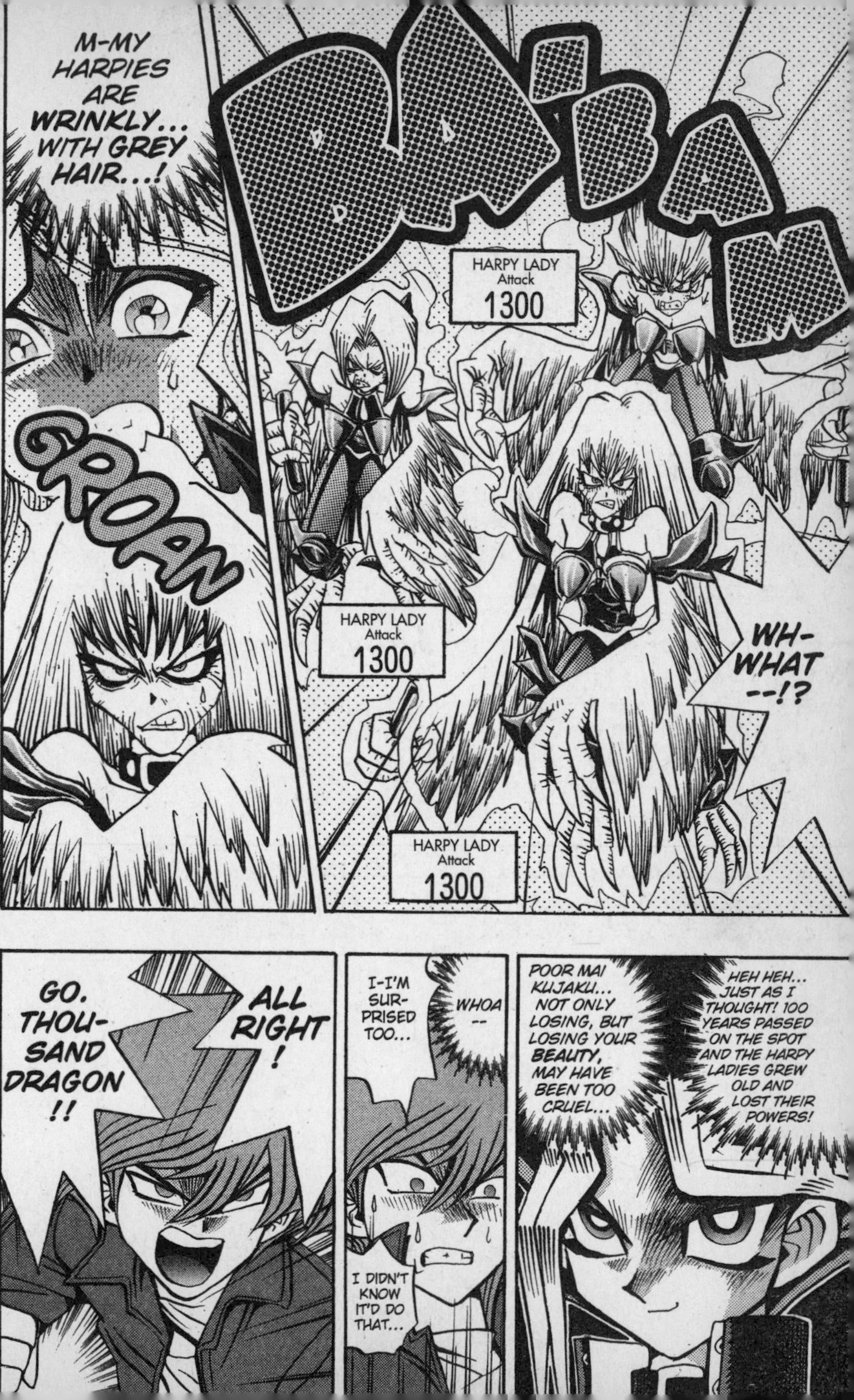
DA'BA'M
HARPY LADY Attack 1300
HARPY LADY Attack 1300
WH-WHAT--!?
HARPY LADY Attack 1300
M-MY HARPIES ARE WRINKLY... WITH GREY HAIR...!
GROAN
HEH HEH... JUST AS I THOUGHT! 100 YEARS PASSED ON THE SPOT AND THE HARPY LADIES GREW OLD AND LOST THEIR POWERS!
POOR MAI KUJAKU... NOT ONLY LOSING, BUT LOSING YOUR BEAUTY, MAY HAVE BEEN TOO CRUEL...
WHOA--
I-I'M SURPRISED TOO...
I DIDN'T KNOW IT'D DO THAT...
ALL RIGHT!
GO. THOUSAND DRAGON!!

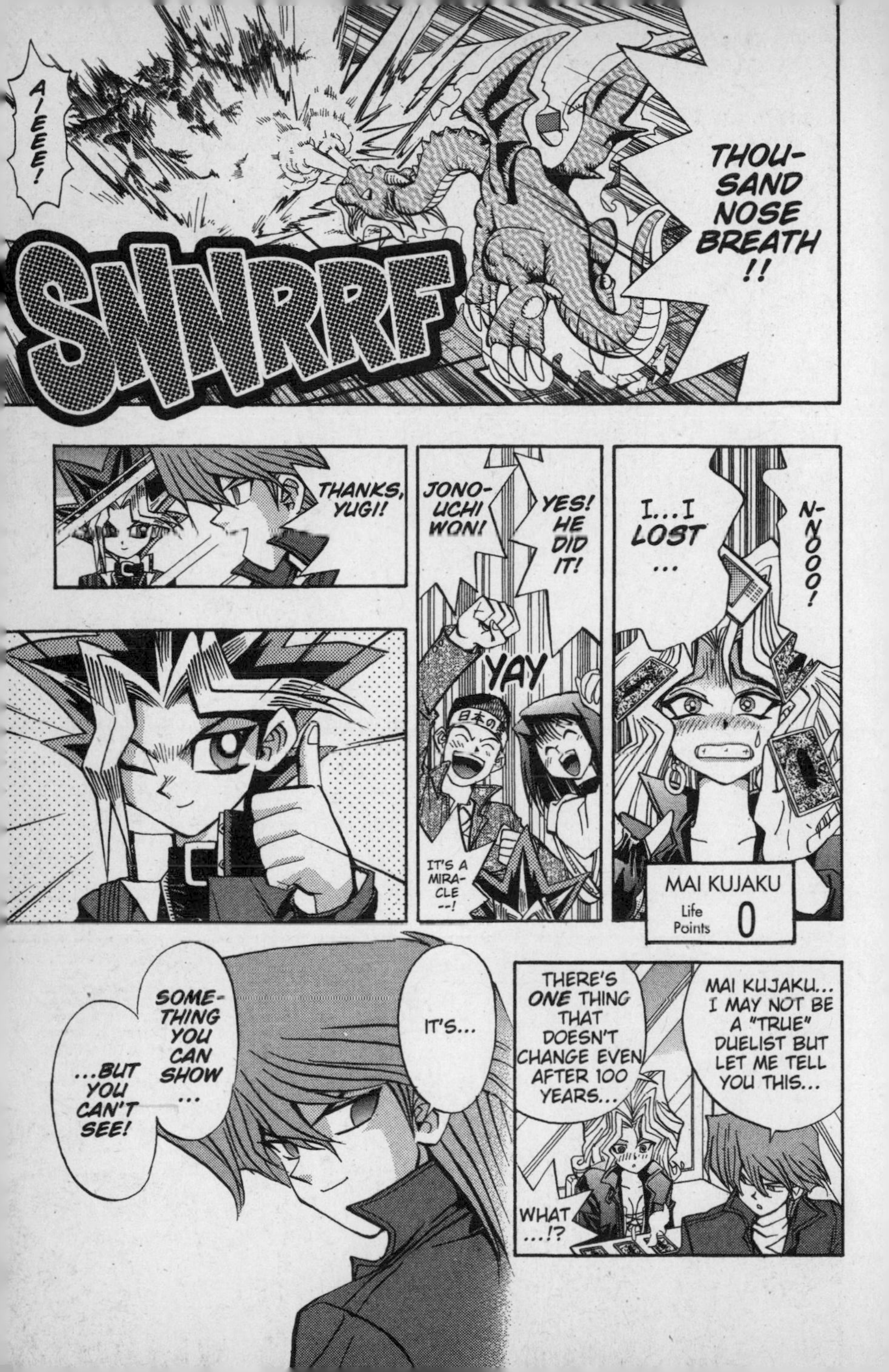

THOU-SAND NOSE BREATH!!
AIEEE!
SNNRRF
N-NOOOO!
I...I LOST...
MAI KUJAKU
Life Points 0
YES! HE DID IT!
JONO-UCHI WON!
YAY
日本の
IT'S A MIRA-CLE--!
THANKS, YUGI!
MAI KUJAKU... I MAY NOT BE A "TRUE" DUELIST BUT LET ME TELL YOU THIS...
THERE'S ONE THING THAT DOESN'T CHANGE EVEN AFTER 100 YEARS...
WHAT...!?
IT'S...
SOME-THING YOU CAN SHOW...
...BUT YOU CAN'T SEE!

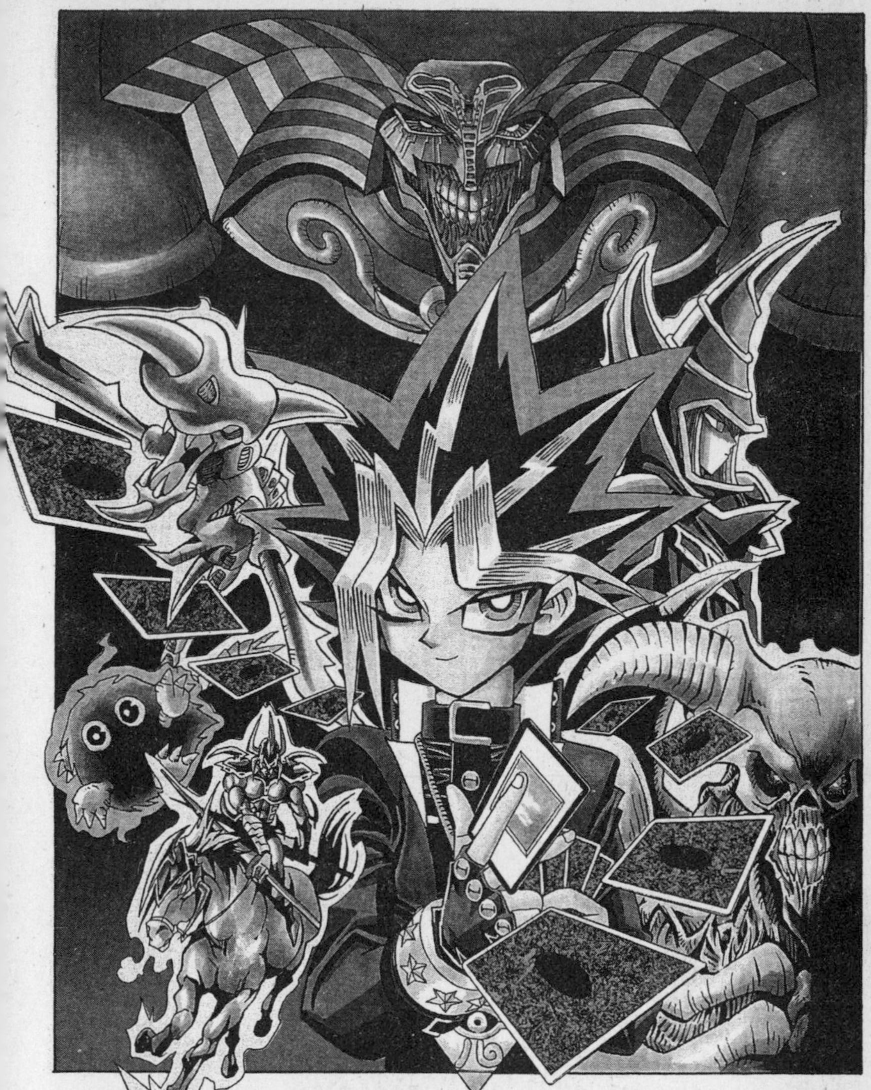

DUEL 12: THE SCOURGE OF THE SEA

READ THIS WAY

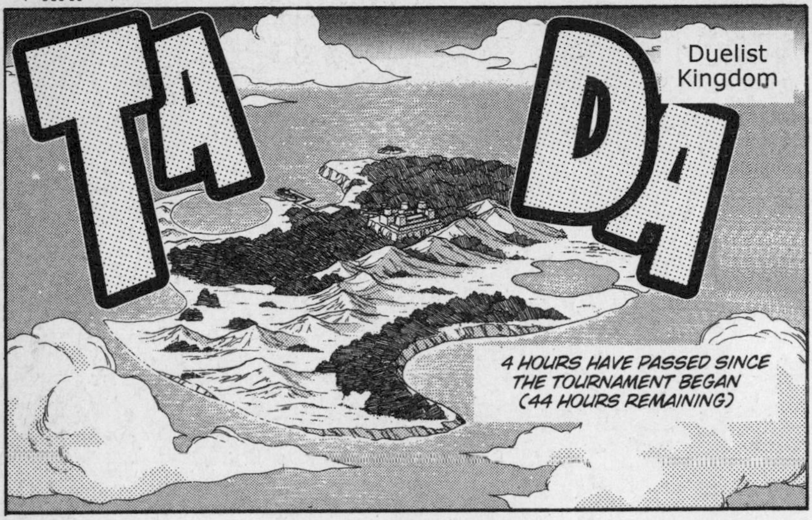
Duelist Kingdom
TA DA
4 HOURS HAVE PASSED SINCE THE TOURNAMENT BEGAN (44 HOURS REMAINING)

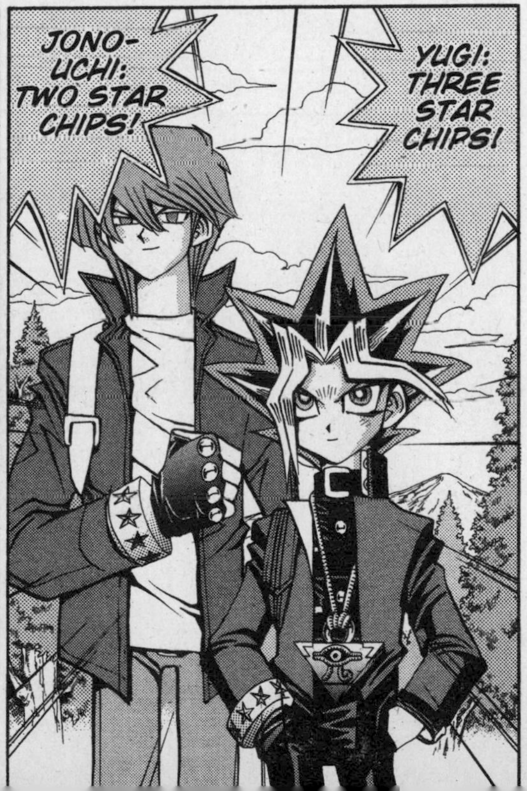
YUGI: THREE STAR CHIPS!
JONO-UCHI: TWO STAR CHIPS!

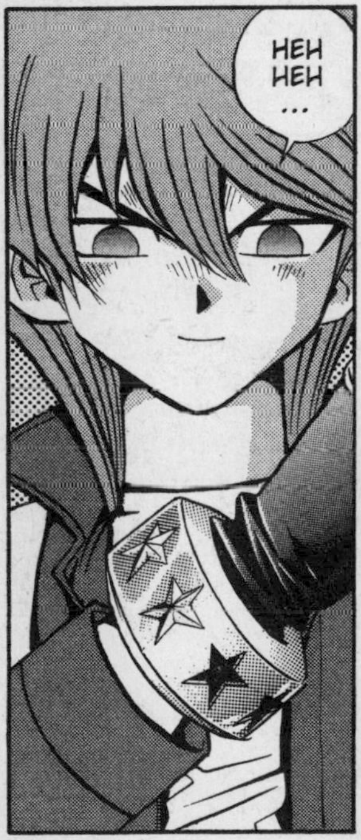
HEH HEH ...

READ THIS WAY

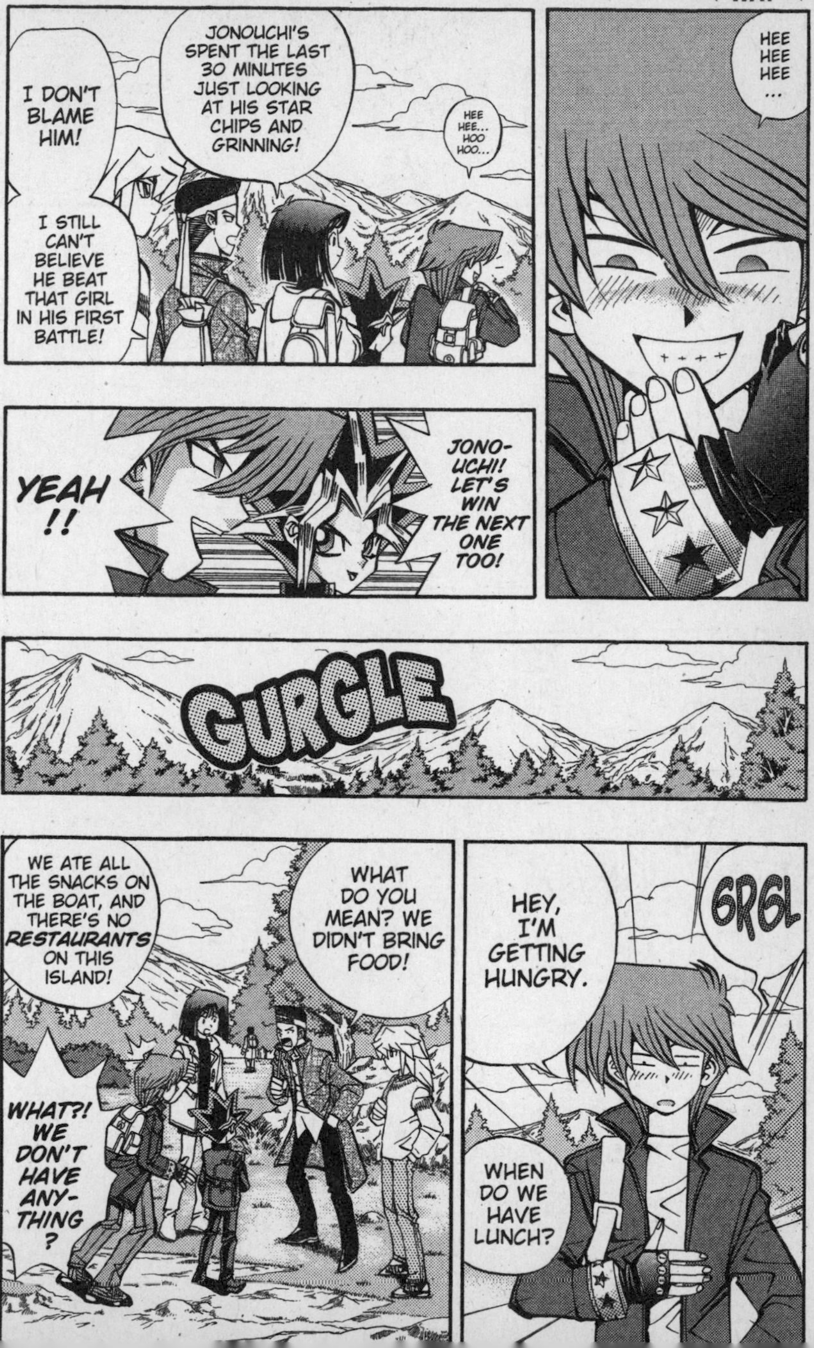
HEE HEE HEE ...
HEE HEE... HOO HOO...
JONOUCHI'S SPENT THE LAST 30 MINUTES JUST LOOKING AT HIS STAR CHIPS AND GRINNING!
I DON'T BLAME HIM!
I STILL CAN'T BELIEVE HE BEAT THAT GIRL IN HIS FIRST BATTLE!
JONOUCHI! LET'S WIN THE NEXT ONE TOO!
YEAH !!
GURGLE
GRGL
HEY, I'M GETTING HUNGRY.
WHEN DO WE HAVE LUNCH?
WHAT DO YOU MEAN? WE DIDN'T BRING FOOD!
WE ATE ALL THE SNACKS ON THE BOAT, AND THERE'S NO *RESTAURANTS* ON THIS ISLAND!
WHAT?! WE DON'T HAVE ANYTHING?

READ THIS WAY

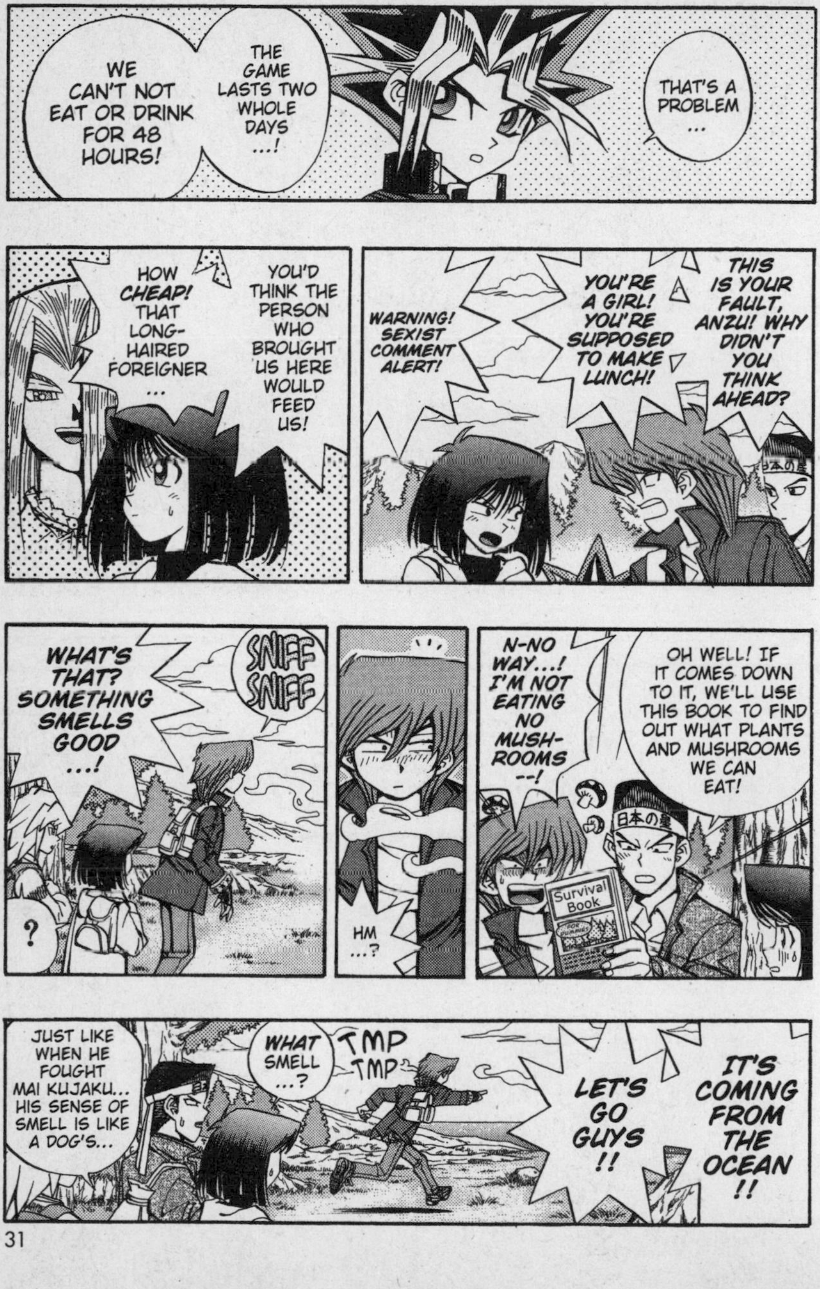
THAT'S A PROBLEM ...
THE GAME LASTS TWO WHOLE DAYS ...!
WE CAN'T NOT EAT OR DRINK FOR 48 HOURS!
THIS IS YOUR FAULT, ANZU! WHY DIDN'T YOU THINK AHEAD?
YOU'RE A GIRL! YOU'RE SUPPOSED TO MAKE LUNCH!
WARNING! SEXIST COMMENT ALERT!
YOU'D THINK THE PERSON WHO BROUGHT US HERE WOULD FEED US!
HOW CHEAP! THAT LONG-HAIRED FOREIGNER ...
OH WELL! IF IT COMES DOWN TO IT, WE'LL USE THIS BOOK TO FIND OUT WHAT PLANTS AND MUSHROOMS WE CAN EAT!
N-NO WAY...! I'M NOT EATING NO MUSH-ROOMS--!
日本の星
Survival Book
HM ...?
SNIFF SNIFF
WHAT'S THAT? SOMETHING SMELLS GOOD ...!
?
IT'S COMING FROM THE OCEAN !!
LET'S GO GUYS !!
TMP TMP
WHAT SMELL ...?
JUST LIKE WHEN HE FOUGHT MAI KUJAKU... HIS SENSE OF SMELL IS LIKE A DOG'S...

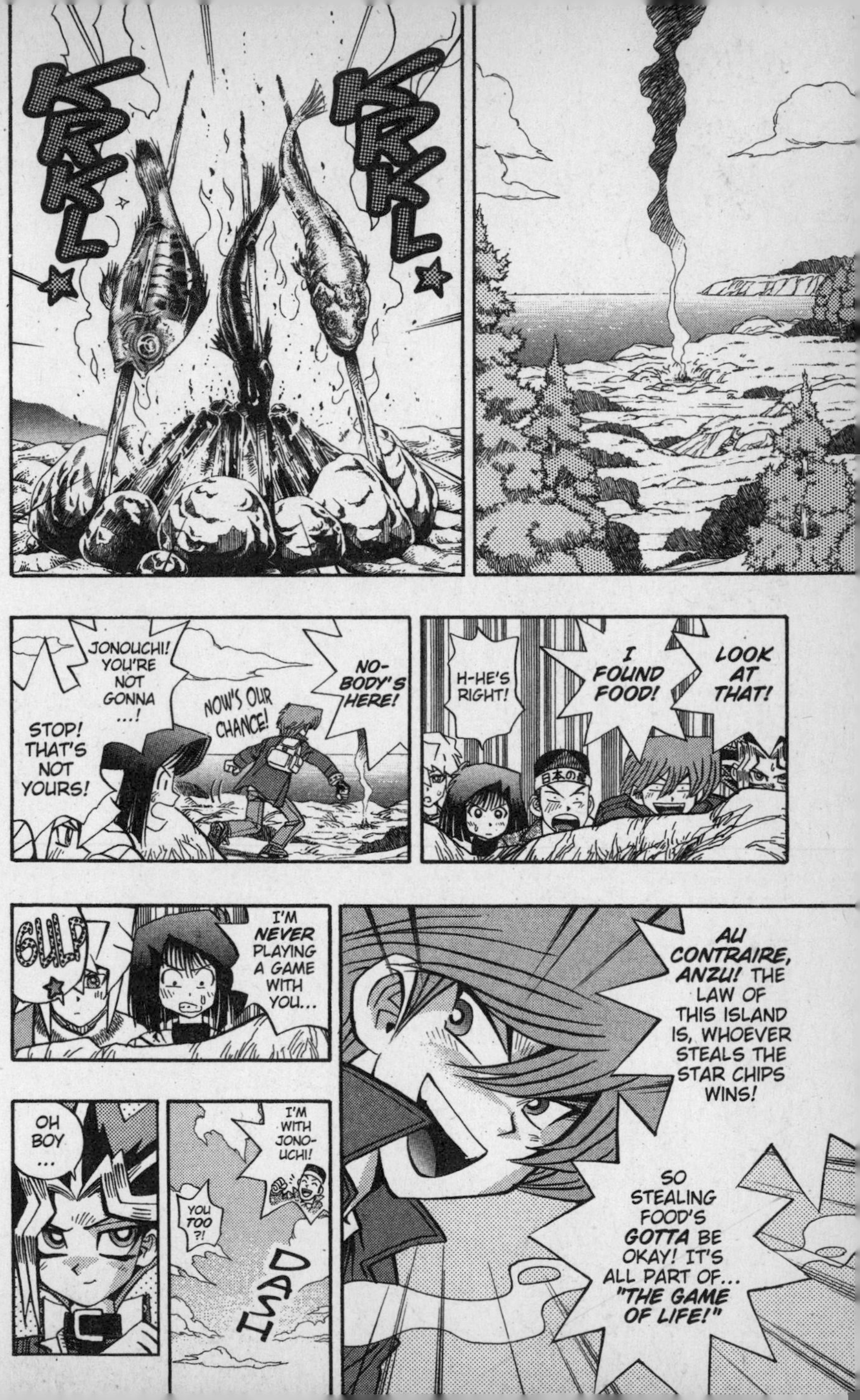
KRKL
KRKL
LOOK AT THAT!
I FOUND FOOD!
H-HE'S RIGHT!
NO-BODY'S HERE!
NOW'S OUR CHANCE!
JONOUCHI! YOU'RE NOT GONNA ...!
STOP! THAT'S NOT YOURS!
AU CONTRAIRE, ANZU! THE LAW OF THIS ISLAND IS, WHOEVER STEALS THE STAR CHIPS WINS!
SO STEALING FOOD'S GOTTA BE OKAY! IT'S ALL PART OF... "THE GAME OF LIFE!"
I'M NEVER PLAYING A GAME WITH YOU...
GULP
I'M WITH JONO-UCHI!
YOU TOO ?!
DASH
OH BOY ...

READ THIS WAY

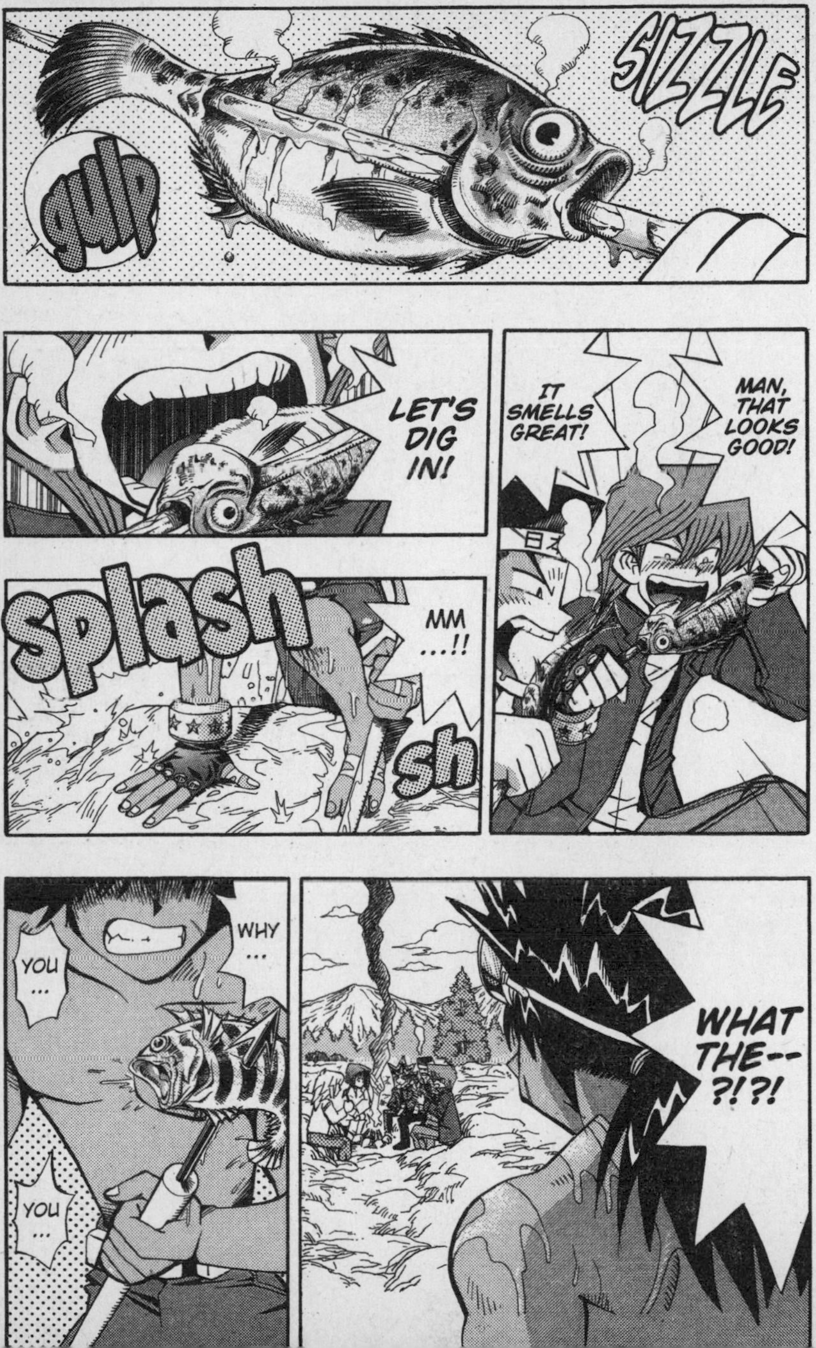
SIZZLE
gulp
MAN, THAT LOOKS GOOD!
IT SMELLS GREAT!
LET'S DIG IN!
MM ...!!
splash
sh
WHAT THE-- ?!?!
WHY ...
YOU ...
YOU ...

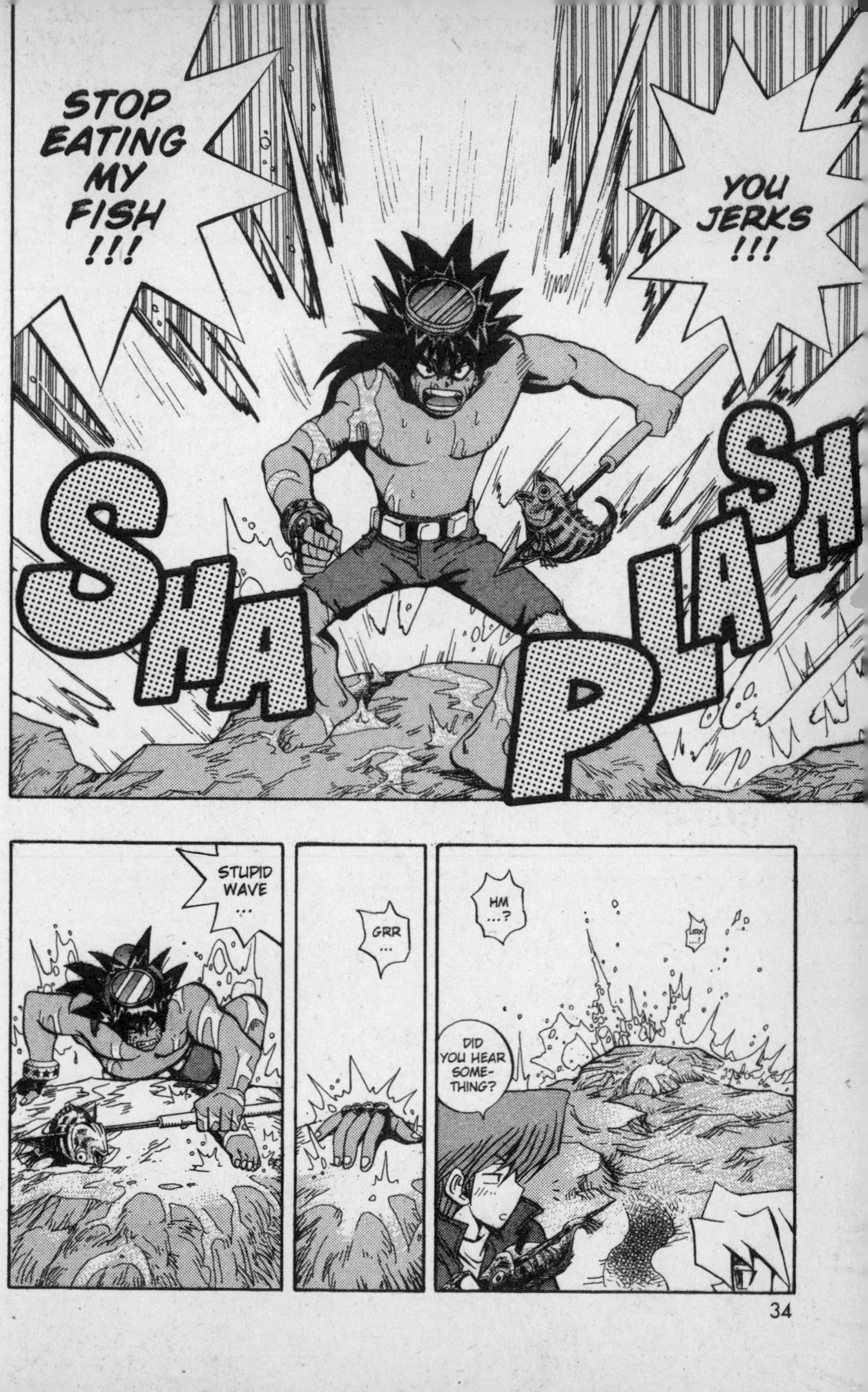
STOP EATING MY FISH !!!
YOU JERKS !!!
SHA PLASH
URK ...!
HM ...?
DID YOU HEAR SOME-THING?
GRR ...
STUPID WAVE ...

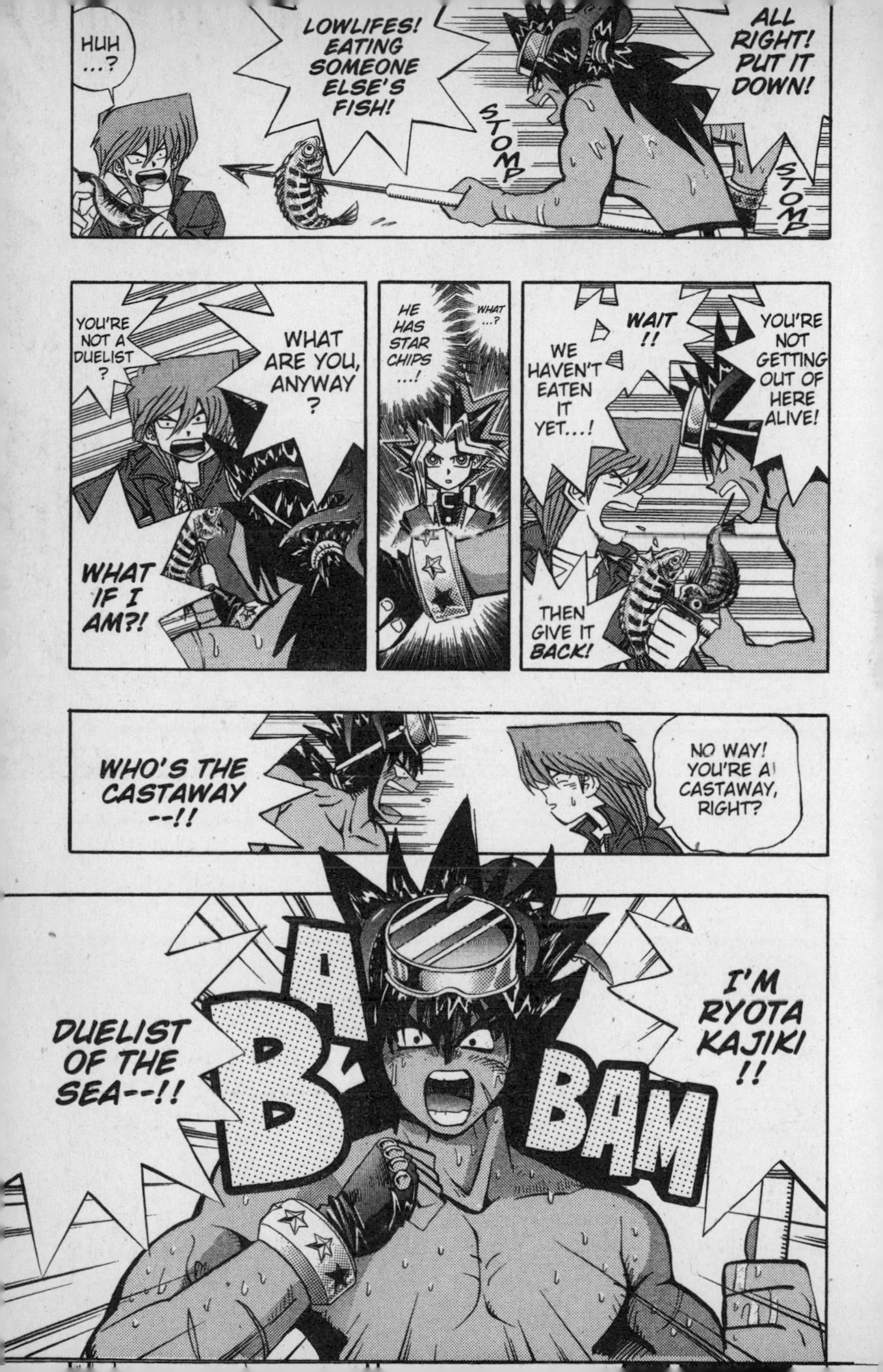
ALL RIGHT! PUT IT DOWN!
STOMP
STOMP
LOWLIFES! EATING SOMEONE ELSE'S FISH!
HUH ...?
YOU'RE NOT GETTING OUT OF HERE ALIVE!
WAIT !!
WE HAVEN'T EATEN IT YET...!
THEN GIVE IT BACK!
WHAT ...?
HE HAS STAR CHIPS ...!
WHAT ARE YOU, ANYWAY ?
YOU'RE NOT A DUELIST ?
WHAT IF I AM?!
NO WAY! YOU'RE A CASTAWAY, RIGHT?
WHO'S THE CASTAWAY --!!
I'M RYOTA KAJIKI !!
BAM
BA
DUELIST OF THE SEA--!!

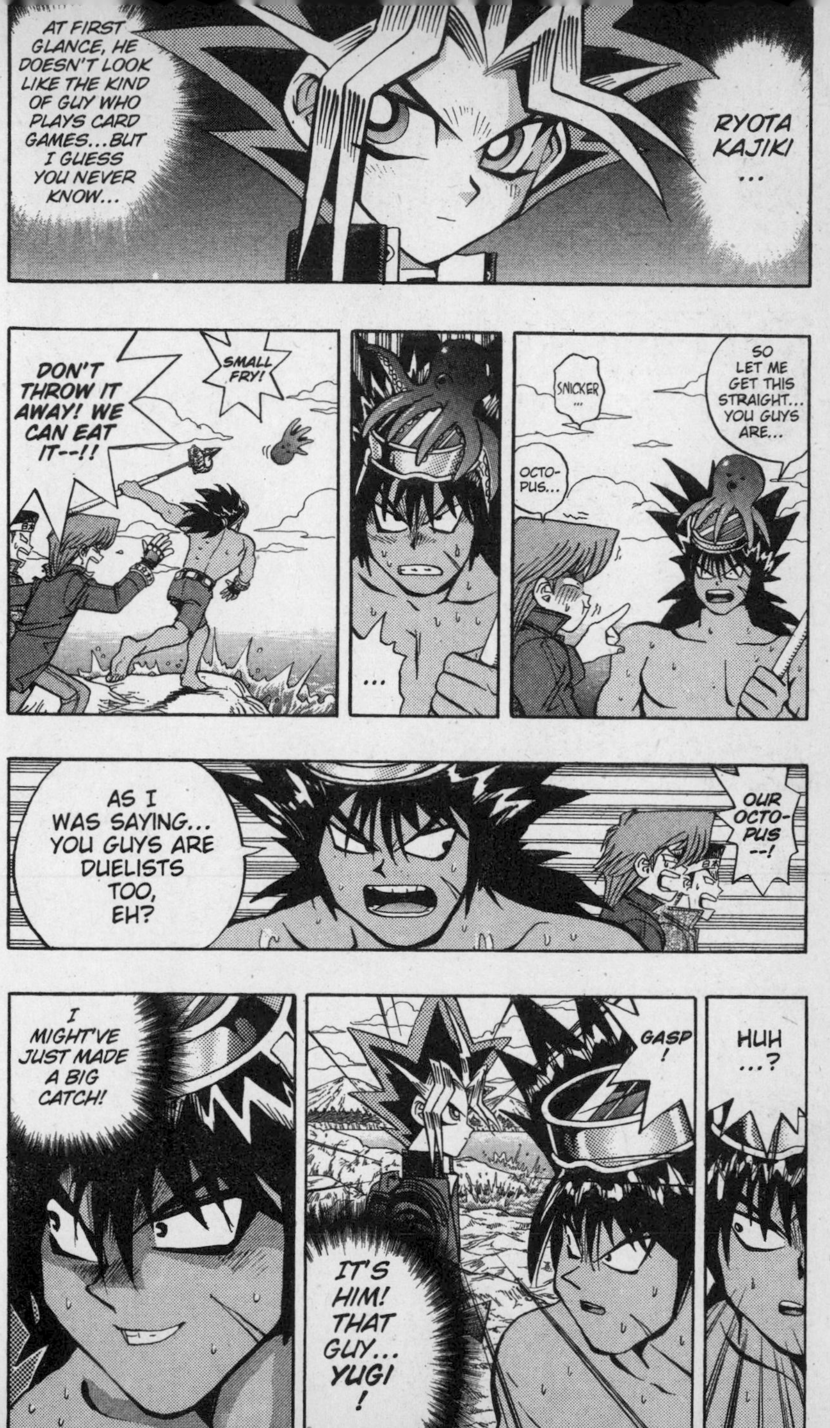
RYOTA KAJIKI ...
AT FIRST GLANCE, HE DOESN'T LOOK LIKE THE KIND OF GUY WHO PLAYS CARD GAMES...BUT I GUESS YOU NEVER KNOW...
SO LET ME GET THIS STRAIGHT... YOU GUYS ARE...
SNICKER ...
OCTO-PUS...
...
SMALL FRY!
DON'T THROW IT AWAY! WE CAN EAT IT--!!
OUR OCTO-PUS --!
AS I WAS SAYING... YOU GUYS ARE DUELISTS TOO, EH?
HUH ...?
GASP !
IT'S HIM! THAT GUY... YUGI !
I MIGHT'VE JUST MADE A BIG CATCH!

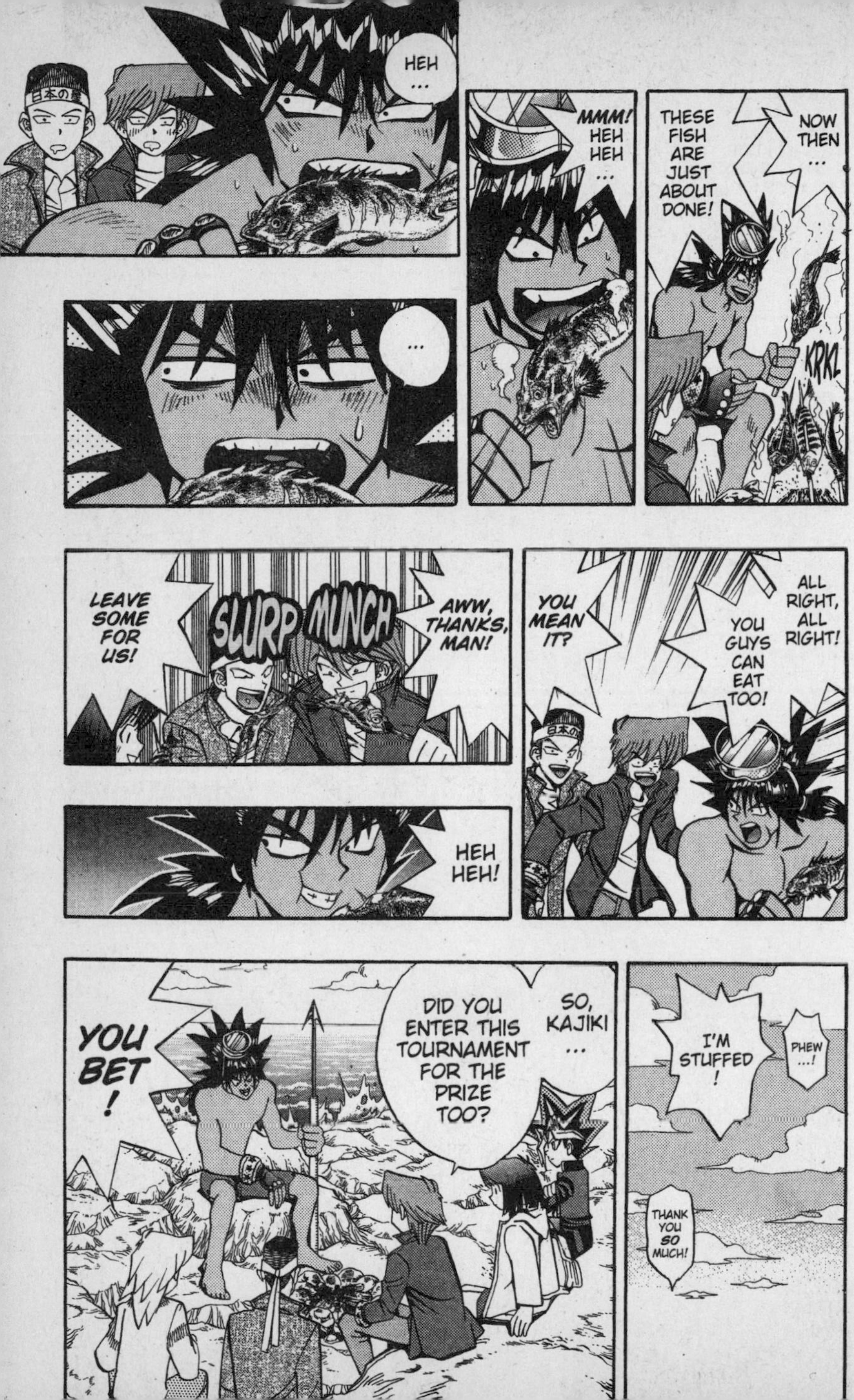
NOW THEN ...
THESE FISH ARE JUST ABOUT DONE!
KRKL
MMM! HEH HEH ...
HEH ...
...
ALL RIGHT, ALL RIGHT!
YOU GUYS CAN EAT TOO!
YOU MEAN IT?
AWW, THANKS, MAN!
MUNCH
SLURP
LEAVE SOME FOR US!
HEH HEH!
PHEW ...!
I'M STUFFED!
THANK YOU SO MUCH!
SO, KAJIKI ...
DID YOU ENTER THIS TOURNAMENT FOR THE PRIZE TOO?
YOU BET!

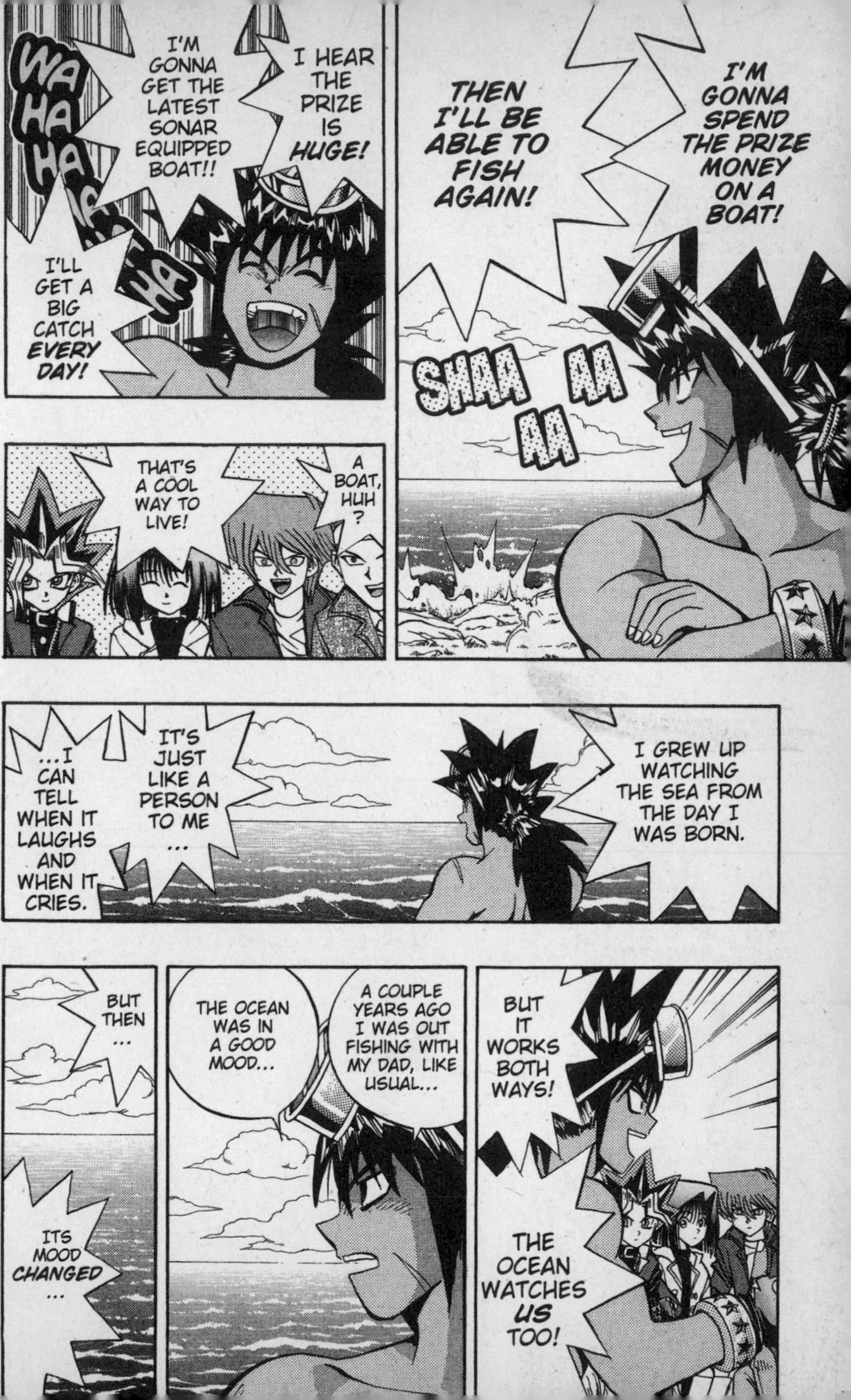
I'M GONNA SPEND THE PRIZE MONEY ON A BOAT!
THEN I'LL BE ABLE TO FISH AGAIN!
SHAA AA AA
I HEAR THE PRIZE IS HUGE!
I'M GONNA GET THE LATEST SONAR EQUIPPED BOAT!!
WA HA HA HA HA
I'LL GET A BIG CATCH EVERY DAY!
A BOAT, HUH?
THAT'S A COOL WAY TO LIVE!
I GREW UP WATCHING THE SEA FROM THE DAY I WAS BORN.
IT'S JUST LIKE A PERSON TO ME...
...I CAN TELL WHEN IT LAUGHS AND WHEN IT CRIES.
BUT IT WORKS BOTH WAYS!
THE OCEAN WATCHES US TOO!
A COUPLE YEARS AGO I WAS OUT FISHING WITH MY DAD, LIKE USUAL...
THE OCEAN WAS IN A GOOD MOOD...
BUT THEN...
ITS MOOD CHANGED...

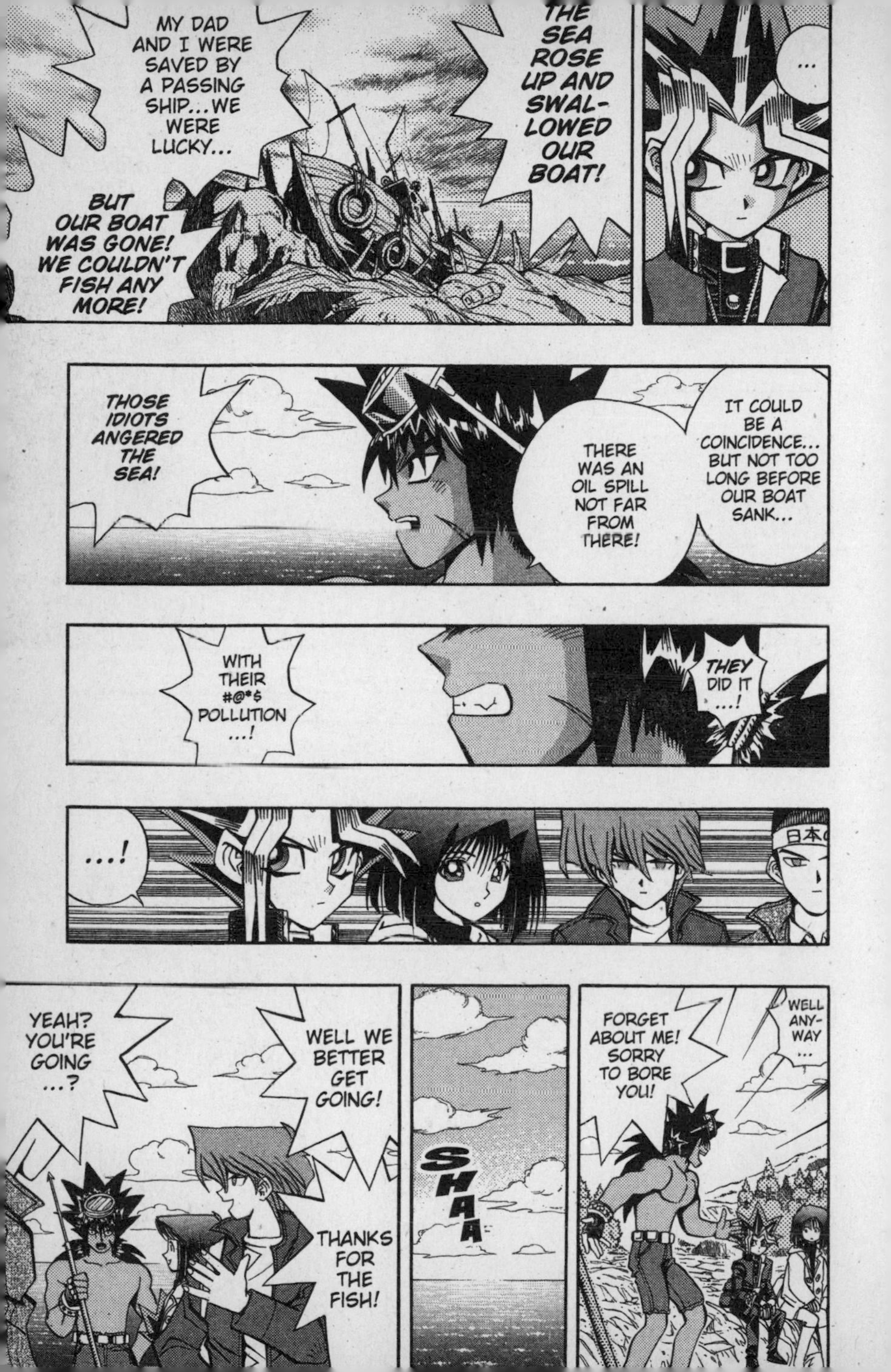
...
THE SEA ROSE UP AND SWAL-LOWED OUR BOAT!
MY DAD AND I WERE SAVED BY A PASSING SHIP...WE WERE LUCKY...
BUT OUR BOAT WAS GONE! WE COULDN'T FISH ANY MORE!
IT COULD BE A COINCIDENCE... BUT NOT TOO LONG BEFORE OUR BOAT SANK...
THERE WAS AN OIL SPILL NOT FAR FROM THERE!
THOSE IDIOTS ANGERED THE SEA!
THEY DID IT ...!
WITH THEIR #@*$ POLLUTION ...!
...!
WELL ANYWAY ...
FORGET ABOUT ME! SORRY TO BORE YOU!
SHAA
WELL WE BETTER GET GOING!
YEAH? YOU'RE GOING ...?
THANKS FOR THE FISH!

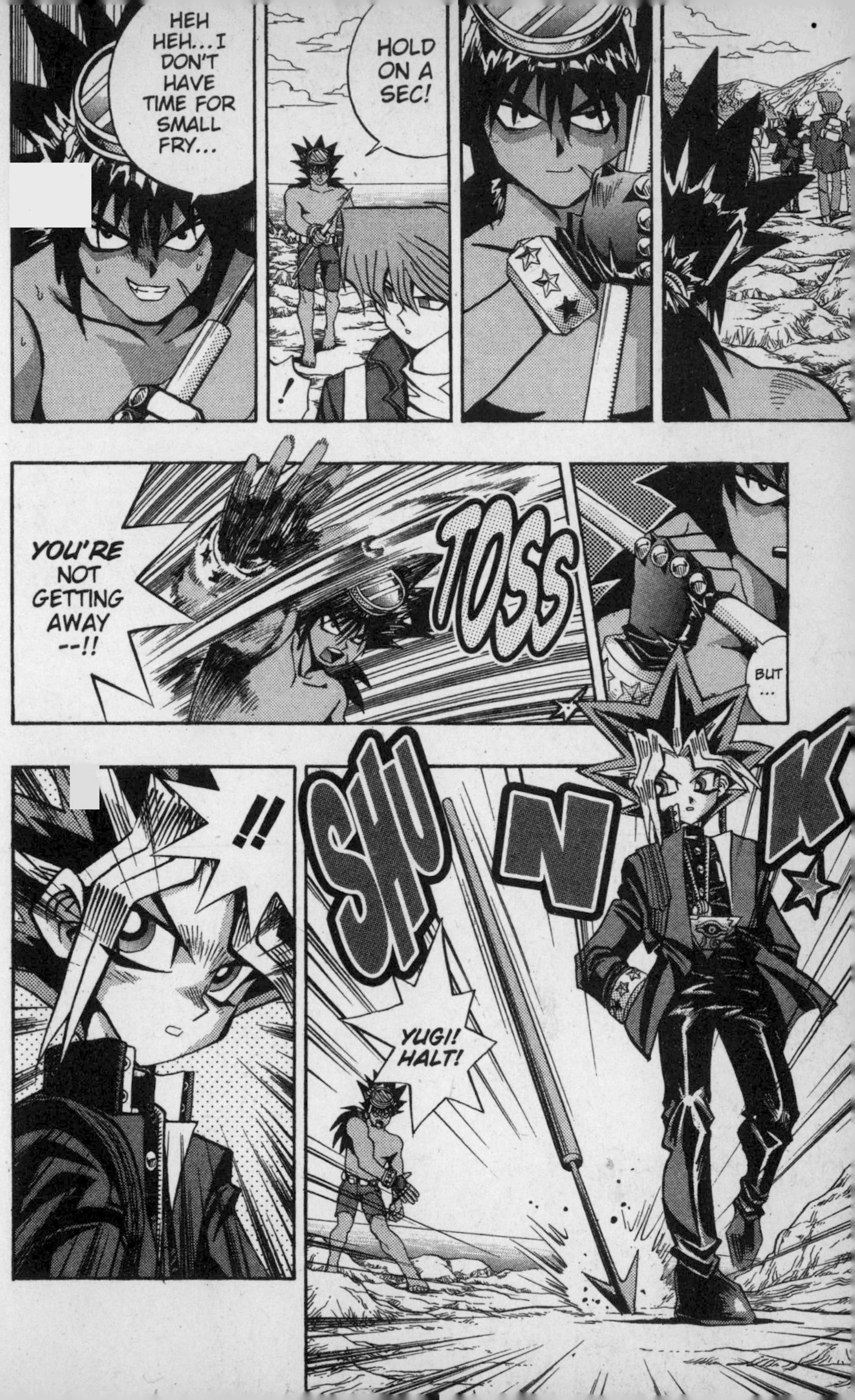
HOLD ON A SEC!
!
HEH HEH...I DON'T HAVE TIME FOR SMALL FRY...
BUT...
TOSS
YOU'RE NOT GETTING AWAY --!!
SHUNK
YUGI! HALT!
!!

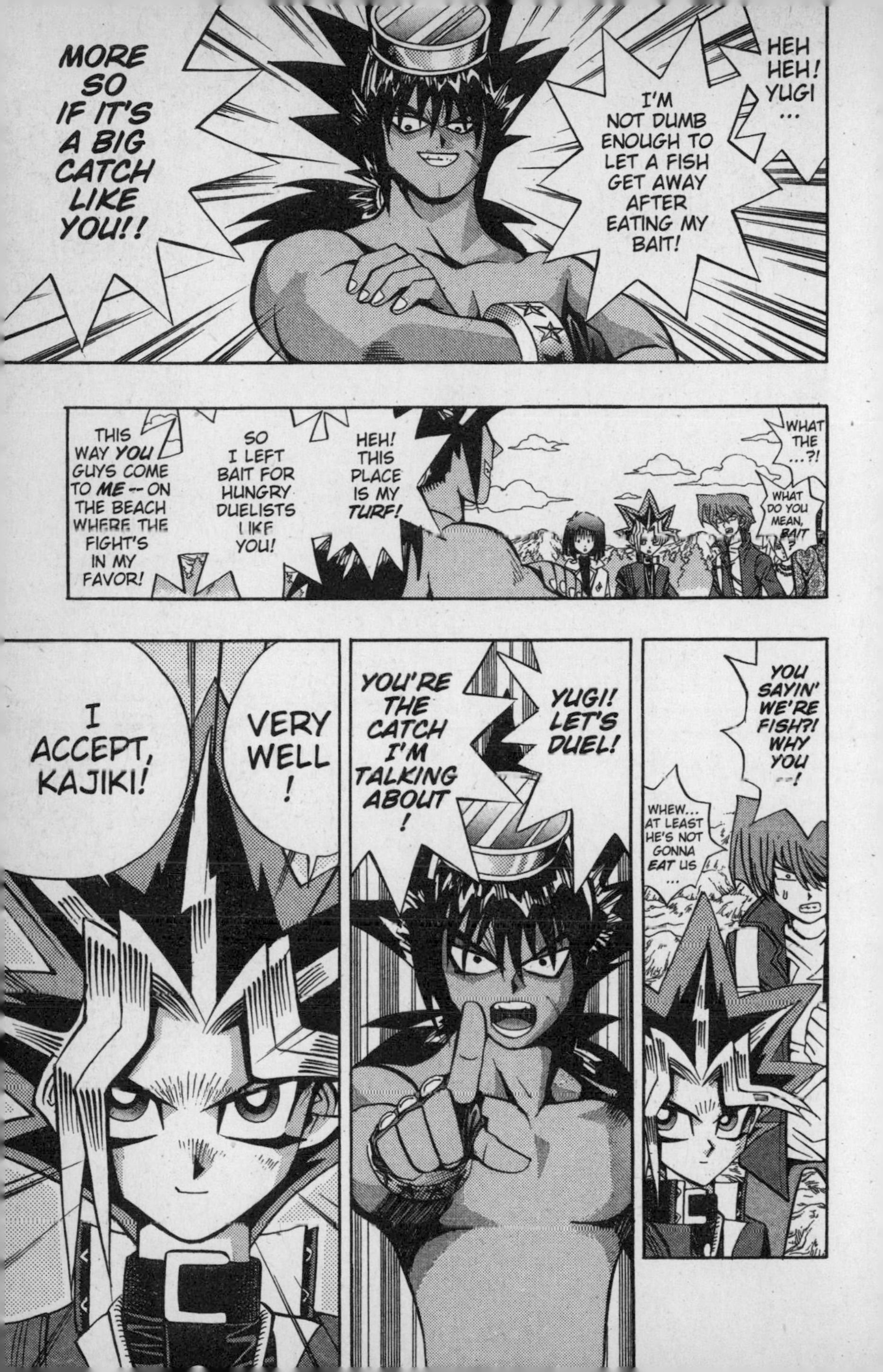
HEH HEH! YUGI ...
I'M NOT DUMB ENOUGH TO LET A FISH GET AWAY AFTER EATING MY BAIT!
MORE SO IF IT'S A BIG CATCH LIKE YOU!!
WHAT THE ...?!
WHAT DO YOU MEAN, BAIT?
HEH! THIS PLACE IS MY TURF!
SO I LEFT BAIT FOR HUNGRY DUELISTS LIKE YOU!
THIS WAY YOU GUYS COME TO ME -- ON THE BEACH WHERE THE FIGHT'S IN MY FAVOR!
YOU SAYIN' WE'RE FISH?! WHY YOU --!
WHEW... AT LEAST HE'S NOT GONNA EAT US ...
YUGI! LET'S DUEL!
YOU'RE THE CATCH I'M TALKING ABOUT!
VERY WELL!
I ACCEPT, KAJIKI!

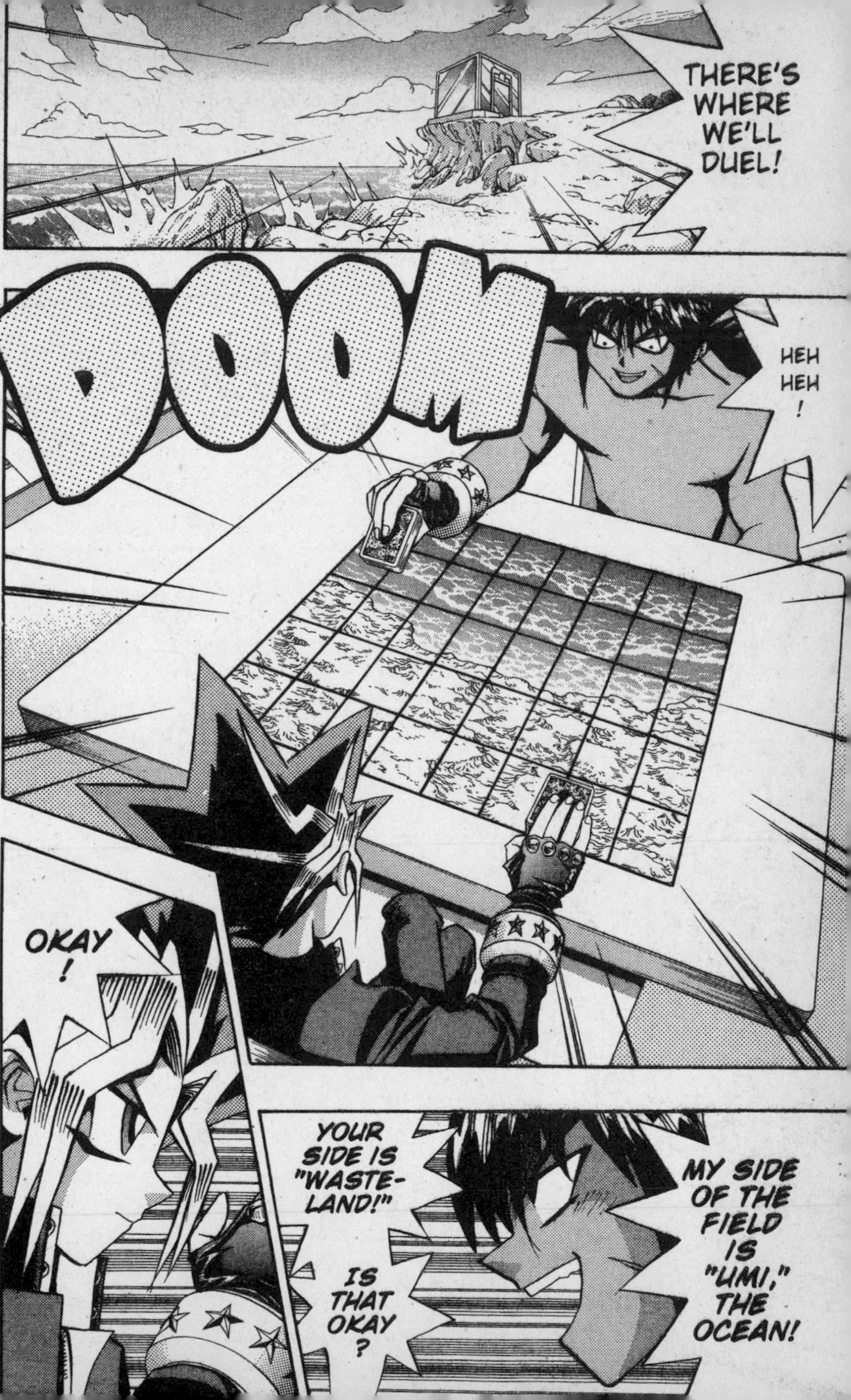
THERE'S WHERE WE'LL DUEL!
HEH HEH!
DOOM
MY SIDE OF THE FIELD IS "UMI," THE OCEAN!
YOUR SIDE IS "WASTE-LAND!"
IS THAT OKAY?
OKAY!

OH YEAH! IN A FIGHT ON MY TERRAIN, YOU'RE AS GOOD AS ALREADY IN MY NET!

SHAA SHAA SHH SHAA

OKAY!

KLIK

I BET TWO STAR CHIPS!

DUEL START !

BEAT THAT SEA DUDE!

GO YUGI!

WSH

READY !!

HERE I GO !!

YUGI	RYOTA KAJIKI
Life Points 2000	Life Points 2000

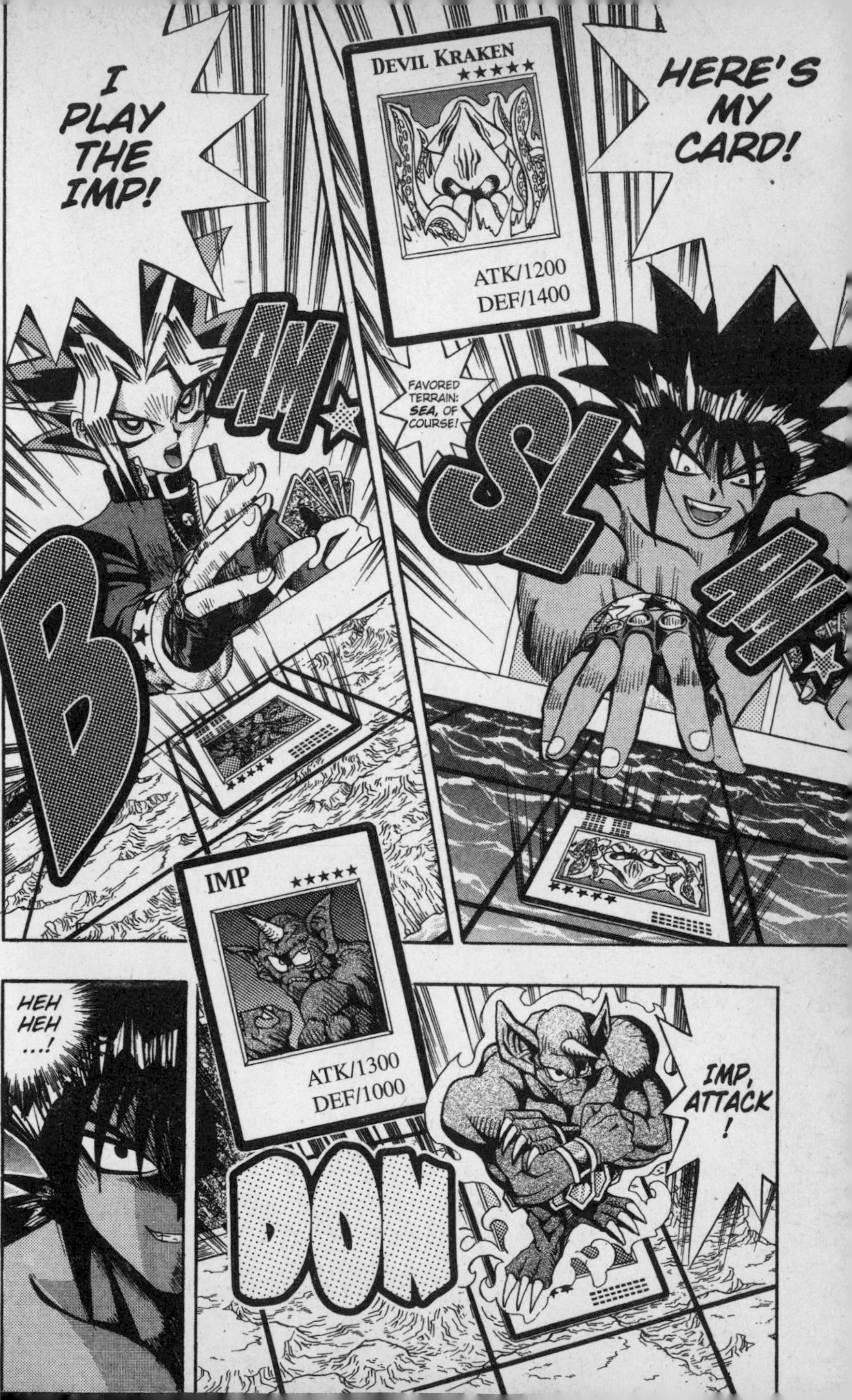
HERE'S MY CARD!
DEVIL KRAKEN
ATK/1200
DEF/1400
FAVORED TERRAIN: SEA, OF COURSE!
SLAM
I PLAY THE IMP!
BAM
IMP
ATK/1300
DEF/1000
IMP, ATTACK!
DON
HEH HEH ...!

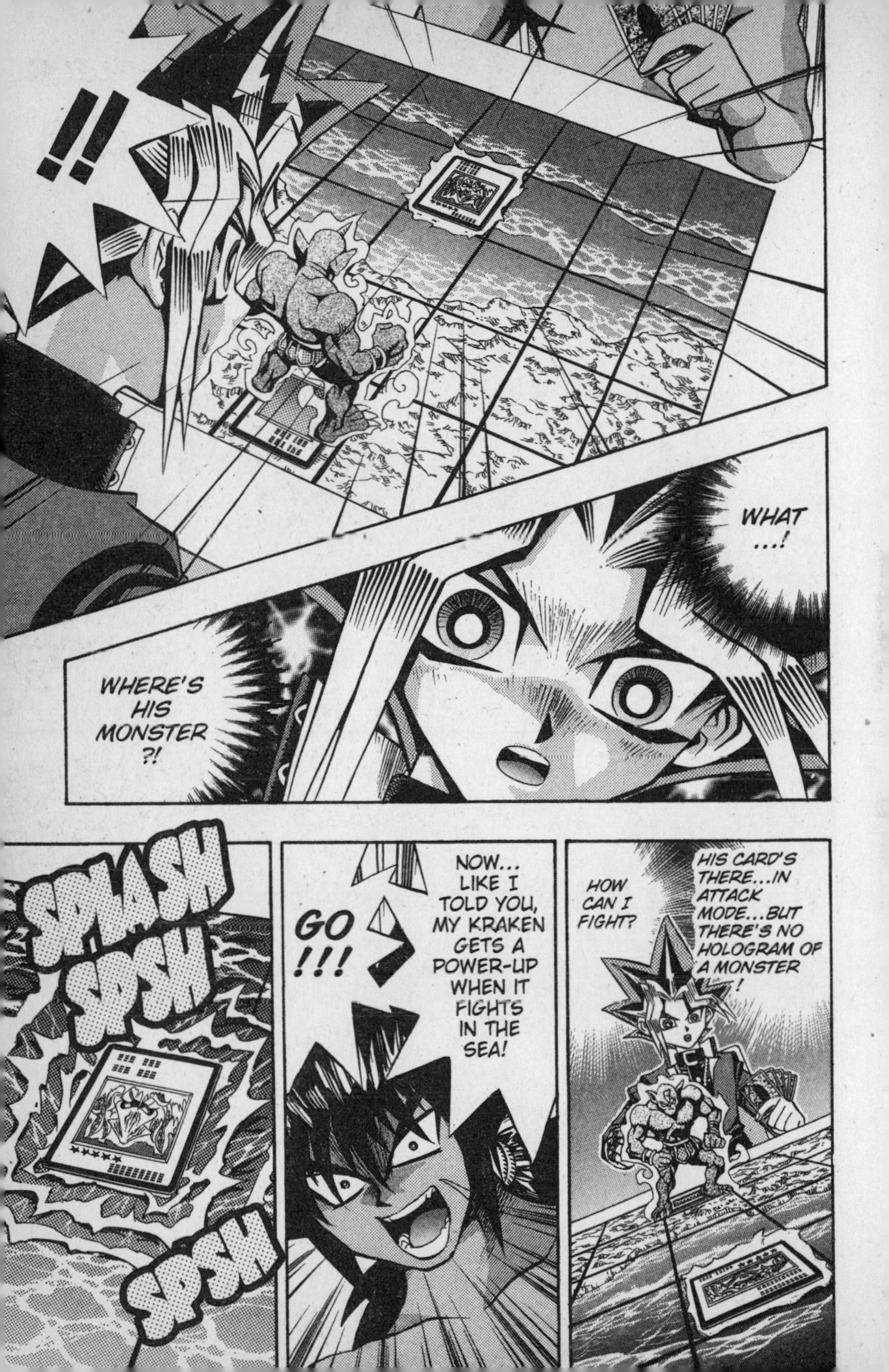
!!
WHAT...!
WHERE'S HIS MONSTER?!
HIS CARD'S THERE...IN ATTACK MODE...BUT THERE'S NO HOLOGRAM OF A MONSTER!
HOW CAN I FIGHT?
NOW... LIKE I TOLD YOU, MY KRAKEN GETS A POWER-UP WHEN IT FIGHTS IN THE SEA!
GO!!!
SPLASH
SPSH
SPSH

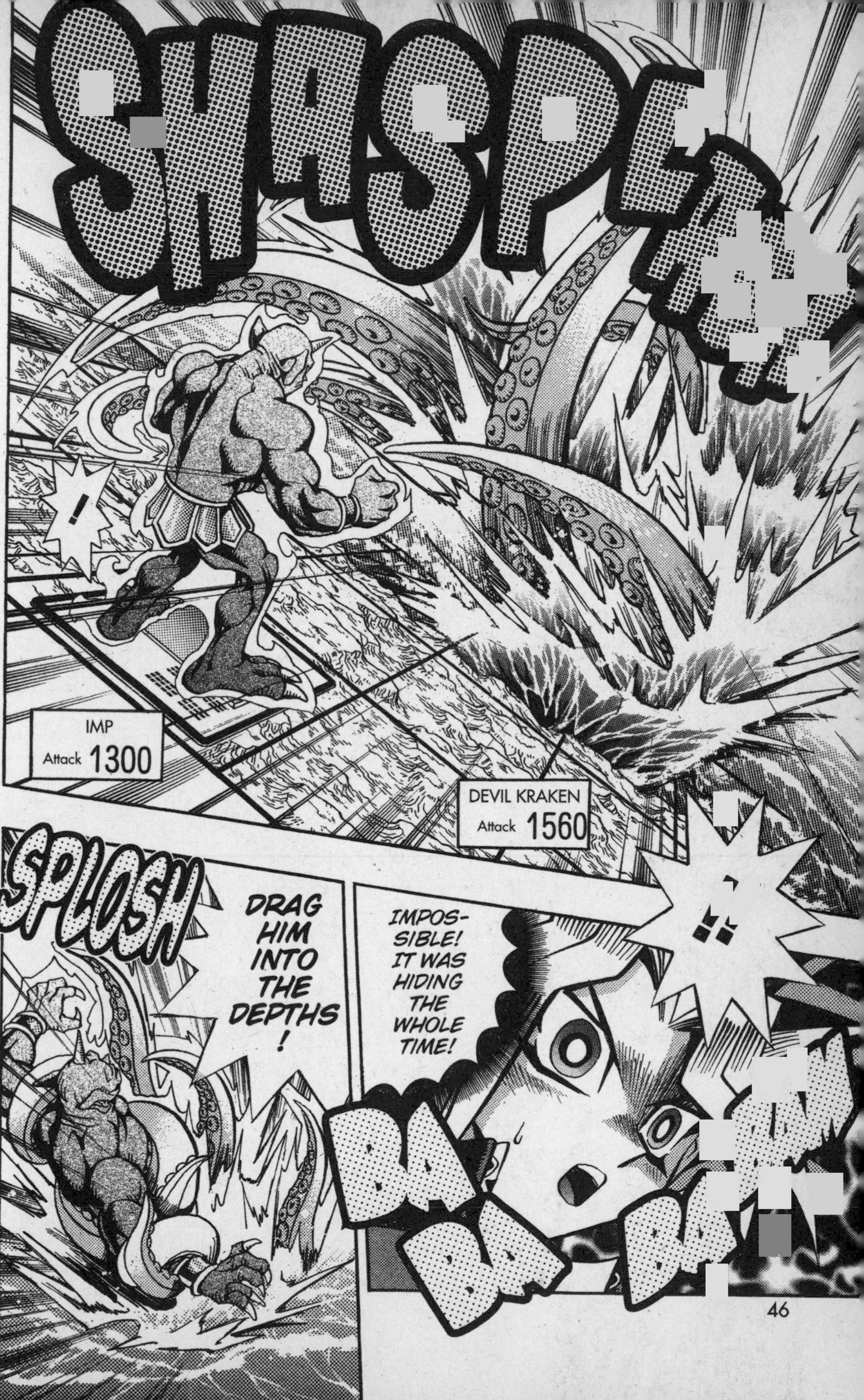
SHASH
!
IMP
Attack 1300
DEVIL KRAKEN
Attack 1560
!!
IMPOSSIBLE! IT WAS HIDING THE WHOLE TIME!
BA DA DA
SPLOSH
DRAG HIM INTO THE DEPTHS!

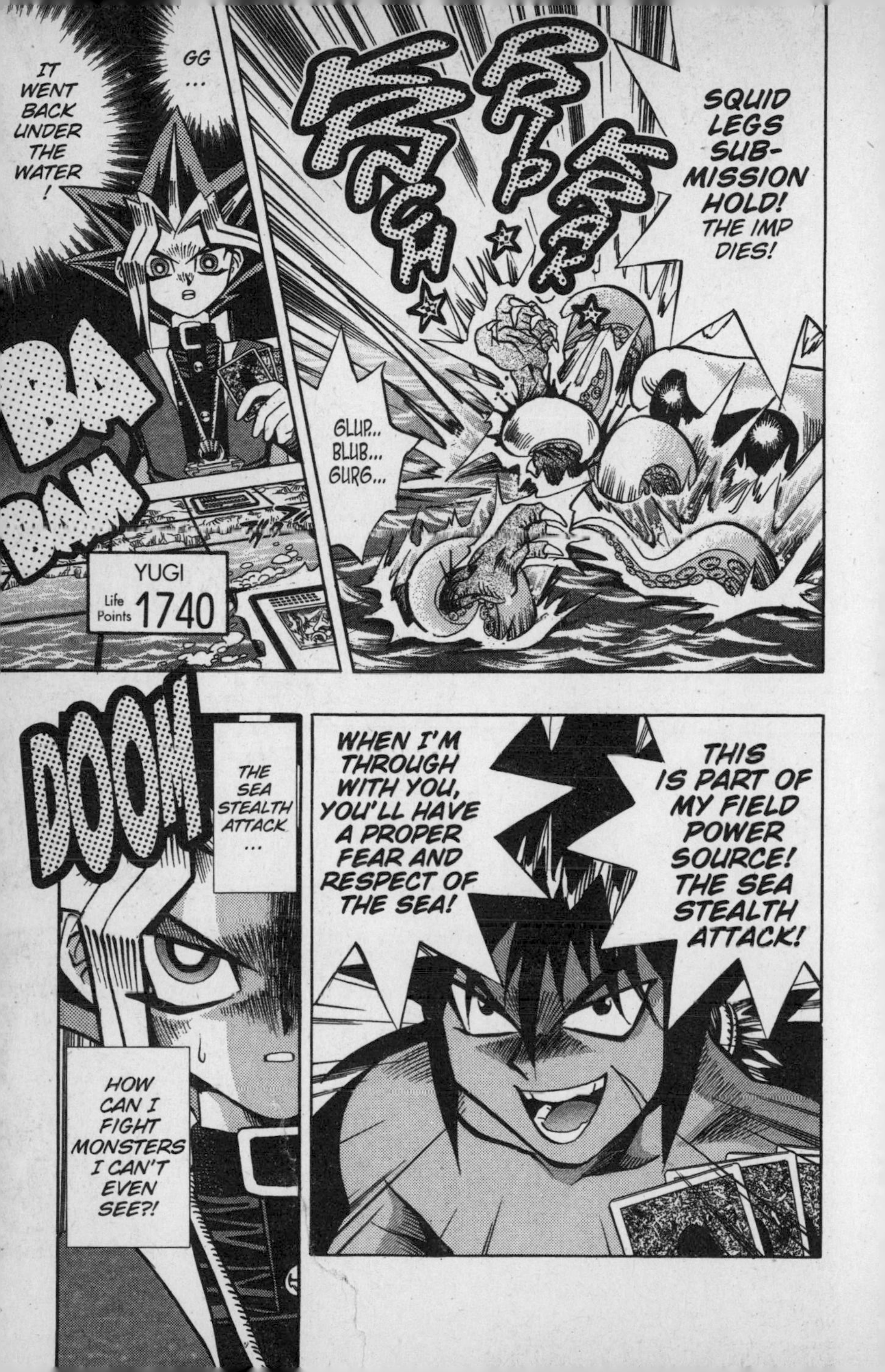
SQUID LEGS SUB-MISSION HOLD! THE IMP DIES!
GLUP... BLUB... GURG...
GG ...
IT WENT BACK UNDER THE WATER!
BA BAM
YUGI Life Points 1740
THIS IS PART OF MY FIELD POWER SOURCE! THE SEA STEALTH ATTACK!
WHEN I'M THROUGH WITH YOU, YOU'LL HAVE A PROPER FEAR AND RESPECT OF THE SEA!
DOOM
THE SEA STEALTH ATTACK ...
HOW CAN I FIGHT MONSTERS I CAN'T EVEN SEE?!

Duel 13: Attack from the Deep

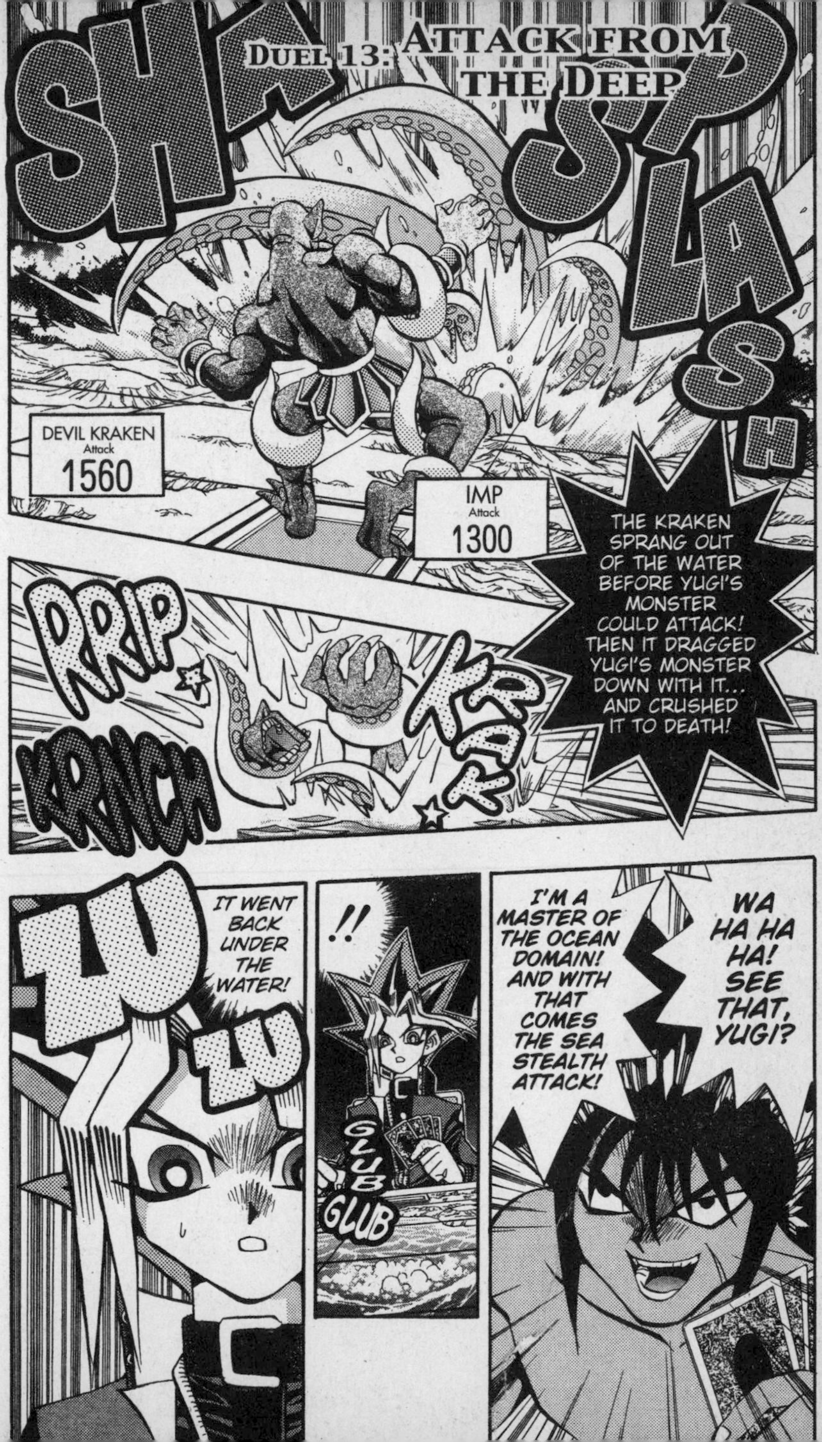
SHA SPLASH
DEVIL KRAKEN Attack 1560
IMP Attack 1300
THE KRAKEN SPRANG OUT OF THE WATER BEFORE YUGI'S MONSTER COULD ATTACK! THEN IT DRAGGED YUGI'S MONSTER DOWN WITH IT... AND CRUSHED IT TO DEATH!
KRAK
RRIP
KRNCH
WA HA HA HA! SEE THAT, YUGI?
I'M A MASTER OF THE OCEAN DOMAIN! AND WITH THAT COMES THE SEA STEALTH ATTACK!
!!
GLUB GLUB
IT WENT BACK UNDER THE WATER!
ZU ZU

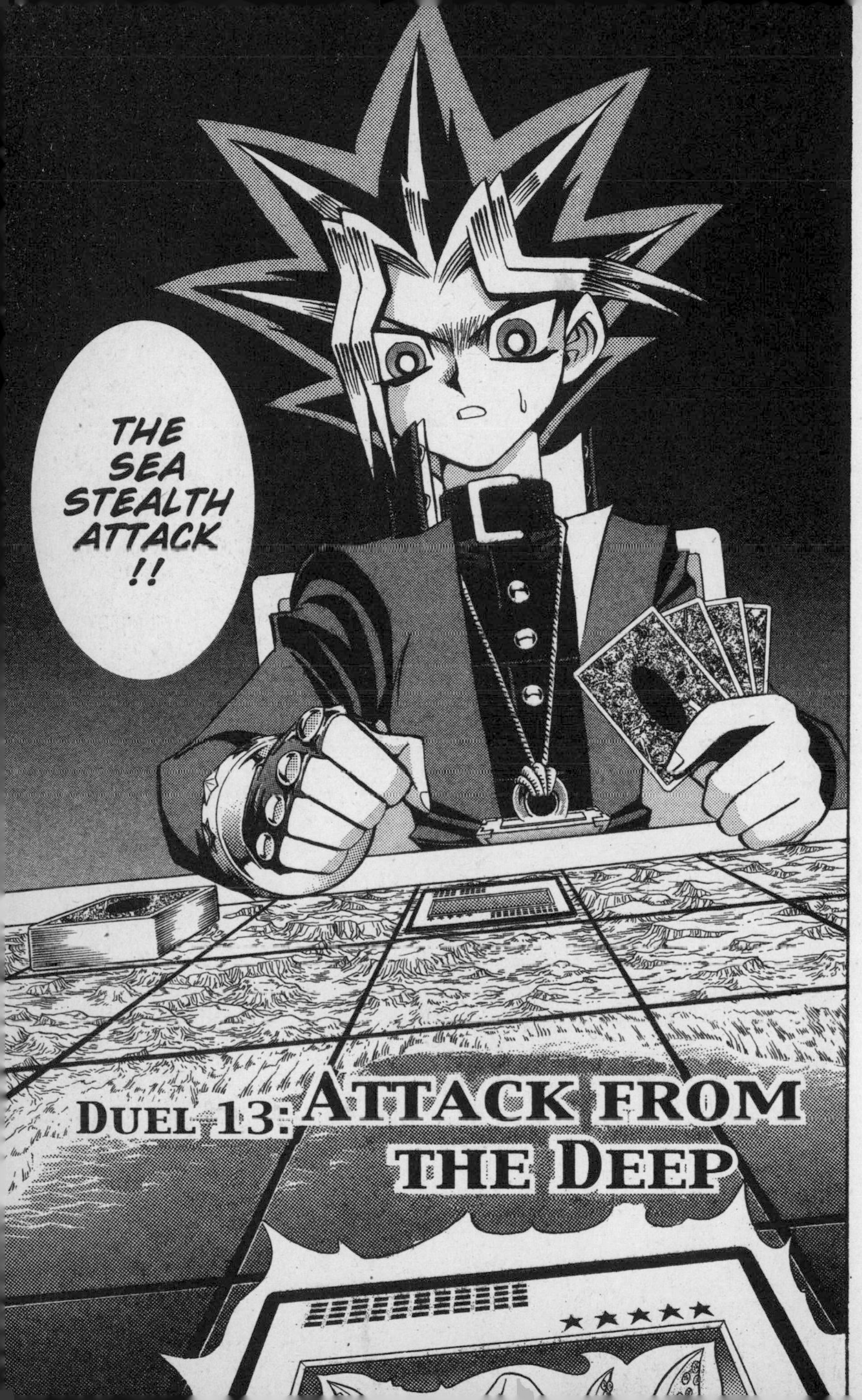
THE SEA STEALTH ATTACK !!
DUEL 13: ATTACK FROM THE DEEP

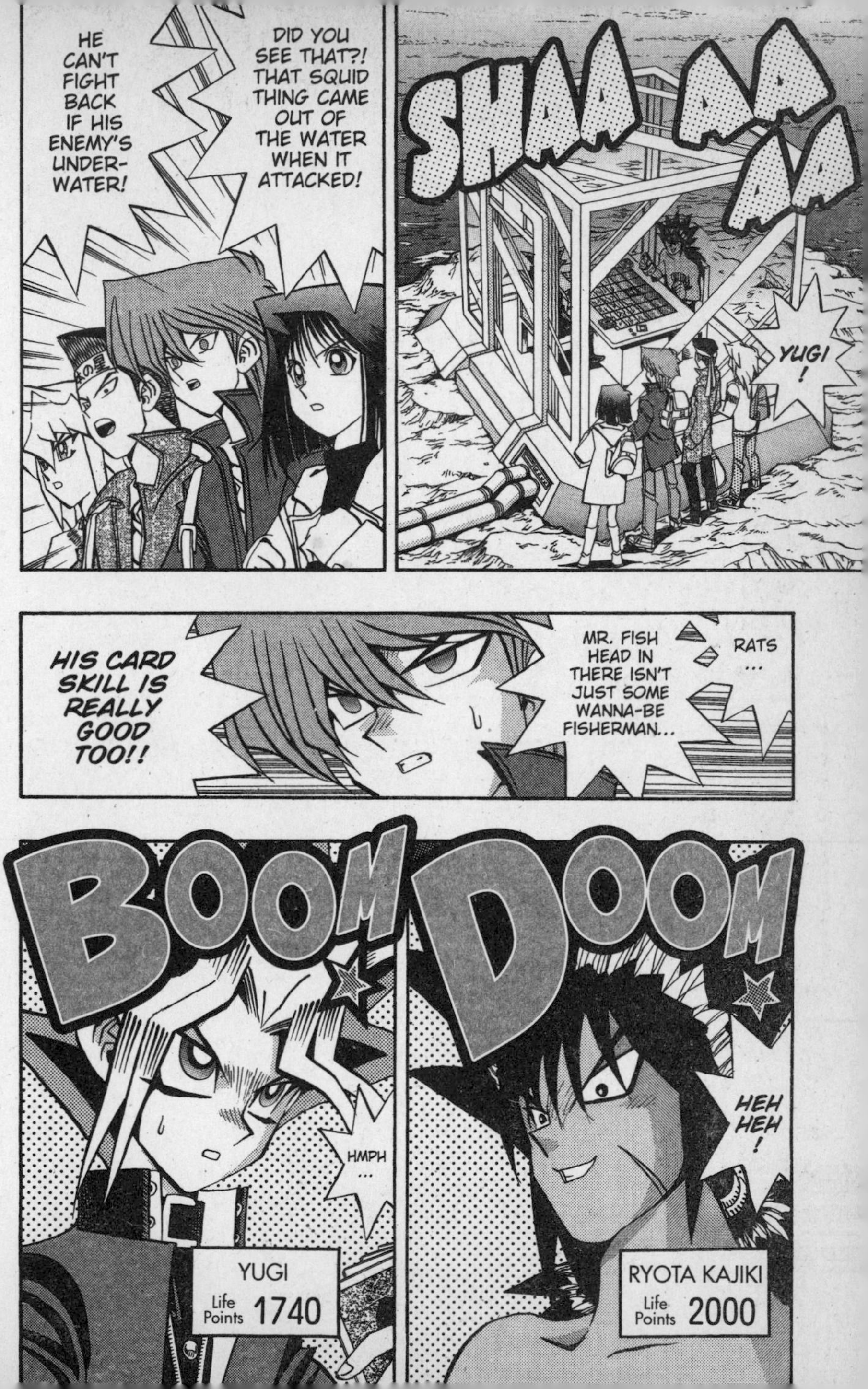
SHAA AAA AAA
YUGI!
DID YOU SEE THAT?! THAT SQUID THING CAME OUT OF THE WATER WHEN IT ATTACKED!
HE CAN'T FIGHT BACK IF HIS ENEMY'S UNDER-WATER!
RATS...
MR. FISH HEAD IN THERE ISN'T JUST SOME WANNA-BE FISHERMAN...
HIS CARD SKILL IS REALLY GOOD TOO!!
DOOM
HEH HEH!
RYOTA KAJIKI
Life Points 2000
BOOM
HMPH...
YUGI
Life Points 1740

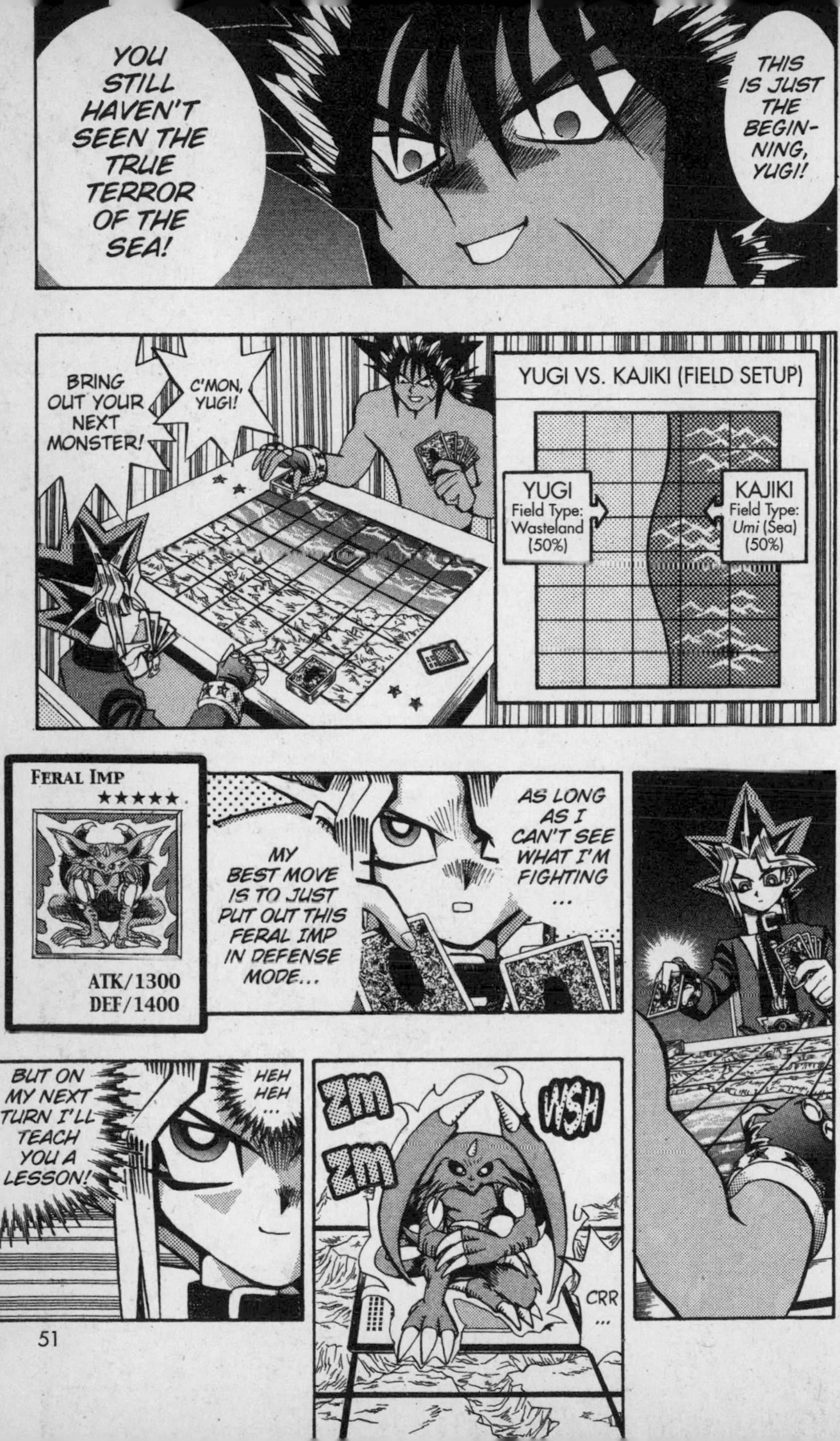
THIS IS JUST THE BEGIN-NING, YUGI!
YOU STILL HAVEN'T SEEN THE TRUE TERROR OF THE SEA!
YUGI VS. KAJIKI (FIELD SETUP)
KAJIKI Field Type: Umi (Sea) (50%)
YUGI Field Type: Wasteland (50%)
C'MON, YUGI!
BRING OUT YOUR NEXT MONSTER!
AS LONG AS I CAN'T SEE WHAT I'M FIGHTING ...
MY BEST MOVE IS TO JUST PUT OUT THIS FERAL IMP IN DEFENSE MODE...
FERAL IMP
★★★★★
ATK/1300
DEF/1400
WSH
ZM
ZM
CRR ...
HEH HEH ...
BUT ON MY NEXT TURN I'LL TEACH YOU A LESSON!

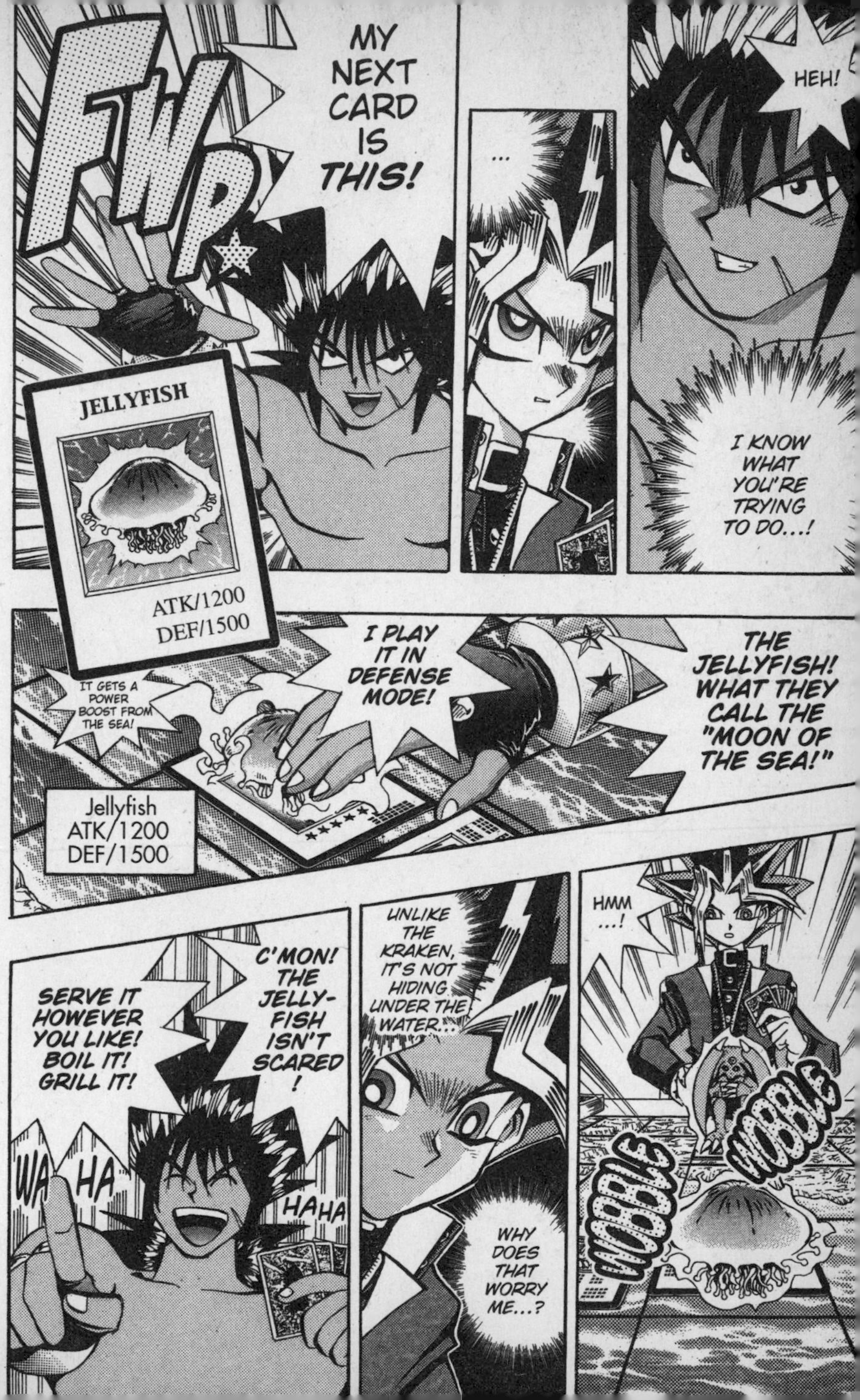
HEH!
I KNOW WHAT YOU'RE TRYING TO DO...!
...
FWP
MY NEXT CARD IS THIS!
JELLYFISH
ATK/1200
DEF/1500
THE JELLYFISH! WHAT THEY CALL THE "MOON OF THE SEA!"
I PLAY IT IN DEFENSE MODE!
IT GETS A POWER BOOST FROM THE SEA!
Jellyfish
ATK/1200
DEF/1500
HMM ...!
WOBBLE
WOBBLE
UNLIKE THE KRAKEN, IT'S NOT HIDING UNDER THE WATER...
WHY DOES THAT WORRY ME...?
C'MON! THE JELLY-FISH ISN'T SCARED!
SERVE IT HOWEVER YOU LIKE! BOIL IT! GRILL IT!
WA HA
HA HA

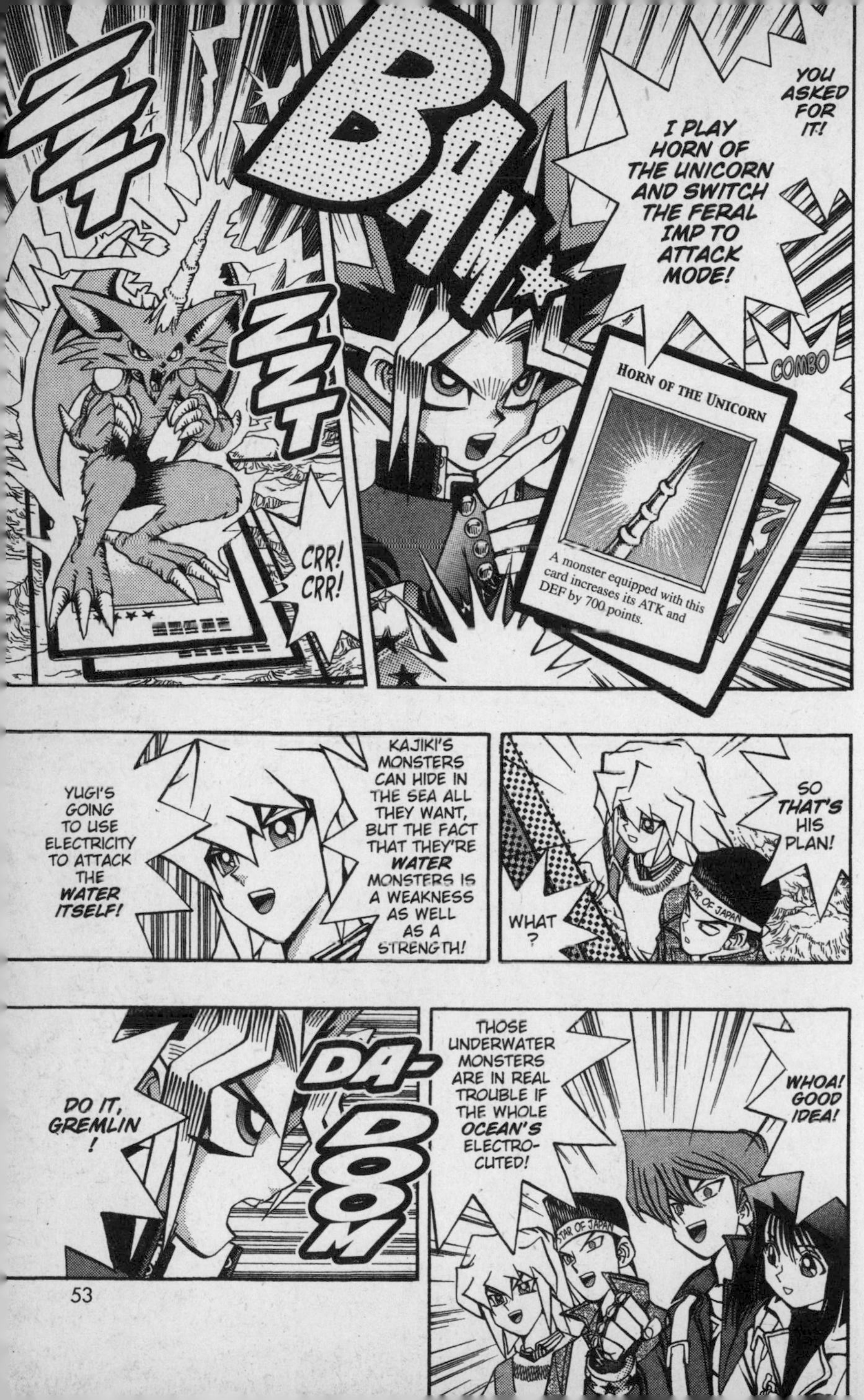

YOU ASKED FOR IT!
I PLAY HORN OF THE UNICORN AND SWITCH THE FERAL IMP TO ATTACK MODE!
BAM
ZZZT
ZZZT
COMBO
HORN OF THE UNICORN
A monster equipped with this card increases its ATK and DEF by 700 points.
CRR! CRR!
SO THAT'S HIS PLAN!
WHAT?
STAR OF JAPAN
KAJIKI'S MONSTERS CAN HIDE IN THE SEA ALL THEY WANT, BUT THE FACT THAT THEY'RE WATER MONSTERS IS A WEAKNESS AS WELL AS A STRENGTH!
YUGI'S GOING TO USE ELECTRICITY TO ATTACK THE WATER ITSELF!
WHOA! GOOD IDEA!
THOSE UNDERWATER MONSTERS ARE IN REAL TROUBLE IF THE WHOLE OCEAN'S ELECTROCUTED!
STAR OF JAPAN
DA-DOOM
DO IT, GREMLIN!

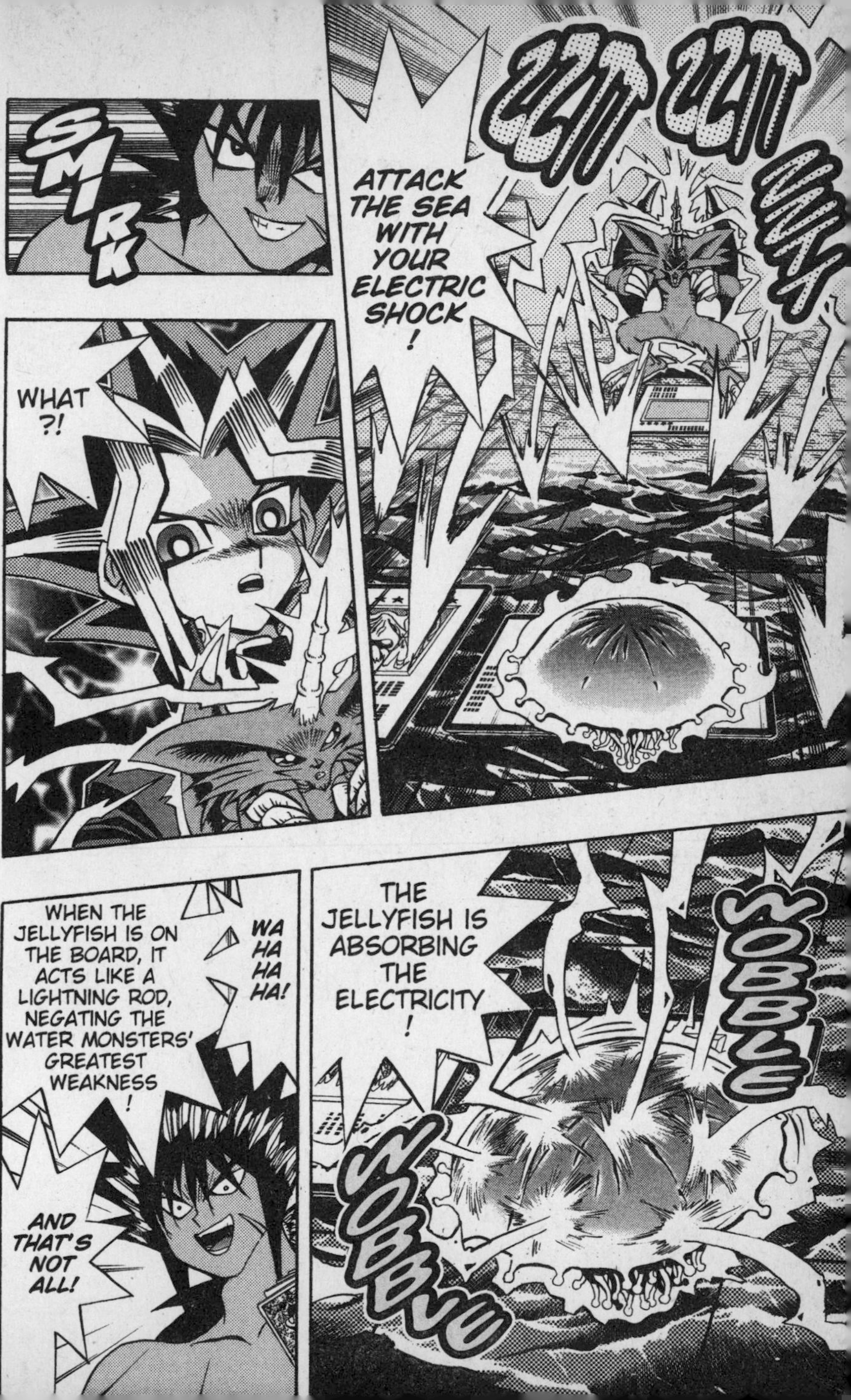
ZZZT ZZZT
ATTACK THE SEA WITH YOUR ELECTRIC SHOCK!
SMIRK
WHAT?!
THE JELLYFISH IS ABSORBING THE ELECTRICITY!
WOBBLE
WOBBLE
WHEN THE JELLYFISH IS ON THE BOARD, IT ACTS LIKE A LIGHTNING ROD, NEGATING THE WATER MONSTERS' GREATEST WEAKNESS!
WA HA HA HA!
AND THAT'S NOT ALL!

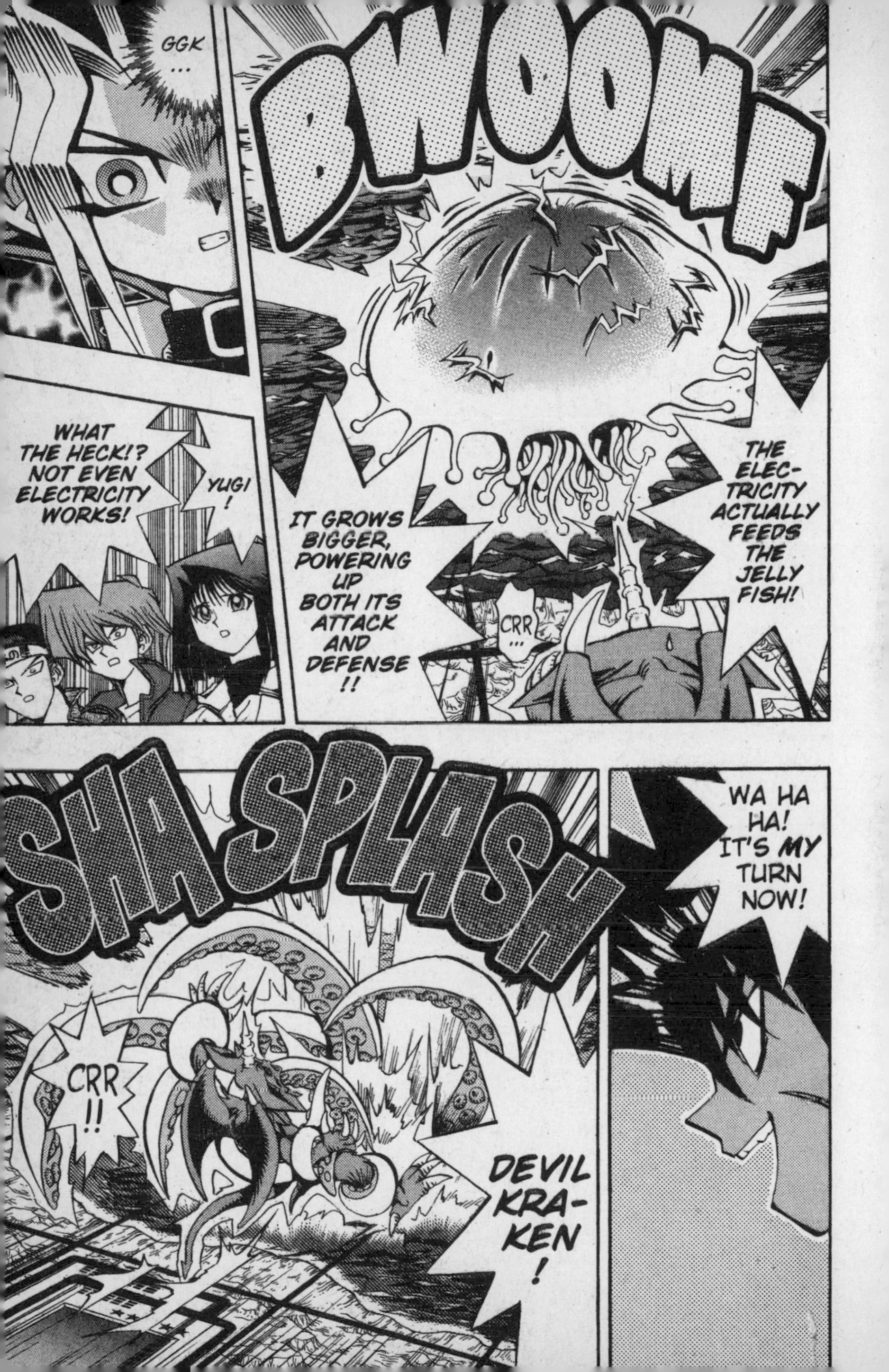

BWOOMF
THE ELECTRICITY ACTUALLY FEEDS THE JELLY FISH!
IT GROWS BIGGER, POWERING UP BOTH ITS ATTACK AND DEFENSE!!
CRR...
GGK...
YUGI!
WHAT THE HECK!? NOT EVEN ELECTRICITY WORKS!
WA HA HA! IT'S MY TURN NOW!
SHA SPLASH
DEVIL KRAKEN!
CRR!!

KRAK RENCH SNAP

SQUID LEGS SUBMISSION HOLD!

THE GREMLIN IS GONE!

BA BA BAM

WAH HA HA HA! NO ONE CAN BEAT ME AT SEA!

BIG FISH! BIG FISH!

BAM

WOBBLE WEEBLE

22T 22T

YUGI
Life Points 1480

GUG GUG

THERE'S NO HOLES IN HIS ATTACK OR DEFENSE!!

HE'S STRONG...

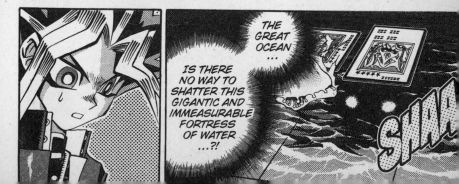

THE GREAT OCEAN...

IS THERE NO WAY TO SHATTER THIS GIGANTIC AND IMMEASURABLE FORTRESS OF WATER...?!

SHAA

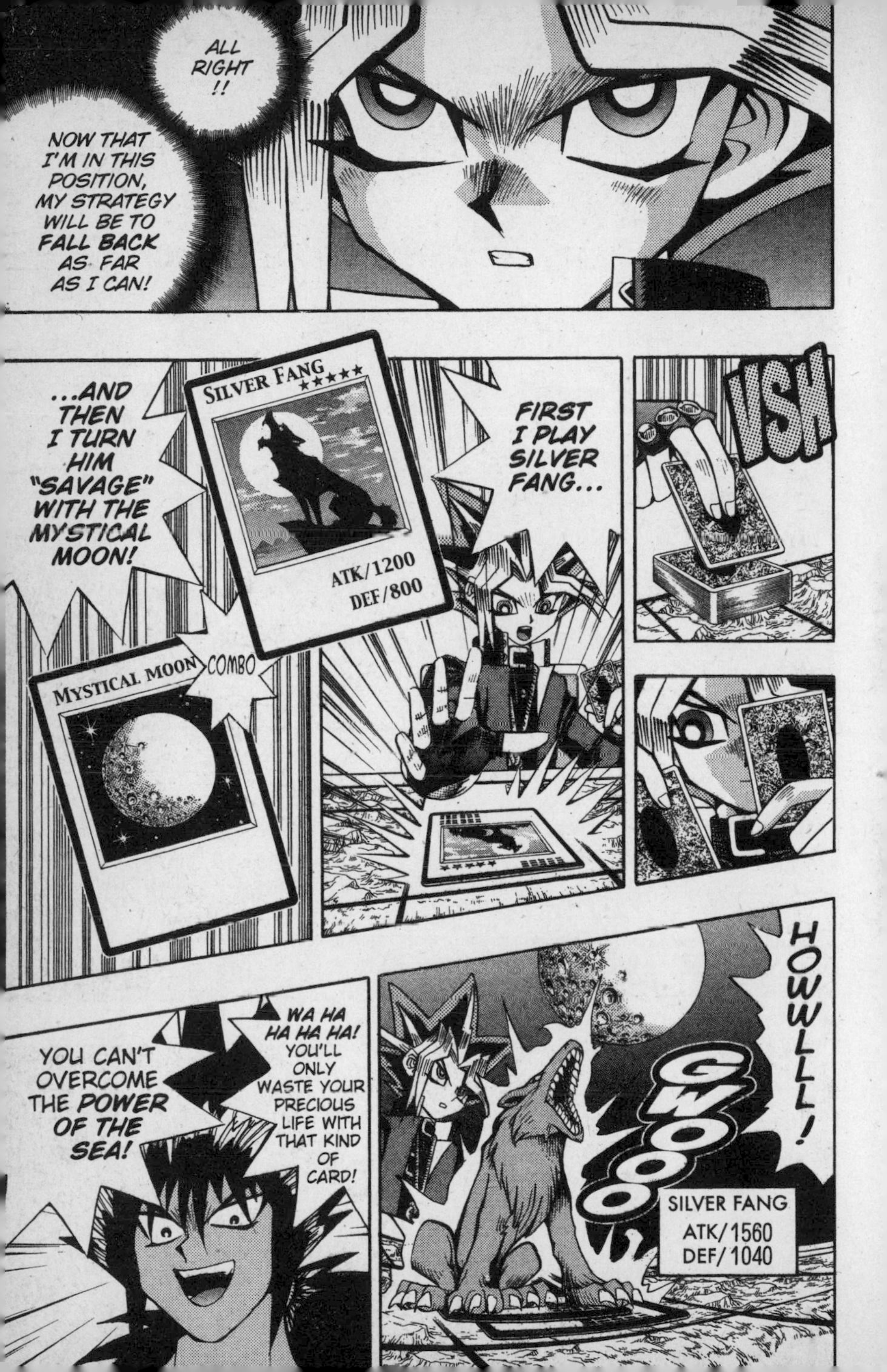
ALL RIGHT!!
NOW THAT I'M IN THIS POSITION, MY STRATEGY WILL BE TO FALL BACK AS FAR AS I CAN!
VSH
FIRST I PLAY SILVER FANG...
...AND THEN I TURN HIM "SAVAGE" WITH THE MYSTICAL MOON!
SILVER FANG
ATK/1200
DEF/800
COMBO
MYSTICAL MOON
HOWWLLL!
GWOOOO
SILVER FANG
ATK/1560
DEF/1040
WA HA HA HA HA! YOU'LL ONLY WASTE YOUR PRECIOUS LIFE WITH THAT KIND OF CARD!
YOU CAN'T OVERCOME THE POWER OF THE SEA!

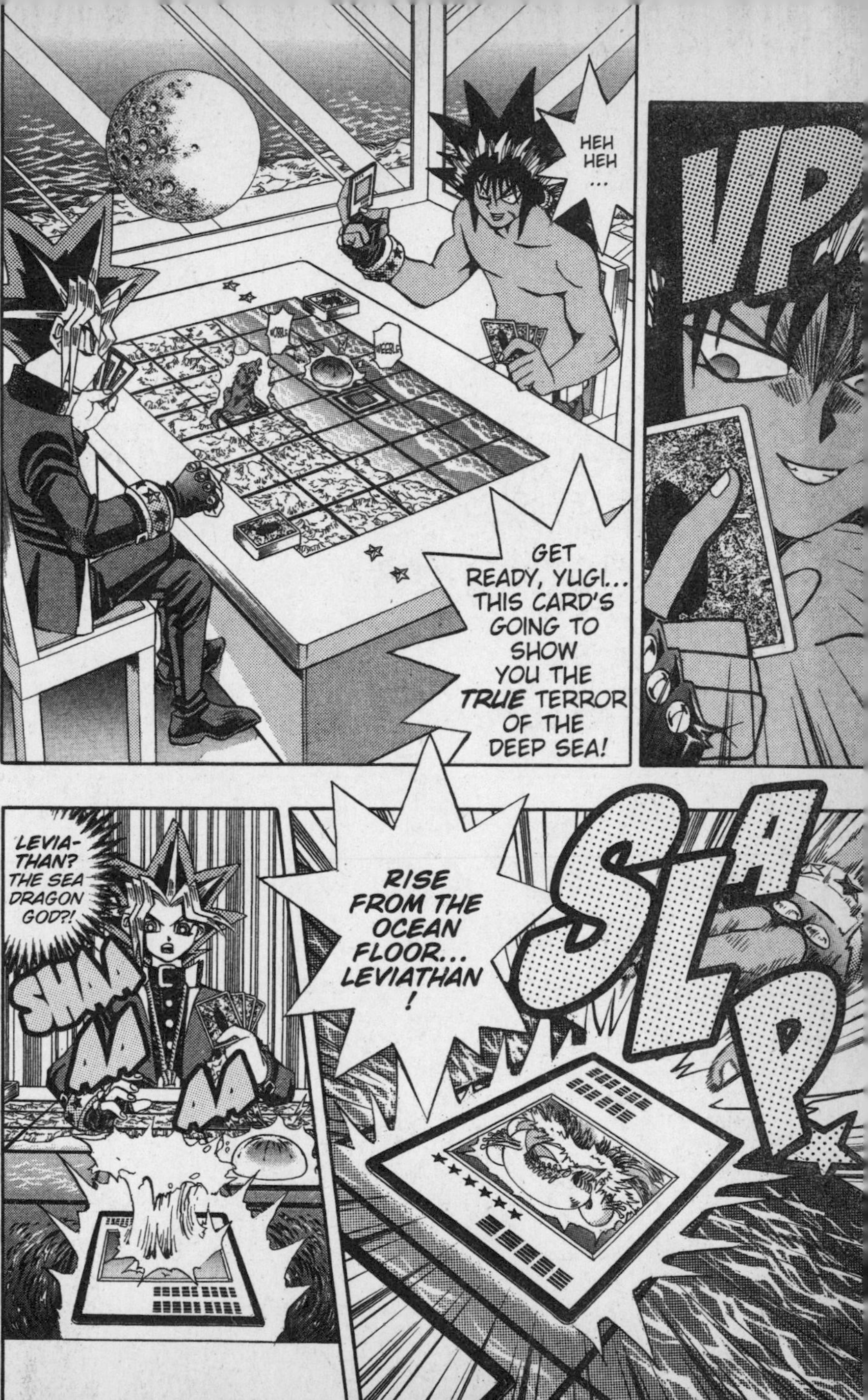
HEH HEH ...
GET READY, YUGI... THIS CARD'S GOING TO SHOW YOU THE TRUE TERROR OF THE DEEP SEA!
RISE FROM THE OCEAN FLOOR... LEVIATHAN !
LEVIA-THAN? THE SEA DRAGON GOD?!

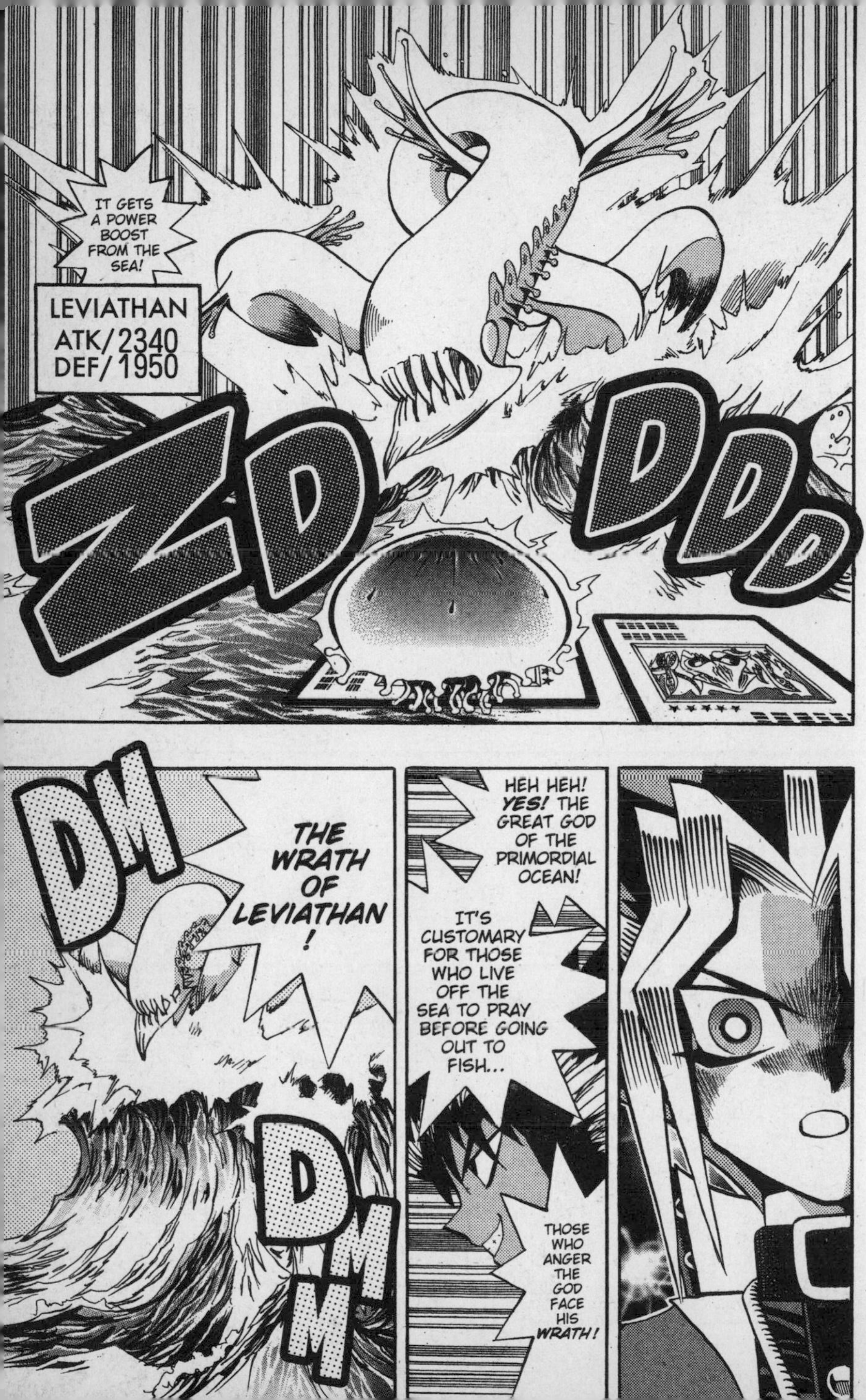
IT GETS A POWER BOOST FROM THE SEA!
LEVIATHAN
ATK/2340
DEF/1950
ZD DDD
HEH HEH! YES! THE GREAT GOD OF THE PRIMORDIAL OCEAN!
IT'S CUSTOMARY FOR THOSE WHO LIVE OFF THE SEA TO PRAY BEFORE GOING OUT TO FISH...
THOSE WHO ANGER THE GOD FACE HIS WRATH!
DM
THE WRATH OF LEVIATHAN!
DMM!

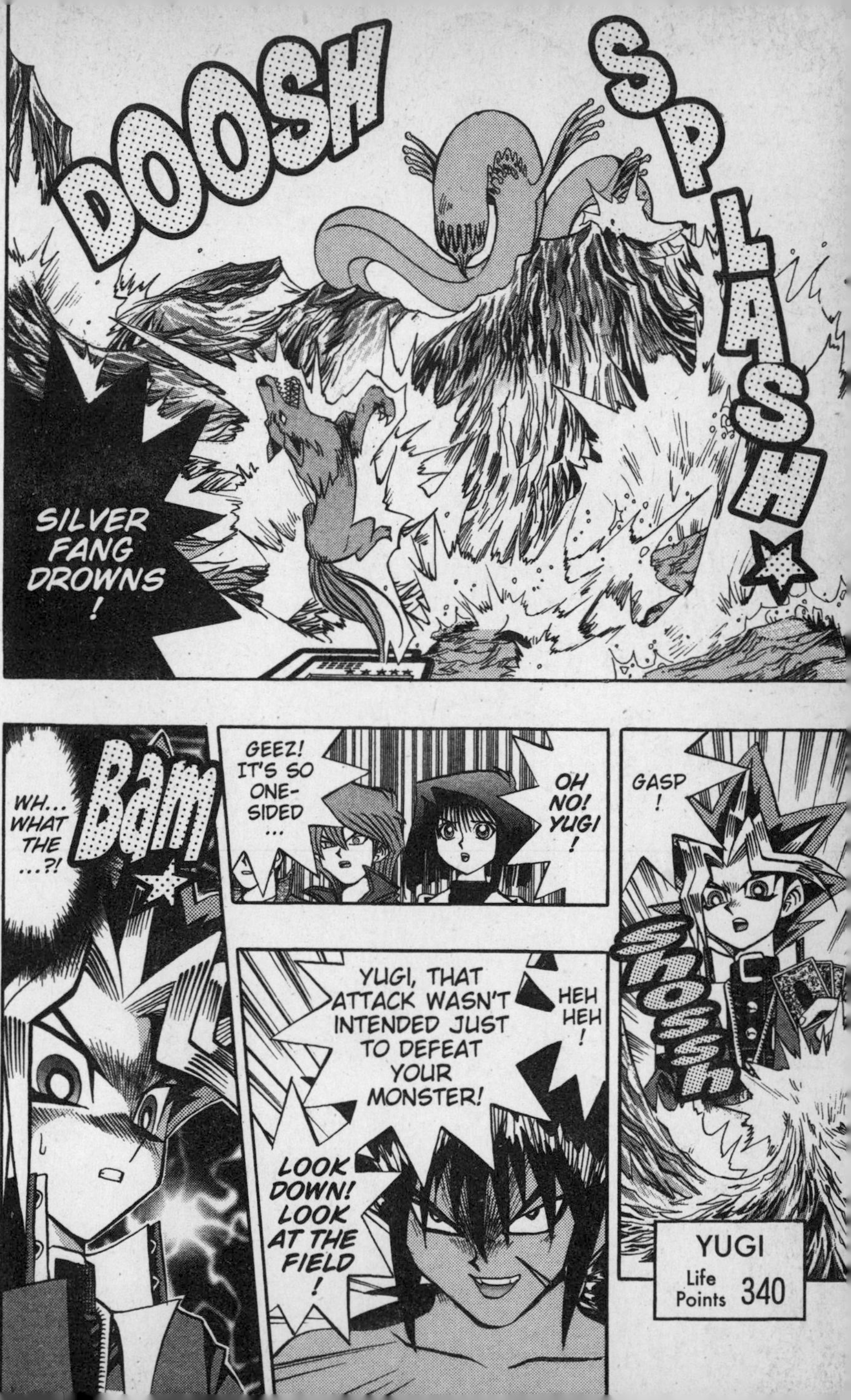
SPLASH
DOOSH
SILVER FANG DROWNS !
GASP !
SWOOSH
YUGI
Life Points 340
OH NO! YUGI !
GEEZ! IT'S SO ONE-SIDED ...
HEH HEH !
YUGI, THAT ATTACK WASN'T INTENDED JUST TO DEFEAT YOUR MONSTER!
LOOK DOWN! LOOK AT THE FIELD !
Bam
WH... WHAT THE ...?!

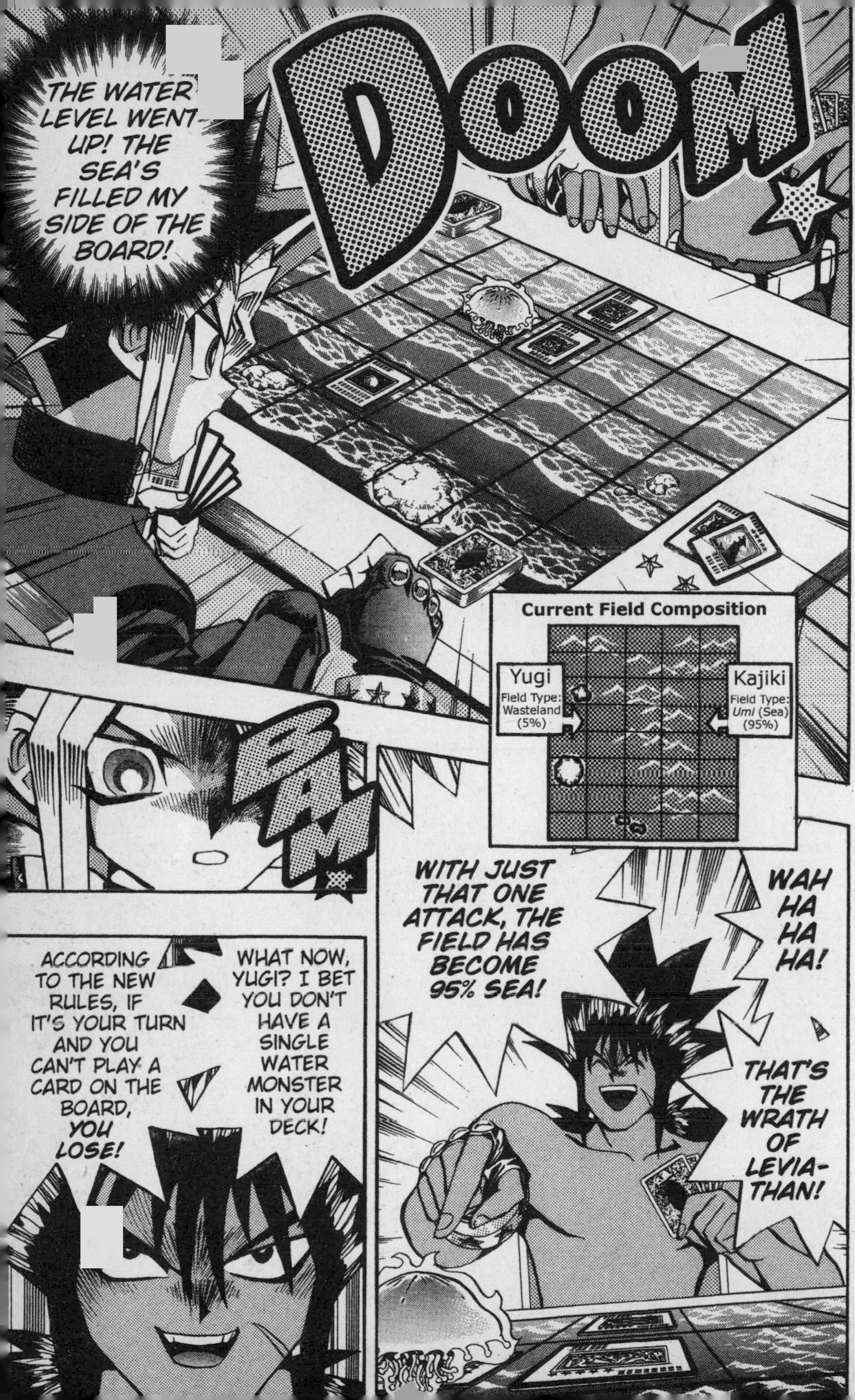
DOOM
THE WATER LEVEL WENT UP! THE SEA'S FILLED MY SIDE OF THE BOARD!
Current Field Composition
Yugi
Field Type: Wasteland (5%)
Kajiki
Field Type: *Umi* (Sea) (95%)
BAM
WITH JUST THAT ONE ATTACK, THE FIELD HAS BECOME 95% SEA!
WAH HA HA HA!
THAT'S THE WRATH OF LEVIA-THAN!
WHAT NOW, YUGI? I BET YOU DON'T HAVE A SINGLE WATER MONSTER IN YOUR DECK!
ACCORDING TO THE NEW RULES, IF IT'S YOUR TURN AND YOU CAN'T PLAY A CARD ON THE BOARD, *YOU LOSE!*

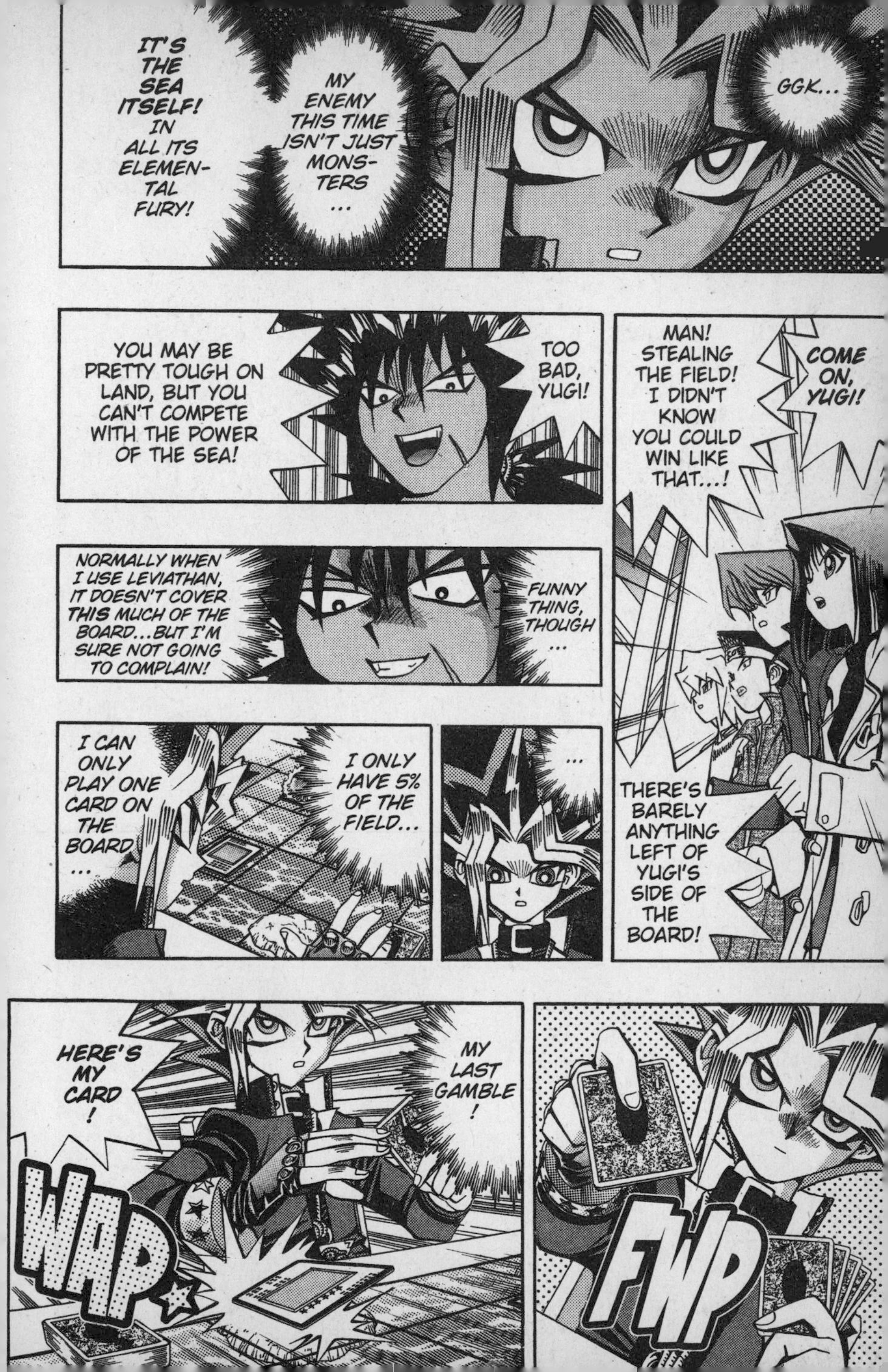
GGK...
MY ENEMY THIS TIME ISN'T JUST MONSTERS...
IT'S THE SEA ITSELF! IN ALL ITS ELEMENTAL FURY!
COME ON, YUGI!
MAN! STEALING THE FIELD! I DIDN'T KNOW YOU COULD WIN LIKE THAT...!
THERE'S BARELY ANYTHING LEFT OF YUGI'S SIDE OF THE BOARD!
TOO BAD, YUGI!
YOU MAY BE PRETTY TOUGH ON LAND, BUT YOU CAN'T COMPETE WITH THE POWER OF THE SEA!
FUNNY THING, THOUGH...
NORMALLY WHEN I USE LEVIATHAN, IT DOESN'T COVER THIS MUCH OF THE BOARD...BUT I'M SURE NOT GOING TO COMPLAIN!
...
I ONLY HAVE 5% OF THE FIELD...
I CAN ONLY PLAY ONE CARD ON THE BOARD...
FWP
MY LAST GAMBLE!
HERE'S MY CARD!
WAP

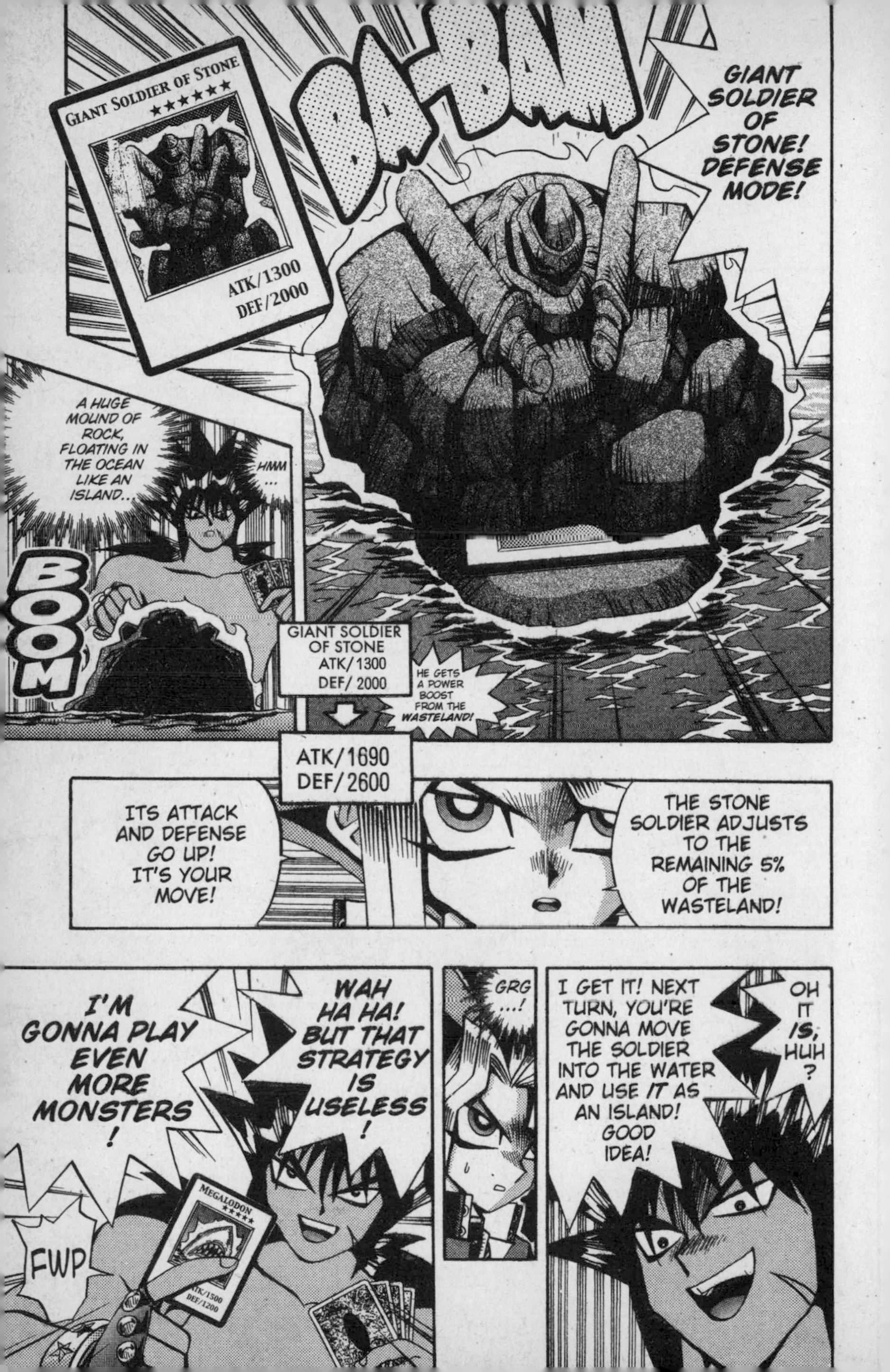
DA-BAM
GIANT SOLDIER OF STONE! DEFENSE MODE!
GIANT SOLDIER OF STONE
ATK/1300
DEF/2000
HMM ...
A HUGE MOUND OF ROCK, FLOATING IN THE OCEAN LIKE AN ISLAND...
BOOM
GIANT SOLDIER OF STONE ATK/1300 DEF/ 2000
HE GETS A POWER BOOST FROM THE WASTELAND!
ATK/1690 DEF/2600
THE STONE SOLDIER ADJUSTS TO THE REMAINING 5% OF THE WASTELAND!
ITS ATTACK AND DEFENSE GO UP! IT'S YOUR MOVE!
OH IT IS, HUH?
I GET IT! NEXT TURN, YOU'RE GONNA MOVE THE SOLDIER INTO THE WATER AND USE IT AS AN ISLAND! GOOD IDEA!
GRG ...!
WAH HA HA! BUT THAT STRATEGY IS USELESS!
I'M GONNA PLAY EVEN MORE MONSTERS!
MEGALODON
ATK/1500
DEF/1200
FWP

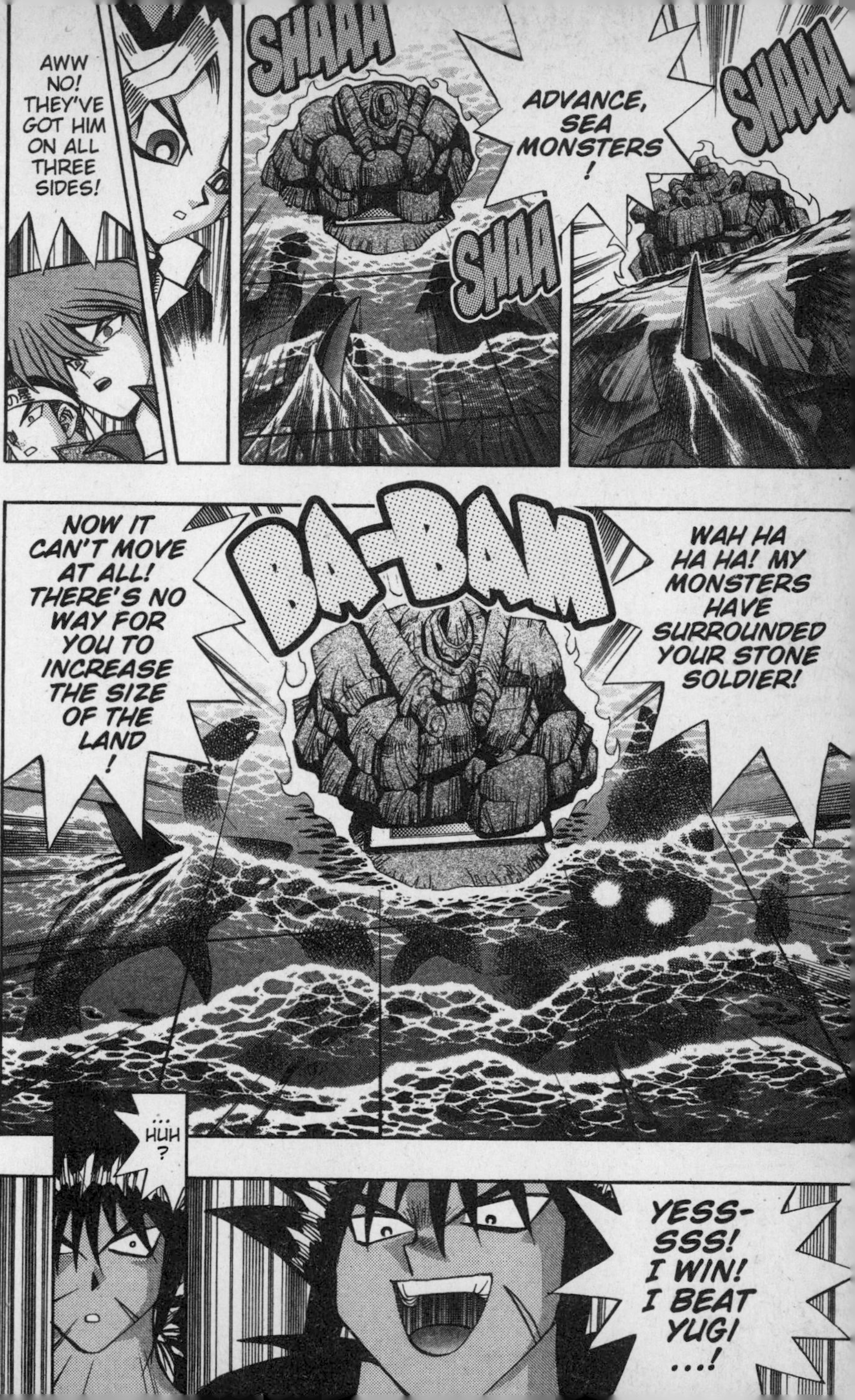
SHAAA
ADVANCE, SEA MONSTERS!
SHAAA
SHAA
AWW NO! THEY'VE GOT HIM ON ALL THREE SIDES!
WAH HA HA HA! MY MONSTERS HAVE SURROUNDED YOUR STONE SOLDIER!
BA-BAM
NOW IT CAN'T MOVE AT ALL! THERE'S NO WAY FOR YOU TO INCREASE THE SIZE OF THE LAND!
YESS-SSS! I WIN! I BEAT YUGI...!
...HUH?

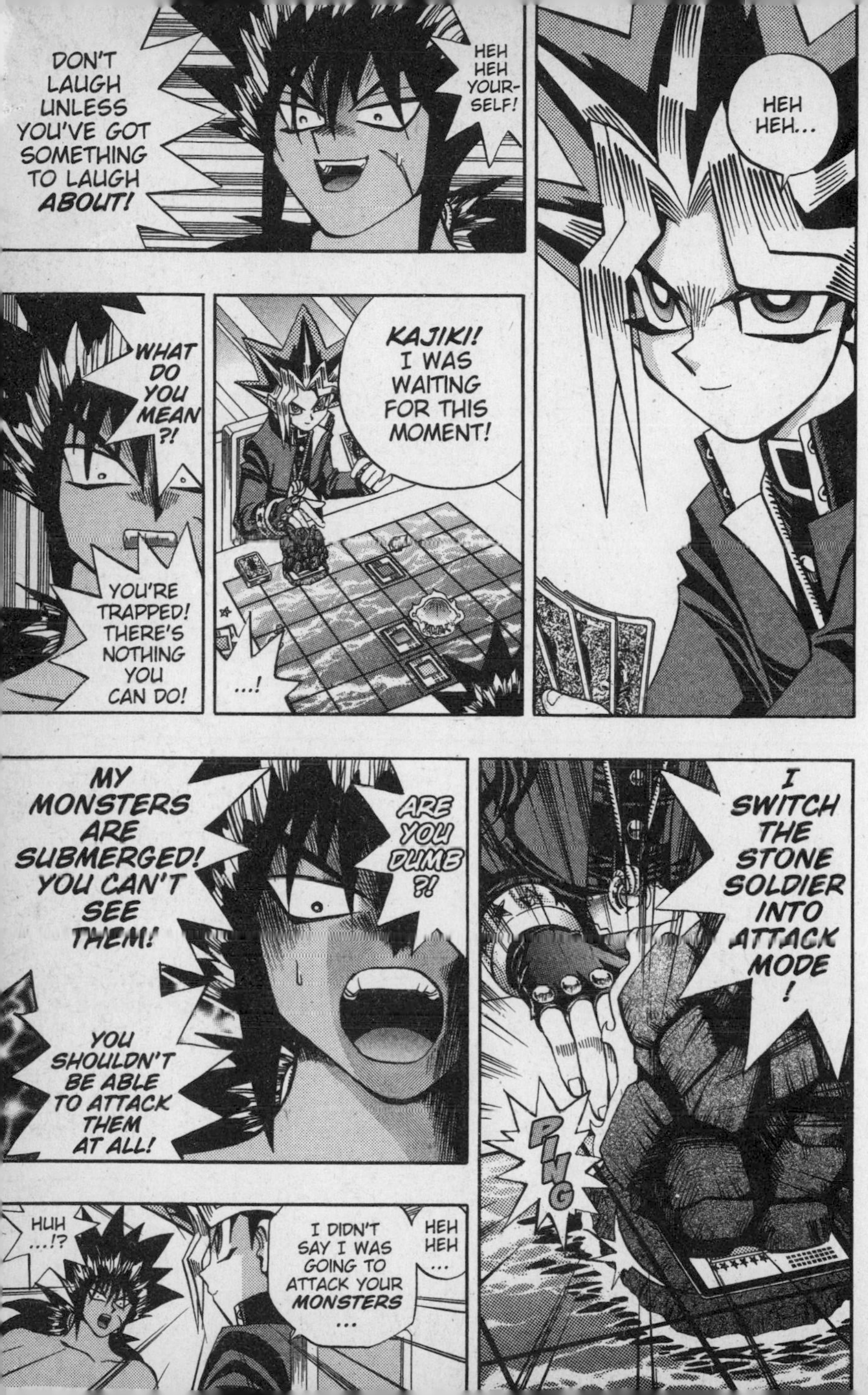
HEH HEH...
HEH HEH YOURSELF!
DON'T LAUGH UNLESS YOU'VE GOT SOMETHING TO LAUGH ABOUT!
KAJIKI! I WAS WAITING FOR THIS MOMENT!
...!
WHAT DO YOU MEAN ?!
YOU'RE TRAPPED! THERE'S NOTHING YOU CAN DO!
I SWITCH THE STONE SOLDIER INTO ATTACK MODE !
PING
ARE YOU DUMB ?!
MY MONSTERS ARE SUBMERGED! YOU CAN'T SEE THEM!
YOU SHOULDN'T BE ABLE TO ATTACK THEM AT ALL!
HEH HEH ...
I DIDN'T SAY I WAS GOING TO ATTACK YOUR MONSTERS ...
HUH ...!?

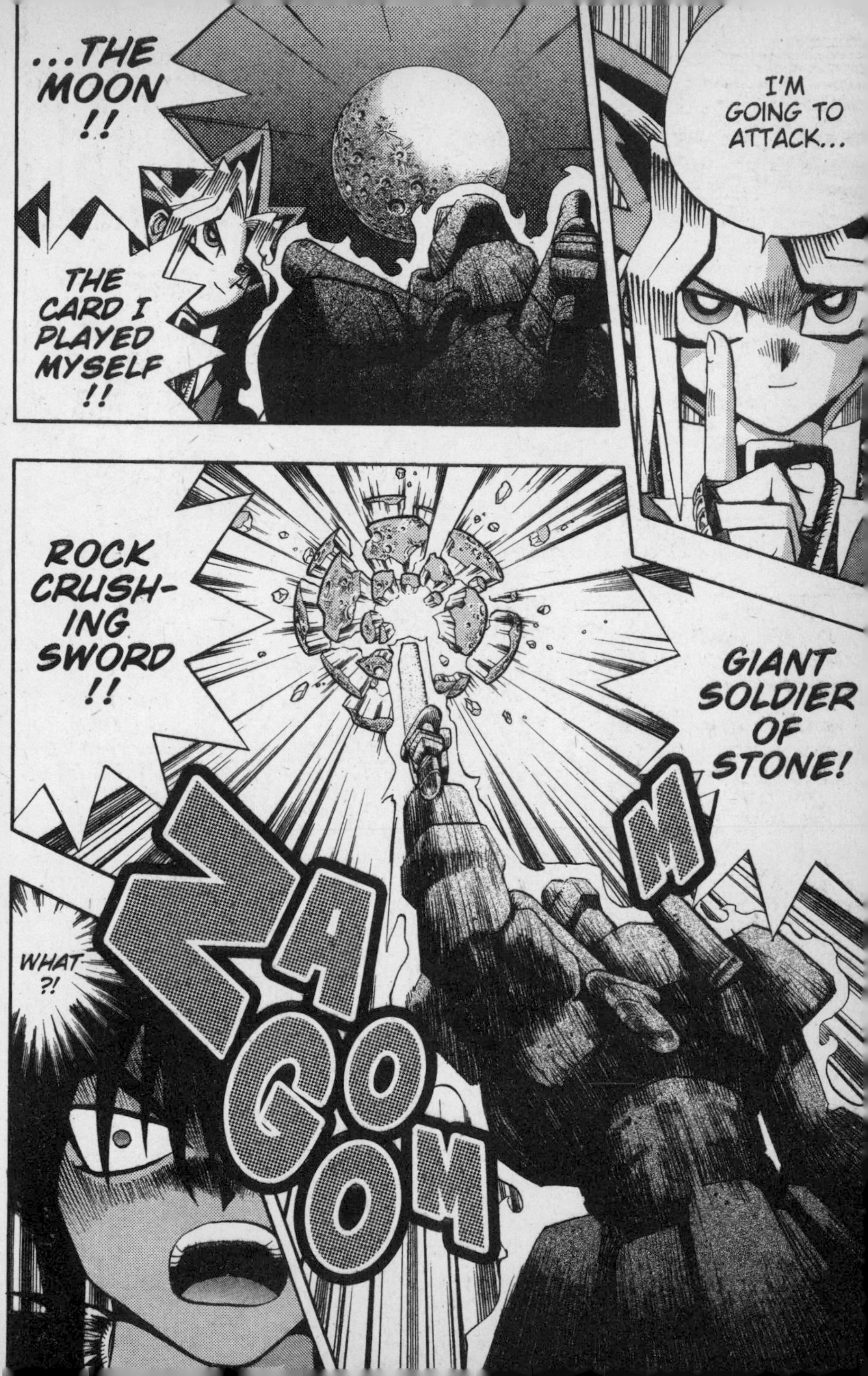
I'M GOING TO ATTACK...
...THE MOON!!
THE CARD I PLAYED MYSELF!!
GIANT SOLDIER OF STONE!
ROCK CRUSHING SWORD!!
M
ZAGOOM
WHAT?!

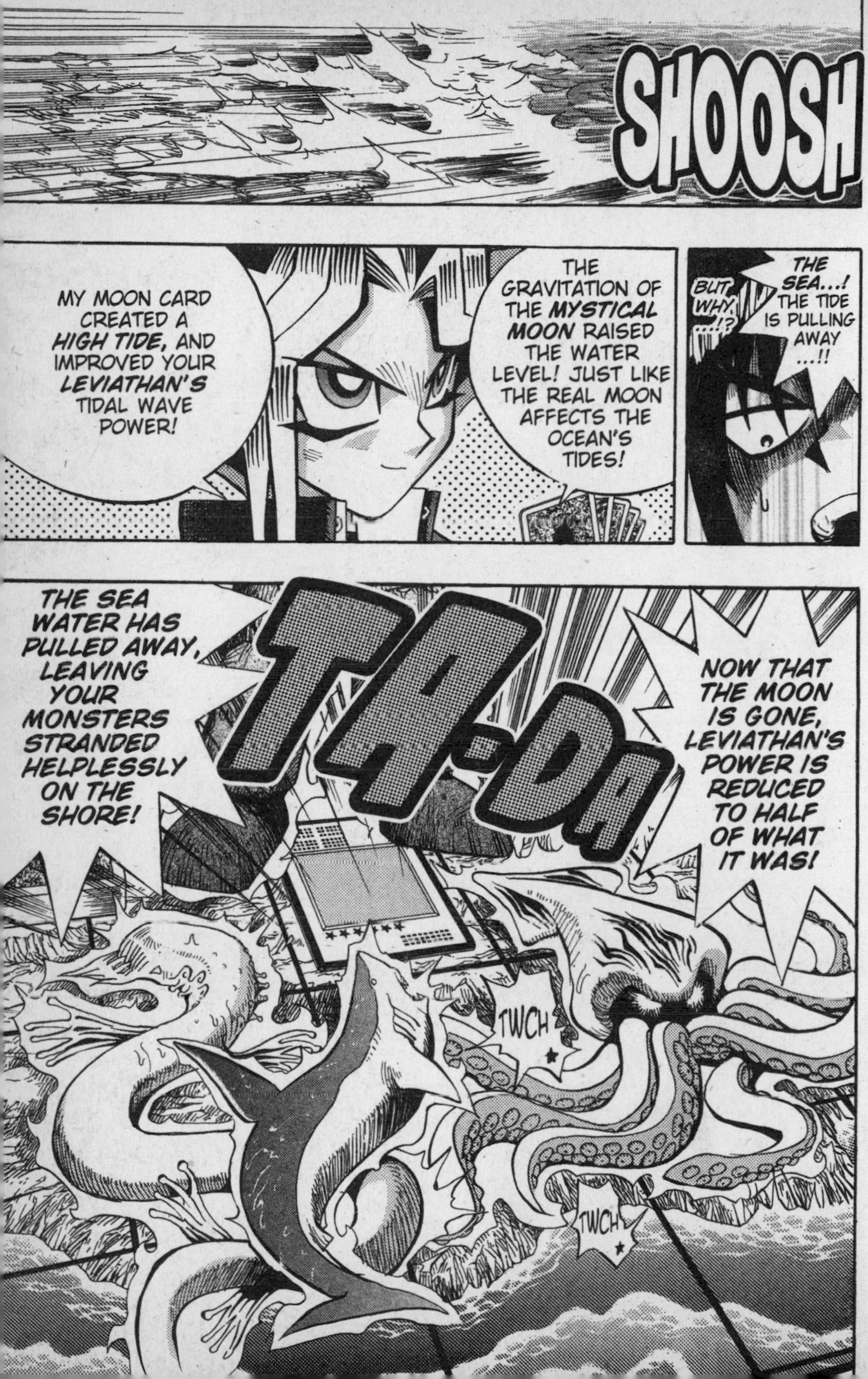
SHOOSH
THE SEA...! THE TIDE IS PULLING AWAY ...!!
BUT WHY ...!?
THE GRAVITATION OF THE MYSTICAL MOON RAISED THE WATER LEVEL! JUST LIKE THE REAL MOON AFFECTS THE OCEAN'S TIDES!
MY MOON CARD CREATED A HIGH TIDE, AND IMPROVED YOUR LEVIATHAN'S TIDAL WAVE POWER!
TA-DA
NOW THAT THE MOON IS GONE, LEVIATHAN'S POWER IS REDUCED TO HALF OF WHAT IT WAS!
THE SEA WATER HAS PULLED AWAY, LEAVING YOUR MONSTERS STRANDED HELPLESSLY ON THE SHORE!
TWCH
TWCH

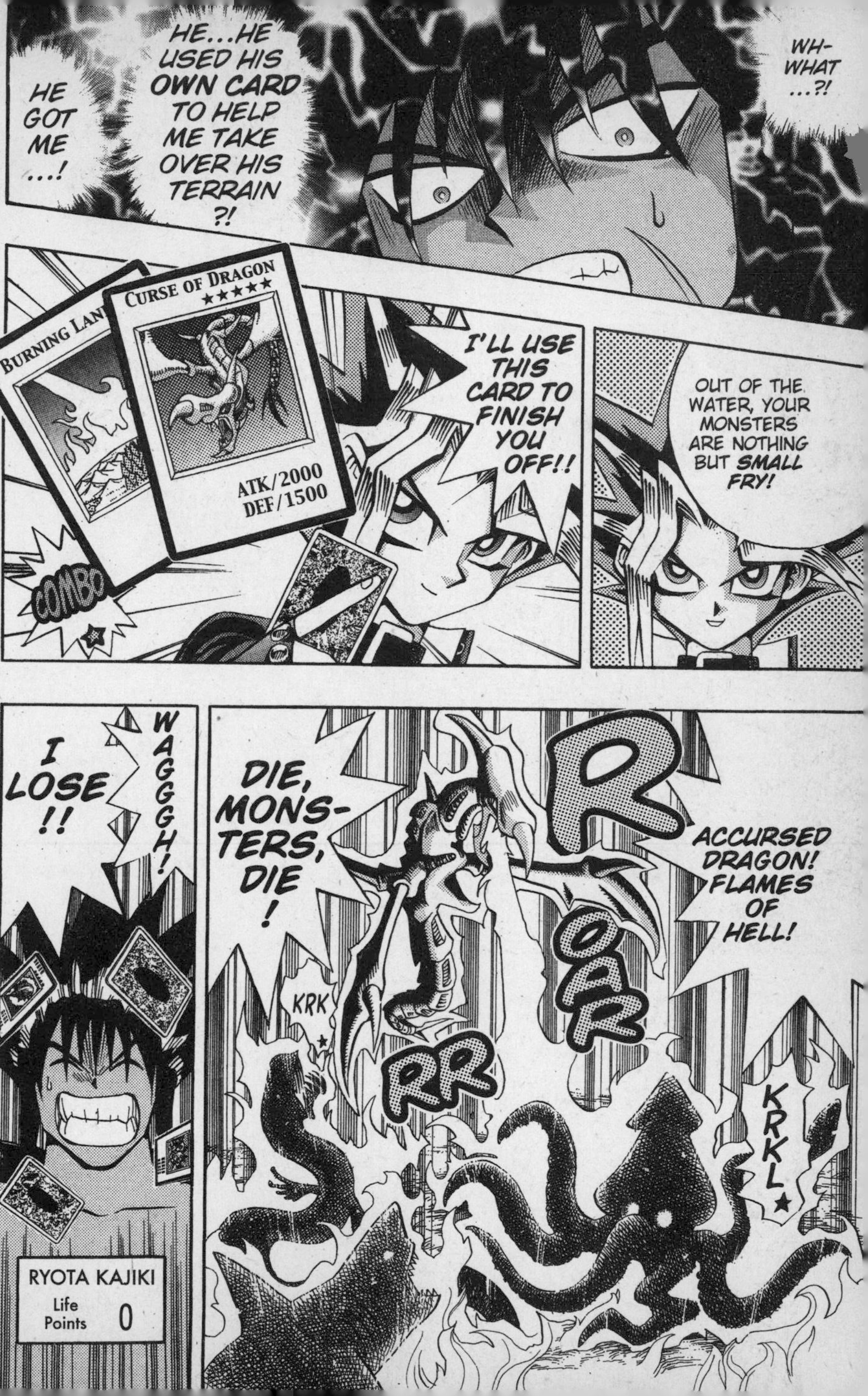
WH- WHAT ...?!
HE...HE USED HIS OWN CARD TO HELP ME TAKE OVER HIS TERRAIN ?!
HE GOT ME ...!
OUT OF THE WATER, YOUR MONSTERS ARE NOTHING BUT SMALL FRY!
I'LL USE THIS CARD TO FINISH YOU OFF!!
BURNING LAN
CURSE OF DRAGON
ATK/2000
DEF/1500
COMBO
ACCURSED DRAGON! FLAMES OF HELL!
ROARRR
DIE, MONSTERS, DIE!
KRKL
KRK
WAGGGH!
I LOSE!!
RYOTA KAJIKI
Life Points 0

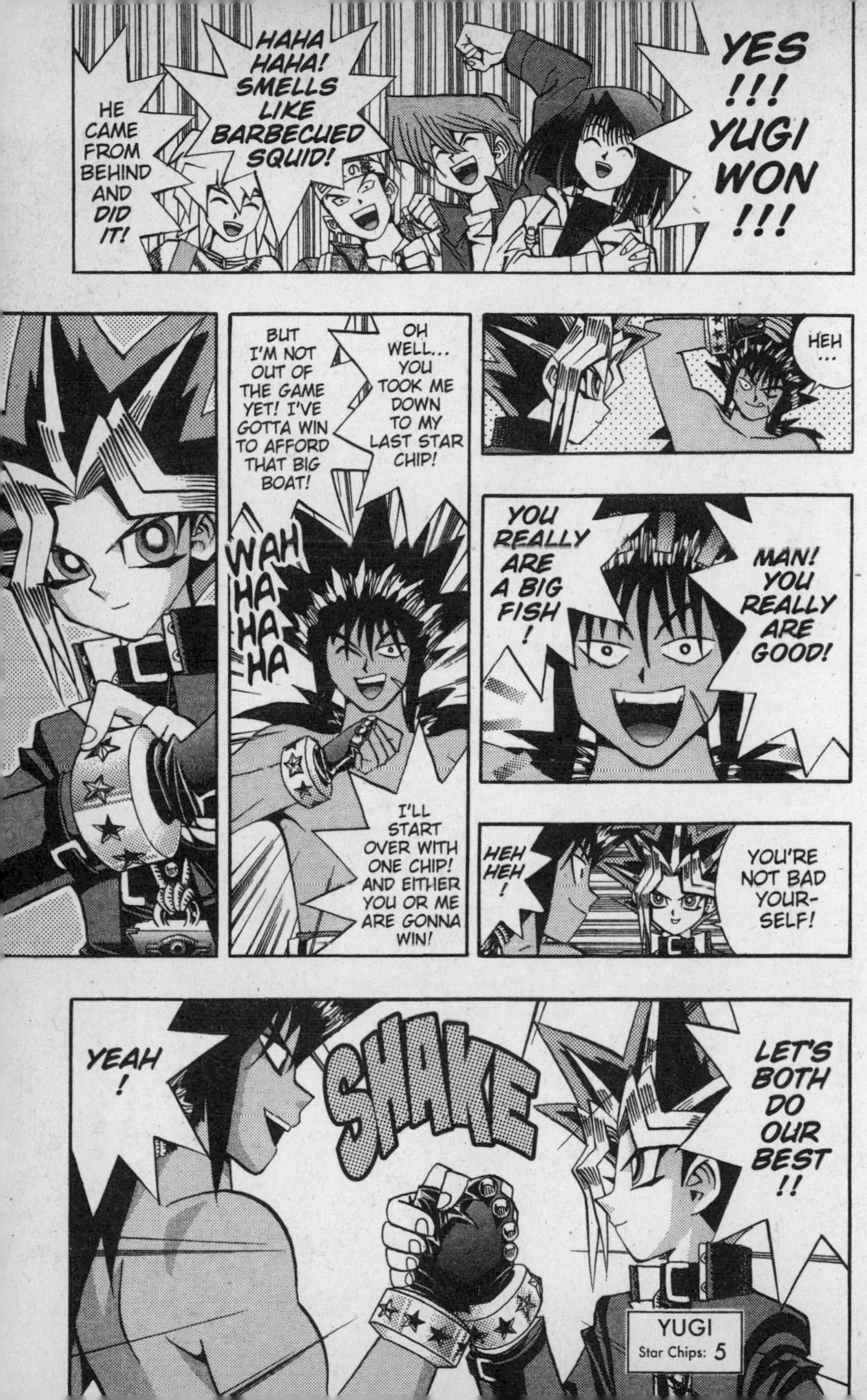
YES!!! YUGI WON!!!
HAHA HAHA! SMELLS LIKE BARBECUED SQUID!
HE CAME FROM BEHIND AND DID IT!
HEH...
MAN! YOU REALLY ARE GOOD!
YOU REALLY ARE A BIG FISH!
YOU'RE NOT BAD YOUR-SELF!
HEH HEH!
OH WELL... YOU TOOK ME DOWN TO MY LAST STAR CHIP!
BUT I'M NOT OUT OF THE GAME YET! I'VE GOTTA WIN TO AFFORD THAT BIG BOAT!
WAH HA HA HA
I'LL START OVER WITH ONE CHIP! AND EITHER YOU OR ME ARE GONNA WIN!
LET'S BOTH DO OUR BEST!!
SHAKE
YEAH!
YUGI
Star Chips: 5

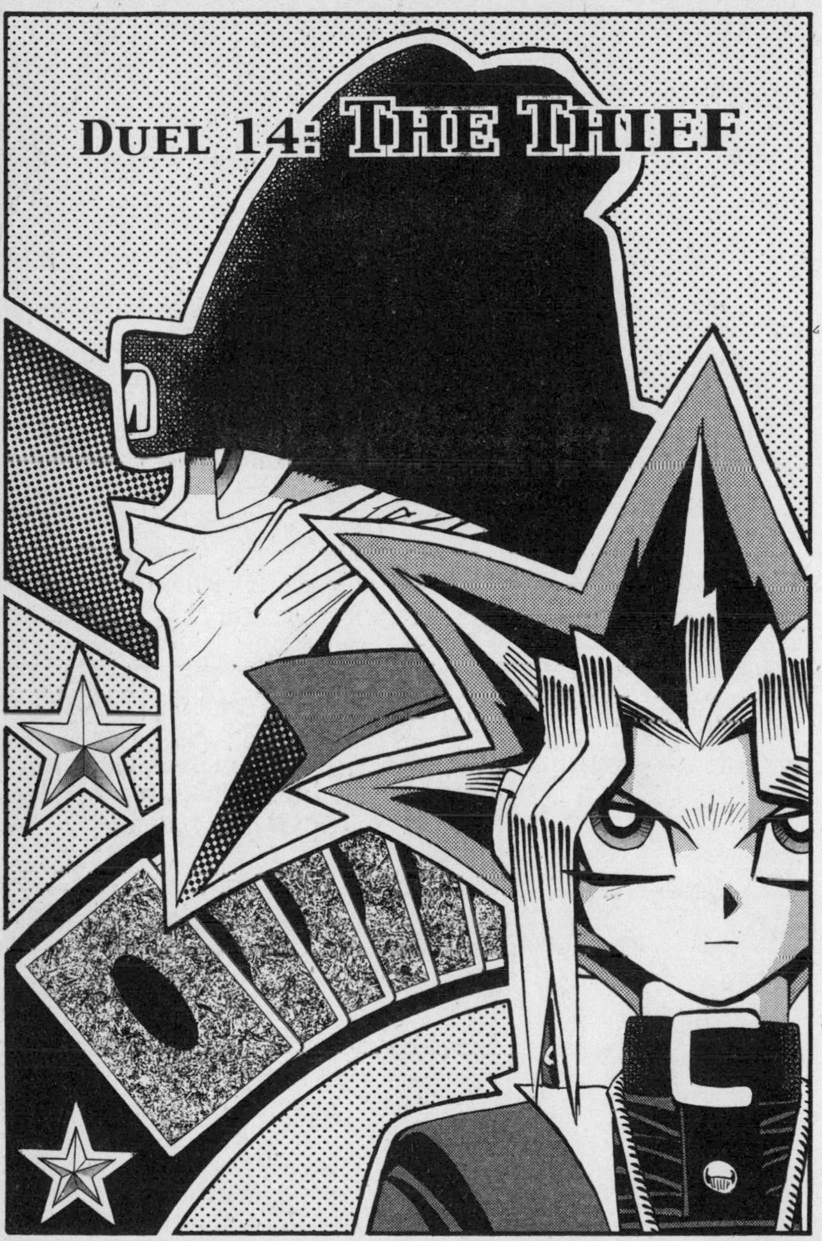
DUEL 14: THE THIEF

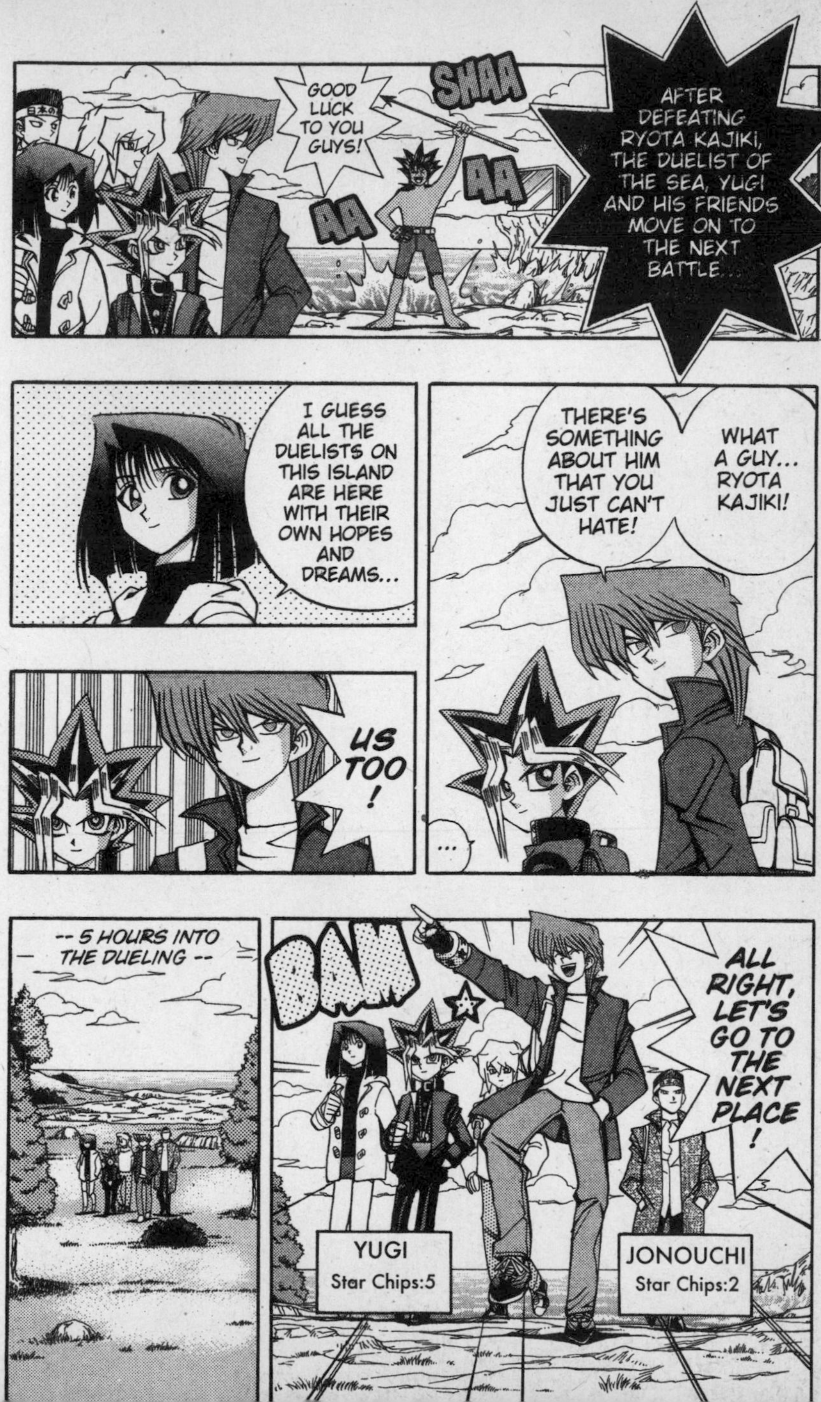
AFTER DEFEATING RYOTA KAJIKI, THE DUELIST OF THE SEA, YUGI AND HIS FRIENDS MOVE ON TO THE NEXT BATTLE...
SHAA
AA
AA
GOOD LUCK TO YOU GUYS!
WHAT A GUY... RYOTA KAJIKI!
THERE'S SOMETHING ABOUT HIM THAT YOU JUST CAN'T HATE!
...
I GUESS ALL THE DUELISTS ON THIS ISLAND ARE HERE WITH THEIR OWN HOPES AND DREAMS...
US TOO!
ALL RIGHT, LET'S GO TO THE NEXT PLACE!
BAM
JONOUCHI
Star Chips:2
YUGI
Star Chips:5
-- 5 HOURS INTO THE DUELING --

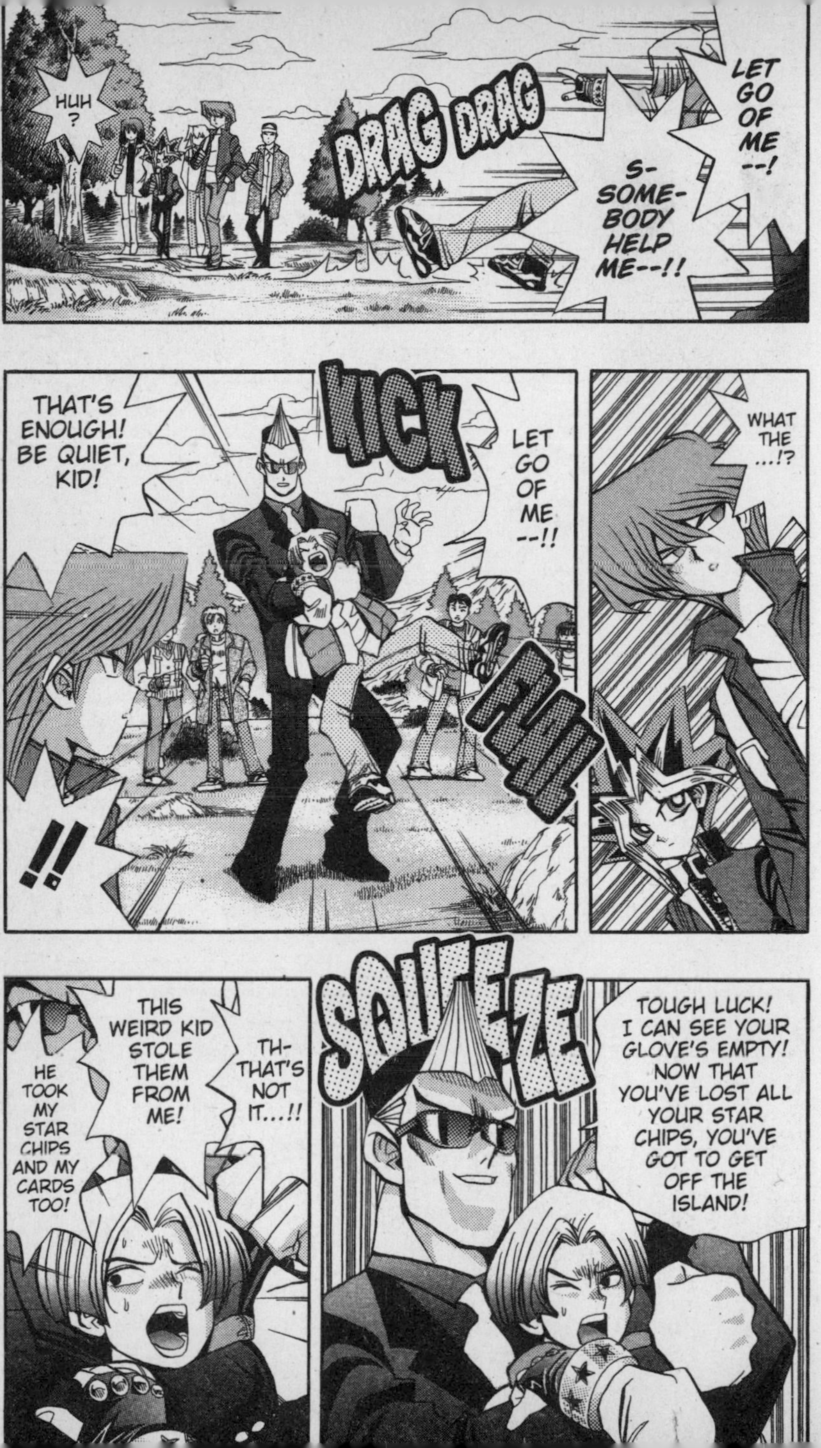
LET GO OF ME--!
S-SOMEBODY HELP ME--!!
DRAG DRAG
HUH?
WHAT THE ...!?
KICK
LET GO OF ME--!!
THAT'S ENOUGH! BE QUIET, KID!
!!
TOUGH LUCK! I CAN SEE YOUR GLOVE'S EMPTY! NOW THAT YOU'VE LOST ALL YOUR STAR CHIPS, YOU'VE GOT TO GET OFF THE ISLAND!
SQUEEZE
TH-THAT'S NOT IT...!!
THIS WEIRD KID STOLE THEM FROM ME!
HE TOOK MY STAR CHIPS AND MY CARDS TOO!

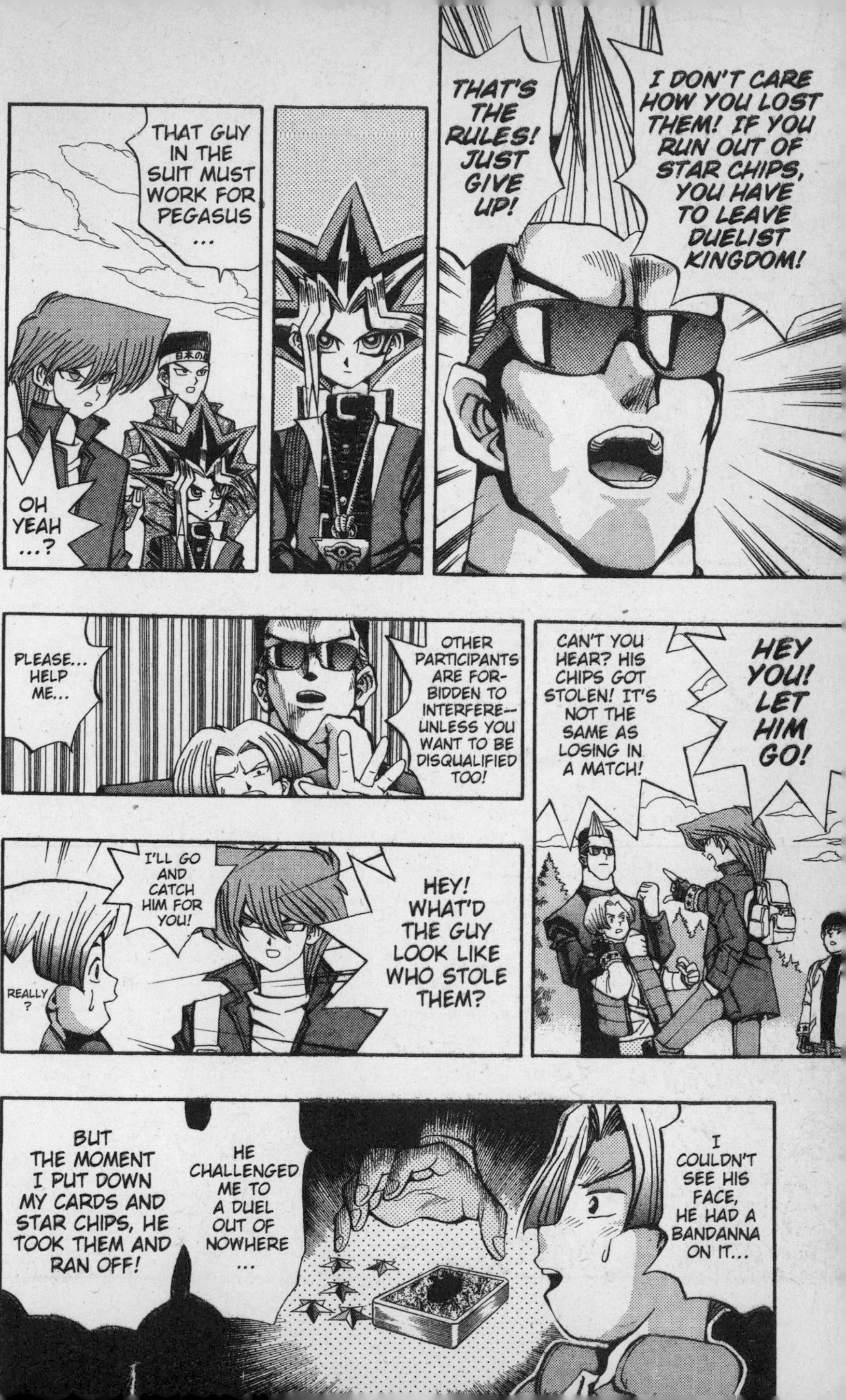
I DON'T CARE HOW YOU LOST THEM! IF YOU RUN OUT OF STAR CHIPS, YOU HAVE TO LEAVE DUELIST KINGDOM!
THAT'S THE RULES! JUST GIVE UP!
THAT GUY IN THE SUIT MUST WORK FOR PEGASUS ...
OH YEAH ...?
HEY YOU! LET HIM GO!
CAN'T YOU HEAR? HIS CHIPS GOT STOLEN! IT'S NOT THE SAME AS LOSING IN A MATCH!
OTHER PARTICIPANTS ARE FOR-BIDDEN TO INTERFERE-- UNLESS YOU WANT TO BE DISQUALIFIED TOO!
PLEASE... HELP ME...
HEY! WHAT'D THE GUY LOOK LIKE WHO STOLE THEM?
I'LL GO AND CATCH HIM FOR YOU!
REALLY ?
I COULDN'T SEE HIS FACE, HE HAD A BANDANNA ON IT...
HE CHALLENGED ME TO A DUEL OUT OF NOWHERE ...
BUT THE MOMENT I PUT DOWN MY CARDS AND STAR CHIPS, HE TOOK THEM AND RAN OFF!

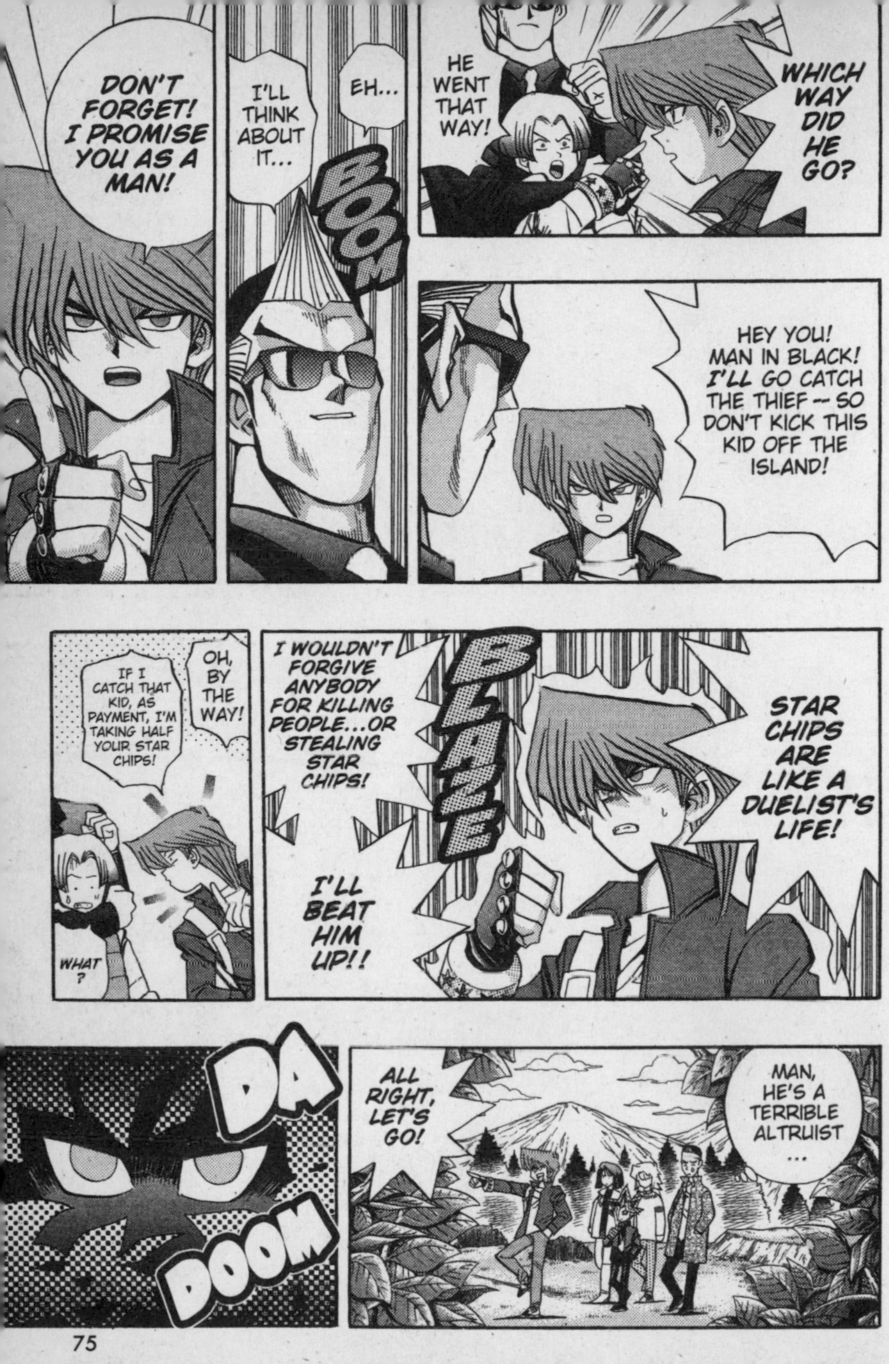
WHICH WAY DID HE GO?
HE WENT THAT WAY!
HEY YOU! MAN IN BLACK! I'LL GO CATCH THE THIEF -- SO DON'T KICK THIS KID OFF THE ISLAND!
EH...
I'LL THINK ABOUT IT...
BOOM
DON'T FORGET! I PROMISE YOU AS A MAN!
STAR CHIPS ARE LIKE A DUELIST'S LIFE!
BLAZE
I WOULDN'T FORGIVE ANYBODY FOR KILLING PEOPLE...OR STEALING STAR CHIPS!
I'LL BEAT HIM UP!!
OH, BY THE WAY!
IF I CATCH THAT KID, AS PAYMENT, I'M TAKING HALF YOUR STAR CHIPS!
WHAT?
MAN, HE'S A TERRIBLE ALTRUIST...
ALL RIGHT, LET'S GO!
DA
DOOM

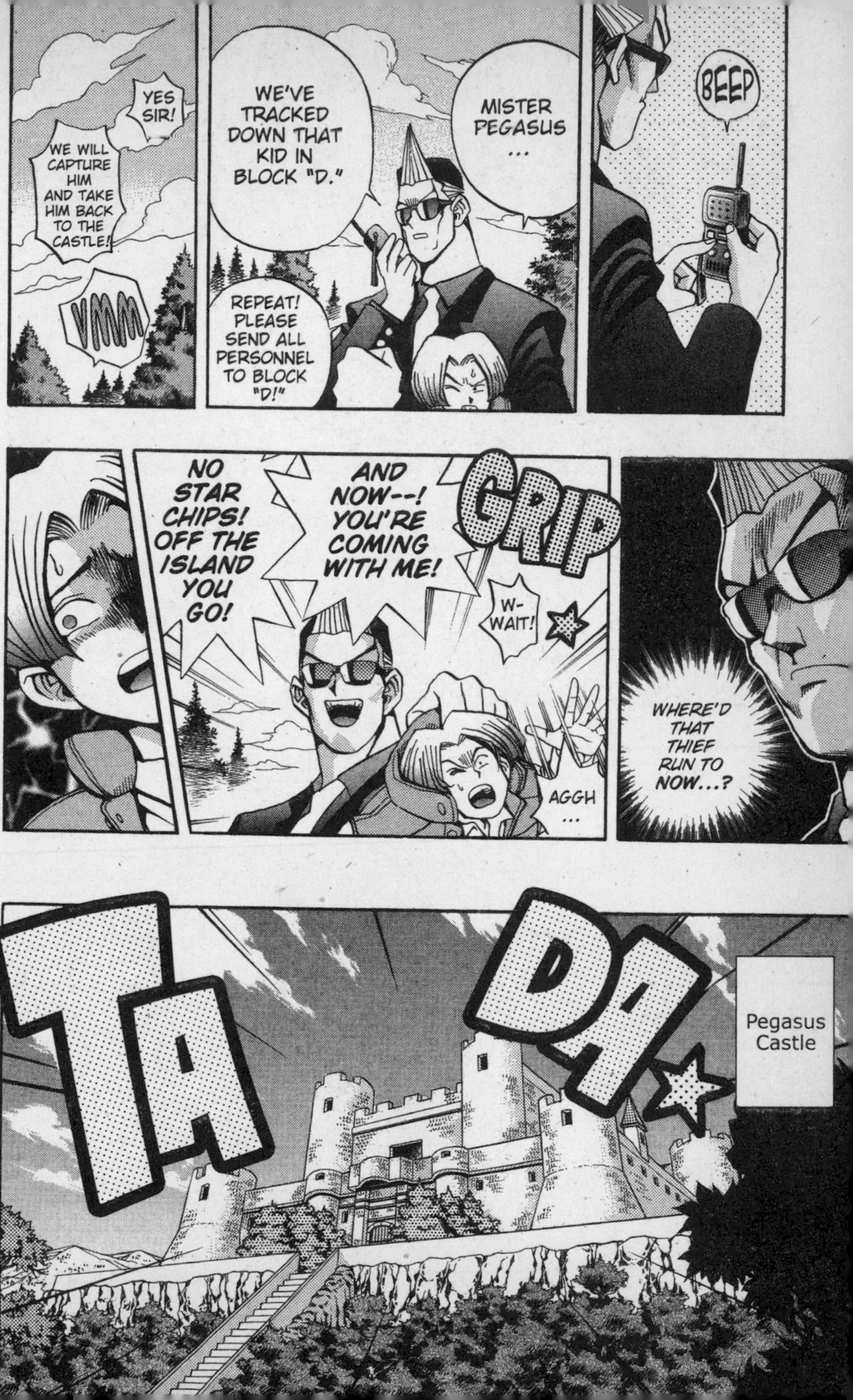
BEEP
MISTER PEGASUS ...
WE'VE TRACKED DOWN THAT KID IN BLOCK "D."
REPEAT! PLEASE SEND ALL PERSONNEL TO BLOCK "D!"
YES SIR!
WE WILL CAPTURE HIM AND TAKE HIM BACK TO THE CASTLE!
VMM
WHERE'D THAT THIEF RUN TO NOW...?
GRIP
AND NOW--! YOU'RE COMING WITH ME!
NO STAR CHIPS! OFF THE ISLAND YOU GO!
W-WAIT!
AGGH ...
Pegasus Castle
TA DA!

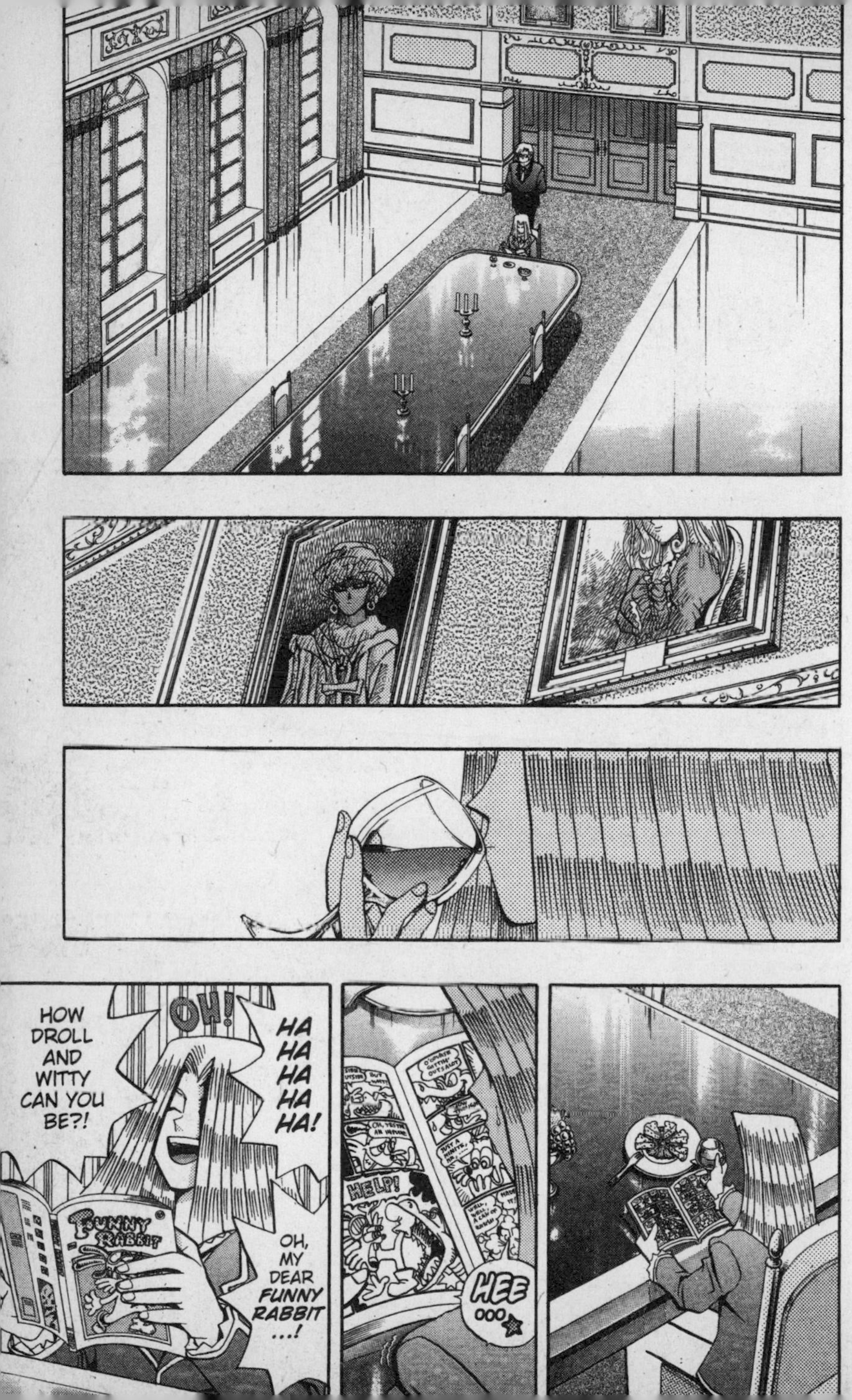
HELP!
HEE ooo
OH!
HA HA HA HA HA!
HOW DROLL AND WITTY CAN YOU BE?!
OH, MY DEAR FUNNY RABBIT ...!
FUNNY RABBIT

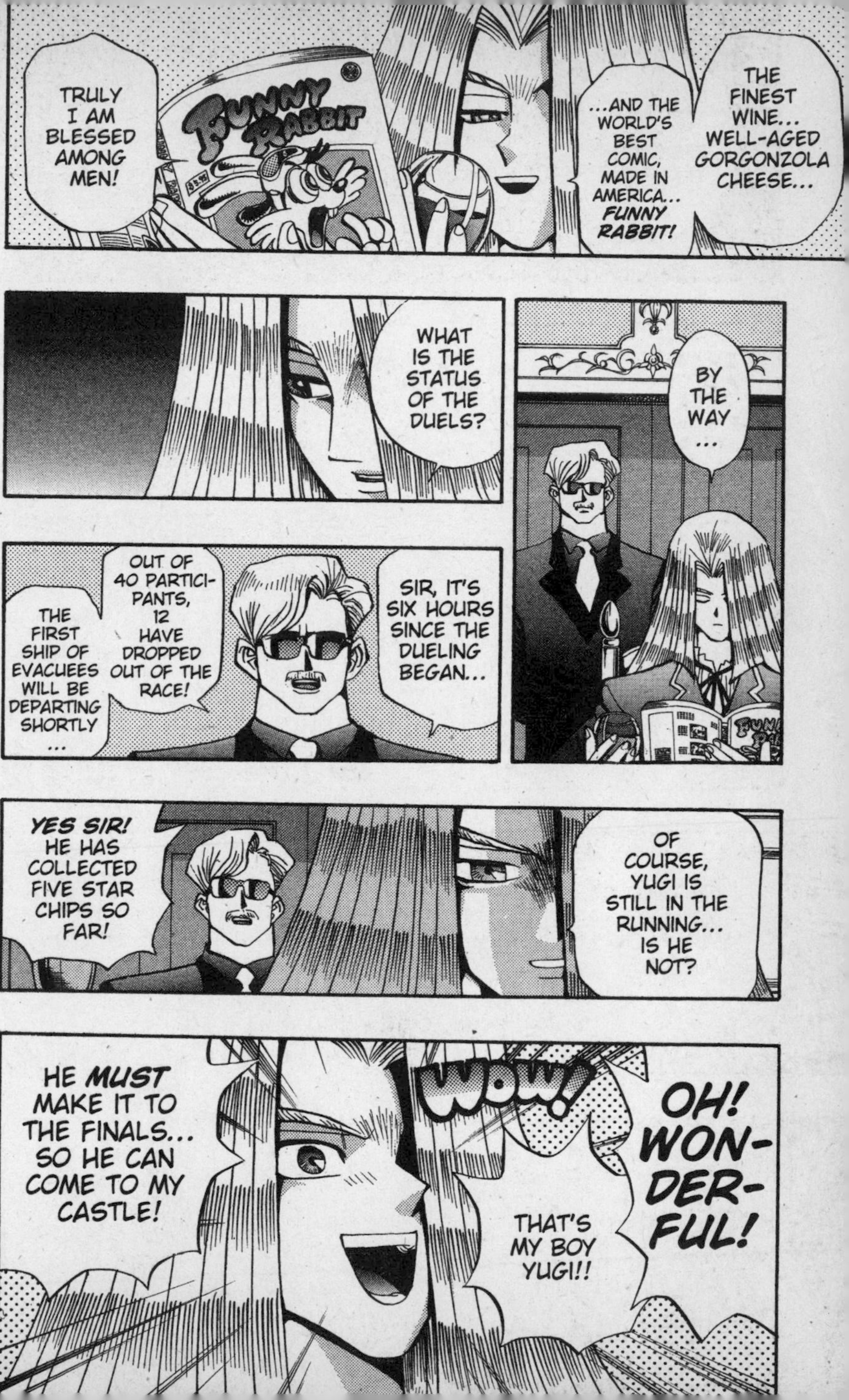
THE FINEST WINE... WELL-AGED GORGONZOLA CHEESE...
...AND THE WORLD'S BEST COMIC, MADE IN AMERICA... *FUNNY RABBIT!*
FUNNY RABBIT
TRULY I AM BLESSED AMONG MEN!
BY THE WAY ...
WHAT IS THE STATUS OF THE DUELS?
SIR, IT'S SIX HOURS SINCE THE DUELING BEGAN...
OUT OF 40 PARTICI-PANTS, 12 HAVE DROPPED OUT OF THE RACE!
THE FIRST SHIP OF EVACUEES WILL BE DEPARTING SHORTLY ...
OF COURSE, YUGI IS STILL IN THE RUNNING... IS HE NOT?
YES SIR! HE HAS COLLECTED FIVE STAR CHIPS SO FAR!
OH! WON-DER-FUL!
THAT'S MY BOY YUGI!!
WOW!
HE *MUST* MAKE IT TO THE FINALS... SO HE CAN COME TO MY CASTLE!

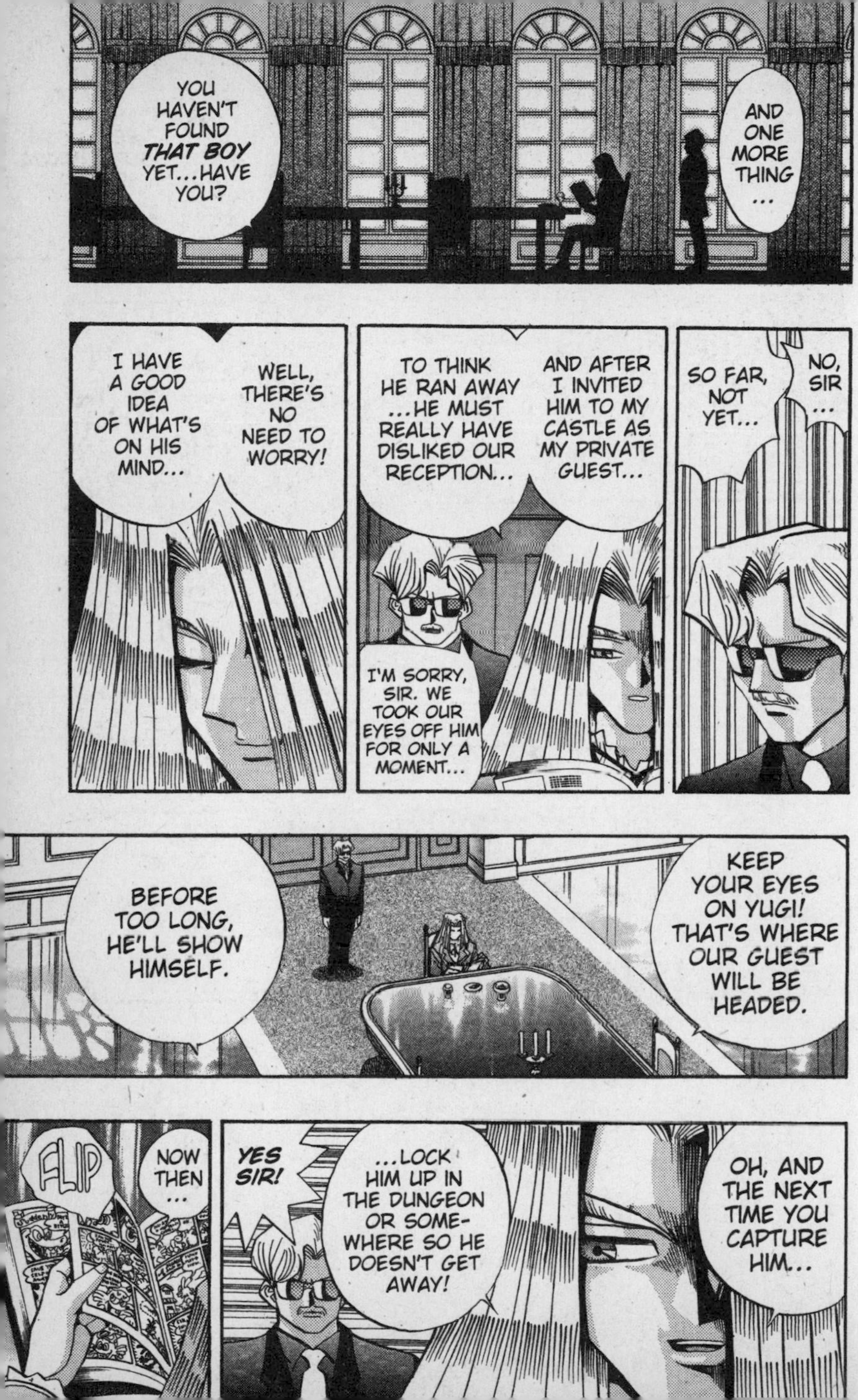
AND ONE MORE THING...
YOU HAVEN'T FOUND THAT BOY YET...HAVE YOU?
NO, SIR...
SO FAR, NOT YET...
AND AFTER I INVITED HIM TO MY CASTLE AS MY PRIVATE GUEST...
TO THINK HE RAN AWAY ...HE MUST REALLY HAVE DISLIKED OUR RECEPTION...
I'M SORRY, SIR. WE TOOK OUR EYES OFF HIM FOR ONLY A MOMENT...
WELL, THERE'S NO NEED TO WORRY!
I HAVE A GOOD IDEA OF WHAT'S ON HIS MIND...
KEEP YOUR EYES ON YUGI! THAT'S WHERE OUR GUEST WILL BE HEADED.
BEFORE TOO LONG, HE'LL SHOW HIMSELF.
OH, AND THE NEXT TIME YOU CAPTURE HIM...
...LOCK HIM UP IN THE DUNGEON OR SOME-WHERE SO HE DOESN'T GET AWAY!
YES SIR!
NOW THEN...
FLIP

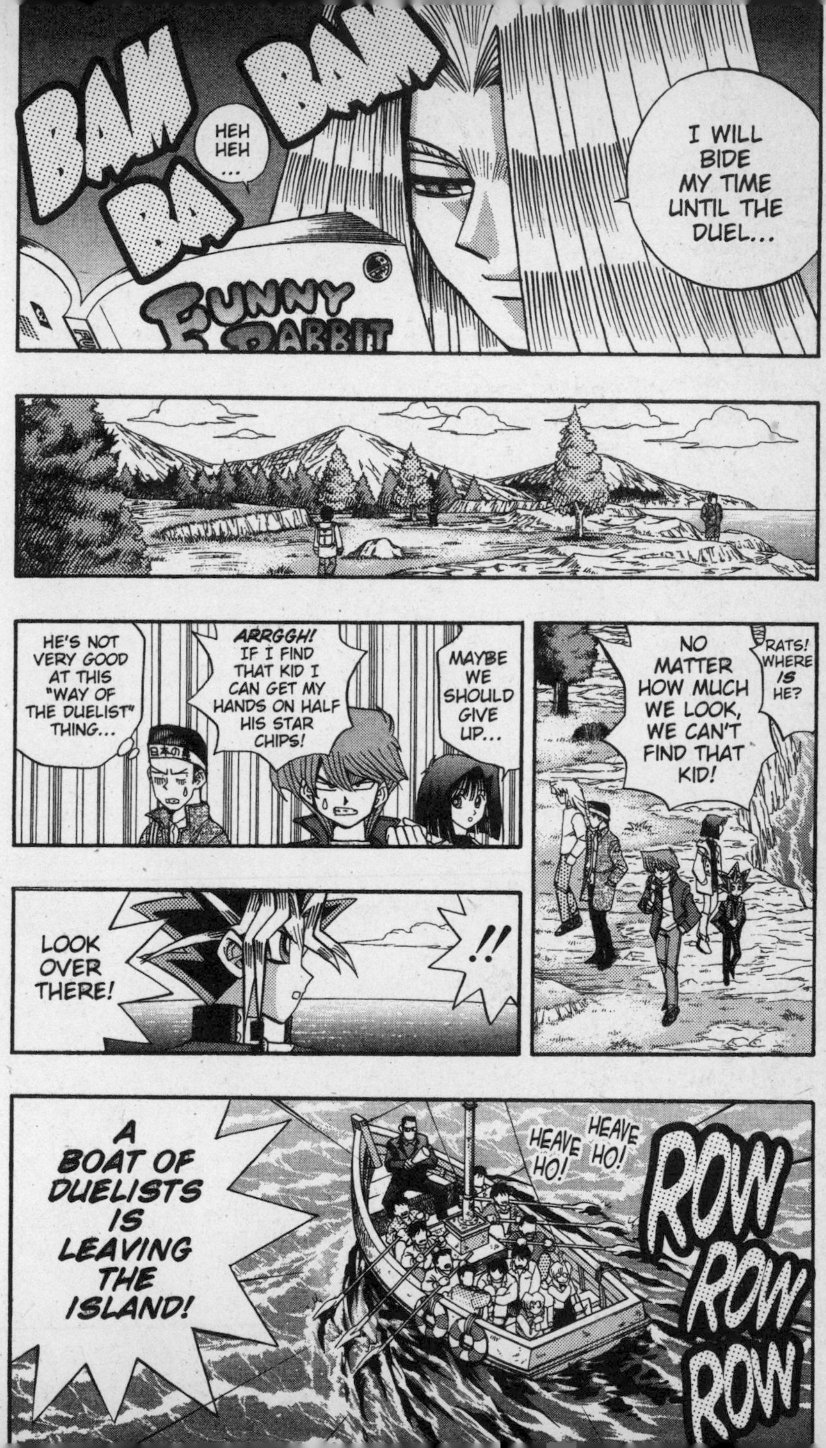

I WILL BIDE MY TIME UNTIL THE DUEL...
BAM
HEH HEH ...
BAM
BA
FUNNY RABBIT
RATS! WHERE IS HE?
NO MATTER HOW MUCH WE LOOK, WE CAN'T FIND THAT KID!
MAYBE WE SHOULD GIVE UP...
ARRGGH! IF I FIND THAT KID I CAN GET MY HANDS ON HALF HIS STAR CHIPS!
HE'S NOT VERY GOOD AT THIS "WAY OF THE DUELIST" THING...
!!
LOOK OVER THERE!
ROW ROW ROW
HEAVE HO!
HEAVE HO!
A BOAT OF DUELISTS IS LEAVING THE ISLAND!

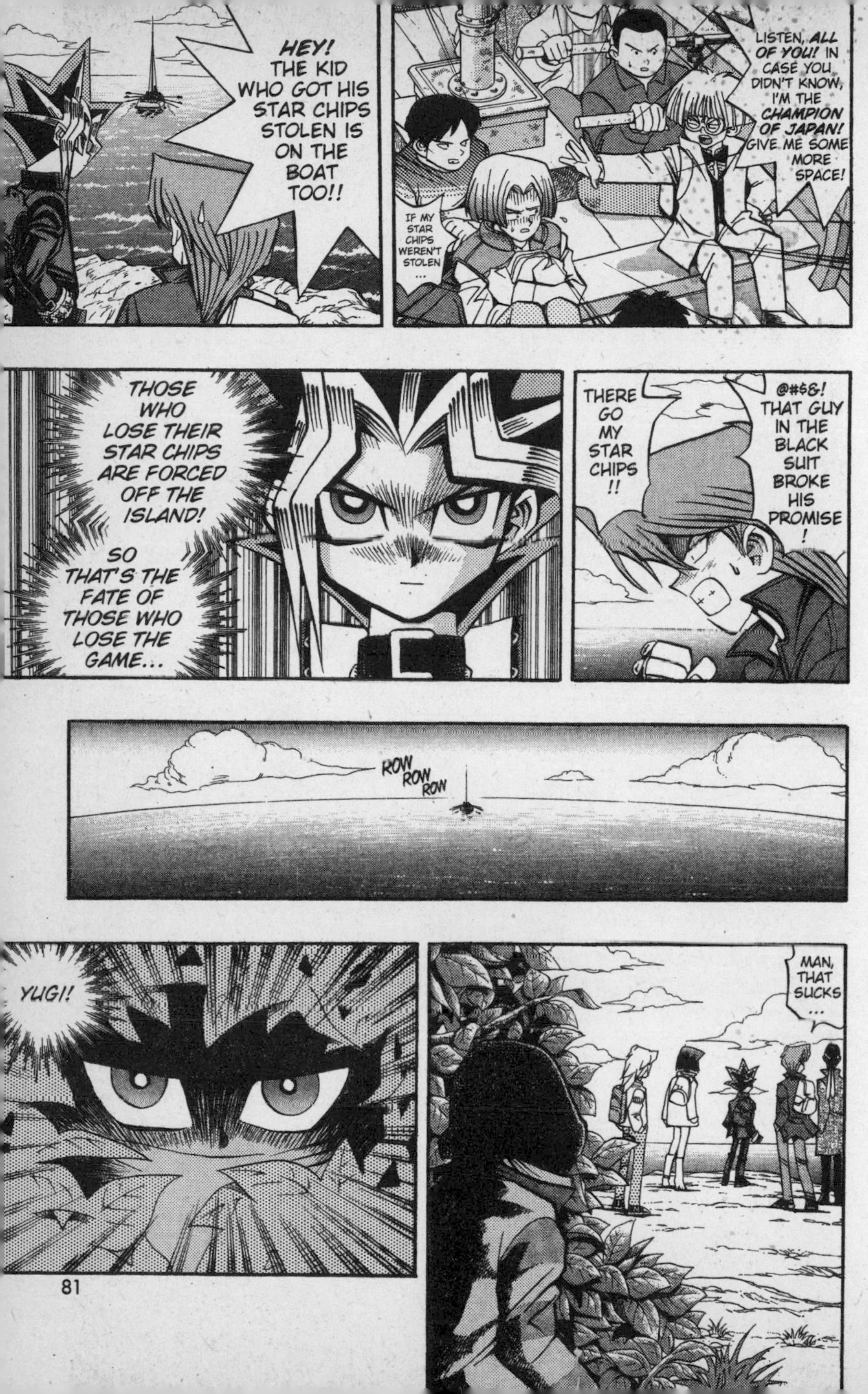

LISTEN, ALL OF YOU! IN CASE YOU DIDN'T KNOW, I'M THE CHAMPION OF JAPAN! GIVE ME SOME MORE SPACE!
IF MY STAR CHIPS WEREN'T STOLEN ...
HEY! THE KID WHO GOT HIS STAR CHIPS STOLEN IS ON THE BOAT TOO!!
@#$&! THAT GUY IN THE BLACK SUIT BROKE HIS PROMISE!
THERE GO MY STAR CHIPS!!
THOSE WHO LOSE THEIR STAR CHIPS ARE FORCED OFF THE ISLAND!
SO THAT'S THE FATE OF THOSE WHO LOSE THE GAME...
ROW ROW ROW
MAN, THAT SUCKS ...
YUGI!

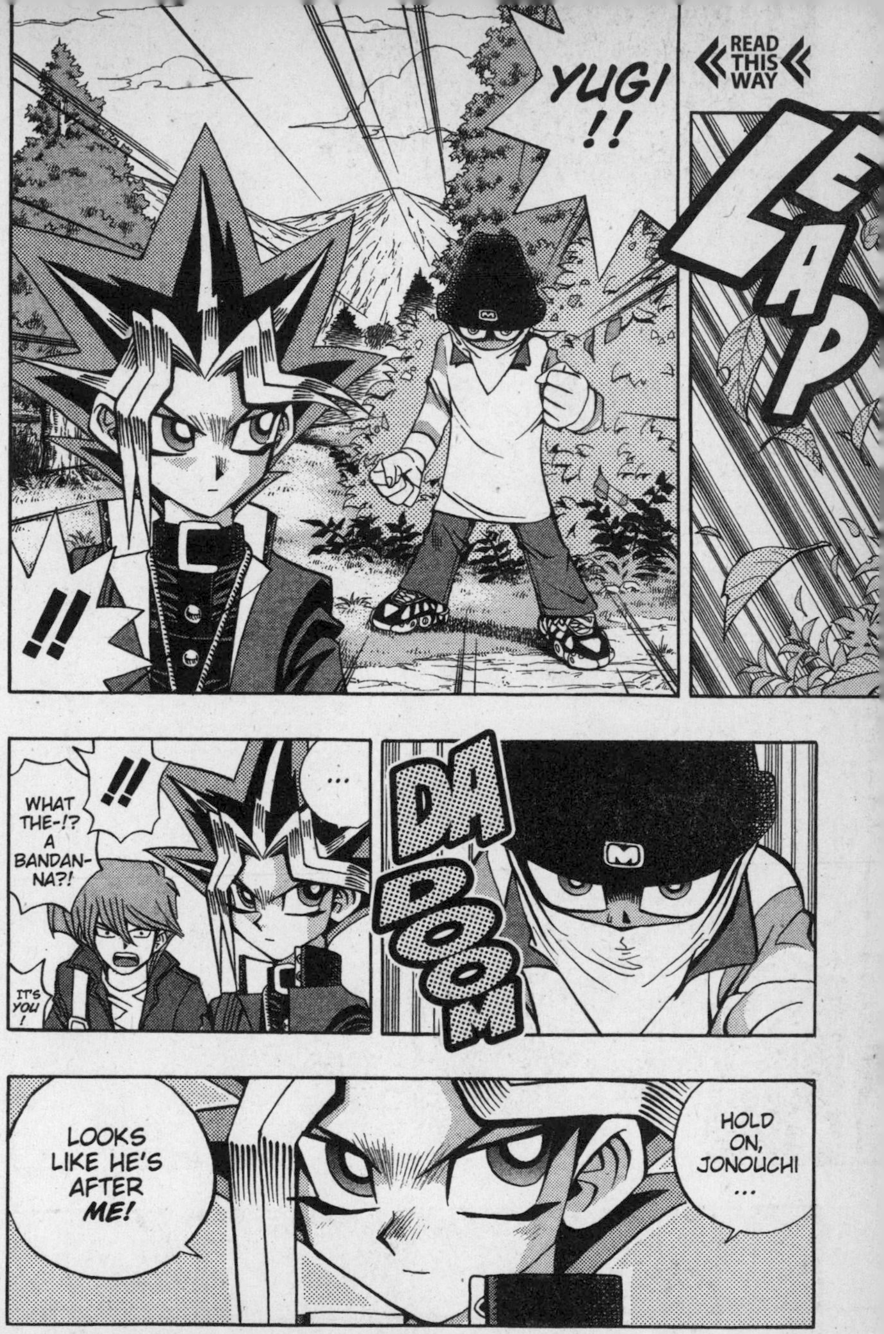
READ THIS WAY
LEAP
YUGI !!
!!
DADOOM
...
!!
WHAT THE-!? A BANDANA?!
IT'S YOU!
HOLD ON, JONOUCHI ...
LOOKS LIKE HE'S AFTER ME!

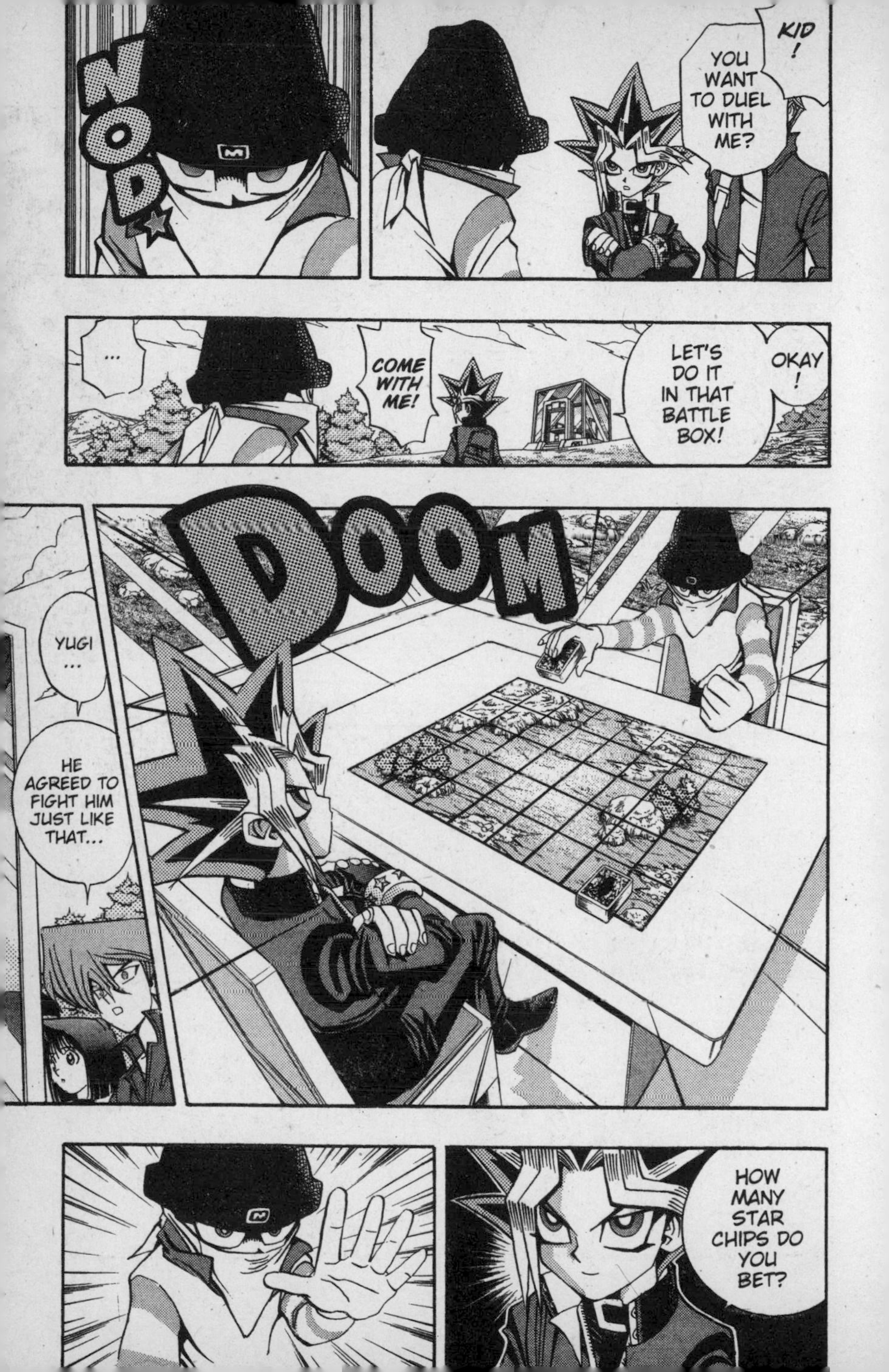
KID!
YOU WANT TO DUEL WITH ME?
NOD
OKAY!
LET'S DO IT IN THAT BATTLE BOX!
COME WITH ME!
...
DOOM
YUGI ...
HE AGREED TO FIGHT HIM JUST LIKE THAT...
HOW MANY STAR CHIPS DO YOU BET?

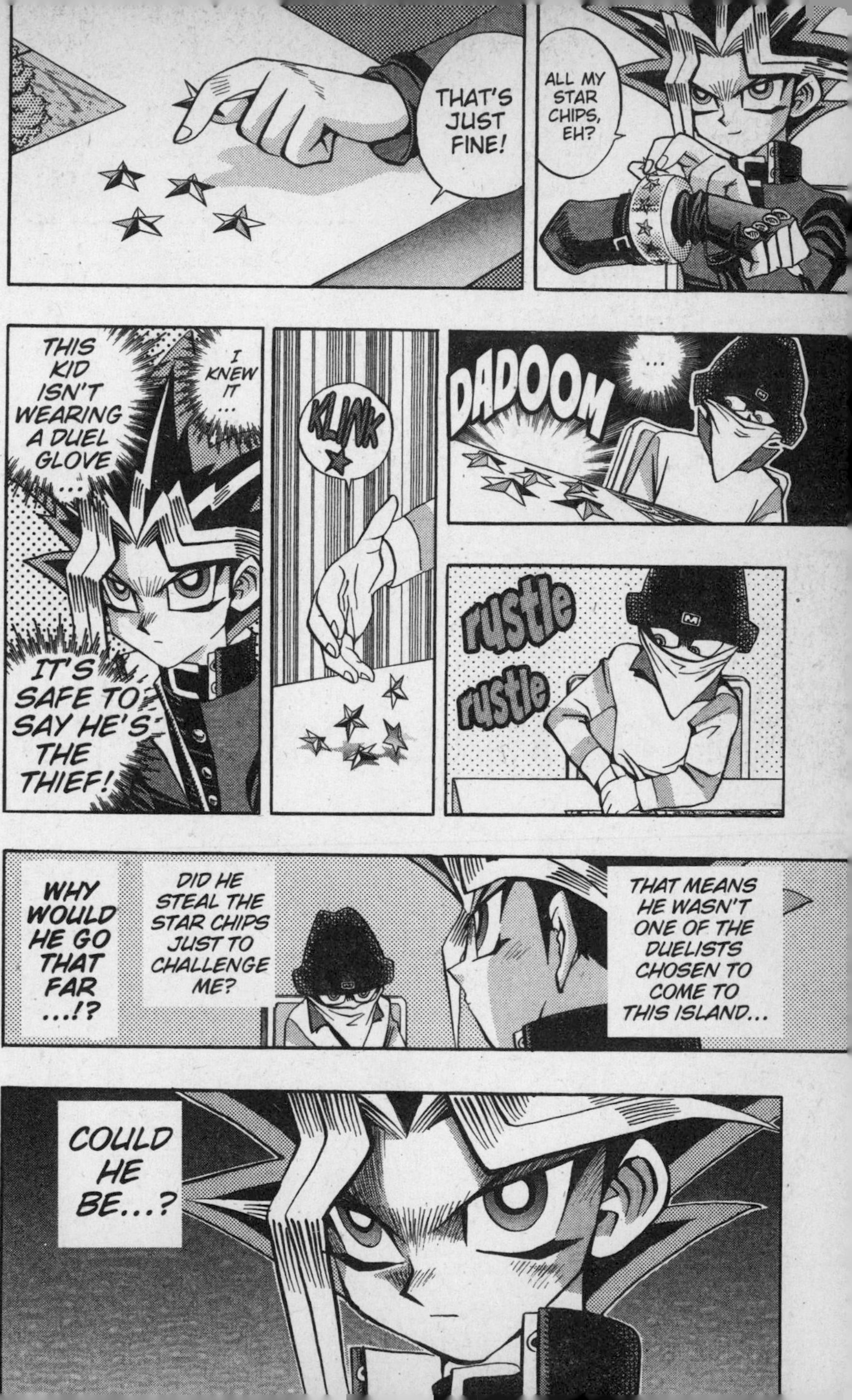
ALL MY STAR CHIPS, EH?
THAT'S JUST FINE!
...
DADOOM
rustle
rustle
KLINK
I KNEW IT ...
THIS KID ISN'T WEARING A DUEL GLOVE ...
IT'S SAFE TO SAY HE'S THE THIEF!
THAT MEANS HE WASN'T ONE OF THE DUELISTS CHOSEN TO COME TO THIS ISLAND...
DID HE STEAL THE STAR CHIPS JUST TO CHALLENGE ME?
WHY WOULD HE GO THAT FAR ...!?
COULD HE BE...?

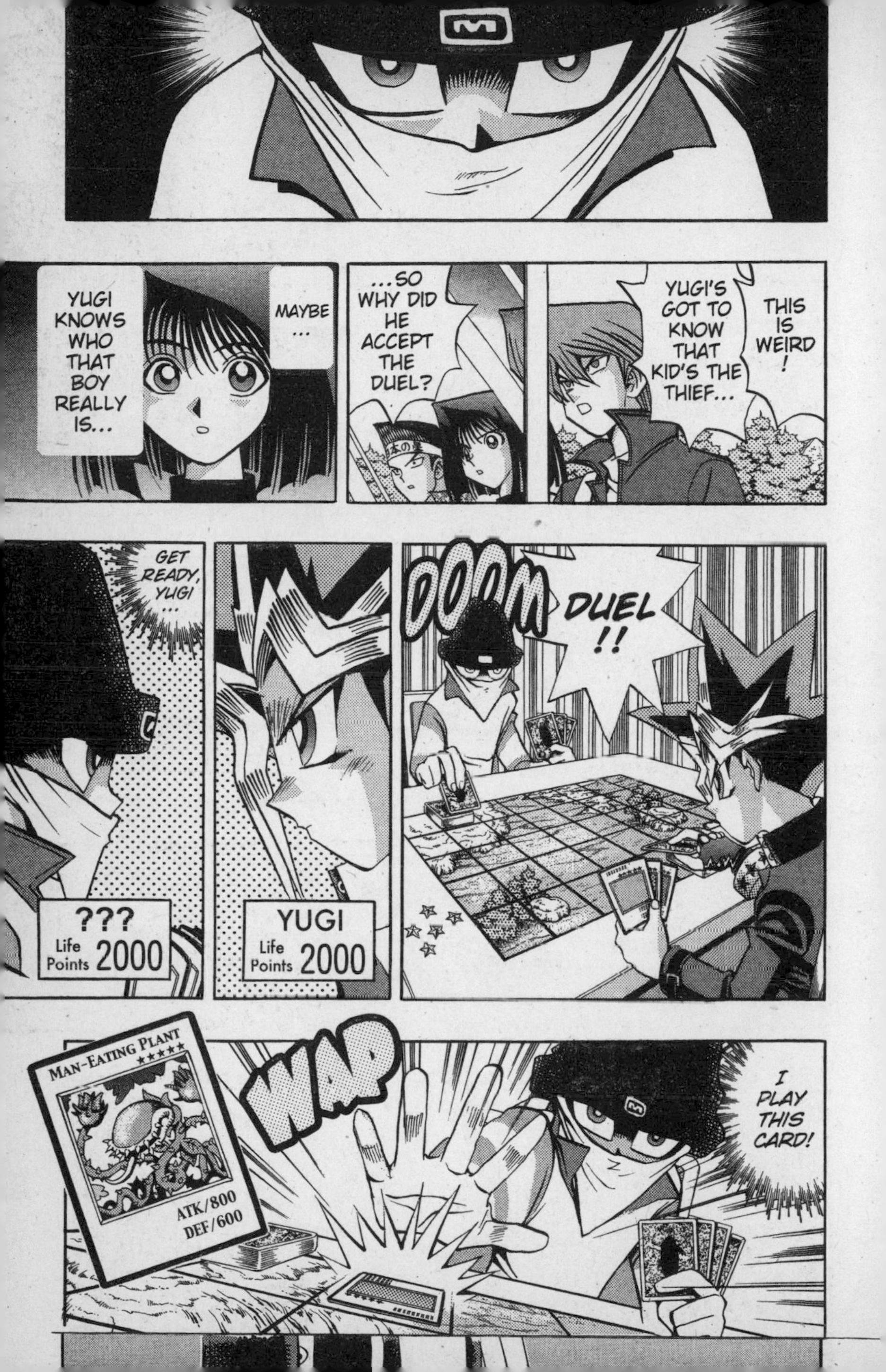
THIS IS WEIRD!
YUGI'S GOT TO KNOW THAT KID'S THE THIEF...
...SO WHY DID HE ACCEPT THE DUEL?
MAYBE...
YUGI KNOWS WHO THAT BOY REALLY IS...
DOOM
DUEL!!
YUGI Life Points 2000
GET READY, YUGI...
??? Life Points 2000
I PLAY THIS CARD!
WAP
MAN-EATING PLANT
ATK/800 DEF/600

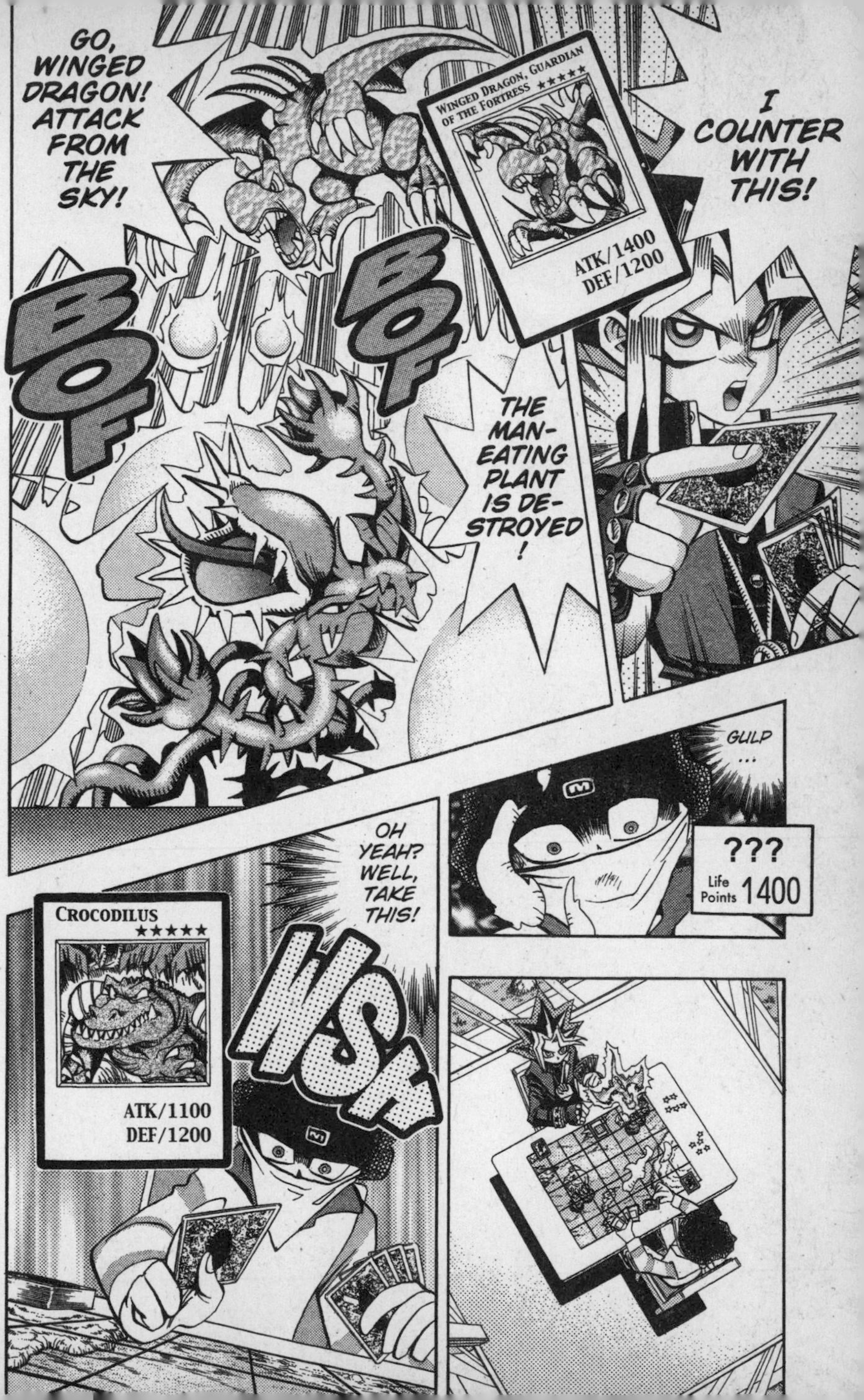
I COUNTER WITH THIS!
GO, WINGED DRAGON! ATTACK FROM THE SKY!
WINGED DRAGON, GUARDIAN OF THE FORTRESS ★★★★★
ATK/1400
DEF/1200
BOF
BOF
THE MAN-EATING PLANT IS DE-STROYED!
GULP...
???
Life Points 1400
OH YEAH? WELL, TAKE THIS!
WSH
CROCODILUS
★★★★★
ATK/1100
DEF/1200

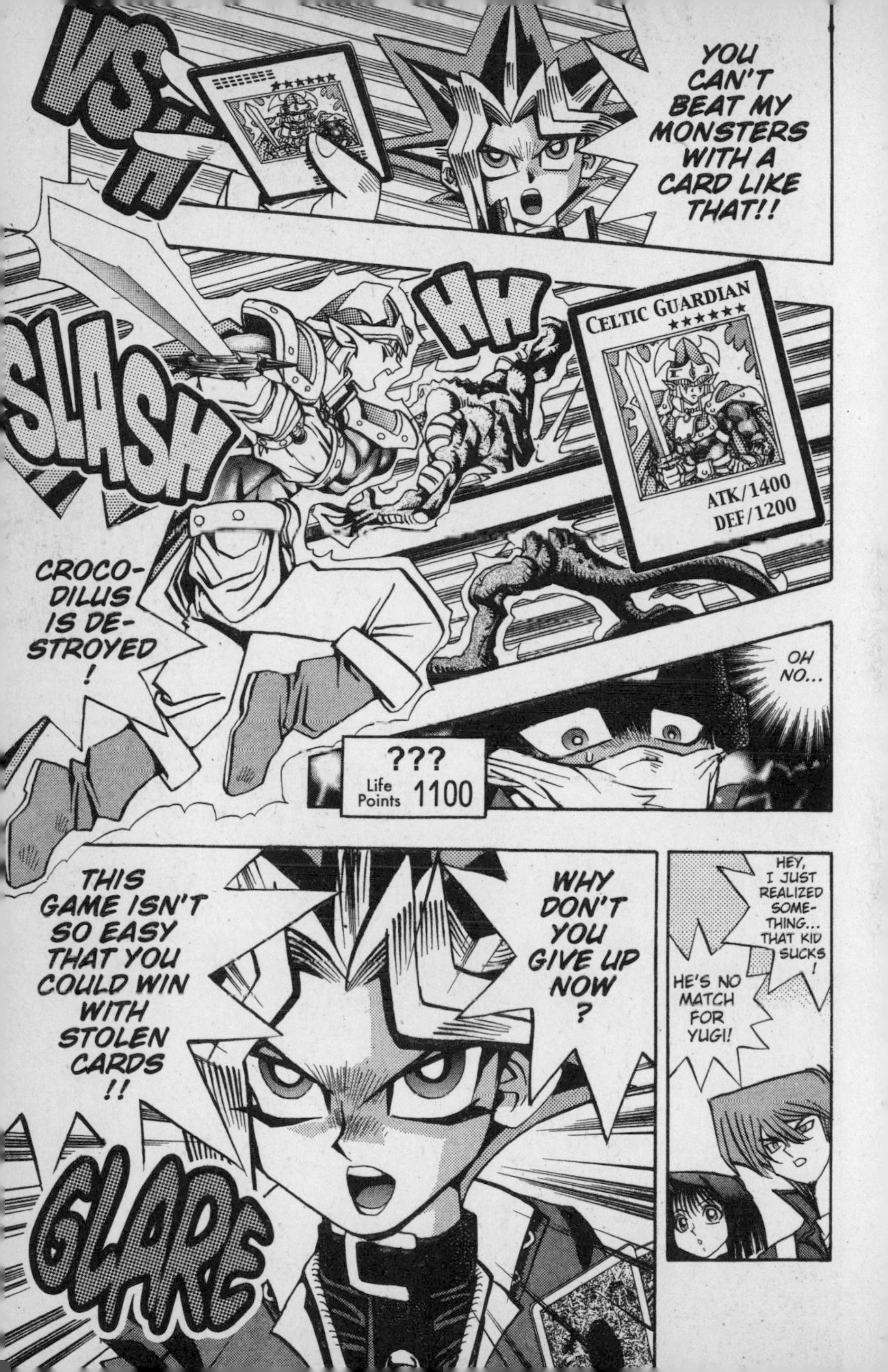

YOU CAN'T BEAT MY MONSTERS WITH A CARD LIKE THAT!!
ISH
CELTIC GUARDIAN
ATK/1400
DEF/1200
HH
SLASH
CROCO-DILUS IS DE-STROYED!
OH NO...
???
Life Points 1100
HEY, I JUST REALIZED SOME-THING... THAT KID SUCKS!
HE'S NO MATCH FOR YUGI!
WHY DON'T YOU GIVE UP NOW?
THIS GAME ISN'T SO EASY THAT YOU COULD WIN WITH STOLEN CARDS!!
GLARE

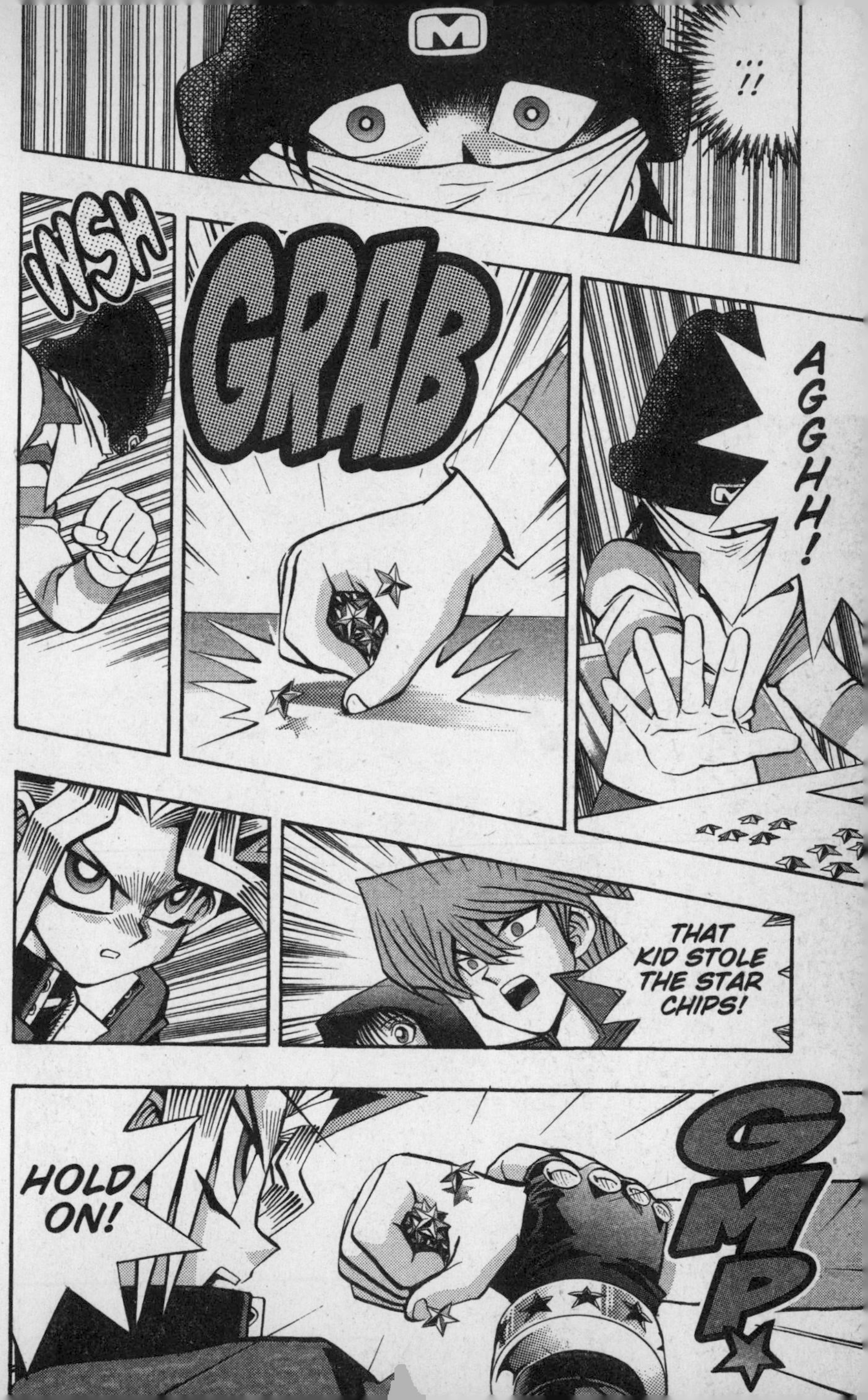
...!!
AGGHH!
GRAB
WSH
THAT KID STOLE THE STAR CHIPS!
GMP
HOLD ON!

READ THIS WAY

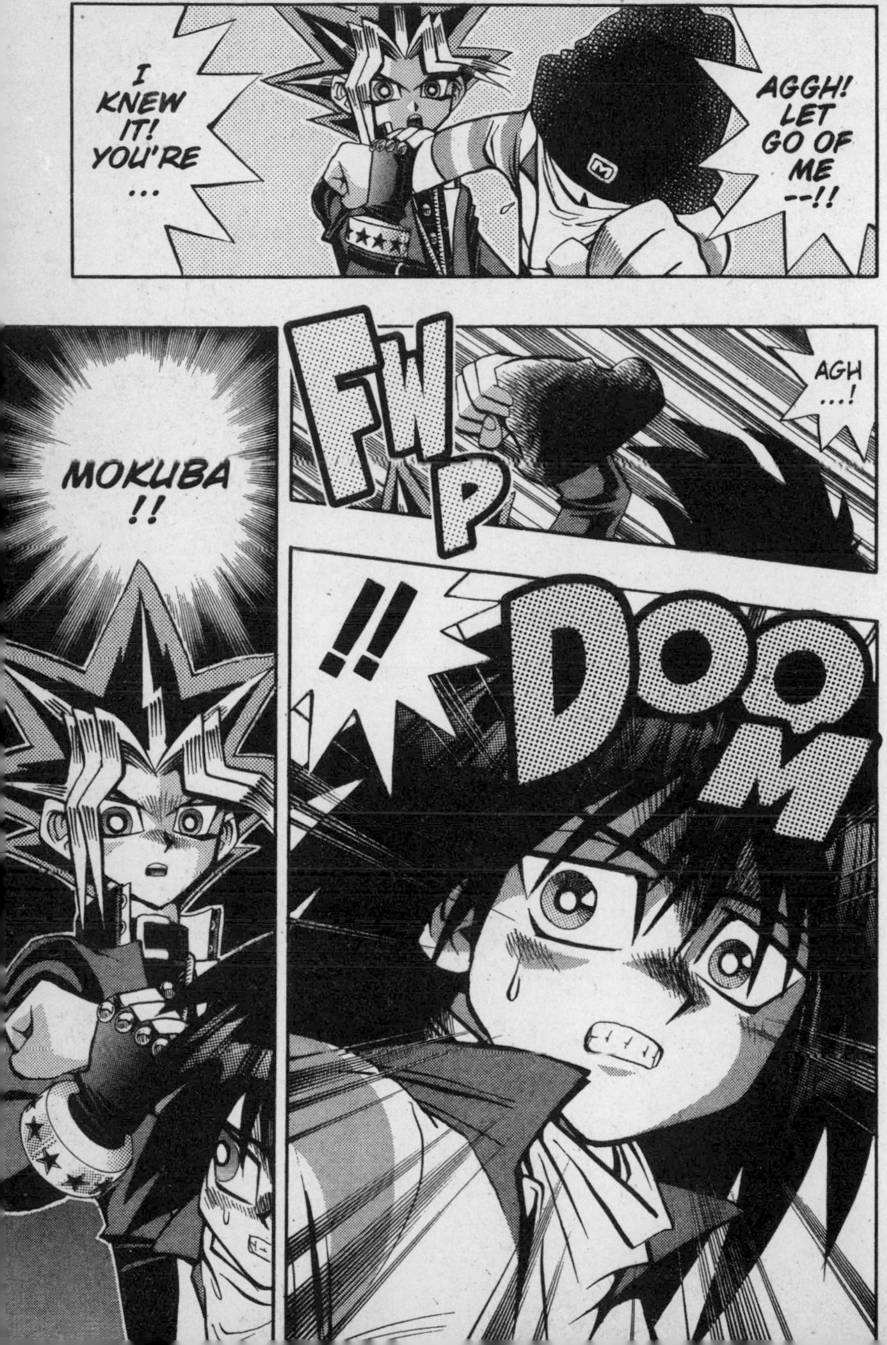
AGGH! LET GO OF ME --!!
I KNEW IT! YOU'RE ...
AGH ...!
FWP
DOOM
!!
MOKUBA !!

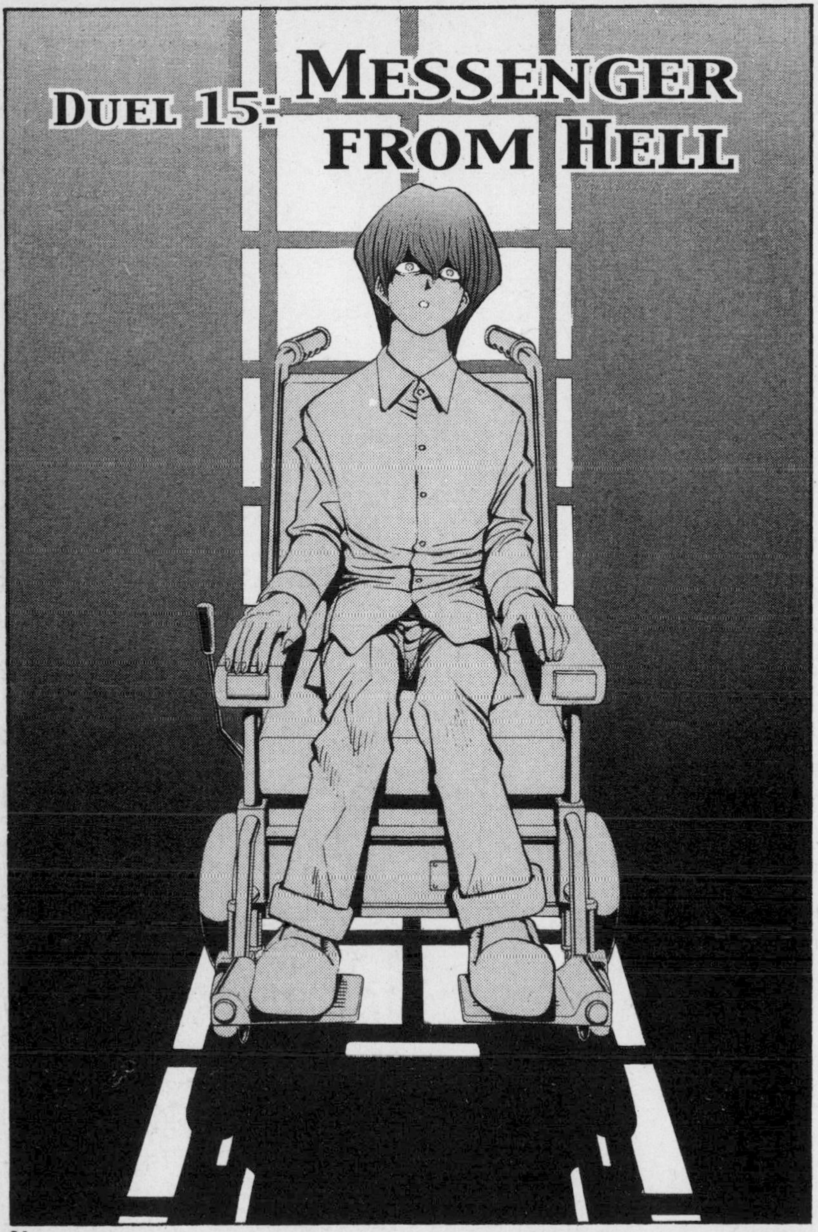
Duel 15: Messenger from Hell

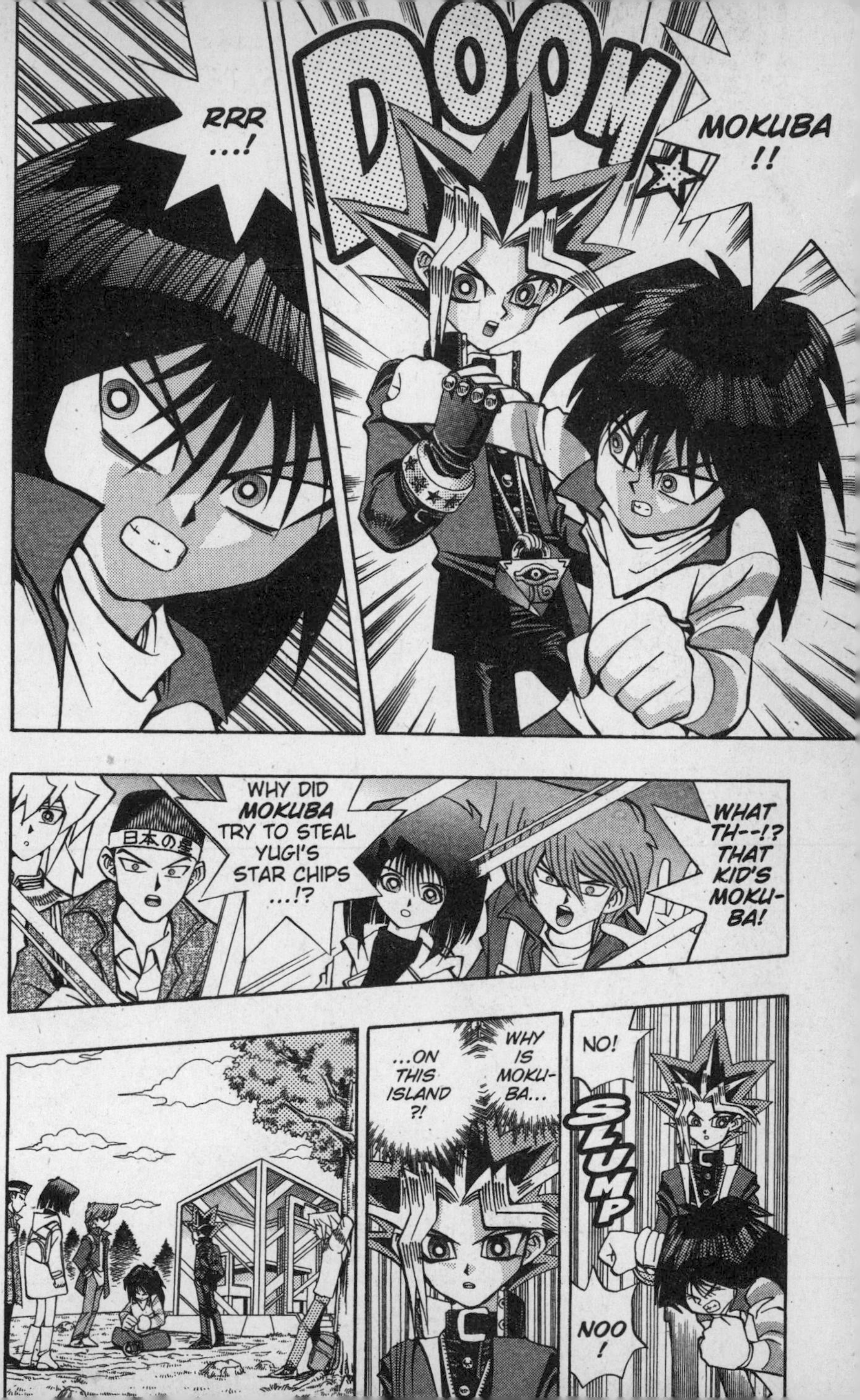
DOOM
MOKUBA!!
RRR...!
WHAT TH--!? THAT KID'S MOKUBA!
WHY DID MOKUBA TRY TO STEAL YUGI'S STAR CHIPS ...!?
日本の星
NO!
SLUMP
NOO!
WHY IS MOKUBA...
...ON THIS ISLAND ?!

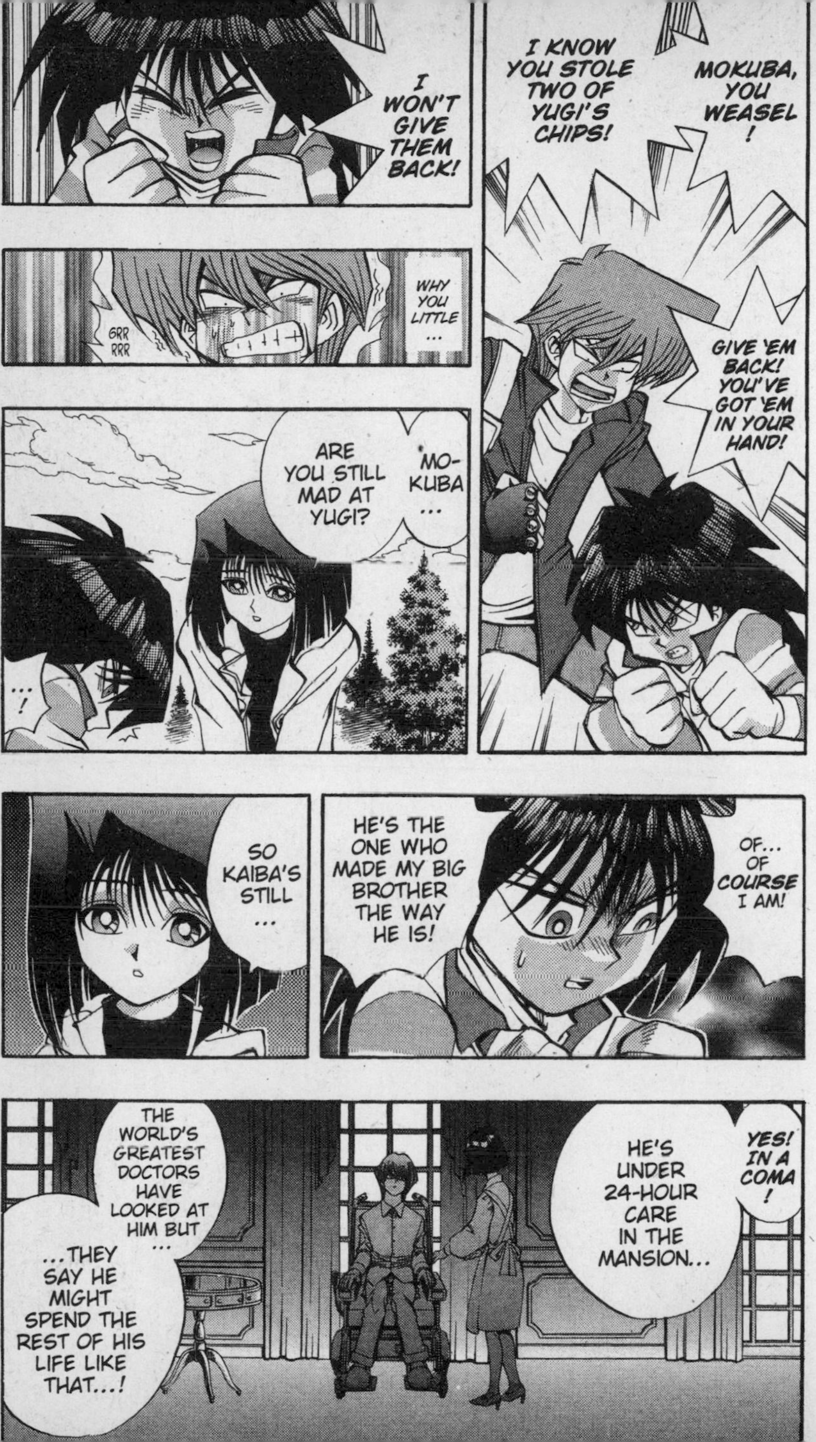
MOKUBA, YOU WEASEL!
I KNOW YOU STOLE TWO OF YUGI'S CHIPS!
GIVE 'EM BACK! YOU'VE GOT 'EM IN YOUR HAND!
I WON'T GIVE THEM BACK!
WHY YOU LITTLE...
GRR RRR
MOKUBA...
ARE YOU STILL MAD AT YUGI?
...!
OF... OF COURSE I AM!
HE'S THE ONE WHO MADE MY BIG BROTHER THE WAY HE IS!
SO KAIBA'S STILL...
YES! IN A COMA!
HE'S UNDER 24-HOUR CARE IN THE MANSION...
THE WORLD'S GREATEST DOCTORS HAVE LOOKED AT HIM BUT...
...THEY SAY HE MIGHT SPEND THE REST OF HIS LIFE LIKE THAT...!

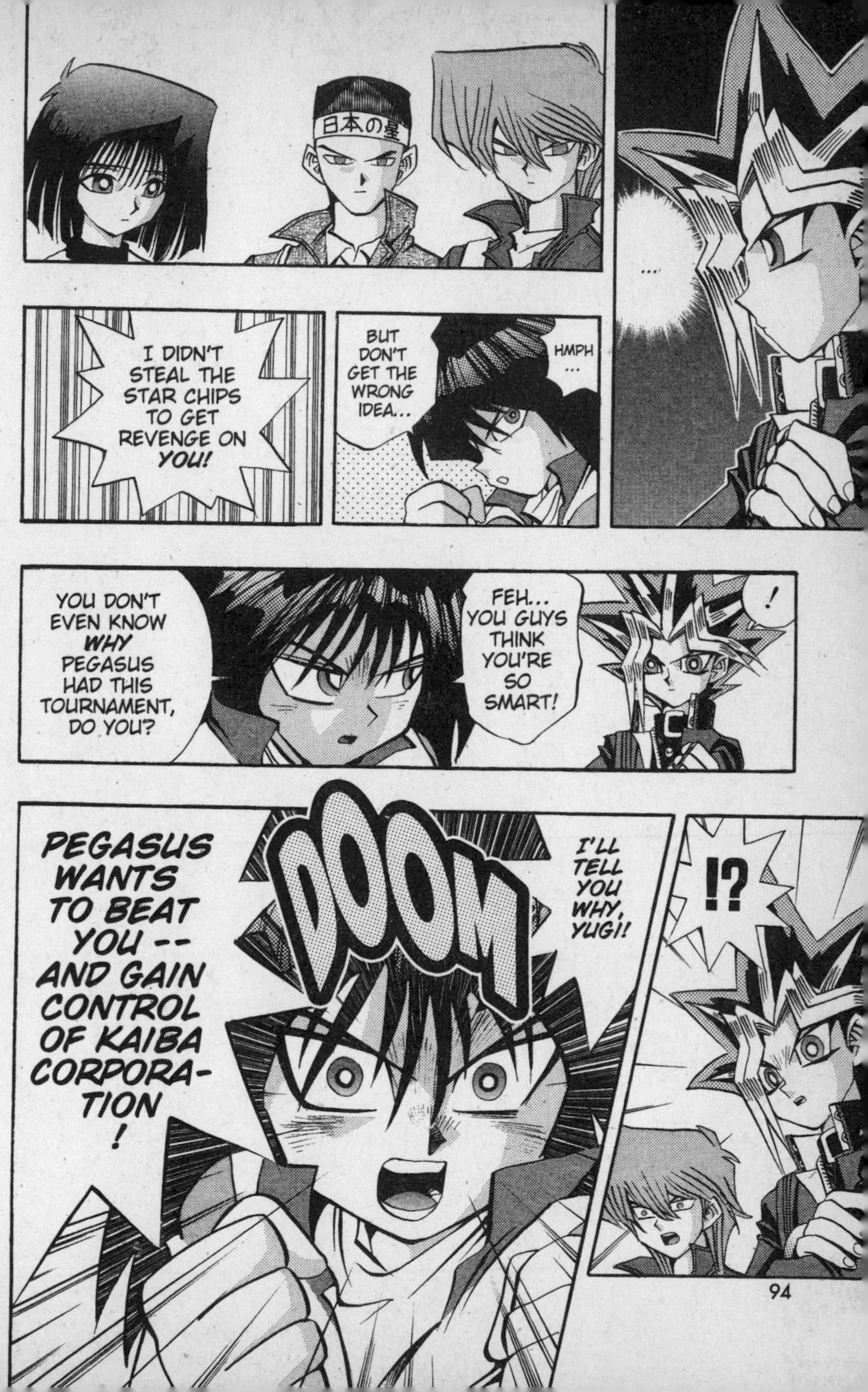
...
HMPH...
BUT DON'T GET THE WRONG IDEA...
I DIDN'T STEAL THE STAR CHIPS TO GET REVENGE ON *YOU!*
!
FEH... YOU GUYS THINK YOU'RE SO SMART!
YOU DON'T EVEN KNOW *WHY* PEGASUS HAD THIS TOURNAMENT, DO YOU?
!?
I'LL TELL YOU WHY, YUGI!
DOOM
PEGASUS WANTS TO BEAT YOU -- AND GAIN CONTROL OF KAIBA CORPORATION!

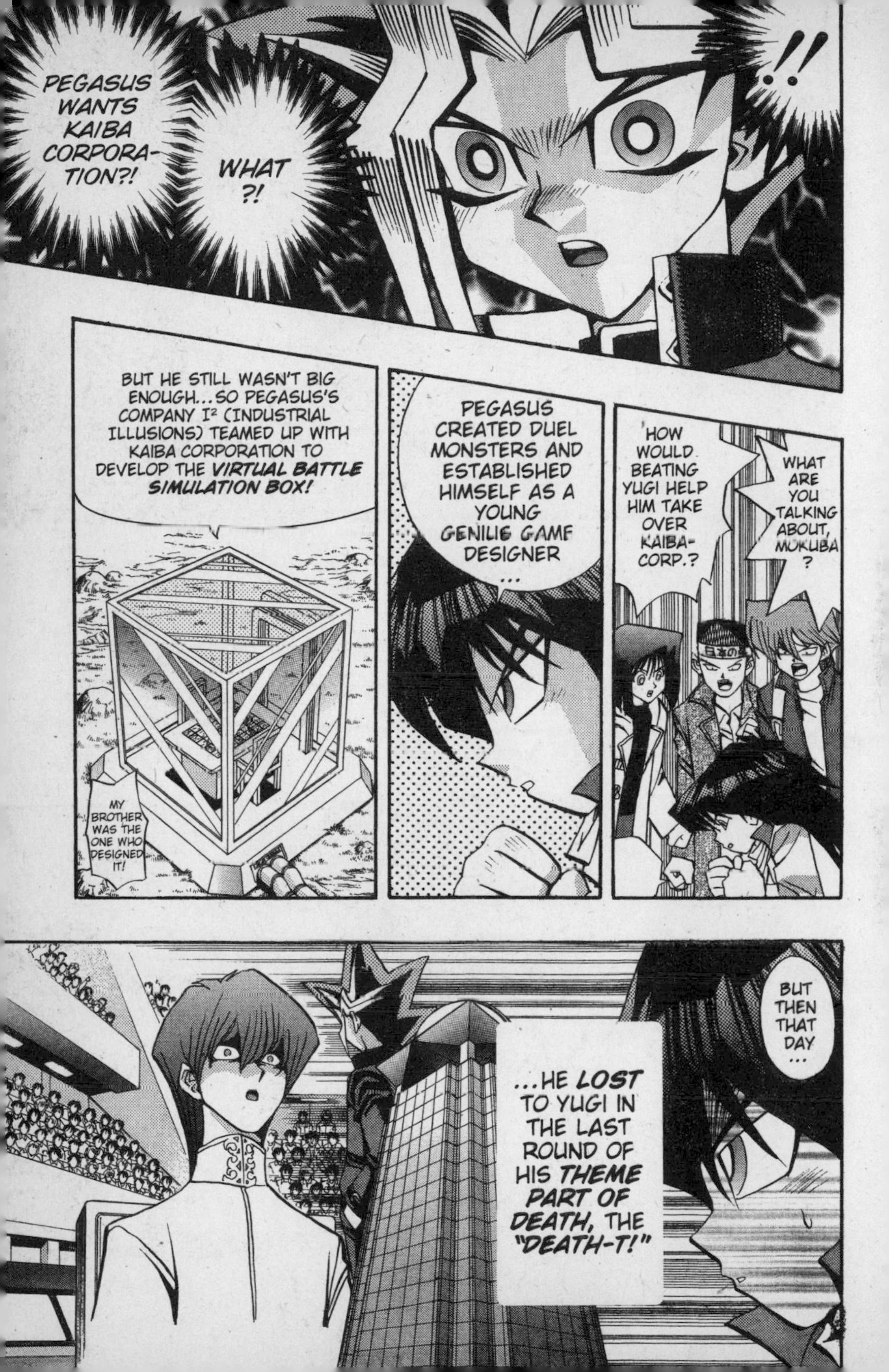
!!
WHAT ?!
PEGASUS WANTS KAIBA CORPORATION?!
WHAT ARE YOU TALKING ABOUT, MOKUBA ?
HOW WOULD BEATING YUGI HELP HIM TAKE OVER KAIBA-CORP.?
PEGASUS CREATED DUEL MONSTERS AND ESTABLISHED HIMSELF AS A YOUNG GENIUS GAME DESIGNER ...
BUT HE STILL WASN'T BIG ENOUGH...SO PEGASUS'S COMPANY I² (INDUSTRIAL ILLUSIONS) TEAMED UP WITH KAIBA CORPORATION TO DEVELOP THE *VIRTUAL BATTLE SIMULATION BOX!*
MY BROTHER WAS THE ONE WHO DESIGNED IT!
BUT THEN THAT DAY ...
...HE *LOST* TO YUGI IN THE LAST ROUND OF HIS *THEME PART OF DEATH,* THE *"DEATH-T!"*

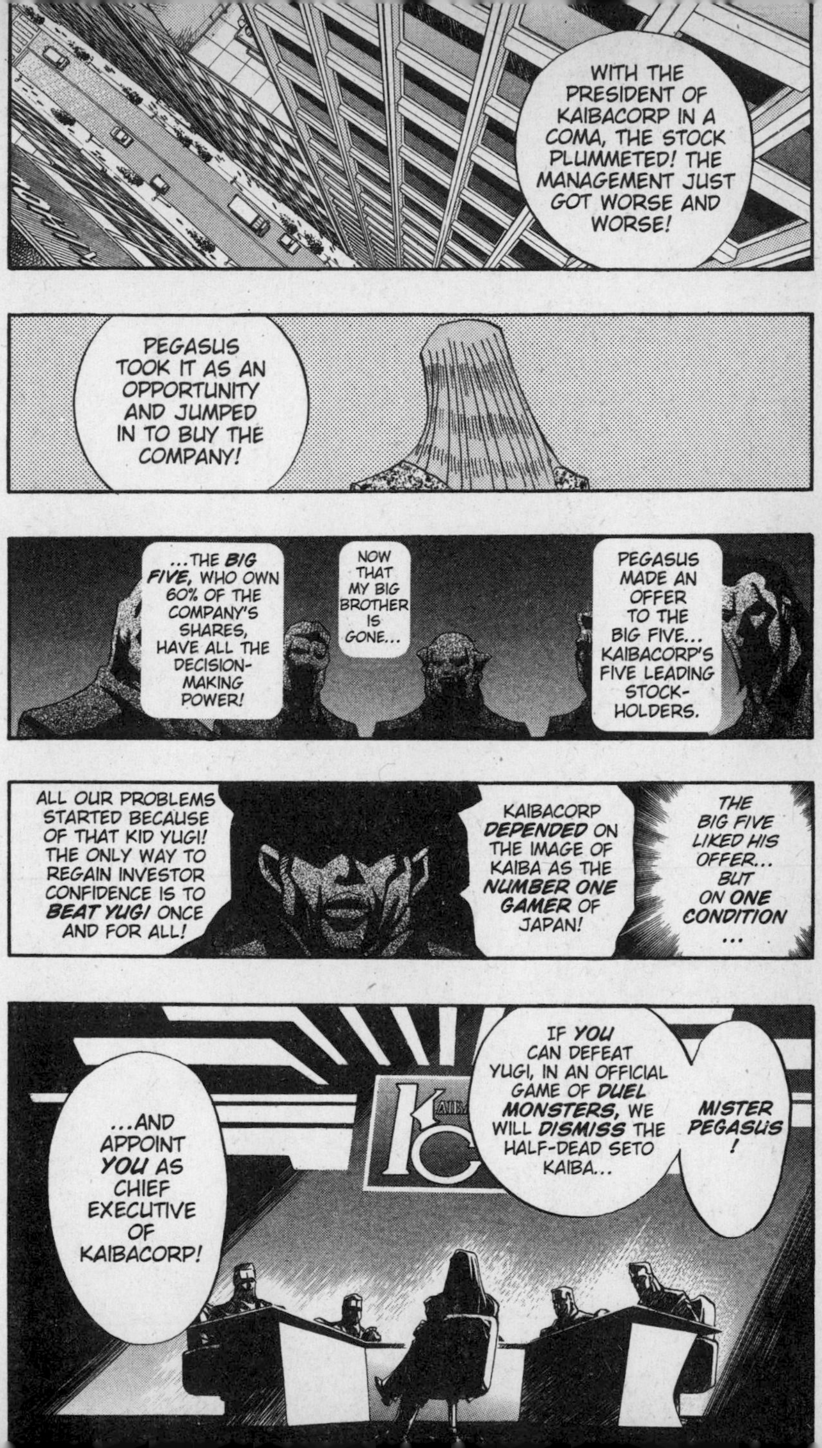
WITH THE PRESIDENT OF KAIBACORP IN A COMA, THE STOCK PLUMMETED! THE MANAGEMENT JUST GOT WORSE AND WORSE!
PEGASUS TOOK IT AS AN OPPORTUNITY AND JUMPED IN TO BUY THE COMPANY!
PEGASUS MADE AN OFFER TO THE BIG FIVE... KAIBACORP'S FIVE LEADING STOCK-HOLDERS.
NOW THAT MY BIG BROTHER IS GONE...
...THE BIG FIVE, WHO OWN 60% OF THE COMPANY'S SHARES, HAVE ALL THE DECISION-MAKING POWER!
THE BIG FIVE LIKED HIS OFFER... BUT ON ONE CONDITION...
KAIBACORP DEPENDED ON THE IMAGE OF KAIBA AS THE NUMBER ONE GAMER OF JAPAN!
ALL OUR PROBLEMS STARTED BECAUSE OF THAT KID YUGI! THE ONLY WAY TO REGAIN INVESTOR CONFIDENCE IS TO BEAT YUGI ONCE AND FOR ALL!
MISTER PEGASUS!
IF YOU CAN DEFEAT YUGI, IN AN OFFICIAL GAME OF DUEL MONSTERS, WE WILL DISMISS THE HALF-DEAD SETO KAIBA...
...AND APPOINT YOU AS CHIEF EXECUTIVE OF KAIBACORP!

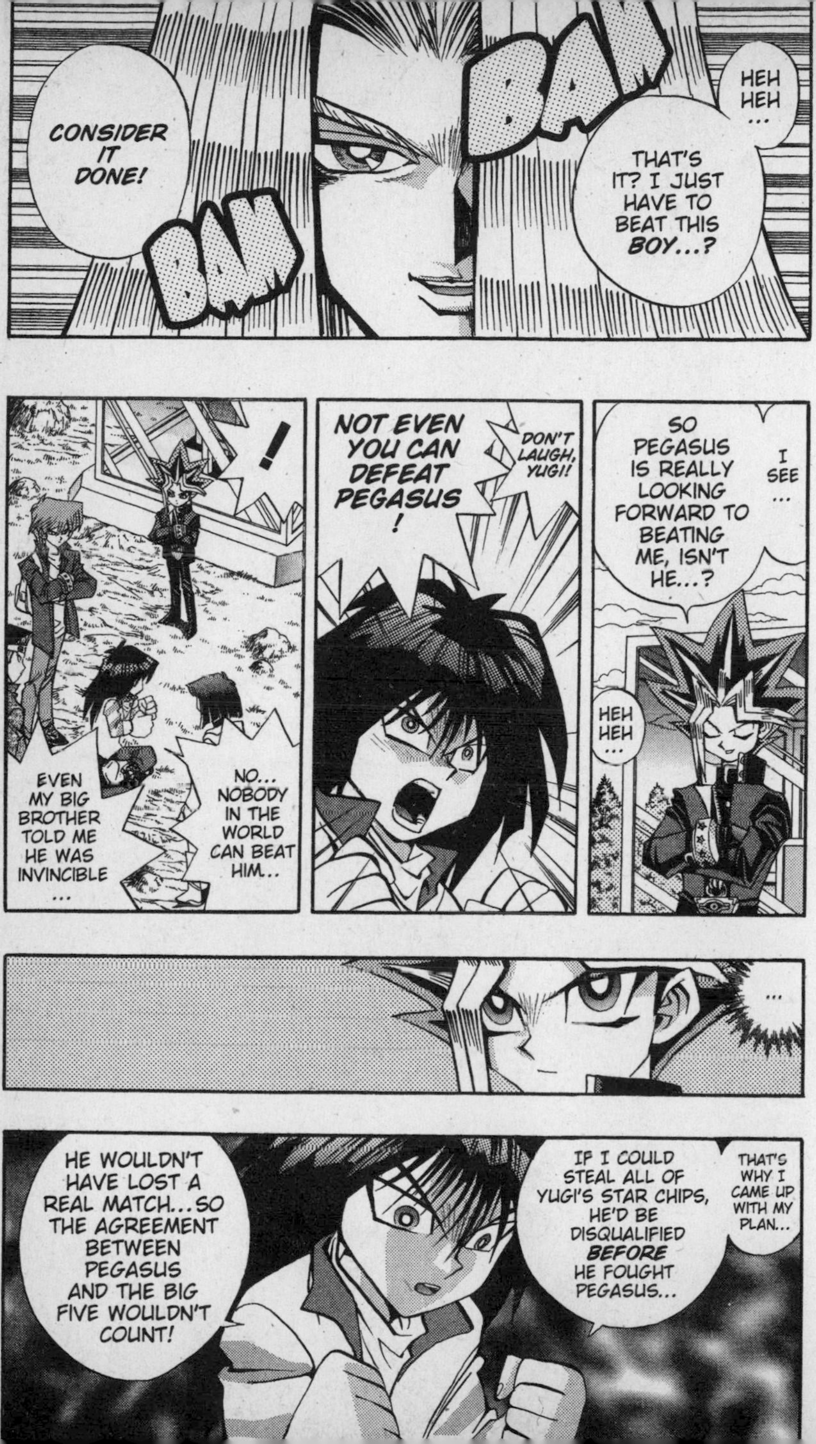
HEH HEH ...
THAT'S IT? I JUST HAVE TO BEAT THIS *BOY*...?
BAM
BAM
CONSIDER IT DONE!
I SEE ...
SO PEGASUS IS REALLY LOOKING FORWARD TO BEATING ME, ISN'T HE...?
HEH HEH ...
DON'T LAUGH, YUGI!
NOT EVEN YOU CAN DEFEAT PEGASUS!
!
NO... NOBODY IN THE WORLD CAN BEAT HIM...
EVEN MY BIG BROTHER TOLD ME HE WAS INVINCIBLE ...
...
THAT'S WHY I CAME UP WITH MY PLAN...
IF I COULD STEAL ALL OF YUGI'S STAR CHIPS, HE'D BE DISQUALIFIED *BEFORE* HE FOUGHT PEGASUS...
HE WOULDN'T HAVE LOST A REAL MATCH...SO THE AGREEMENT BETWEEN PEGASUS AND THE BIG FIVE WOULDN'T COUNT!

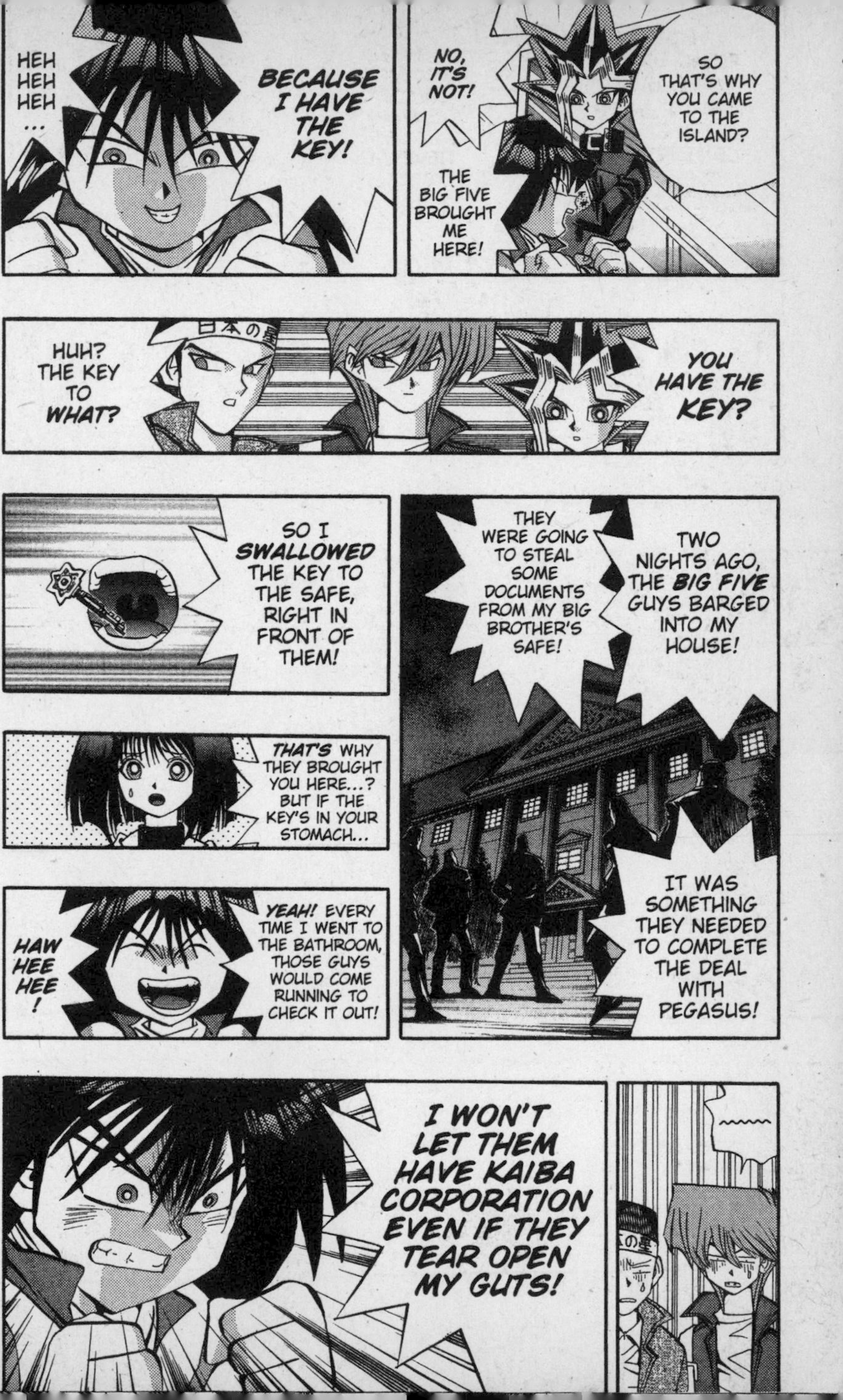
SO THAT'S WHY YOU CAME TO THE ISLAND?
NO, IT'S NOT!
THE BIG FIVE BROUGHT ME HERE!
BECAUSE I HAVE THE KEY!
HEH HEH HEH ...
YOU HAVE THE KEY?
HUH? THE KEY TO WHAT?
TWO NIGHTS AGO, THE BIG FIVE GUYS BARGED INTO MY HOUSE!
THEY WERE GOING TO STEAL SOME DOCUMENTS FROM MY BIG BROTHER'S SAFE!
IT WAS SOMETHING THEY NEEDED TO COMPLETE THE DEAL WITH PEGASUS!
SO I SWALLOWED THE KEY TO THE SAFE, RIGHT IN FRONT OF THEM!
THAT'S WHY THEY BROUGHT YOU HERE...? BUT IF THE KEY'S IN YOUR STOMACH...
YEAH! EVERY TIME I WENT TO THE BATHROOM, THOSE GUYS WOULD COME RUNNING TO CHECK IT OUT!
HAW HEE HEE!
I WON'T LET THEM HAVE KAIBA CORPORATION EVEN IF THEY TEAR OPEN MY GUTS!

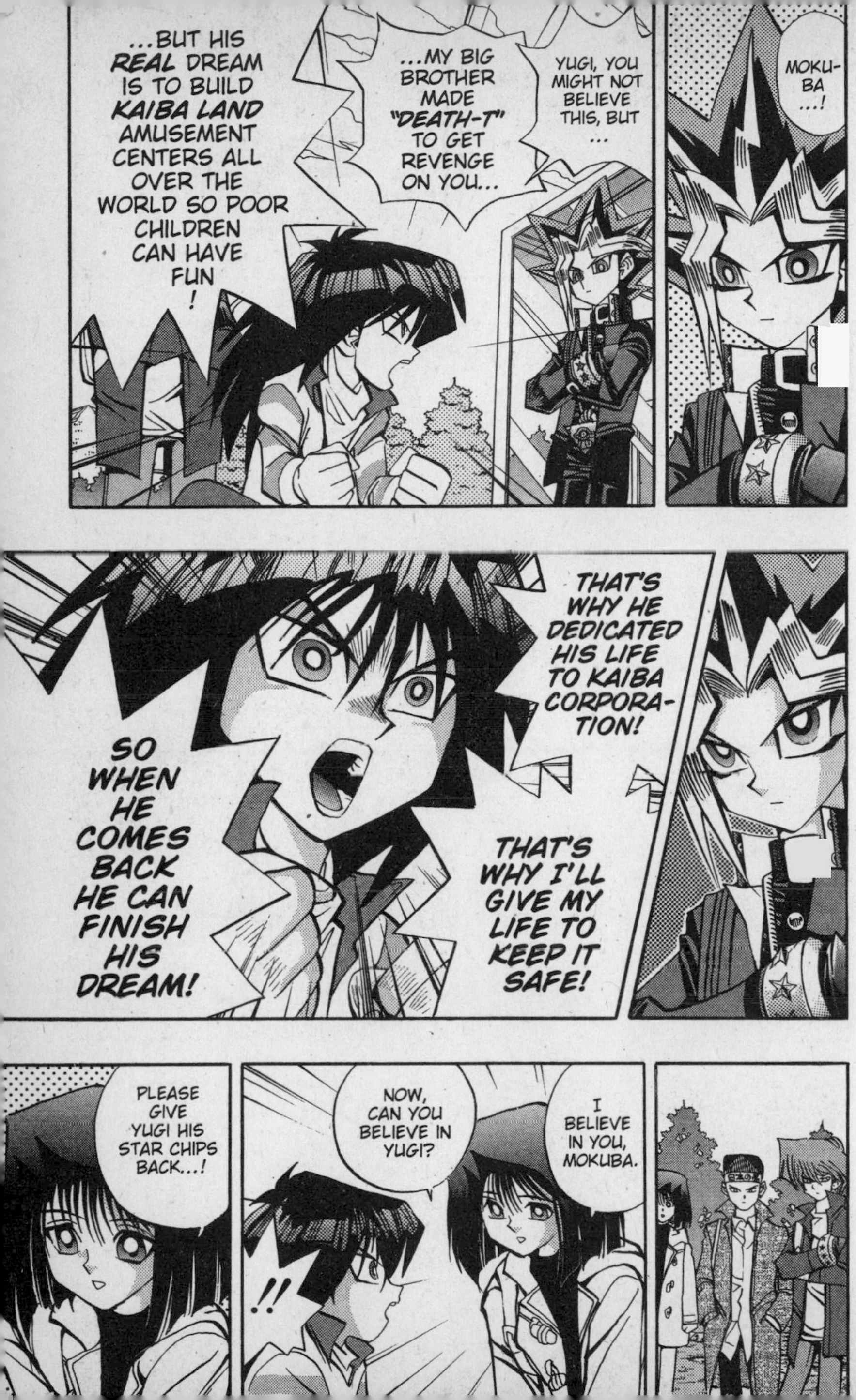
MOKU-BA ...!
YUGI, YOU MIGHT NOT BELIEVE THIS, BUT ...
...MY BIG BROTHER MADE "DEATH-T" TO GET REVENGE ON YOU...
...BUT HIS REAL DREAM IS TO BUILD KAIBA LAND AMUSEMENT CENTERS ALL OVER THE WORLD SO POOR CHILDREN CAN HAVE FUN!
THAT'S WHY HE DEDICATED HIS LIFE TO KAIBA CORPORATION!
SO WHEN HE COMES BACK HE CAN FINISH HIS DREAM!
THAT'S WHY I'LL GIVE MY LIFE TO KEEP IT SAFE!
I BELIEVE IN YOU, MOKUBA.
NOW, CAN YOU BELIEVE IN YUGI?
!!
PLEASE GIVE YUGI HIS STAR CHIPS BACK...!

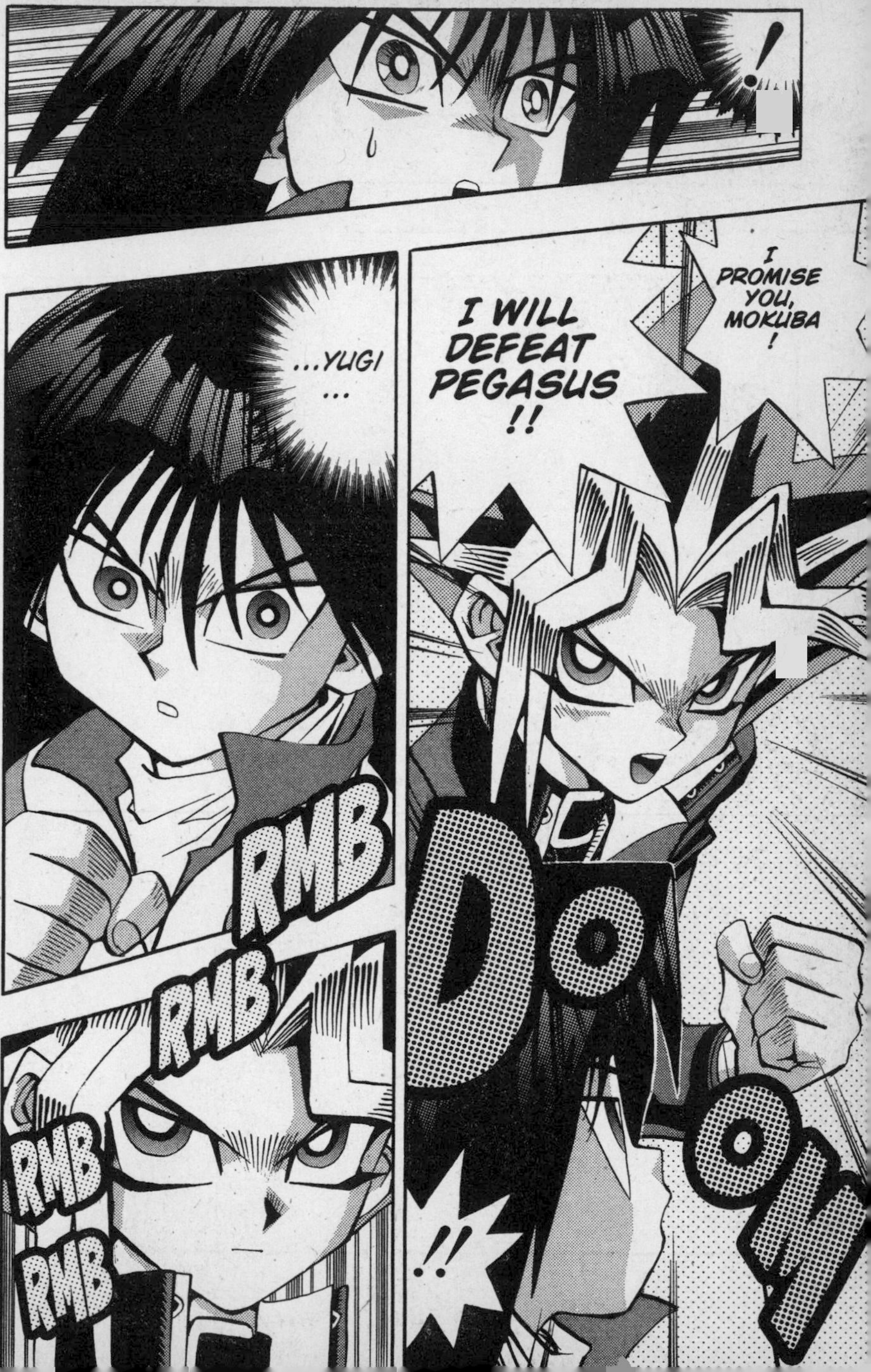
!
I PROMISE YOU, MOKUBA!
I WILL DEFEAT PEGASUS!!
DOOM
!!
...YUGI...
RMB
RMB
RMB
RMB

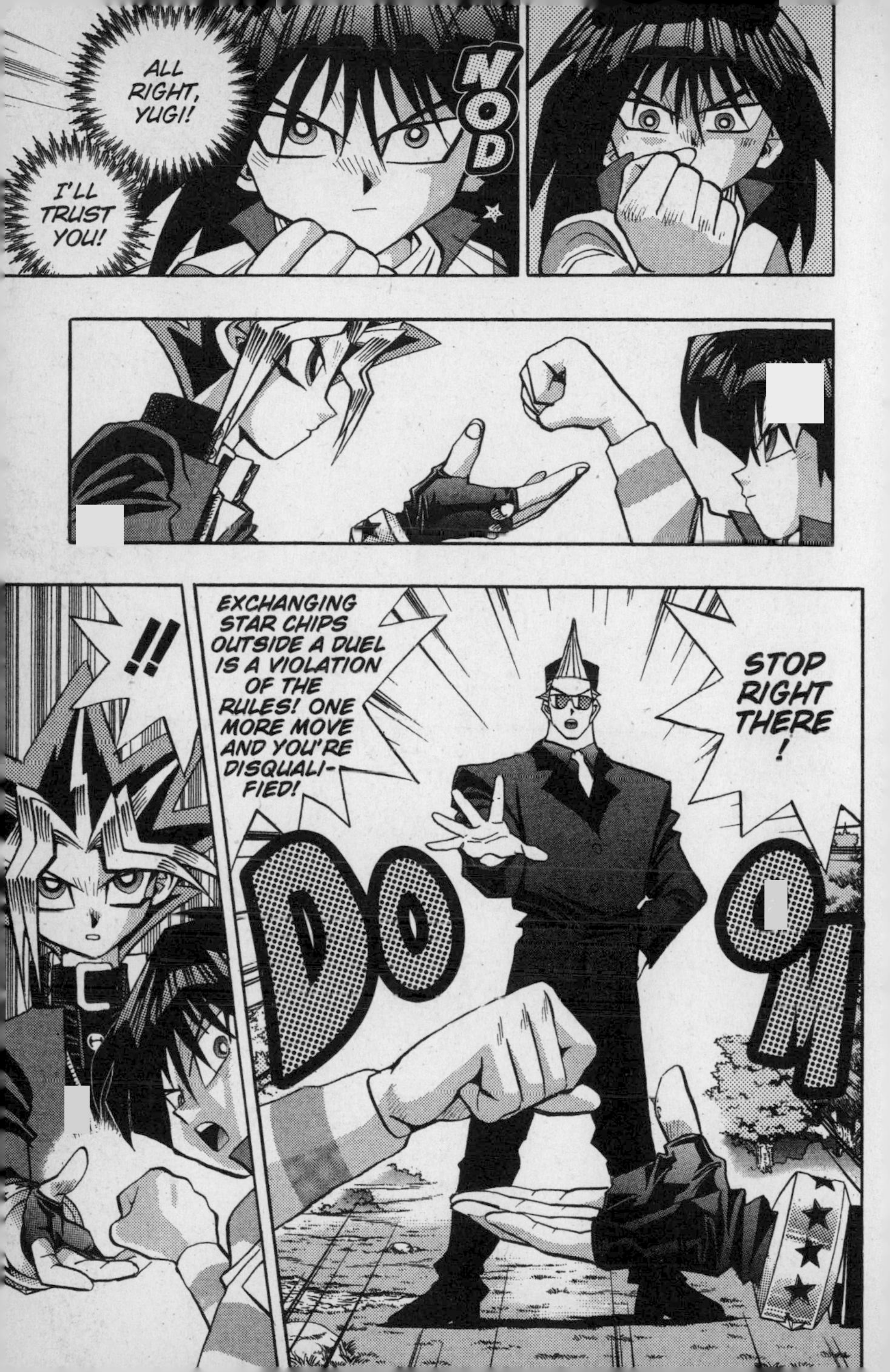
NOD
ALL RIGHT, YUGI!
I'LL TRUST YOU!
STOP RIGHT THERE!
EXCHANGING STAR CHIPS OUTSIDE A DUEL IS A VIOLATION OF THE RULES! ONE MORE MOVE AND YOU'RE DISQUALIFIED!
DOOM
!!

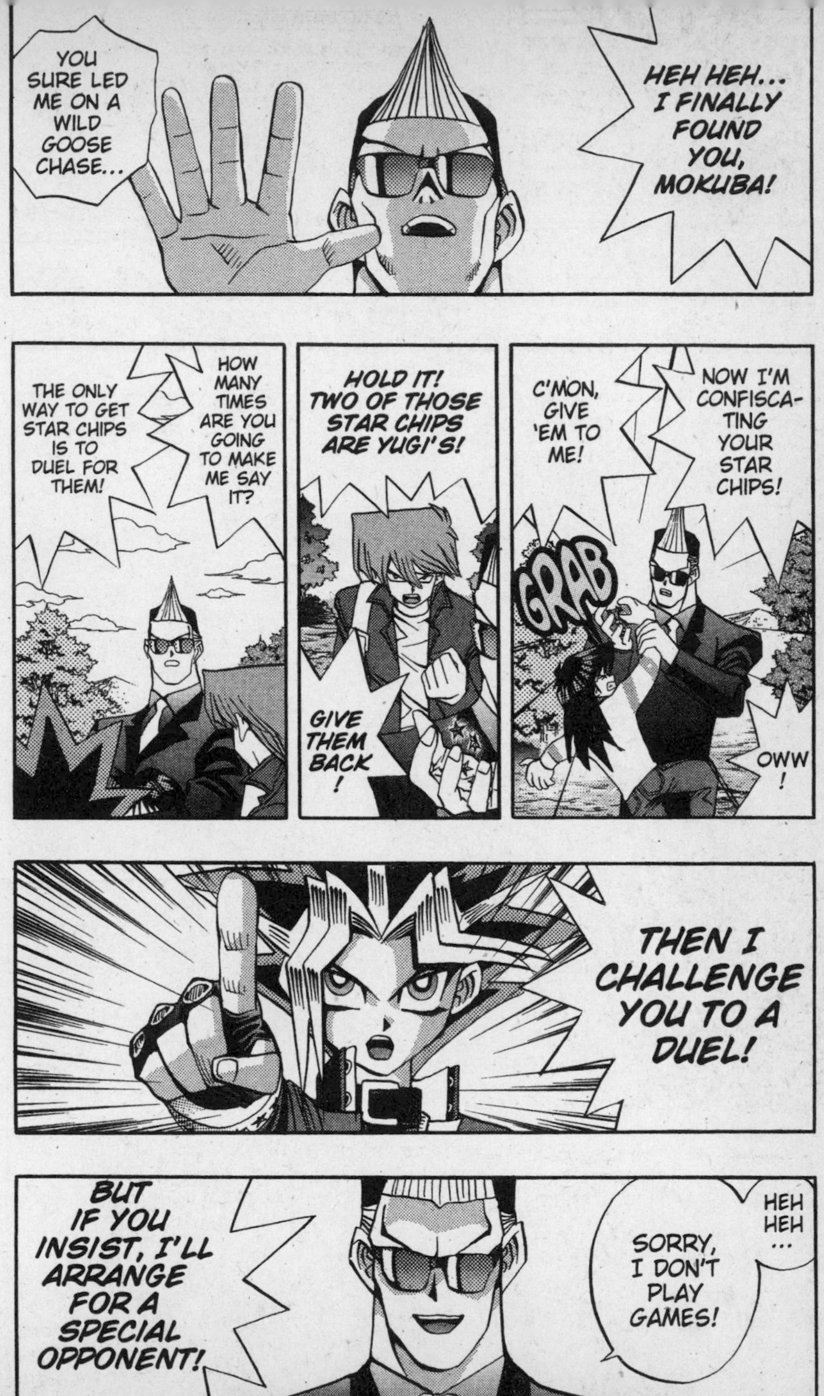
HEH HEH... I FINALLY FOUND YOU, MOKUBA!
YOU SURE LED ME ON A WILD GOOSE CHASE...
NOW I'M CONFISCA-TING YOUR STAR CHIPS!
C'MON, GIVE 'EM TO ME!
GRAB
OWW!
HOLD IT! TWO OF THOSE STAR CHIPS ARE YUGI'S!
GIVE THEM BACK!
HOW MANY TIMES ARE YOU GOING TO MAKE ME SAY IT?
THE ONLY WAY TO GET STAR CHIPS IS TO DUEL FOR THEM!
THEN I CHALLENGE YOU TO A DUEL!
HEH HEH...
SORRY, I DON'T PLAY GAMES!
BUT IF YOU INSIST, I'LL ARRANGE FOR A SPECIAL OPPONENT!

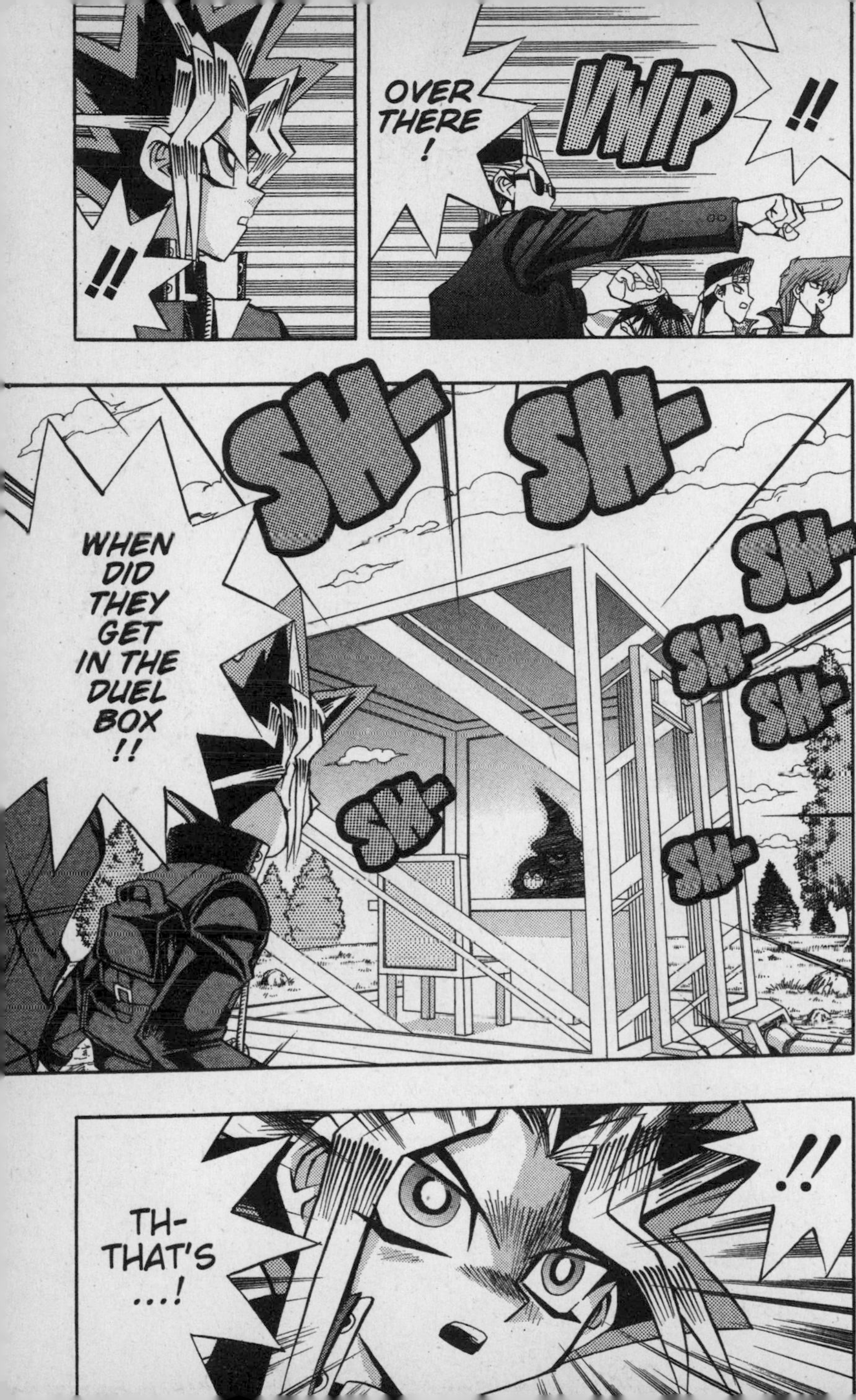
WHIP
!!
OVER THERE!
!!
SH-
SH-
SH-
SH-
SH-
SH-
SH-
WHEN DID THEY GET IN THE DUEL BOX!!
!!
TH-THAT'S...!

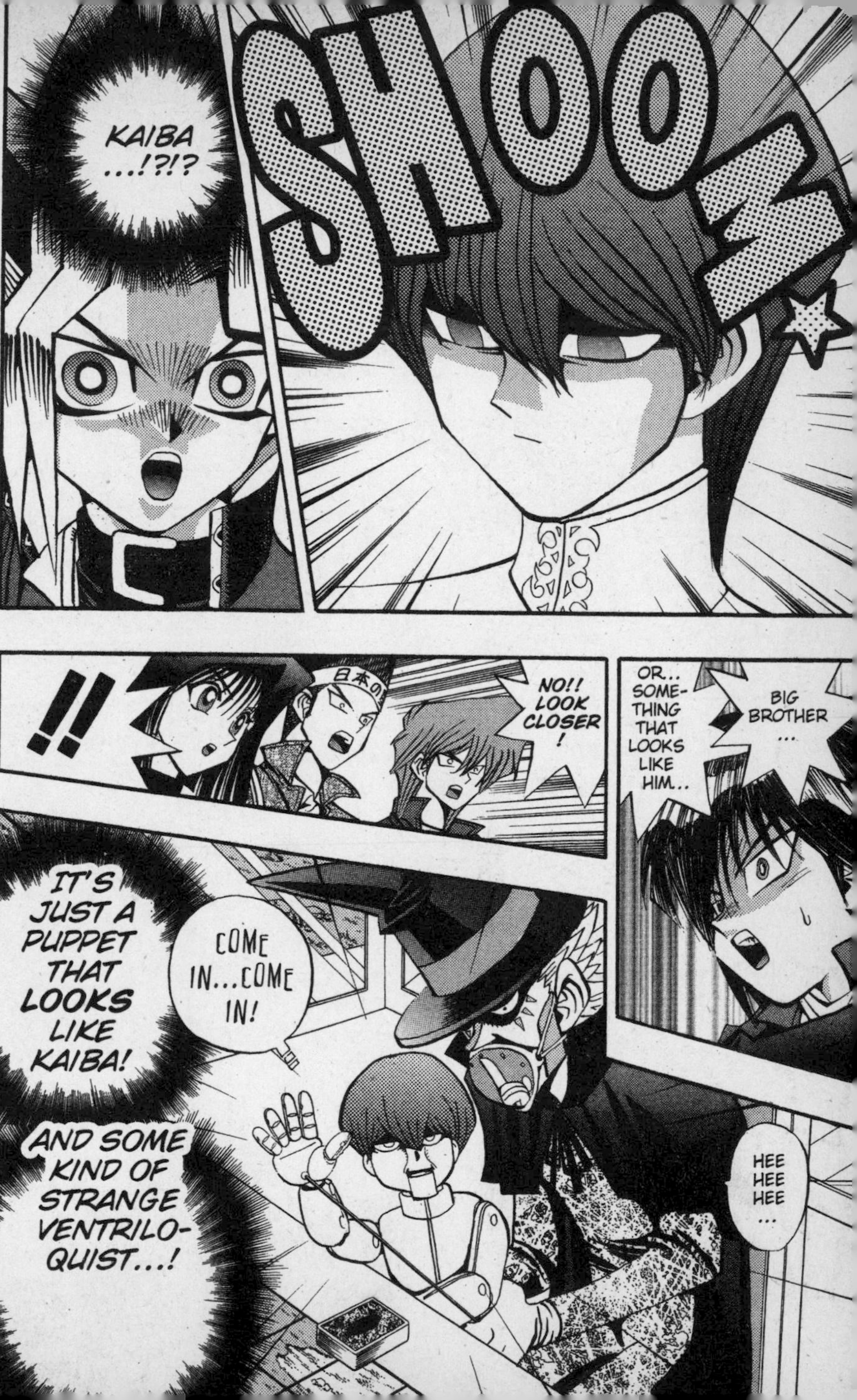
SHOOM
KAIBA ...!?!?
BIG BROTHER ...
OR.. SOME-THING THAT LOOKS LIKE HIM..
NO!! LOOK CLOSER!
!!
HEE HEE HEE ...
COME IN...COME IN!
IT'S JUST A PUPPET THAT LOOKS LIKE KAIBA!
AND SOME KIND OF STRANGE VENTRILO-QUIST...!

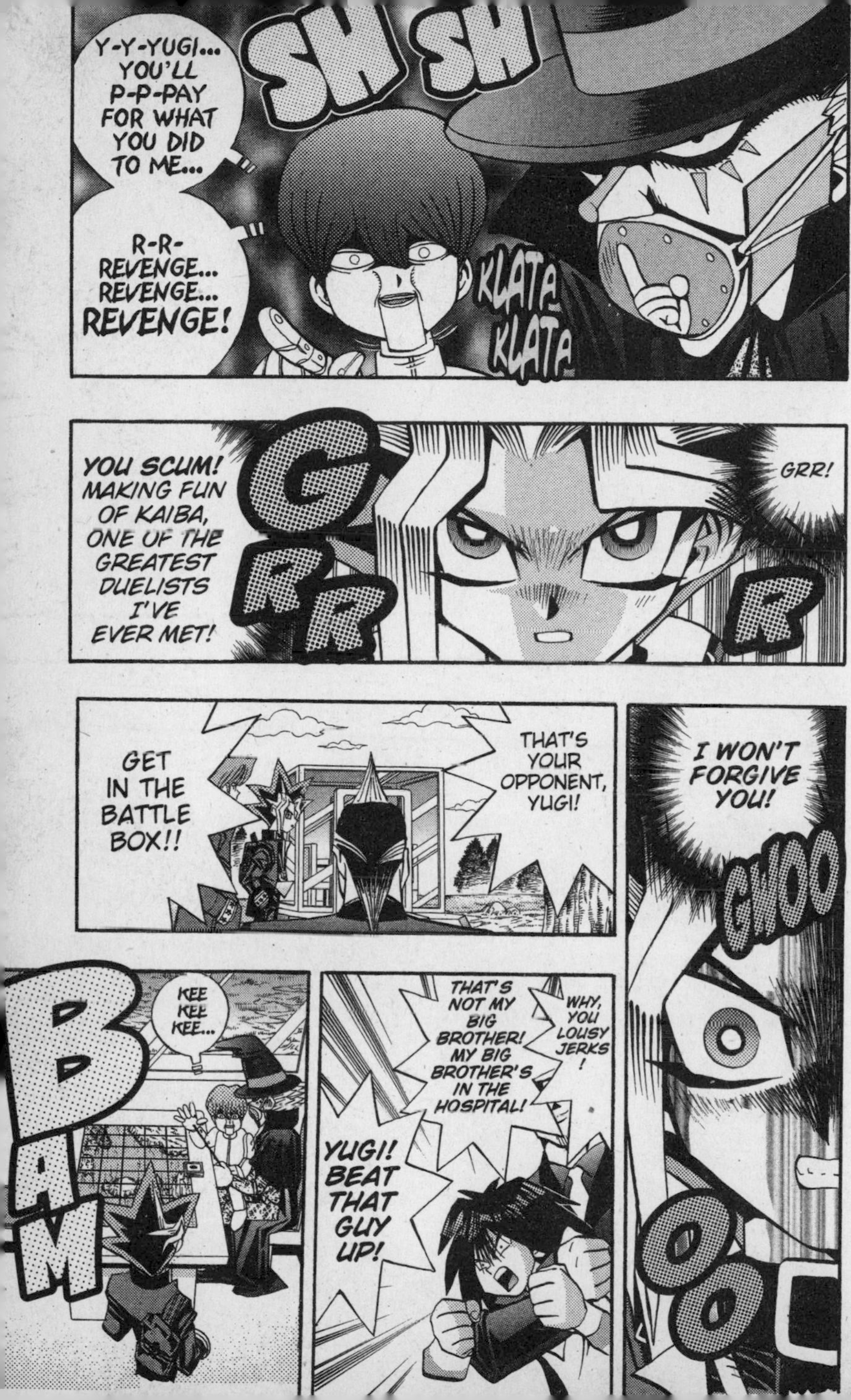
SH SH
Y-Y-YUGI... YOU'LL P-P-PAY FOR WHAT YOU DID TO ME...
KLATA KLATA
R-R-REVENGE... REVENGE... REVENGE!
GRR!
GRRR
YOU SCUM! MAKING FUN OF KAIBA, ONE OF THE GREATEST DUELISTS I'VE EVER MET!
I WON'T FORGIVE YOU!
GWOOOO
THAT'S YOUR OPPONENT, YUGI!
GET IN THE BATTLE BOX!!
WHY, YOU LOUSY JERKS!
THAT'S NOT MY BIG BROTHER! MY BIG BROTHER'S IN THE HOSPITAL!
YUGI! BEAT THAT GUY UP!
KEE KEE KEE...
BAM

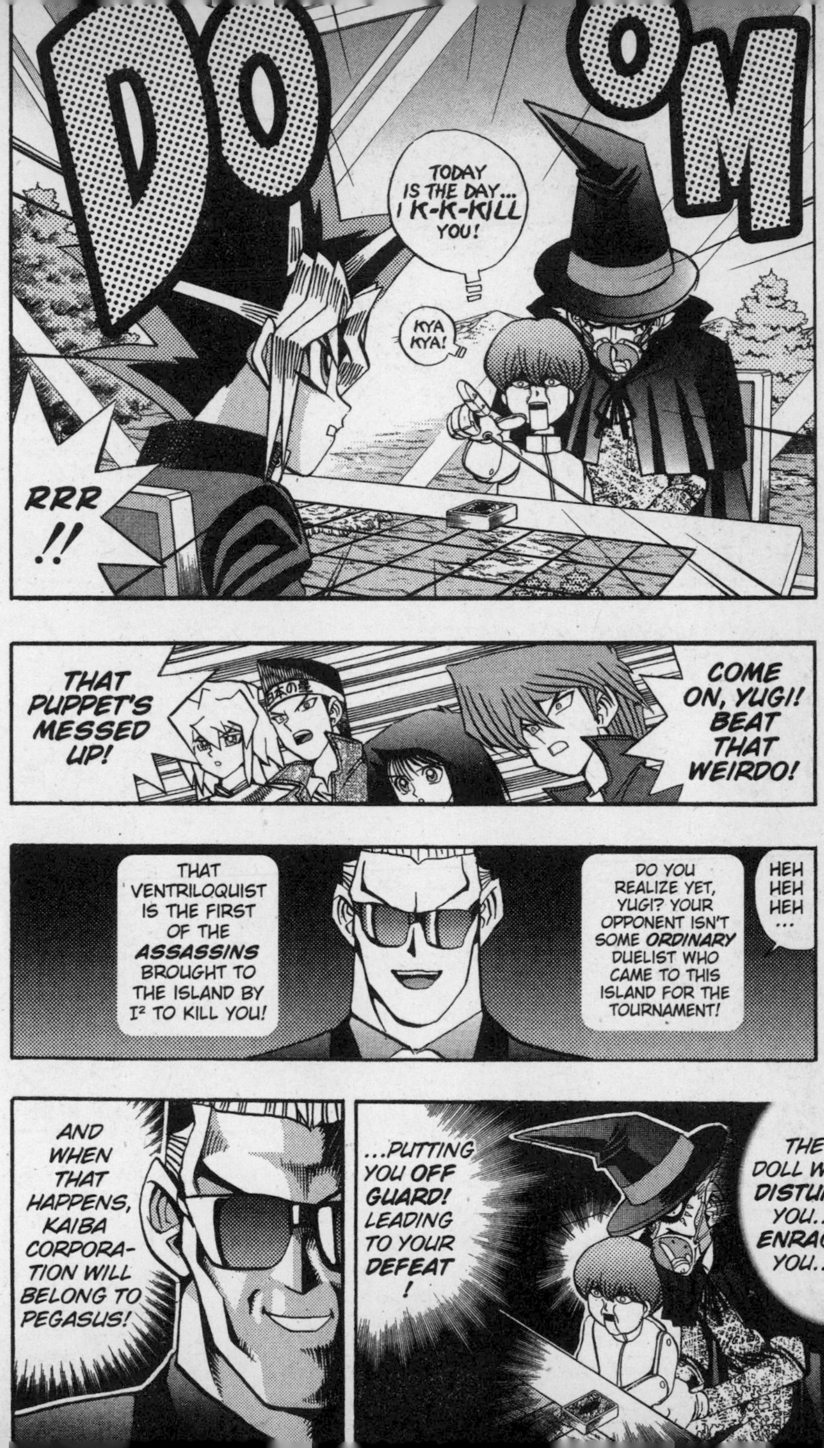
DOOM
TODAY IS THE DAY... I K-K-KILL YOU!
KYA KYA!
RRR!!
COME ON, YUGI! BEAT THAT WEIRDO!
THAT PUPPET'S MESSED UP!
HEH HEH HEH ...
DO YOU REALIZE YET, YUGI? YOUR OPPONENT ISN'T SOME ORDINARY DUELIST WHO CAME TO THIS ISLAND FOR THE TOURNAMENT!
THAT VENTRILOQUIST IS THE FIRST OF THE ASSASSINS BROUGHT TO THE ISLAND BY I^2 TO KILL YOU!
THE DOLL WILL DISTURB YOU... ENRAGE YOU...
...PUTTING YOU OFF GUARD! LEADING TO YOUR DEFEAT!
AND WHEN THAT HAPPENS, KAIBA CORPORATION WILL BELONG TO PEGASUS!

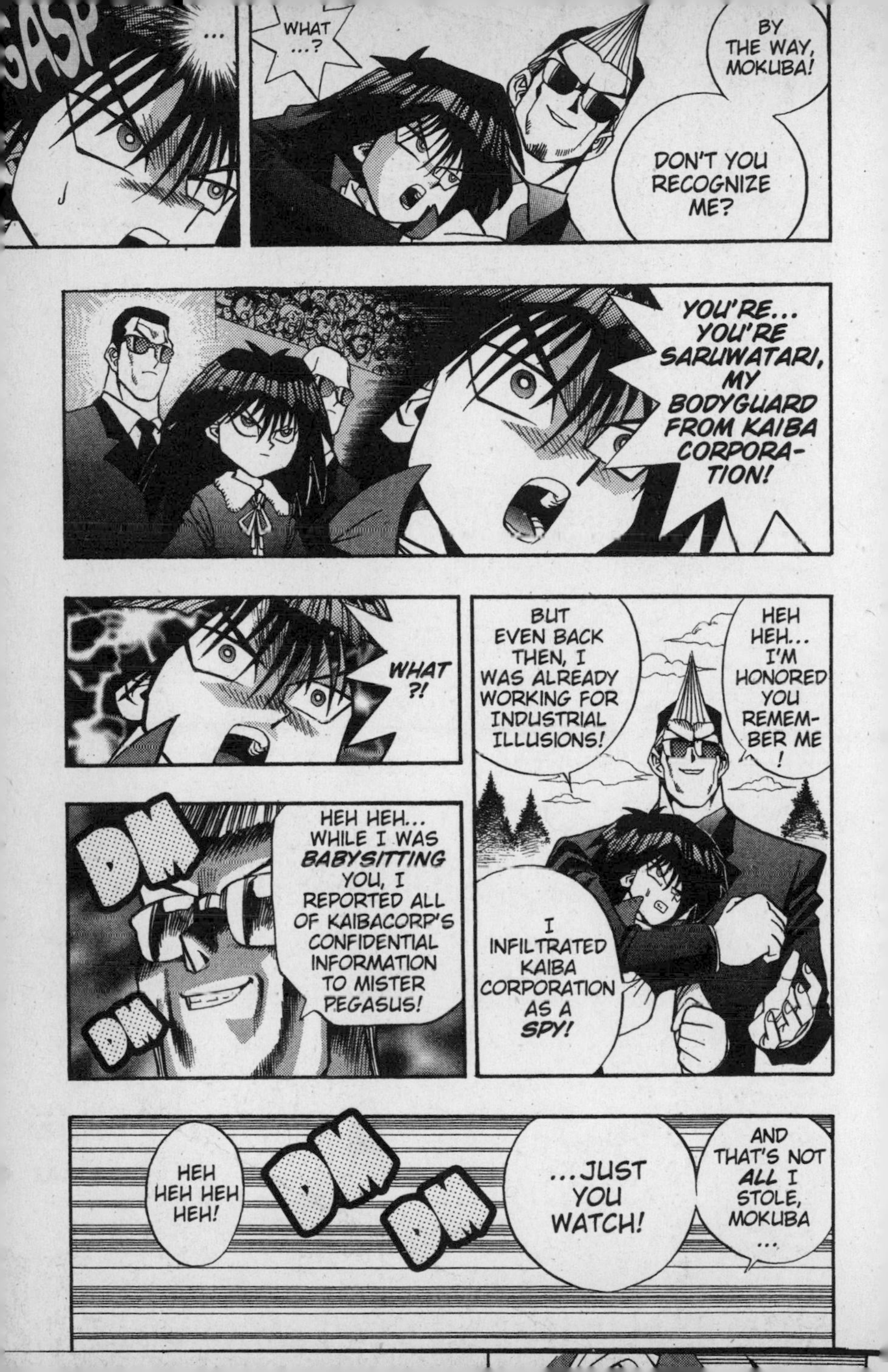
BY THE WAY, MOKUBA!
DON'T YOU RECOGNIZE ME?
WHAT ...?
GASP
...
YOU'RE... YOU'RE SARUWATARI, MY BODYGUARD FROM KAIBA CORPORA-TION!
HEH HEH... I'M HONORED YOU REMEM-BER ME!
BUT EVEN BACK THEN, I WAS ALREADY WORKING FOR INDUSTRIAL ILLUSIONS!
I INFILTRATED KAIBA CORPORATION AS A SPY!
WHAT ?!
HEH HEH... WHILE I WAS BABYSITTING YOU, I REPORTED ALL OF KAIBACORP'S CONFIDENTIAL INFORMATION TO MISTER PEGASUS!
DM
DM
AND THAT'S NOT ALL I STOLE, MOKUBA ...
...JUST YOU WATCH!
DM
DM
HEH HEH HEH HEH!

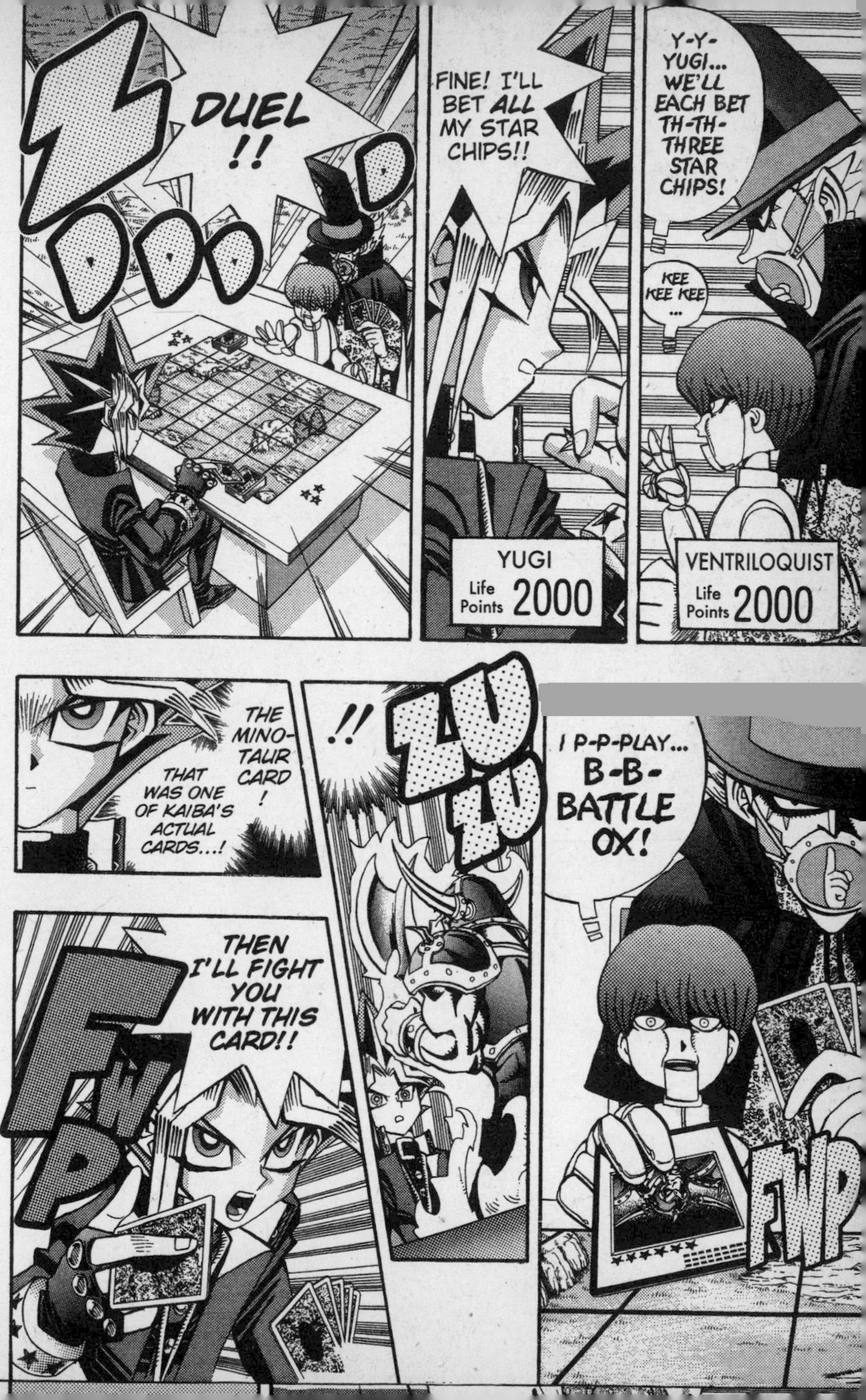
Y-Y-YUGI... WE'LL EACH BET TH-TH-THREE STAR CHIPS!
KEE KEE KEE ...
VENTRILOQUIST Life Points 2000
FINE! I'LL BET ALL MY STAR CHIPS!!
YUGI Life Points 2000
DUEL !!
DDDD
I P-P-PLAY... B-B-BATTLE OX!
FWP
ZU ZU
!!
THE MINO-TAUR CARD!
THAT WAS ONE OF KAIBA'S ACTUAL CARDS...!
THEN I'LL FIGHT YOU WITH THIS CARD!!
FWP

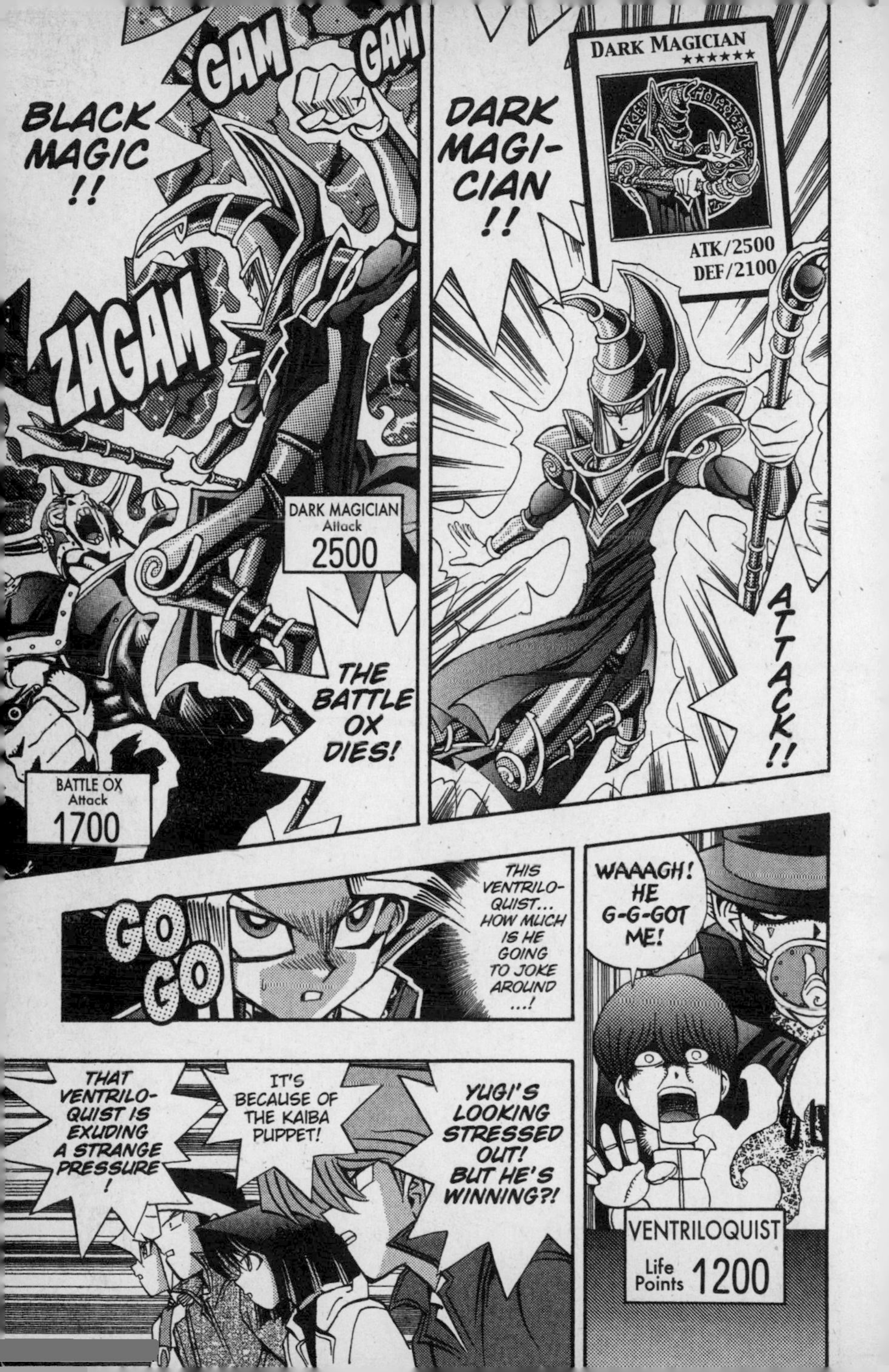
DARK MAGICIAN
ATK/2500
DEF/2100
DARK MAGICIAN!!
ATTACK!!
GAM
GAM
BLACK MAGIC!!
ZAGAM
DARK MAGICIAN Attack 2500
THE BATTLE OX DIES!
BATTLE OX Attack 1700
WAAAGH! HE G-G-GOT ME!
VENTRILOQUIST Life Points 1200
THIS VENTRILOQUIST... HOW MUCH IS HE GOING TO JOKE AROUND...!
GO GO
GO GO
YUGI'S LOOKING STRESSED OUT! BUT HE'S WINNING?!
IT'S BECAUSE OF THE KAIBA PUPPET!
THAT VENTRILOQUIST IS EXUDING A STRANGE PRESSURE!

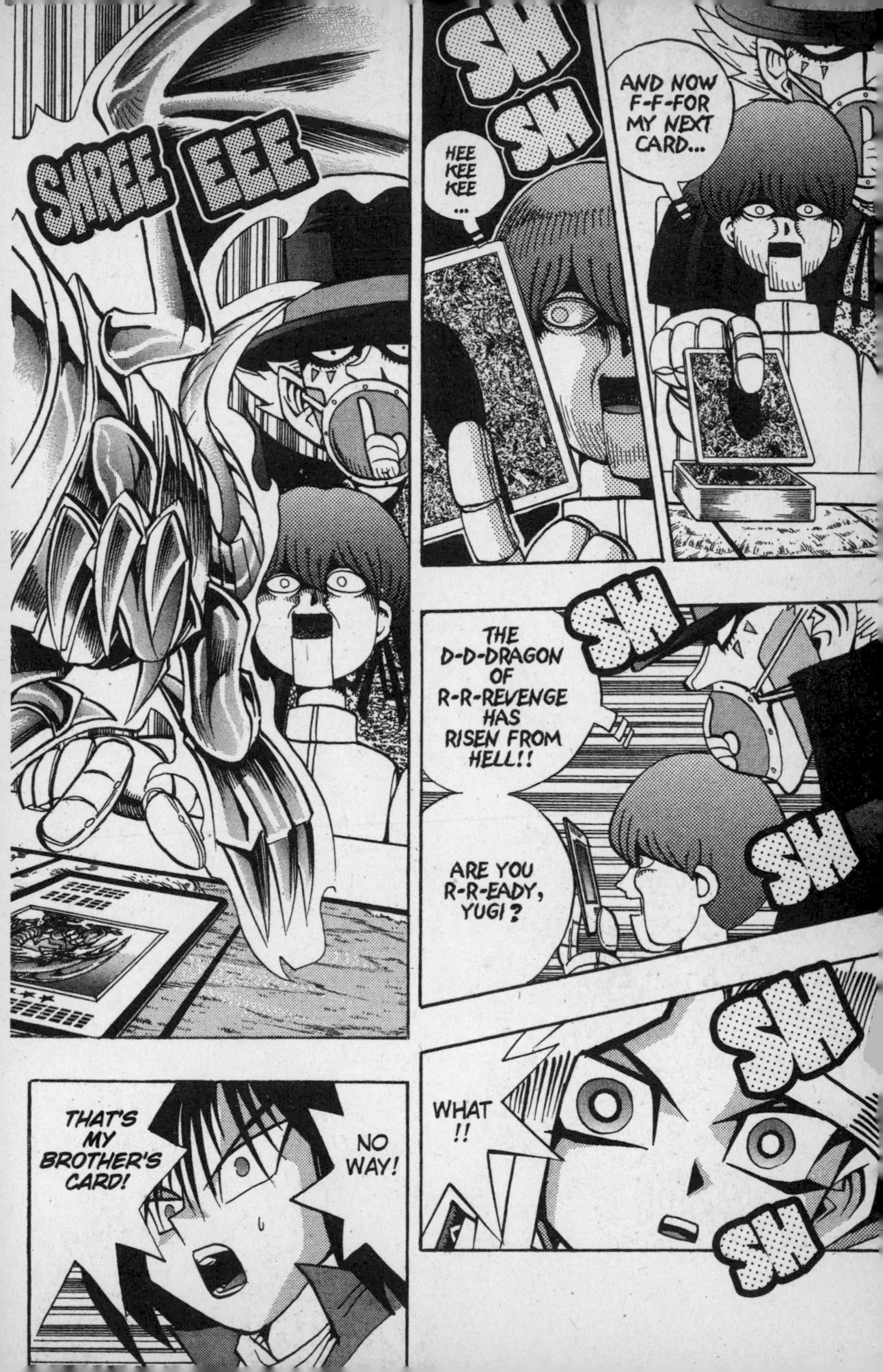
AND NOW F-F-FOR MY NEXT CARD...
SH SH
HEE KEE KEE ...
SH
THE D-D-DRAGON OF R-R-REVENGE HAS RISEN FROM HELL!!
ARE YOU R-R-EADY, YUGI?
SH
SHREE EEE
SH
WHAT!!
SH
NO WAY!
THAT'S MY BROTHER'S CARD!

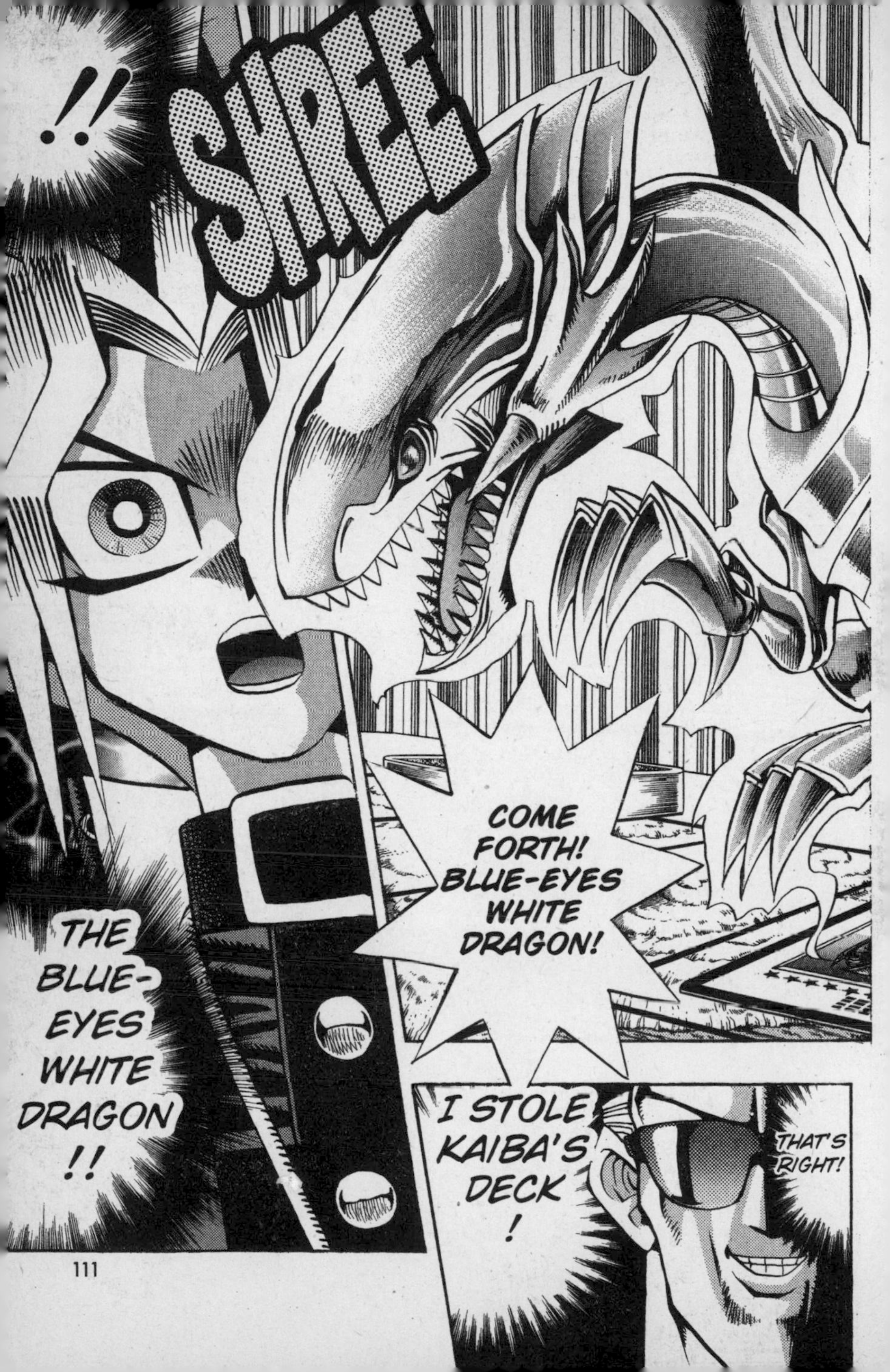
SHREE!
!!
COME FORTH! BLUE-EYES WHITE DRAGON!
THE BLUE-EYES WHITE DRAGON !!
THAT'S RIGHT!
I STOLE KAIBA'S DECK !

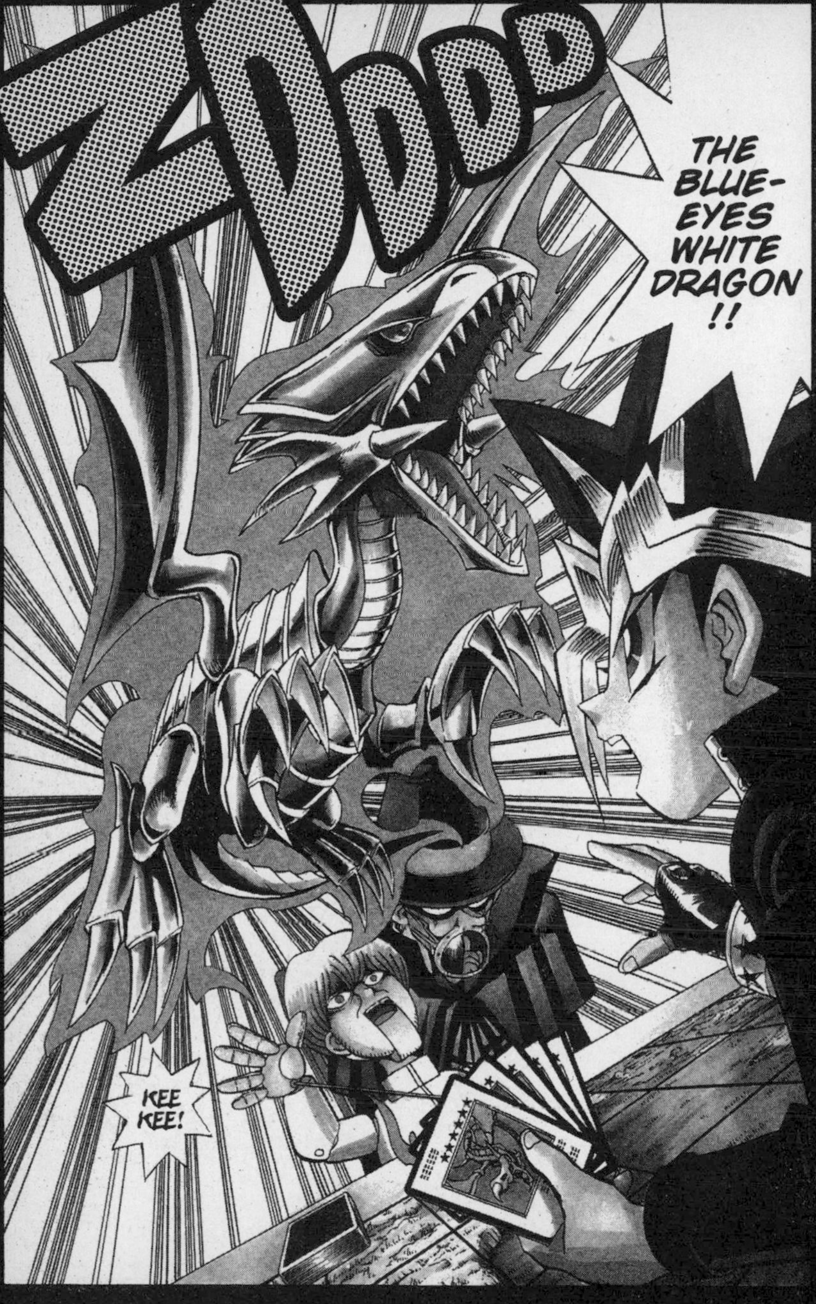
ZDDDP
THE BLUE-EYES WHITE DRAGON!!
KEE KEE!

Duel 16: The Cards Bare Their Teeth

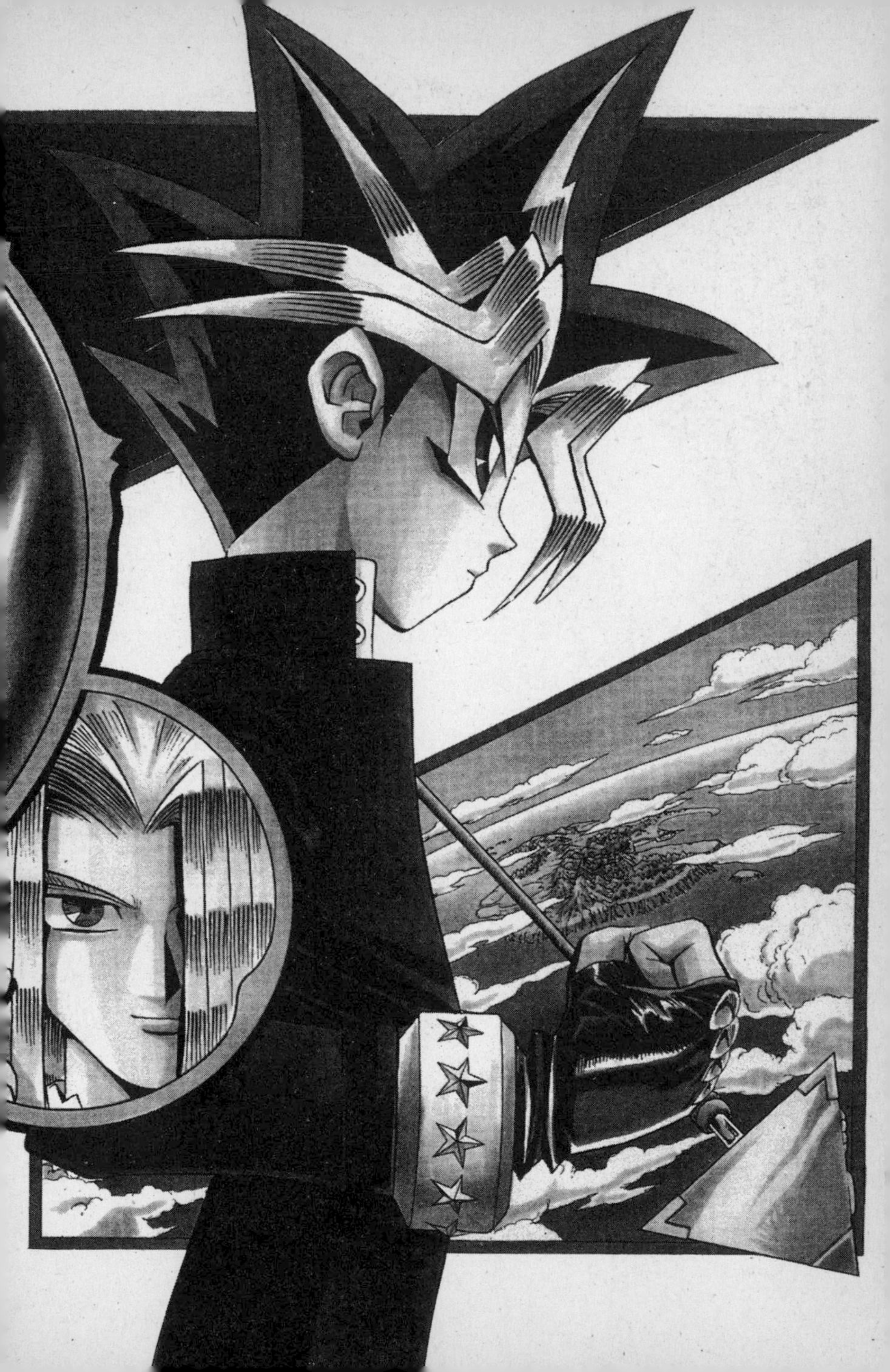

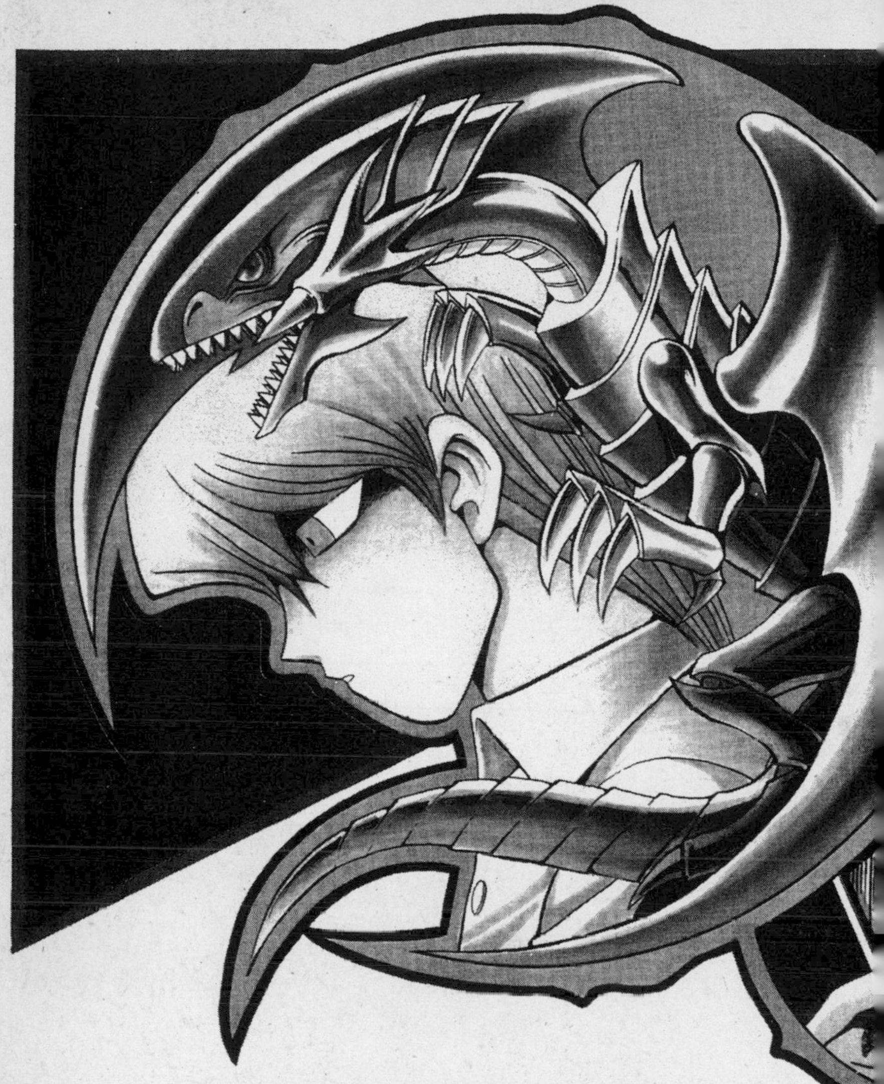

Duel 16: The Cards Bare Their Teeth

READ THIS WAY

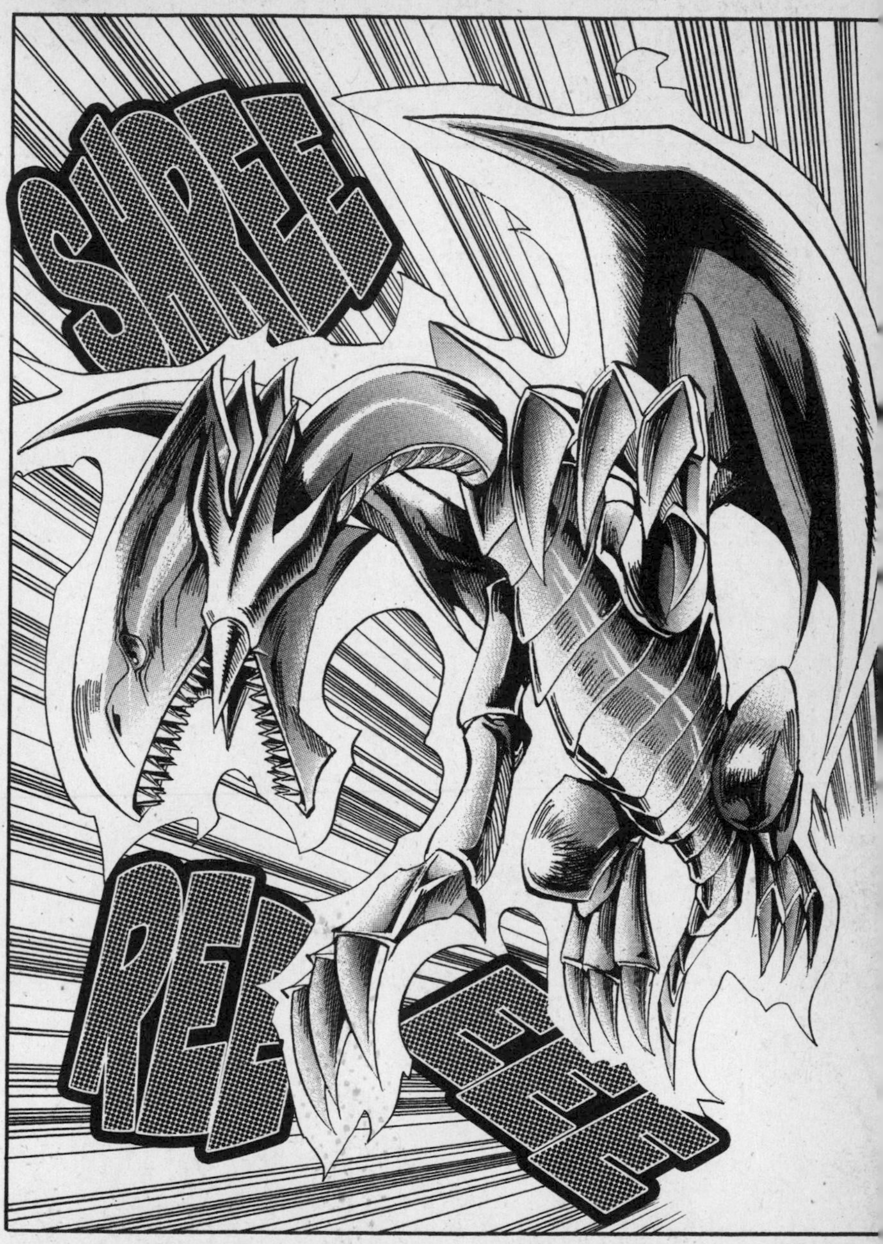
SHREE!
REE-EEE

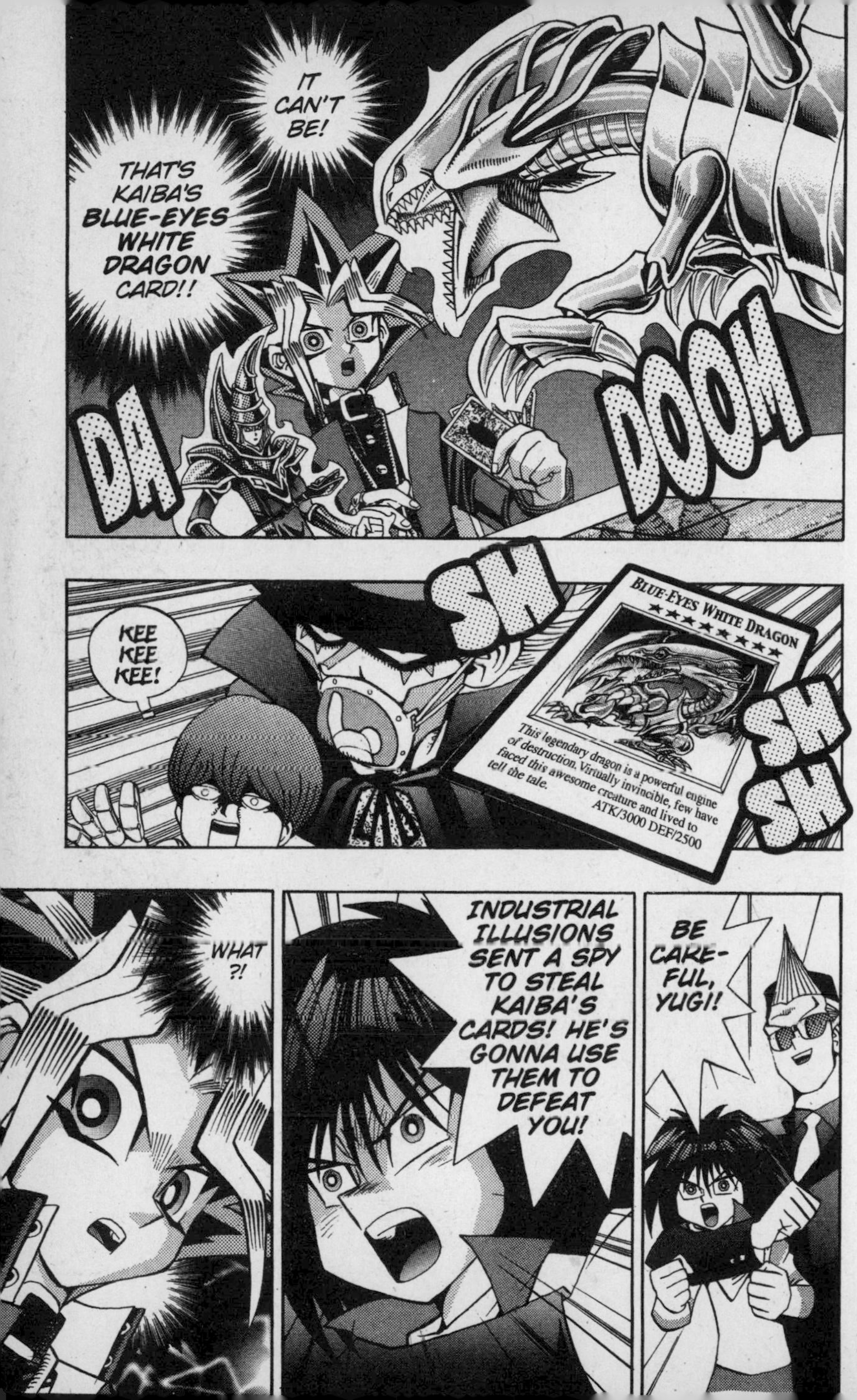
IT CAN'T BE!
THAT'S KAIBA'S BLUE-EYES WHITE DRAGON CARD!!
DA
DOOM
SH
BLUE-EYES WHITE DRAGON
This legendary dragon is a powerful engine of destruction. Virtually invincible, few have faced this awesome creature and lived to tell the tale.
ATK/3000 DEF/2500
SH
SH
KEE KEE KEE!
BE CARE-FUL, YUGI!
INDUSTRIAL ILLUSIONS SENT A SPY TO STEAL KAIBA'S CARDS! HE'S GONNA USE THEM TO DEFEAT YOU!
WHAT?!

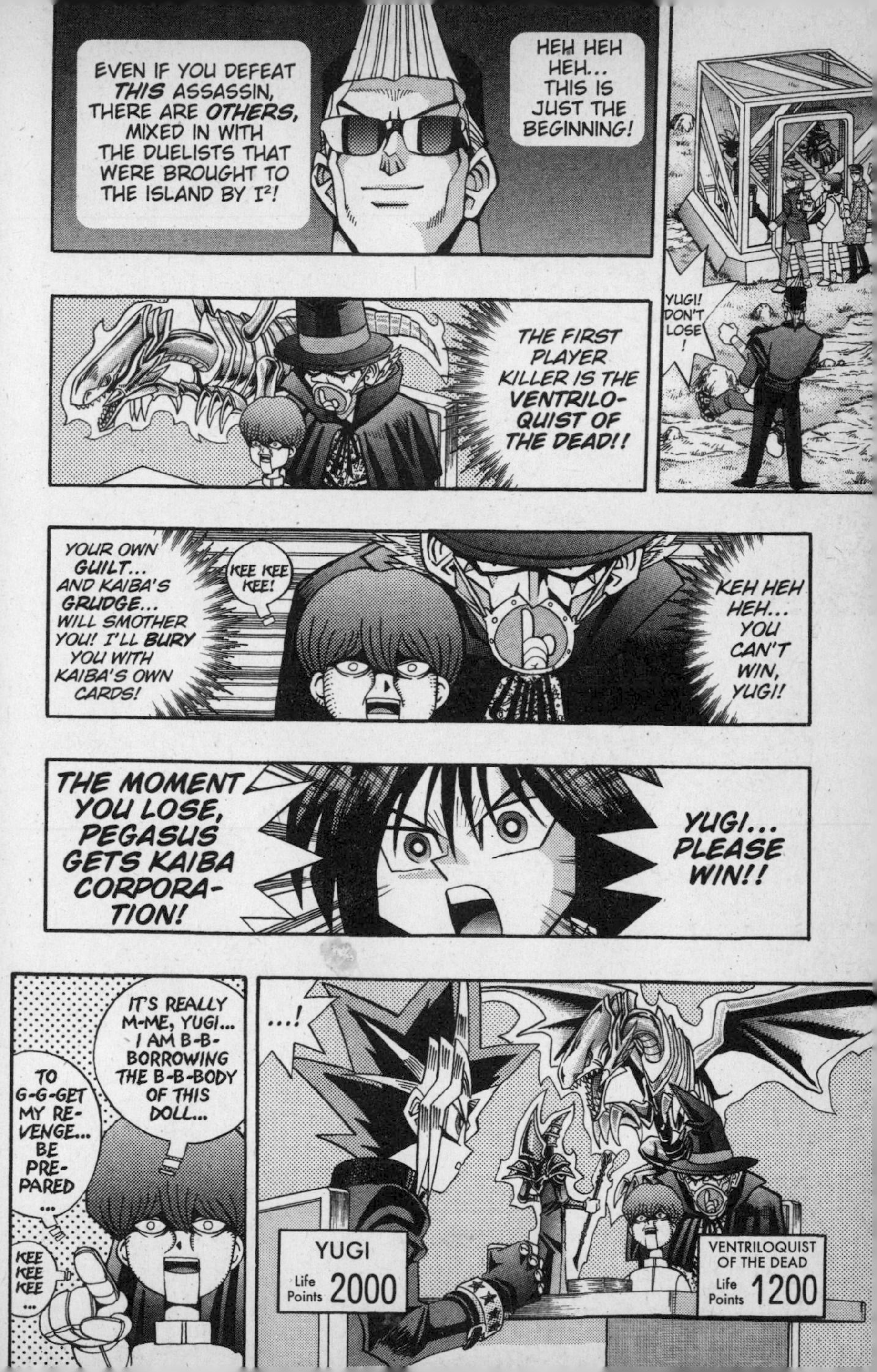
YUGI! DON'T LOSE!
HEH HEH HEH... THIS IS JUST THE BEGINNING!
EVEN IF YOU DEFEAT *THIS* ASSASSIN, THERE ARE *OTHERS*, MIXED IN WITH THE DUELISTS THAT WERE BROUGHT TO THE ISLAND BY I²!
THE FIRST PLAYER KILLER IS THE VENTRILOQUIST OF THE DEAD!!
KEH HEH HEH... YOU CAN'T WIN, YUGI!
KEE KEE KEE!
YOUR OWN GUILT... AND KAIBA'S GRUDGE... WILL SMOTHER YOU! I'LL BURY YOU WITH KAIBA'S OWN CARDS!
YUGI... PLEASE WIN!!
THE MOMENT YOU LOSE, PEGASUS GETS KAIBA CORPORATION!
...!
VENTRILOQUIST OF THE DEAD Life Points 1200
YUGI Life Points 2000
IT'S REALLY M-ME, YUGI... I AM B-B-BORROWING THE B-B-BODY OF THIS DOLL...
TO G-G-GET MY REVENGE... BE PREPARED...
KEE KEE KEE...

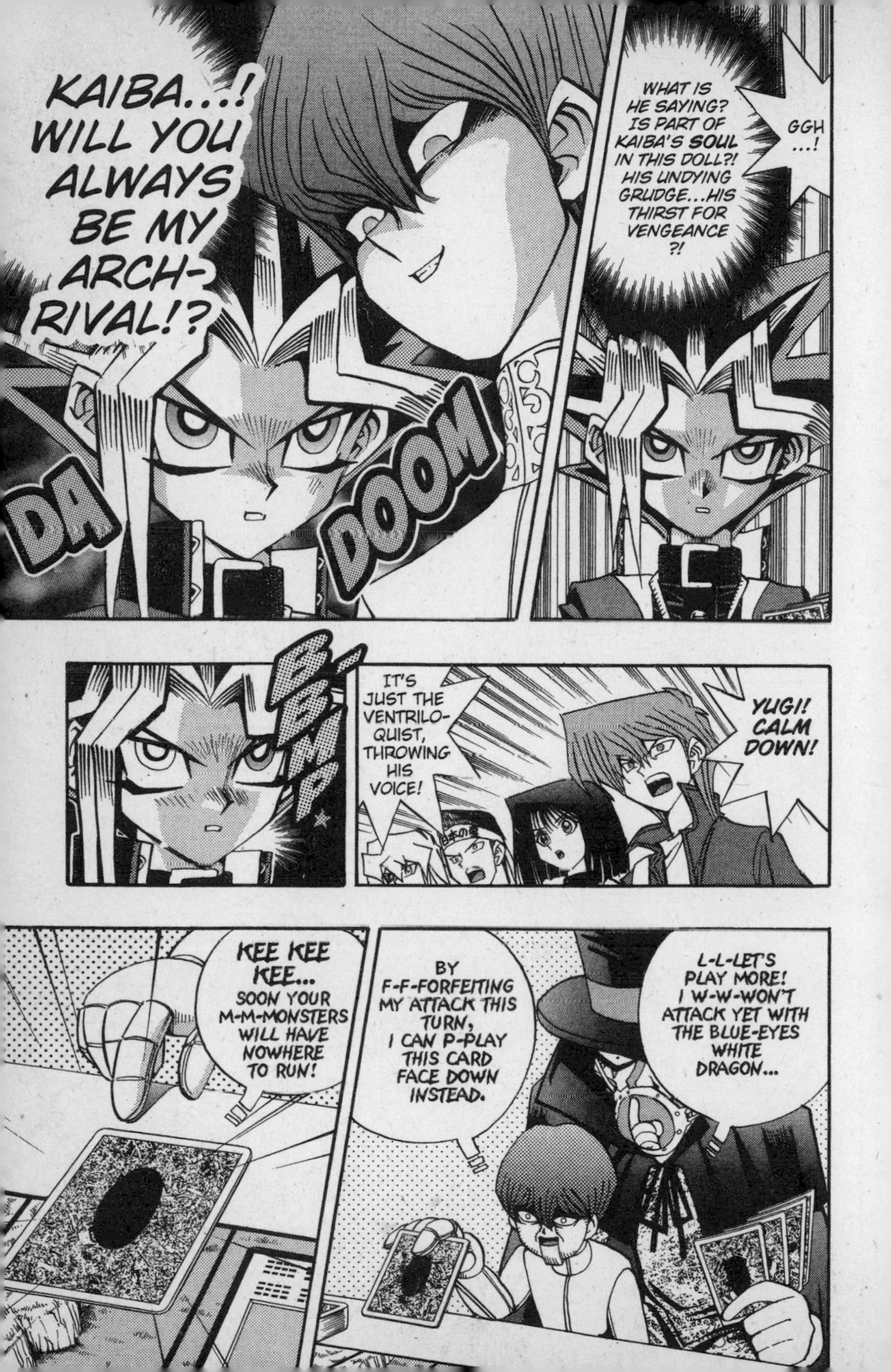
WHAT IS HE SAYING? IS PART OF KAIBA'S **SOUL** IN THIS DOLL?! HIS UNDYING GRUDGE...HIS THIRST FOR VENGEANCE ?!
GGH ...!
KAIBA...! WILL YOU ALWAYS BE MY ARCH-RIVAL!?
DA
DOOM
YUGI! CALM DOWN!
IT'S JUST THE VENTRILO-QUIST, THROWING HIS VOICE!
L-L-LET'S PLAY MORE! I W-W-WON'T ATTACK YET WITH THE BLUE-EYES WHITE DRAGON...
BY F-F-FORFEITING MY ATTACK THIS TURN, I CAN P-PLAY THIS CARD FACE DOWN INSTEAD.
KEE KEE KEE... SOON YOUR M-M-MONSTERS WILL HAVE NOWHERE TO RUN!

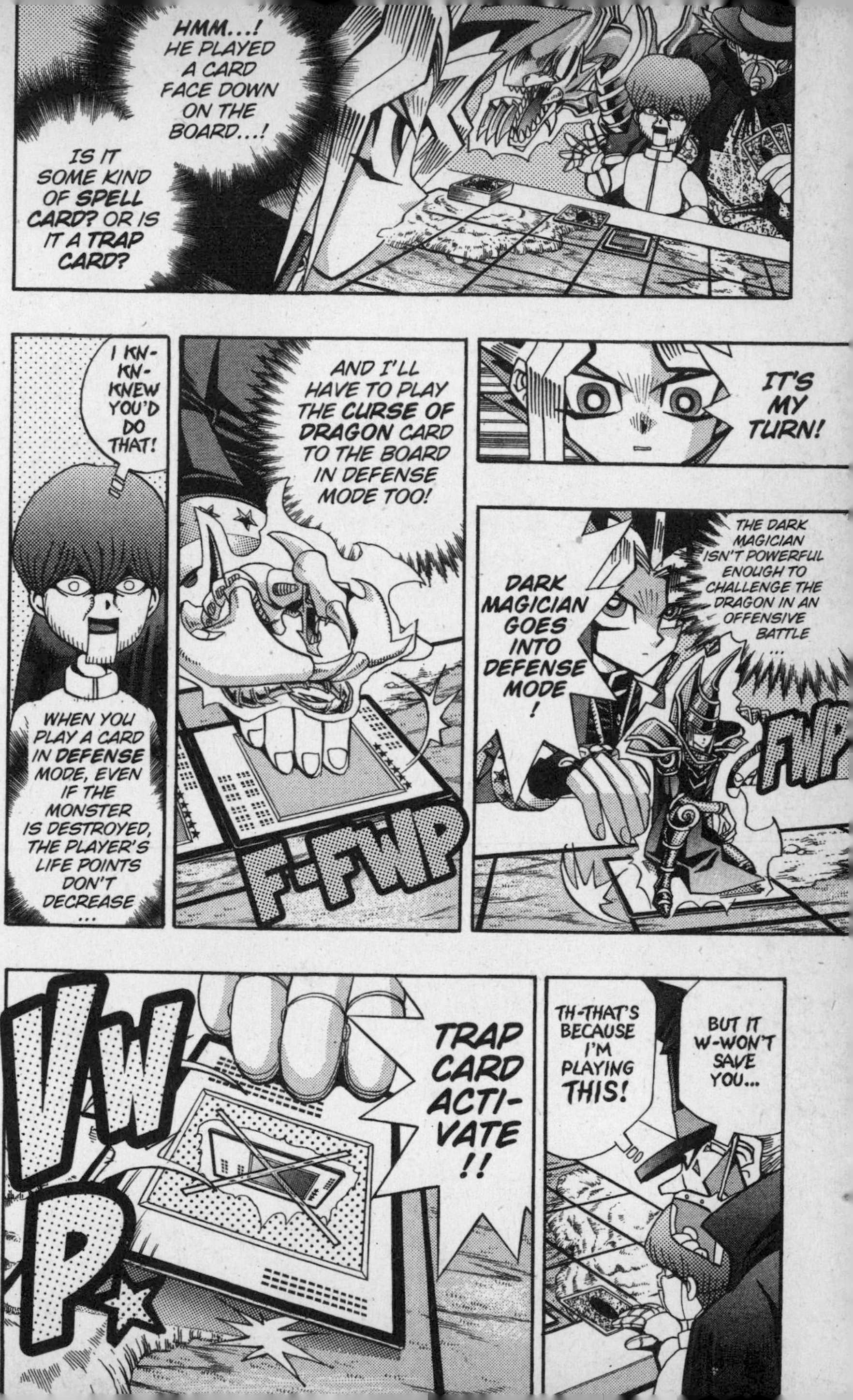
HMM...! HE PLAYED A CARD FACE DOWN ON THE BOARD...!
IS IT SOME KIND OF SPELL CARD? OR IS IT A TRAP CARD?
IT'S MY TURN!
THE DARK MAGICIAN ISN'T POWERFUL ENOUGH TO CHALLENGE THE DRAGON IN AN OFFENSIVE BATTLE...
DARK MAGICIAN GOES INTO DEFENSE MODE!
FWP
AND I'LL HAVE TO PLAY THE CURSE OF DRAGON CARD TO THE BOARD IN DEFENSE MODE TOO!
F-FWP
I KN-KN-KNEW YOU'D DO THAT!
WHEN YOU PLAY A CARD IN DEFENSE MODE, EVEN IF THE MONSTER IS DESTROYED, THE PLAYER'S LIFE POINTS DON'T DECREASE...
BUT IT W-WON'T SAVE YOU...
TH-THAT'S BECAUSE I'M PLAYING THIS!
TRAP CARD ACTIVATE!!
VWP

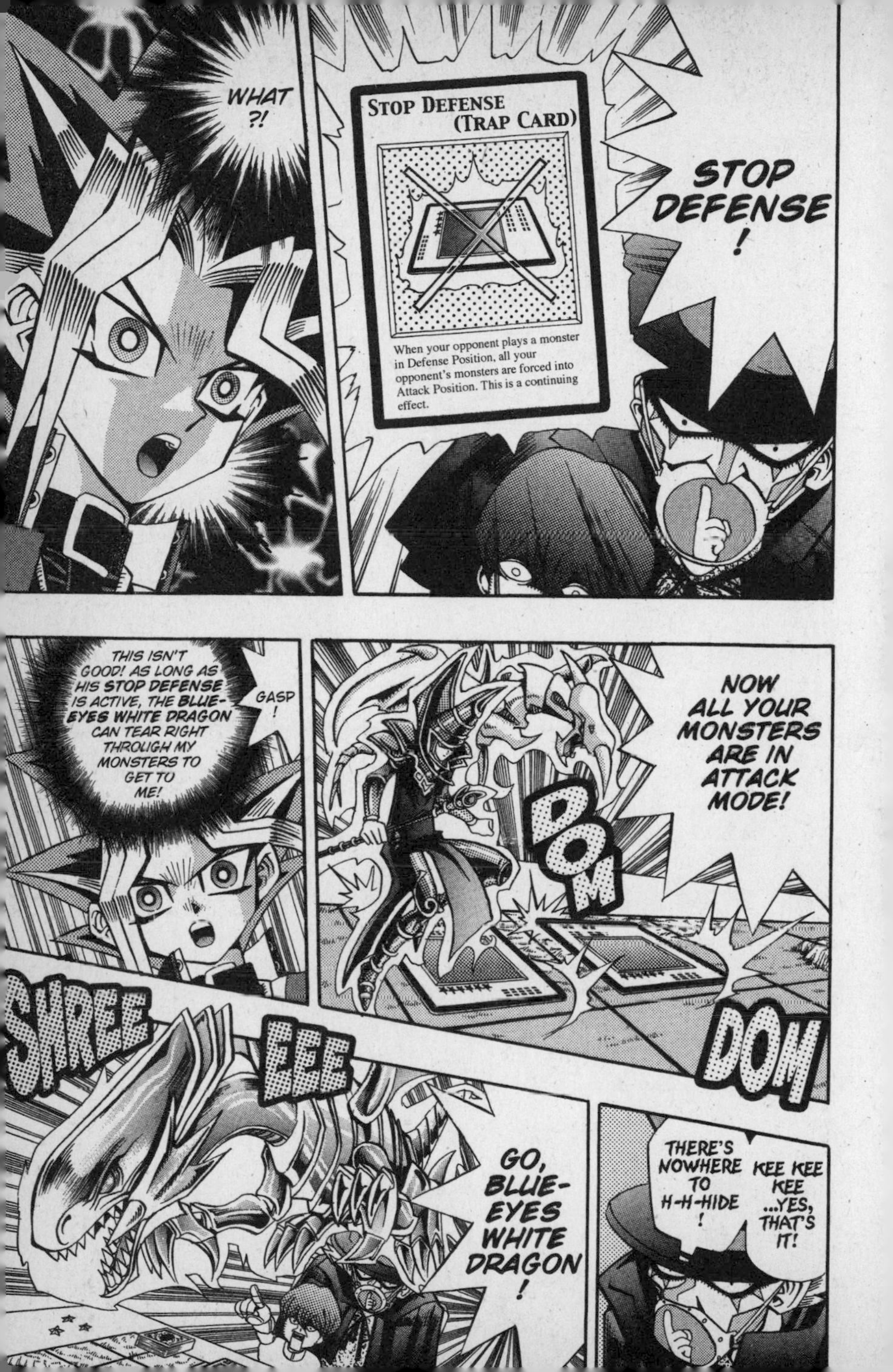
STOP DEFENSE!
STOP DEFENSE (TRAP CARD)
When your opponent plays a monster in Defense Position, all your opponent's monsters are forced into Attack Position. This is a continuing effect.
WHAT ?!
NOW ALL YOUR MONSTERS ARE IN ATTACK MODE!
DOM
DOM
GASP!
THIS ISN'T GOOD! AS LONG AS HIS STOP DEFENSE IS ACTIVE, THE BLUE-EYES WHITE DRAGON CAN TEAR RIGHT THROUGH MY MONSTERS TO GET TO ME!
THERE'S NOWHERE TO H-H-HIDE!
KEE KEE KEE ...YES, THAT'S IT!
SHREE
EEE
GO, BLUE-EYES WHITE DRAGON!

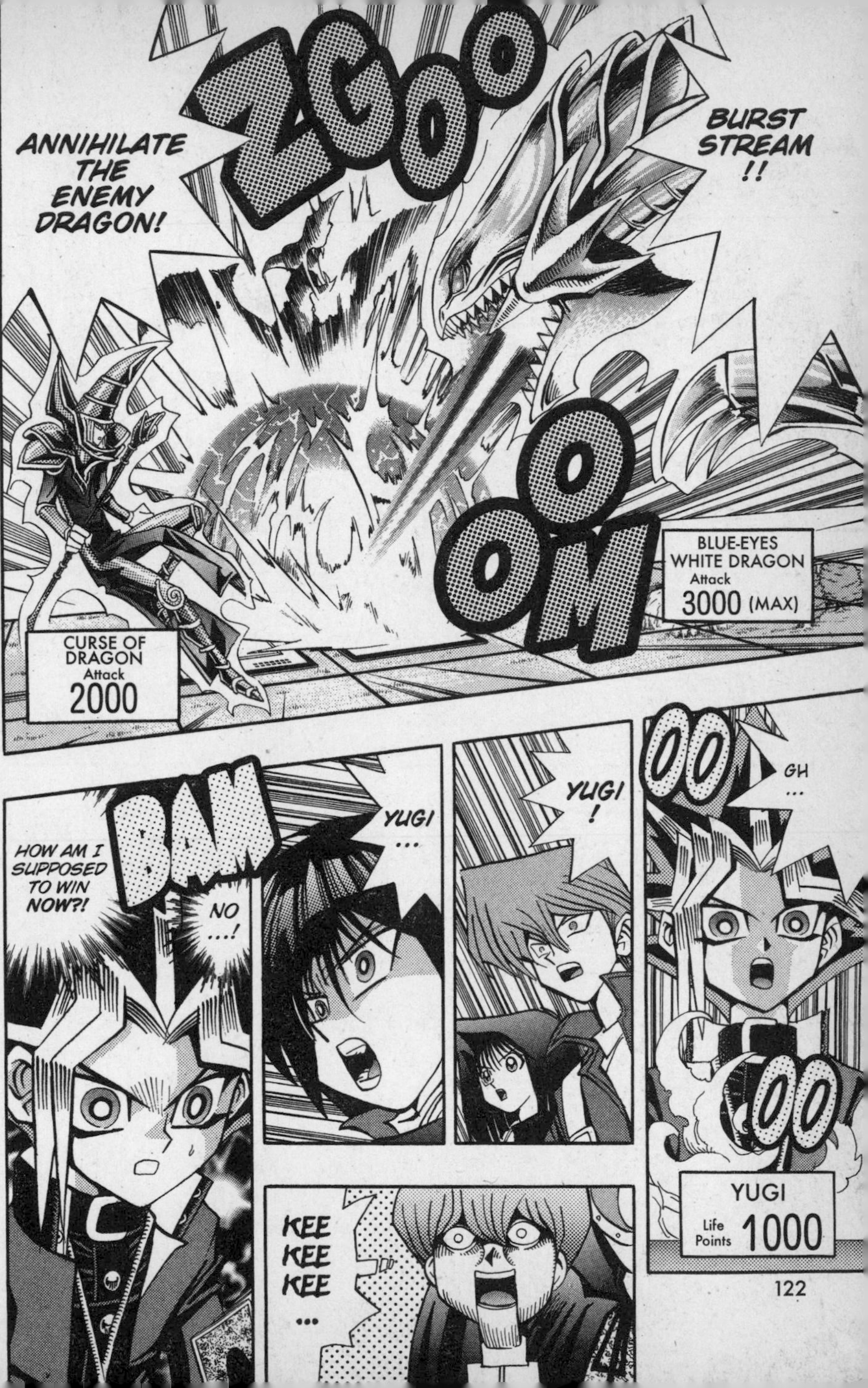
BURST STREAM !!
ZGOOO
ANNIHILATE THE ENEMY DRAGON!
OOOM
BLUE-EYES WHITE DRAGON Attack 3000 (MAX)
CURSE OF DRAGON Attack 2000
OO
GH ...
OO
YUGI Life Points 1000
YUGI !
YUGI ...
KEE KEE KEE ...
BAM
HOW AM I SUPPOSED TO WIN NOW?!
NO ...!

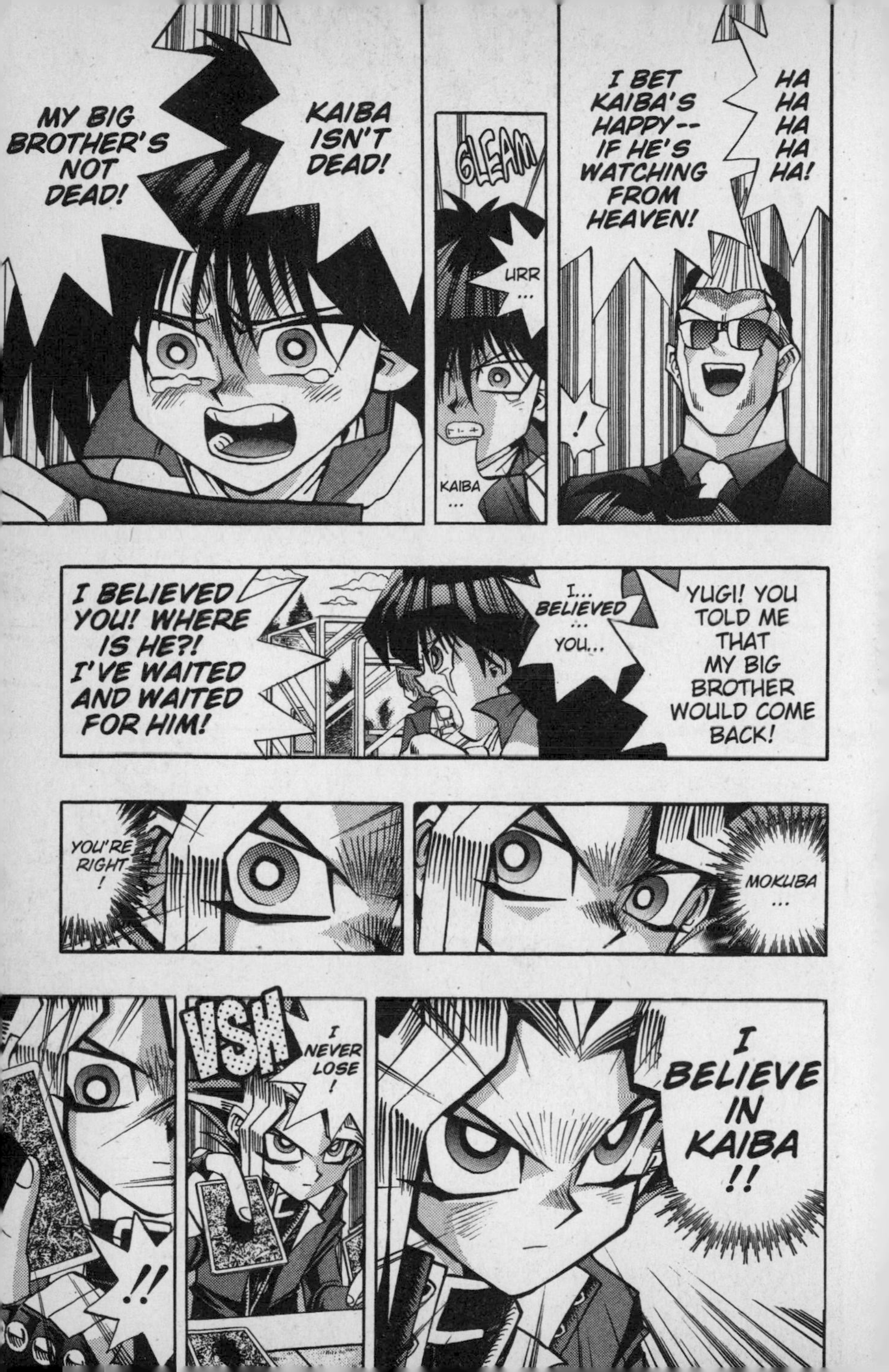
I BET KAIBA'S HAPPY-- IF HE'S WATCHING FROM HEAVEN!
HA HA HA HA HA!
!
GLEAM
URR ...
KAIBA ...
KAIBA ISN'T DEAD!
MY BIG BROTHER'S NOT DEAD!
YUGI! YOU TOLD ME THAT MY BIG BROTHER WOULD COME BACK!
I... BELIEVED ... YOU...
I BELIEVED YOU! WHERE IS HE?! I'VE WAITED AND WAITED FOR HIM!
MOKUBA ...
YOU'RE RIGHT !
I BELIEVE IN KAIBA !!
VSH
I NEVER LOSE !
!!

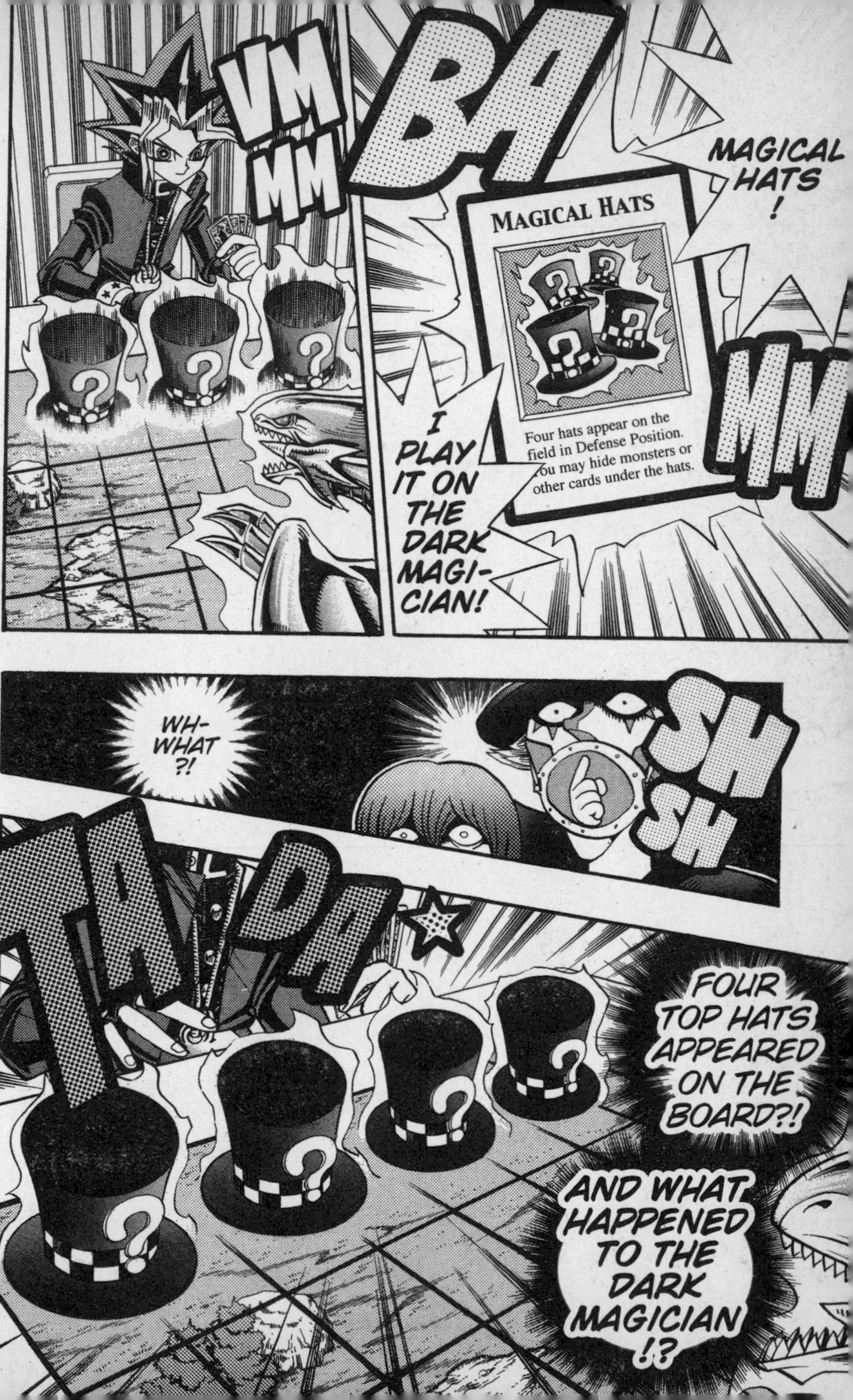
BA
MAGICAL HATS!
MAGICAL HATS
Four hats appear on the field in Defense Position.
ou may hide monsters or other cards under the hats.
MM
I PLAY IT ON THE DARK MAGICIAN!
VM MM
SH SH
WH-WHAT?!
TAPA
FOUR TOP HATS APPEARED ON THE BOARD?!
AND WHAT HAPPENED TO THE DARK MAGICIAN!?

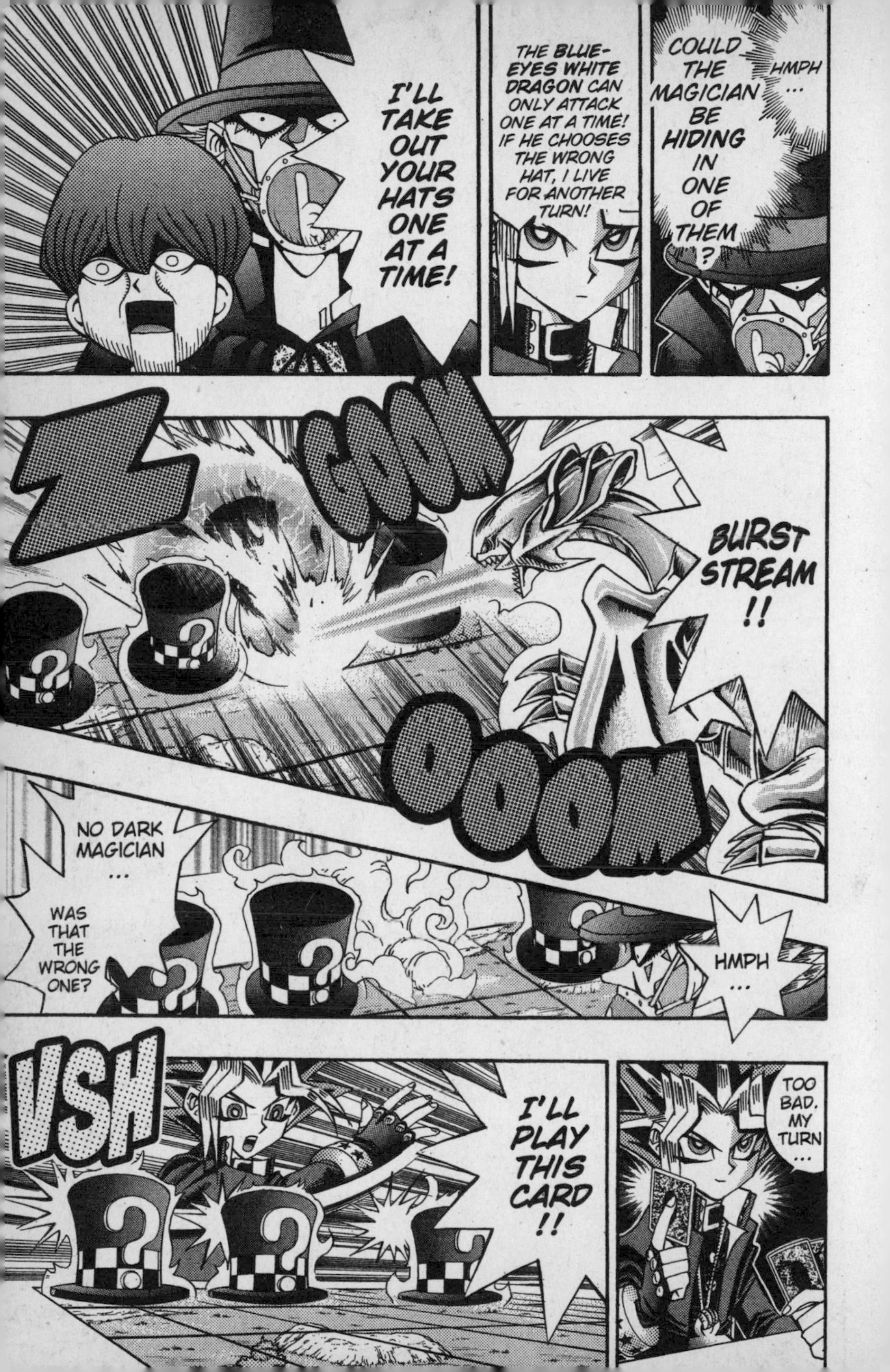
COULD THE MAGICIAN BE HIDING IN ONE OF THEM?
HMPH...
THE BLUE-EYES WHITE DRAGON CAN ONLY ATTACK ONE AT A TIME! IF HE CHOOSES THE WRONG HAT, I LIVE FOR ANOTHER TURN!
I'LL TAKE OUT YOUR HATS ONE AT A TIME!
BURST STREAM!!
ZGOOM
OOOM
HMPH...
NO DARK MAGICIAN...
WAS THAT THE WRONG ONE?
TOO BAD. MY TURN...
I'LL PLAY THIS CARD!!
VSH

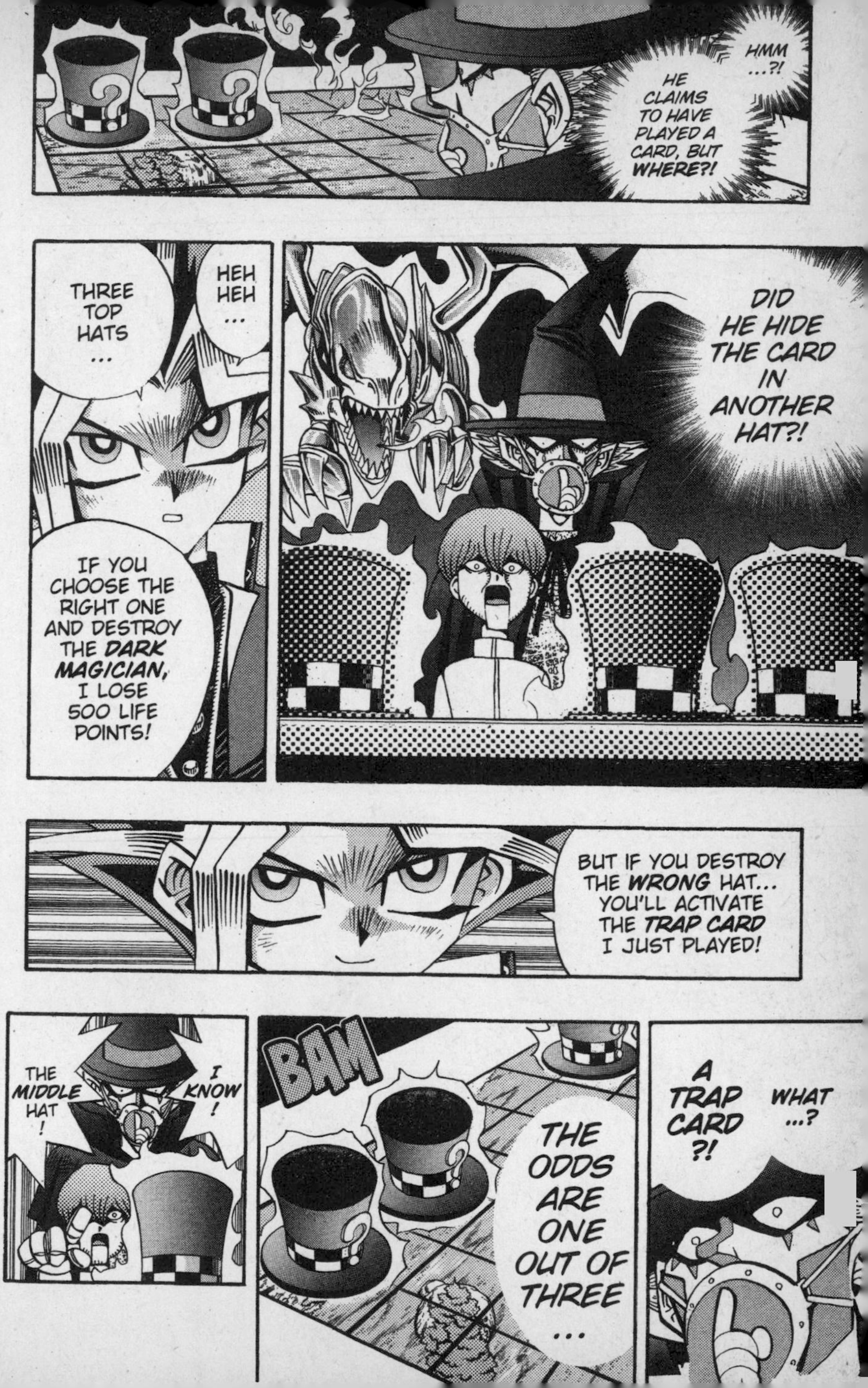
HMM ...?!
HE CLAIMS TO HAVE PLAYED A CARD, BUT WHERE?!
DID HE HIDE THE CARD IN ANOTHER HAT?!
HEH HEH ...
THREE TOP HATS ...
IF YOU CHOOSE THE RIGHT ONE AND DESTROY THE DARK MAGICIAN, I LOSE 500 LIFE POINTS!
BUT IF YOU DESTROY THE WRONG HAT... YOU'LL ACTIVATE THE TRAP CARD I JUST PLAYED!
WHAT ...?
A TRAP CARD ?!
BAM
THE ODDS ARE ONE OUT OF THREE ...
I KNOW !
THE MIDDLE HAT !

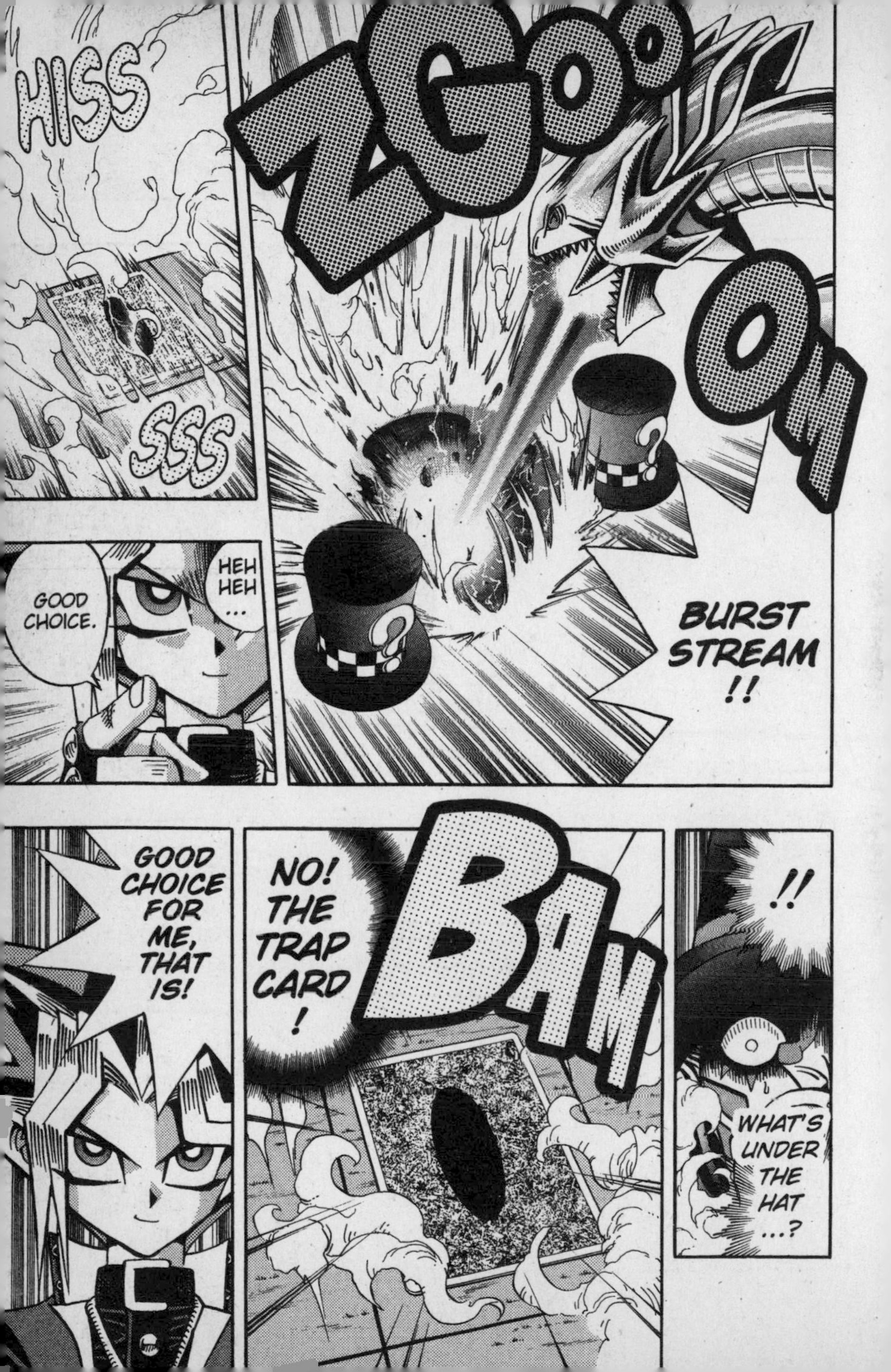
ZGOOOOM
BURST STREAM !!
HISS SSSS
HEH HEH ...
GOOD CHOICE.
!!
WHAT'S UNDER THE HAT ...?
BAM
NO! THE TRAP CARD !
GOOD CHOICE FOR ME, THAT IS!

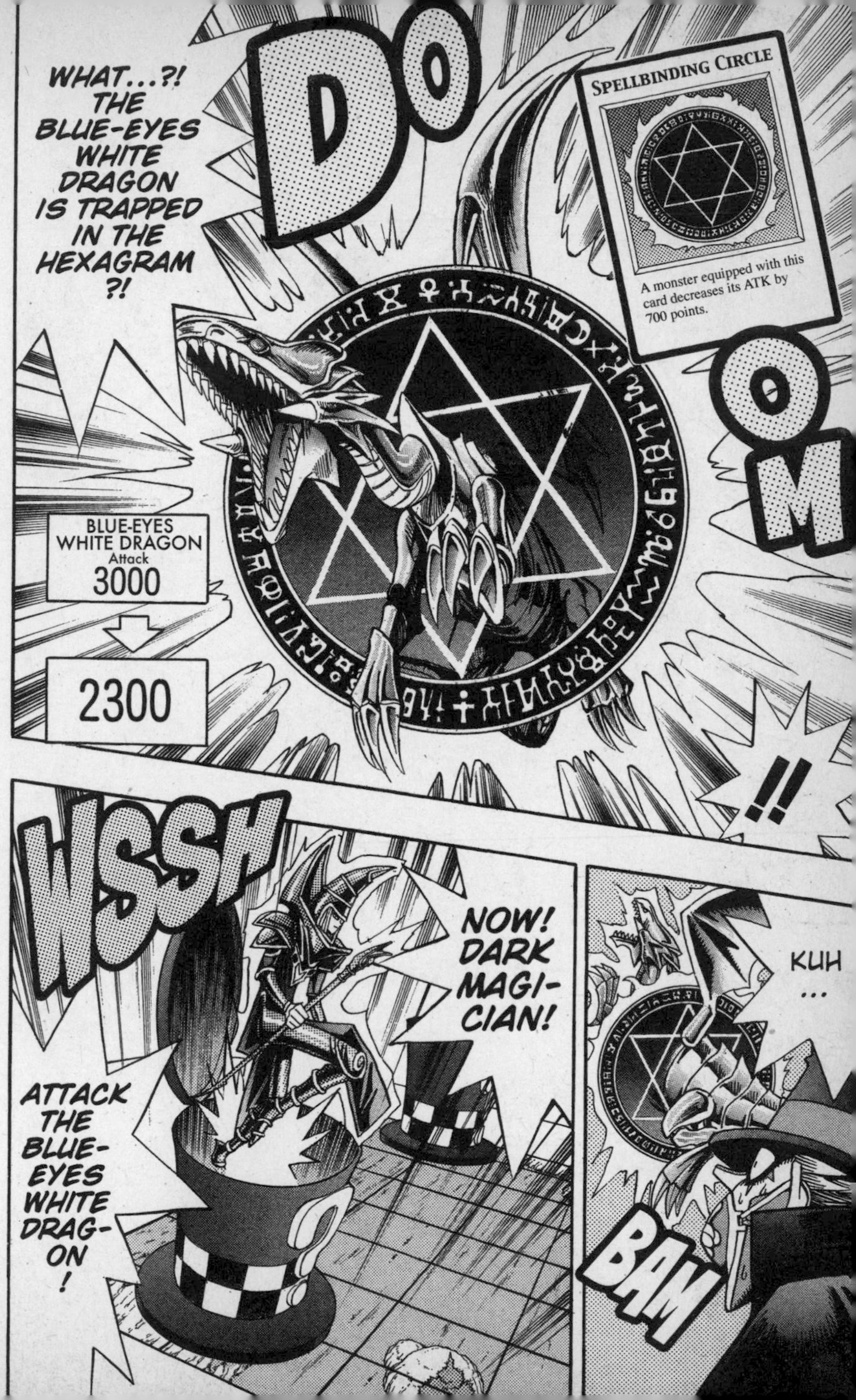
DO
OM
SPELLBINDING CIRCLE
A monster equipped with this card decreases its ATK by 700 points.
WHAT...?! THE BLUE-EYES WHITE DRAGON IS TRAPPED IN THE HEXAGRAM ?!
BLUE-EYES WHITE DRAGON Attack 3000
2300
!!
KUH ...
BAM
WSSH
NOW! DARK MAGI-CIAN!
ATTACK THE BLUE-EYES WHITE DRAG-ON !

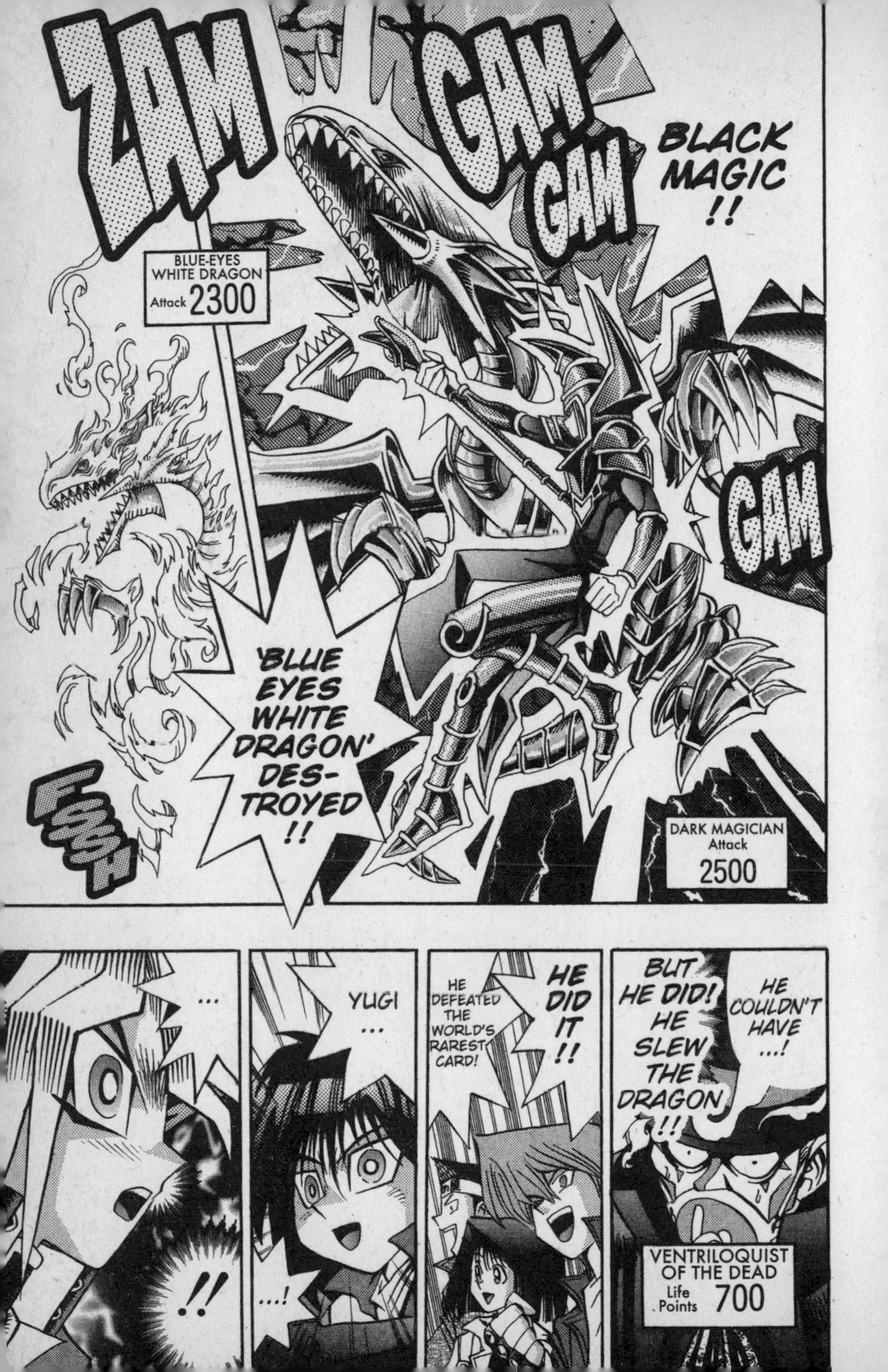
BLACK MAGIC !!
GAM
GAM
GAM
ZAM
BLUE-EYES WHITE DRAGON Attack 2300
'BLUE EYES WHITE DRAGON' DES-TROYED !!
DARK MAGICIAN Attack 2500
HE COULDN'T HAVE ...!
BUT HE DID! HE SLEW THE DRAGON !!
VENTRILOQUIST OF THE DEAD Life Points 700
HE DID IT !!
HE DEFEATED THE WORLD'S RAREST CARD!
YUGI ...
...!
...
!!

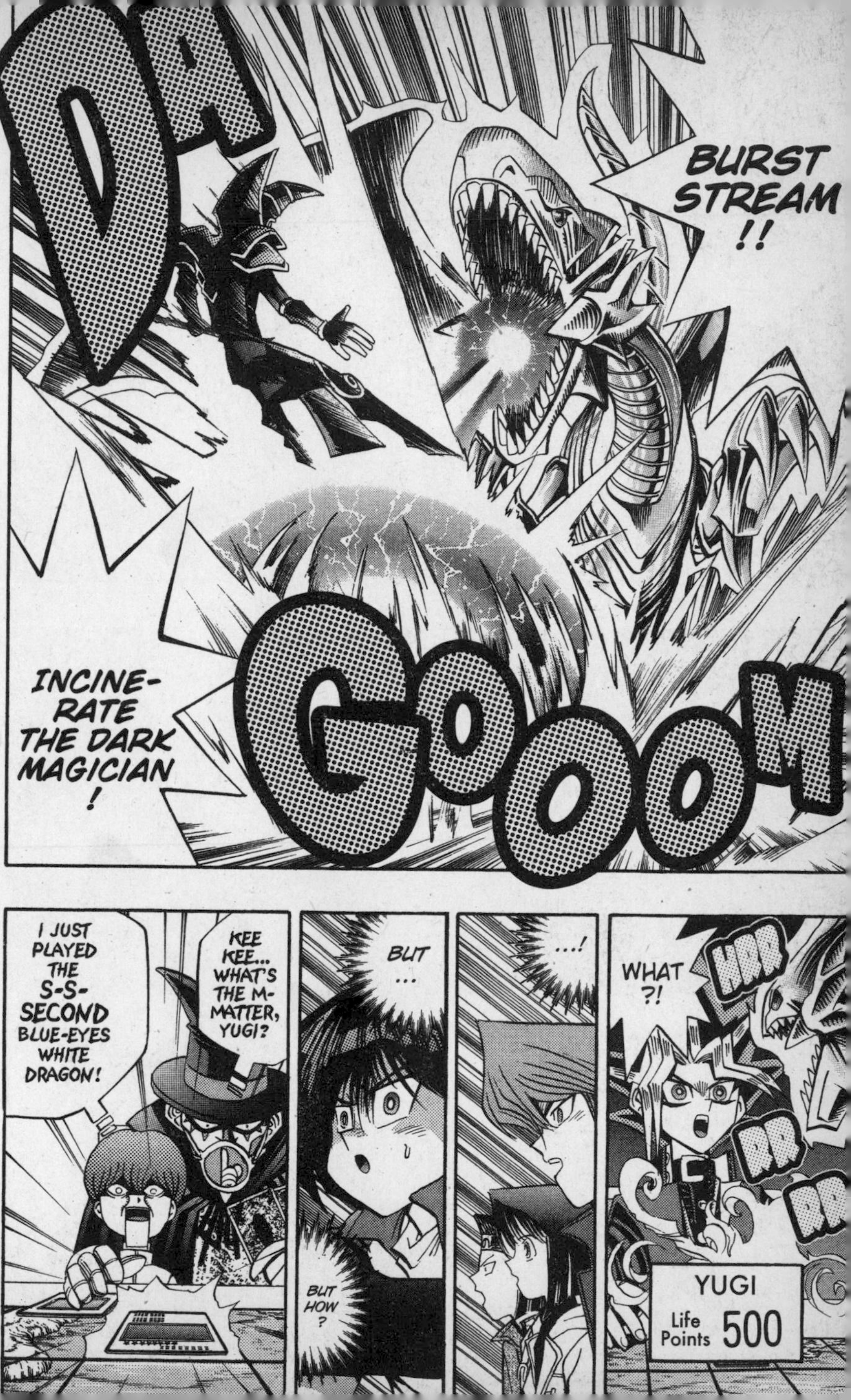
BURST STREAM !!
DA
INCINE-RATE THE DARK MAGICIAN !
GOOOM
WHAT ?!
HRR
RR
RR
YUGI
Life Points 500
...!
BUT ...
BUT HOW ?
KEE KEE... WHAT'S THE M-MATTER, YUGI?
I JUST PLAYED THE S-S-SECOND BLUE-EYES WHITE DRAGON!

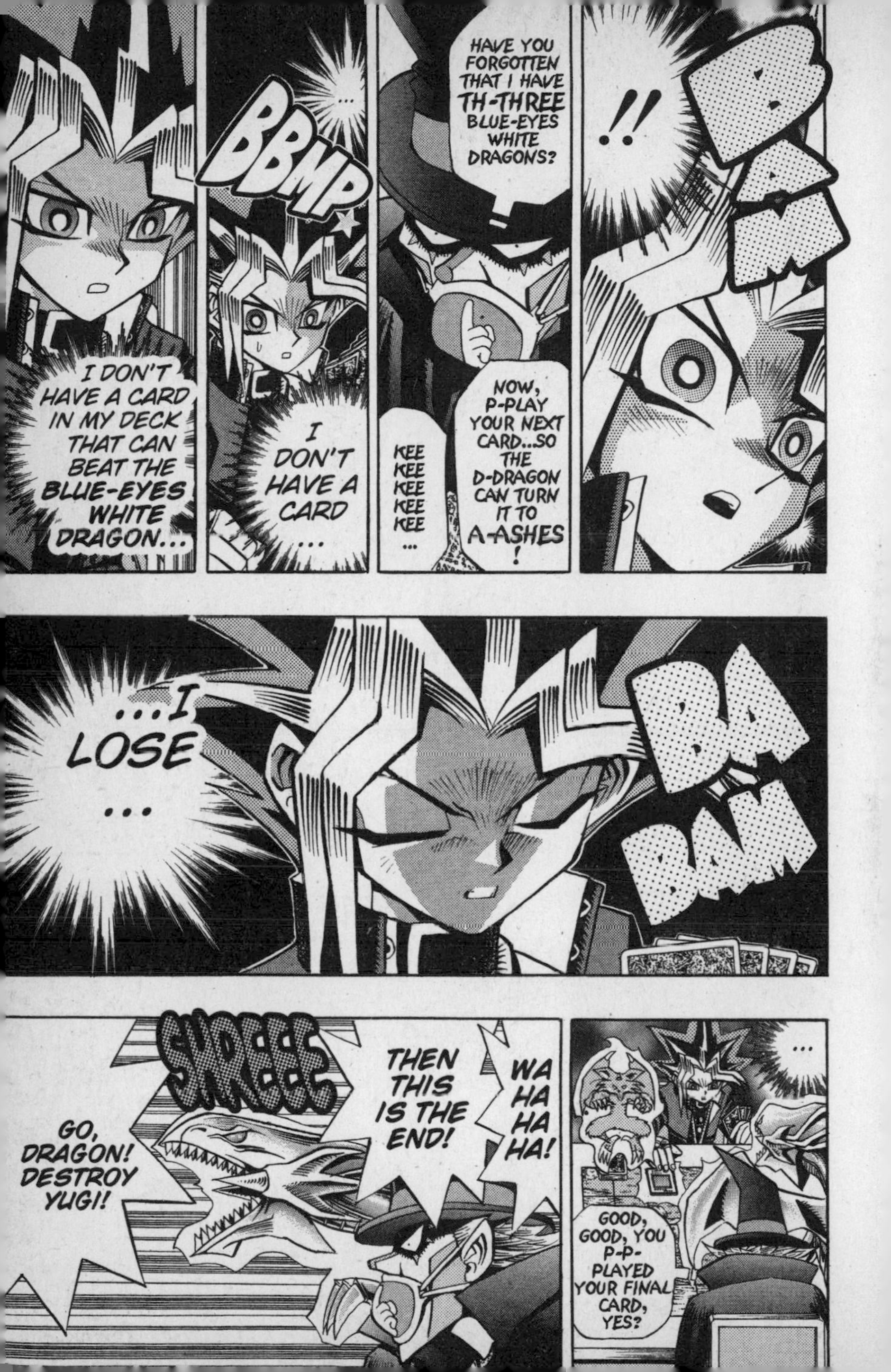
!!
HAVE YOU FORGOTTEN THAT I HAVE TH-THREE BLUE-EYES WHITE DRAGONS?
NOW, P-PLAY YOUR NEXT CARD...SO THE D-DRAGON CAN TURN IT TO A-ASHES!
KEE KEE KEE KEE KEE ...
BBMP
...
I DON'T HAVE A CARD ...
I DON'T HAVE A CARD IN MY DECK THAT CAN BEAT THE BLUE-EYES WHITE DRAGON...
BA DAM
...I LOSE ...
...
GOOD, GOOD, YOU P-P-PLAYED YOUR FINAL CARD, YES?
WA HA HA HA HA!
THEN THIS IS THE END!
SHREEE
GO, DRAGON! DESTROY YUGI!

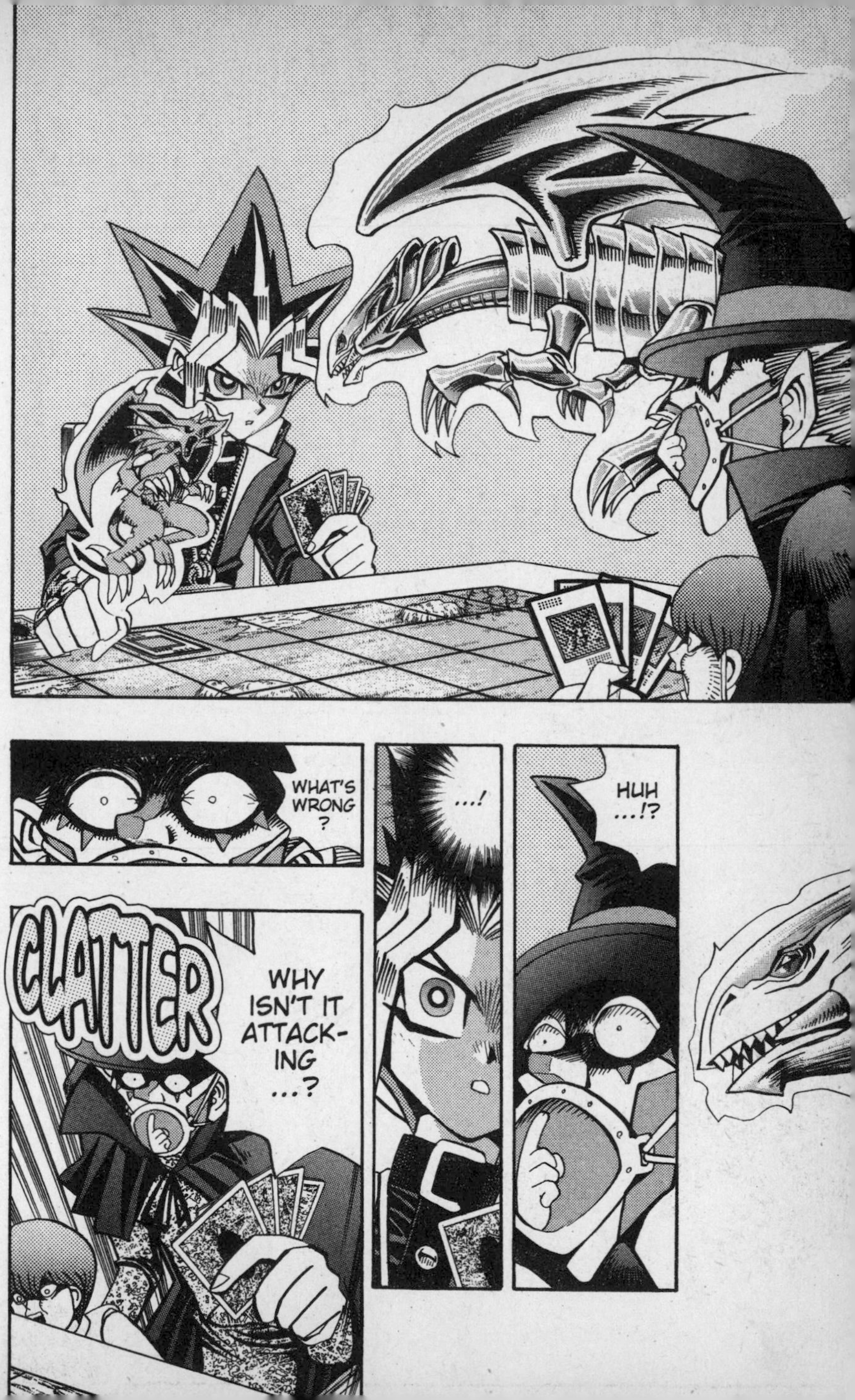
HUH ...!?
...!
WHAT'S WRONG ?
CLATTER
WHY ISN'T IT ATTACK-ING ...?

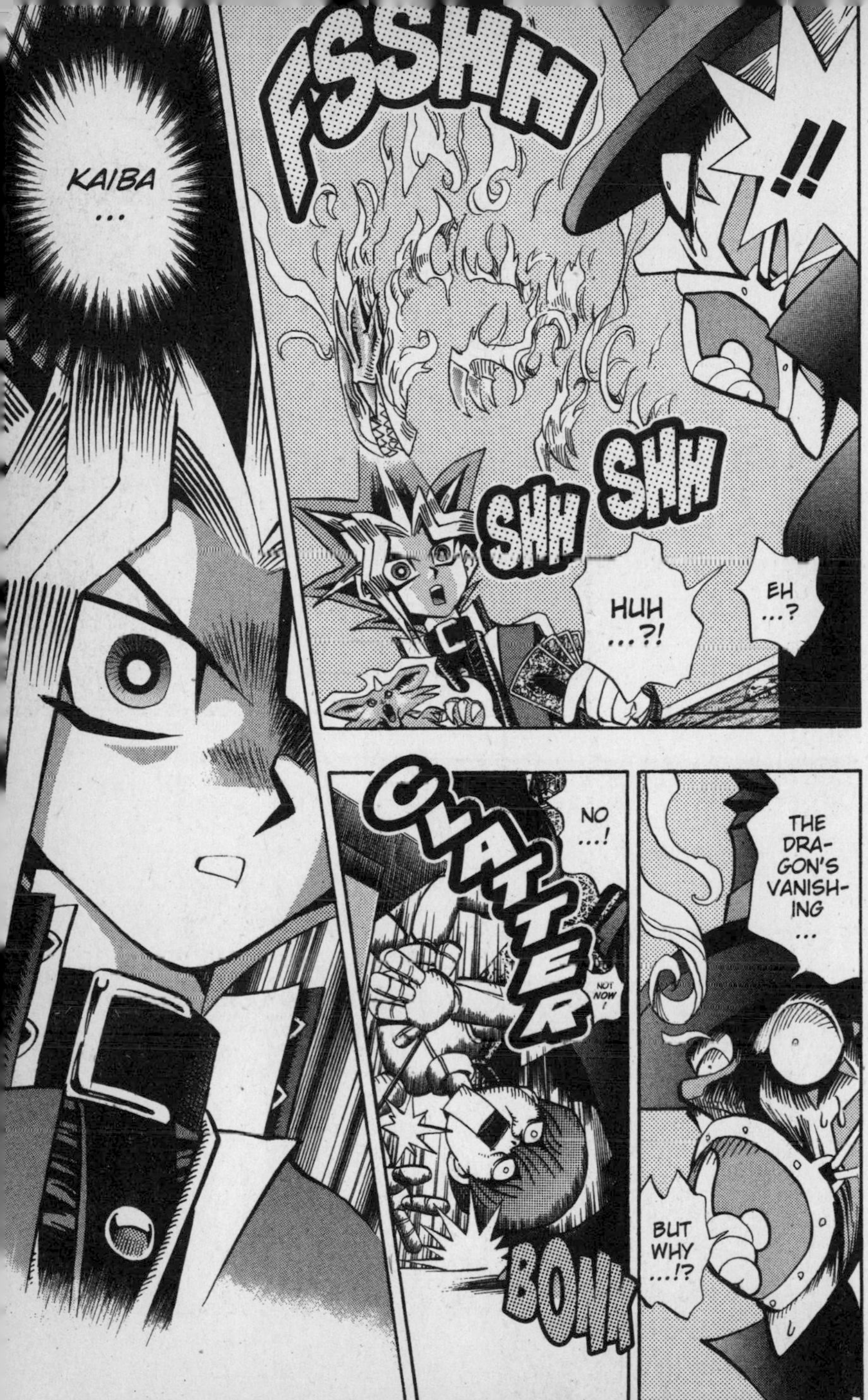
!!
FSSHH
SHH SHH
EH ...?
HUH ...?!
THE DRA-GON'S VANISH-ING ...
BUT WHY ...!?
NO ...!
CLATTER
NOT NOW!
BONK
KAIBA ...

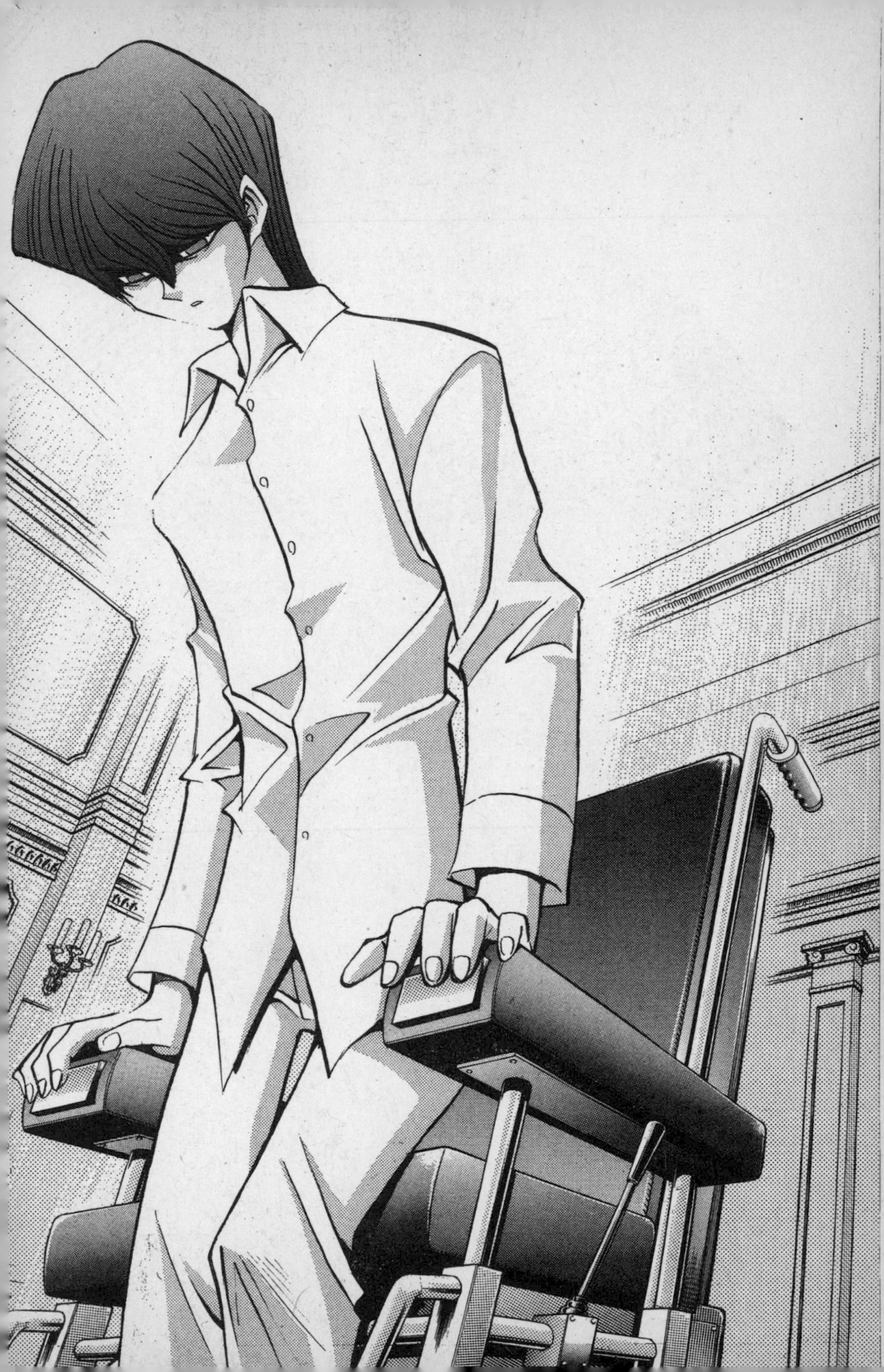

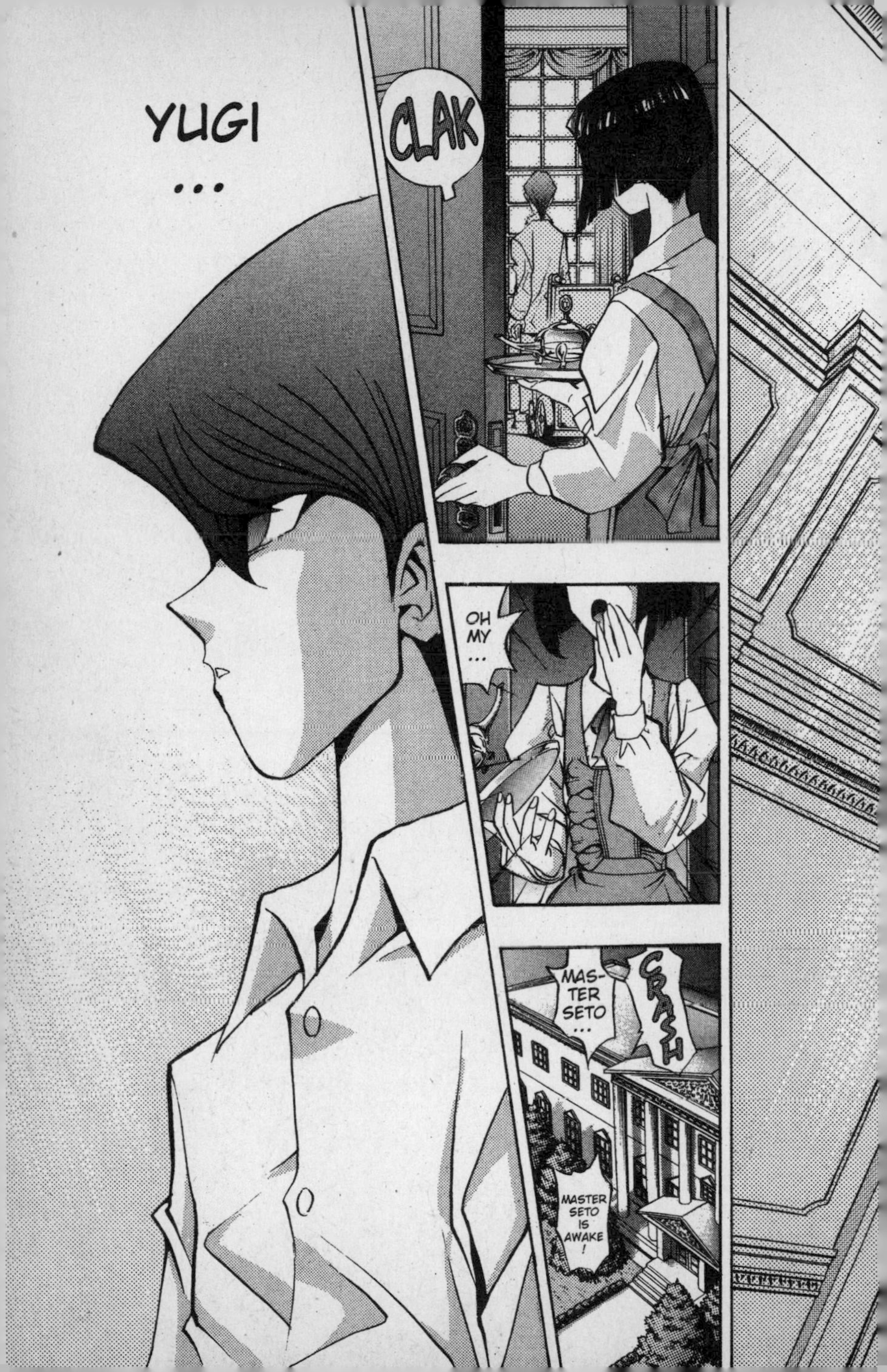
CLAK
OH MY ...
MAS-TER SETO ...
CRASH
MASTER SETO IS AWAKE !
YUGI ...

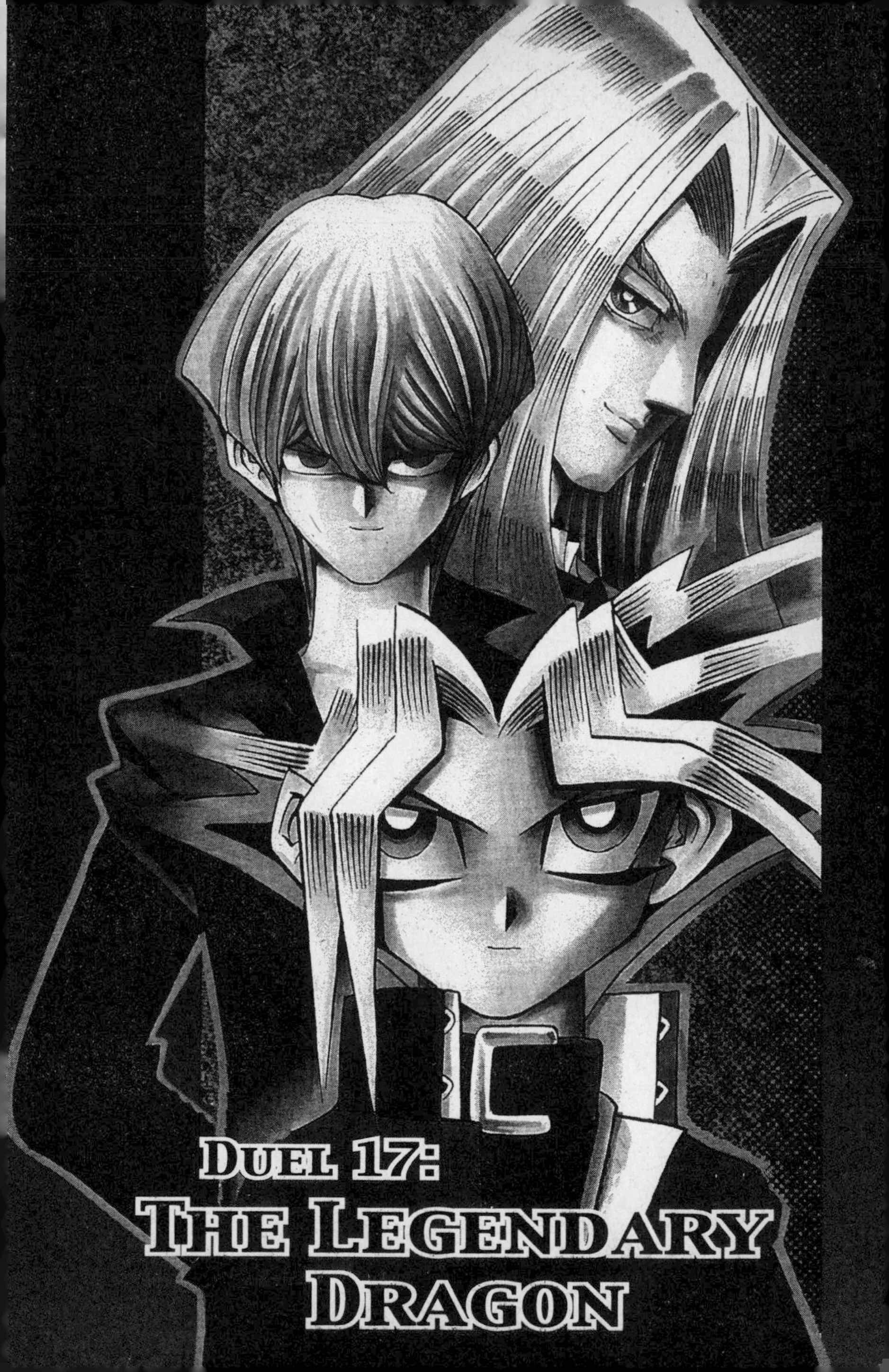

Duel 17: The Legendary Dragon

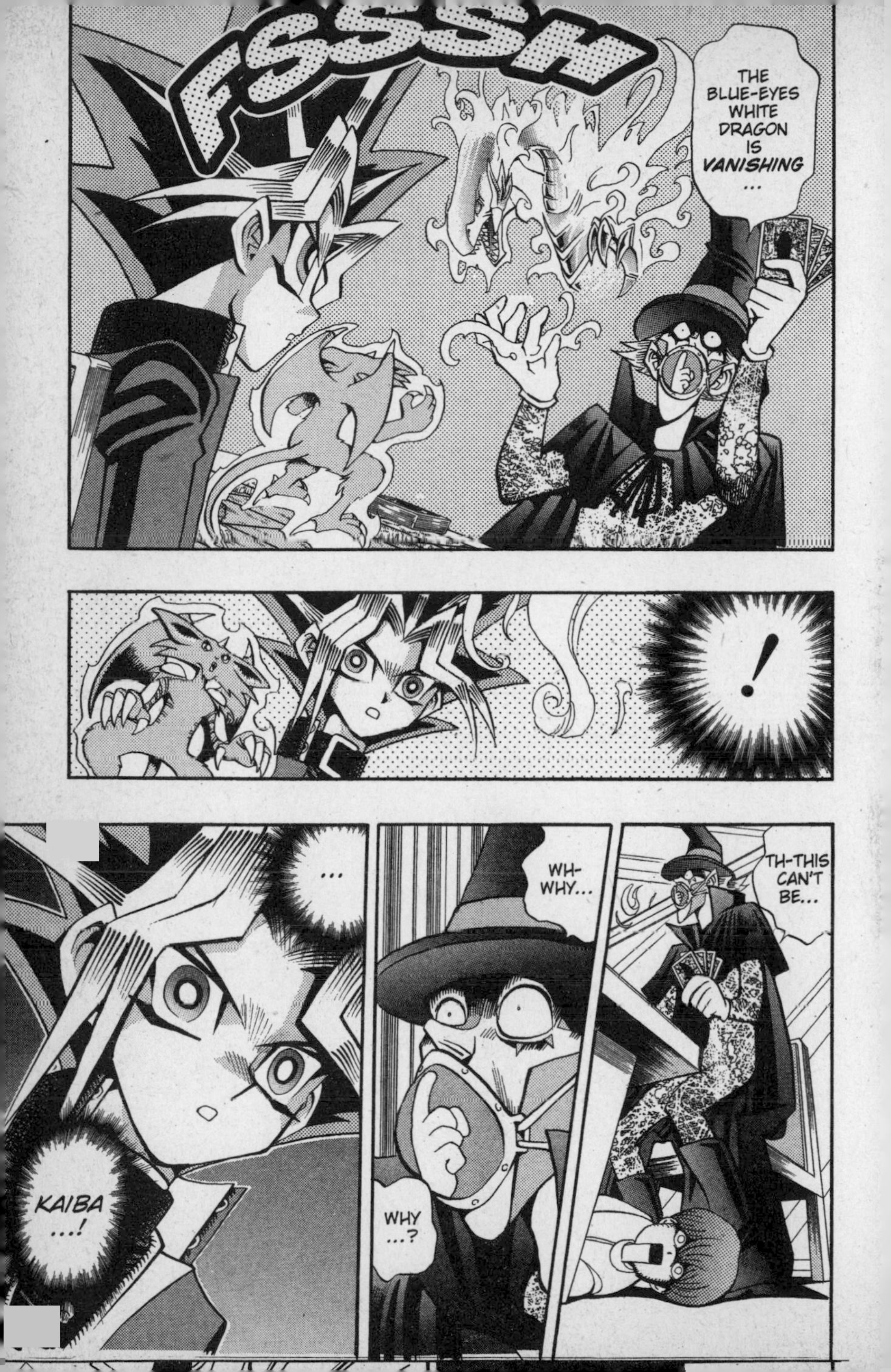
THE BLUE-EYES WHITE DRAGON IS *VANISHING* ...
FSSSH
!
TH-THIS CAN'T BE...
WH- WHY...
WHY ...?
...
KAIBA ...!

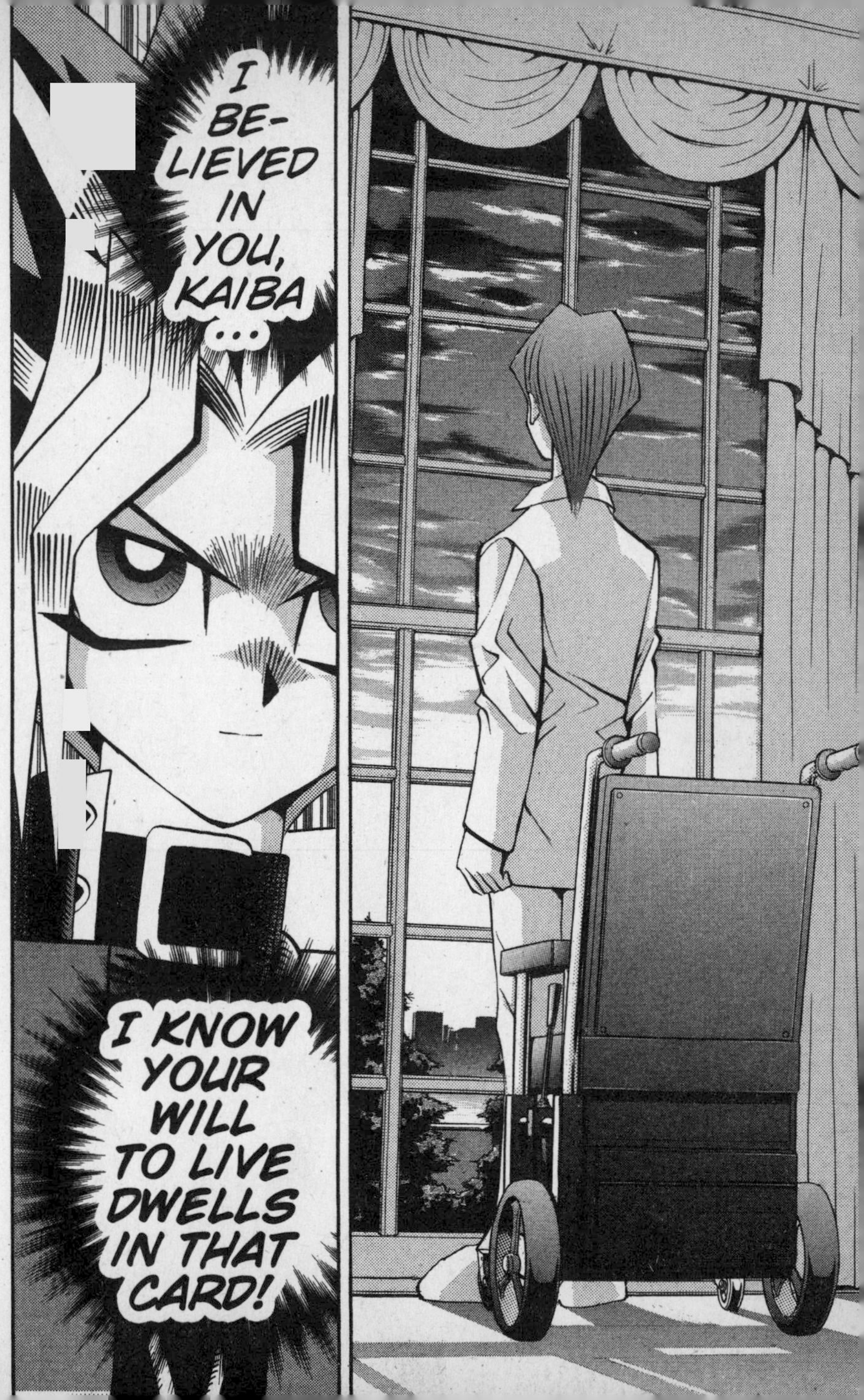
I BE-LIEVED IN YOU, KAIBA ...
I KNOW YOUR WILL TO LIVE DWELLS IN THAT CARD!

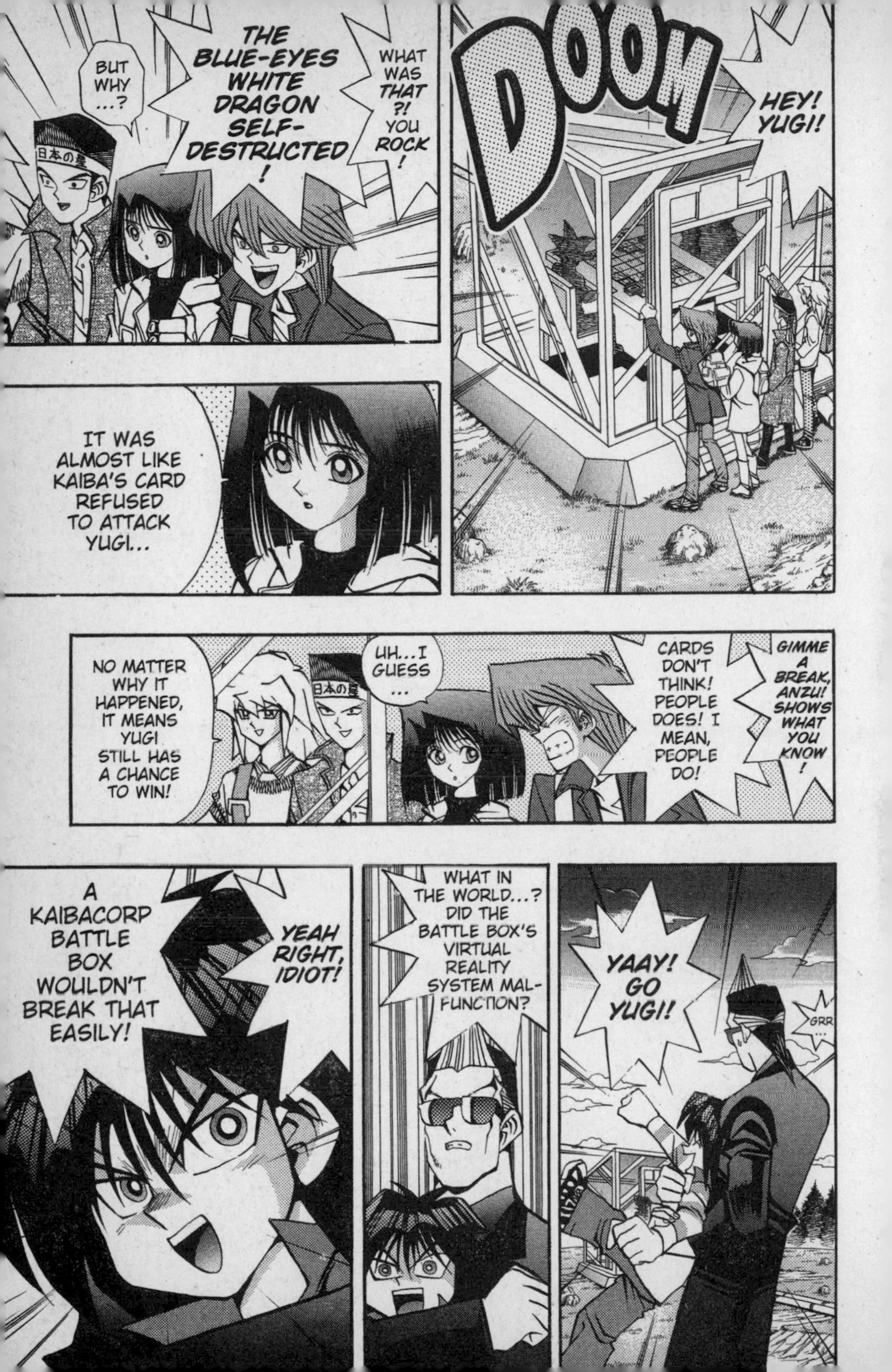
DOOM
HEY! YUGI!
WHAT WAS THAT?! YOU ROCK!
THE BLUE-EYES WHITE DRAGON SELF-DESTRUCTED!
BUT WHY...?
IT WAS ALMOST LIKE KAIBA'S CARD REFUSED TO ATTACK YUGI...
GIMME A BREAK, ANZU! SHOWS WHAT YOU KNOW!
CARDS DON'T THINK! PEOPLE DOES! I MEAN, PEOPLE DO!
UH...I GUESS...
NO MATTER WHY IT HAPPENED, IT MEANS YUGI STILL HAS A CHANCE TO WIN!
YAAY! GO YUGI!
GRR...
WHAT IN THE WORLD...? DID THE BATTLE BOX'S VIRTUAL REALITY SYSTEM MAL-FUNCTION?
A KAIBACORP BATTLE BOX WOULDN'T BREAK THAT EASILY!
YEAH RIGHT, IDIOT!

SERVES THAT CLOWN RIGHT!

HEH!

BIG BROTHER'S CARD CAN'T BE USED JUST BY ANYBODY!

...BUT THERE'S ONE MORE BLUE-EYES WHITE DRAGON IN THAT DECK!

HE MAY HAVE LASTED THIS LONG...

GRR...

KILL THE VENTRILO-QUIST!

YUGI! DO IT!

WHY YOU...

CURSE HIM...

...

ENOUGH TALK! LET'S GAME!

VENTRILOQUIST OF THE DEAD	YUGI
Life Points 700	Life Points 500

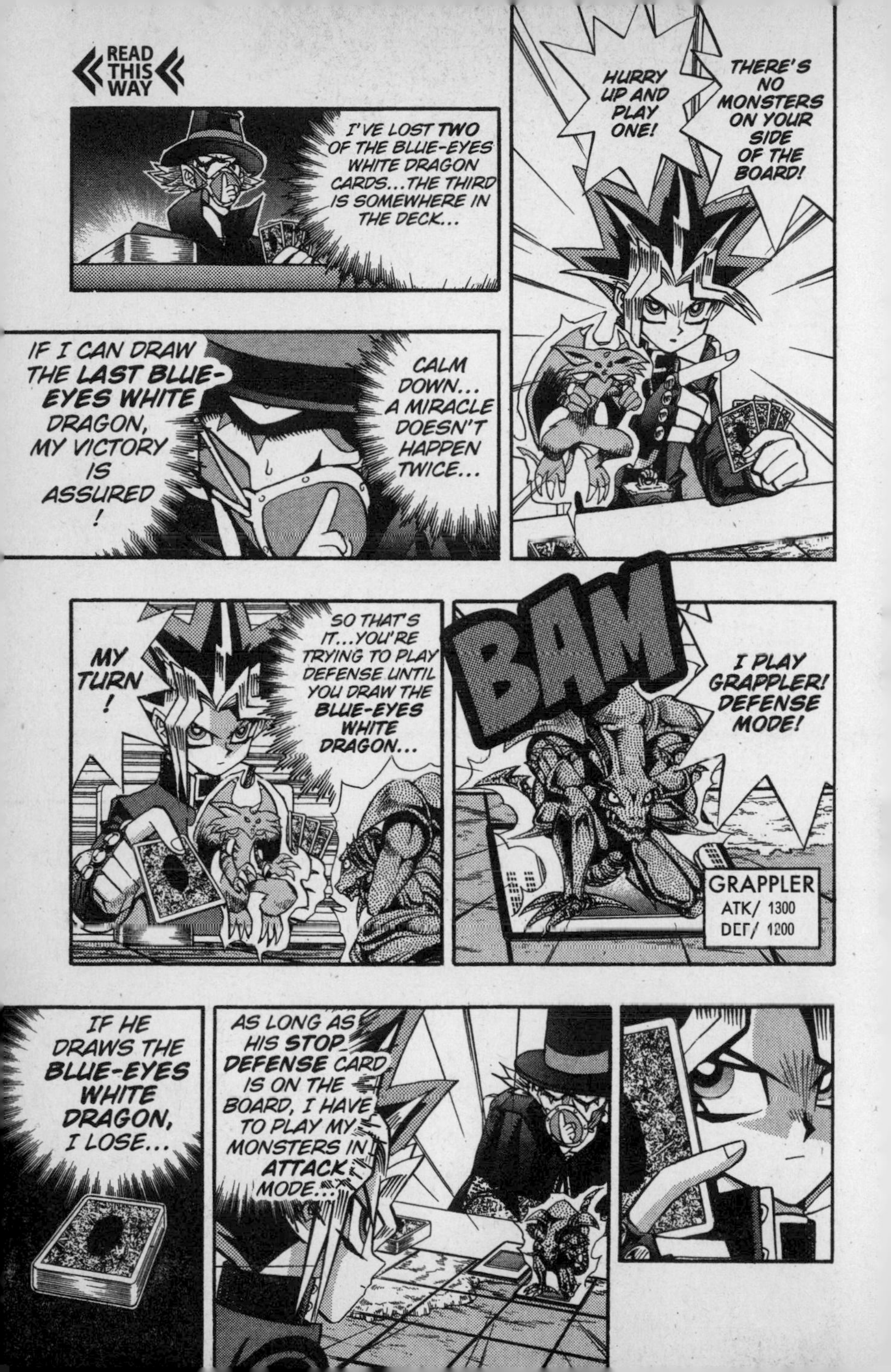
READ THIS WAY
THERE'S NO MONSTERS ON YOUR SIDE OF THE BOARD!
HURRY UP AND PLAY ONE!
I'VE LOST TWO OF THE BLUE-EYES WHITE DRAGON CARDS...THE THIRD IS SOMEWHERE IN THE DECK...
CALM DOWN... A MIRACLE DOESN'T HAPPEN TWICE...
IF I CAN DRAW THE LAST BLUE-EYES WHITE DRAGON, MY VICTORY IS ASSURED!
BAM
I PLAY GRAPPLER! DEFENSE MODE!
GRAPPLER
ATK/ 1300
DEF/ 1200
SO THAT'S IT...YOU'RE TRYING TO PLAY DEFENSE UNTIL YOU DRAW THE BLUE-EYES WHITE DRAGON...
MY TURN!
AS LONG AS HIS STOP DEFENSE CARD IS ON THE BOARD, I HAVE TO PLAY MY MONSTERS IN ATTACK MODE...
IF HE DRAWS THE BLUE-EYES WHITE DRAGON, I LOSE...

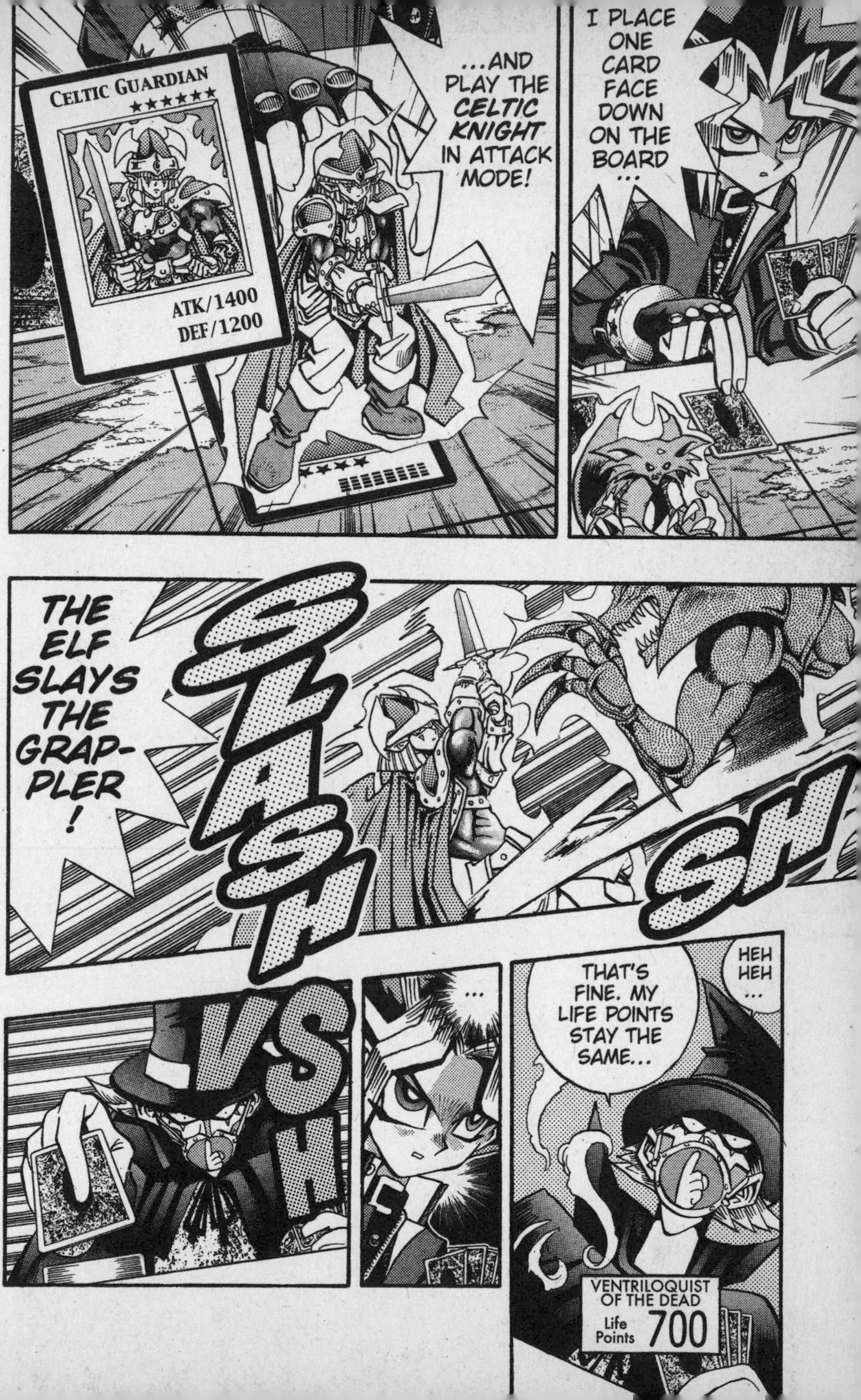
I PLACE ONE CARD FACE DOWN ON THE BOARD ...
...AND PLAY THE CELTIC KNIGHT IN ATTACK MODE!
CELTIC GUARDIAN
ATK/1400
DEF/1200
SH
SLASH
THE ELF SLAYS THE GRAPPLER!
HEH HEH ...
THAT'S FINE. MY LIFE POINTS STAY THE SAME...
VENTRILOQUIST OF THE DEAD
Life Points 700
...
VSH

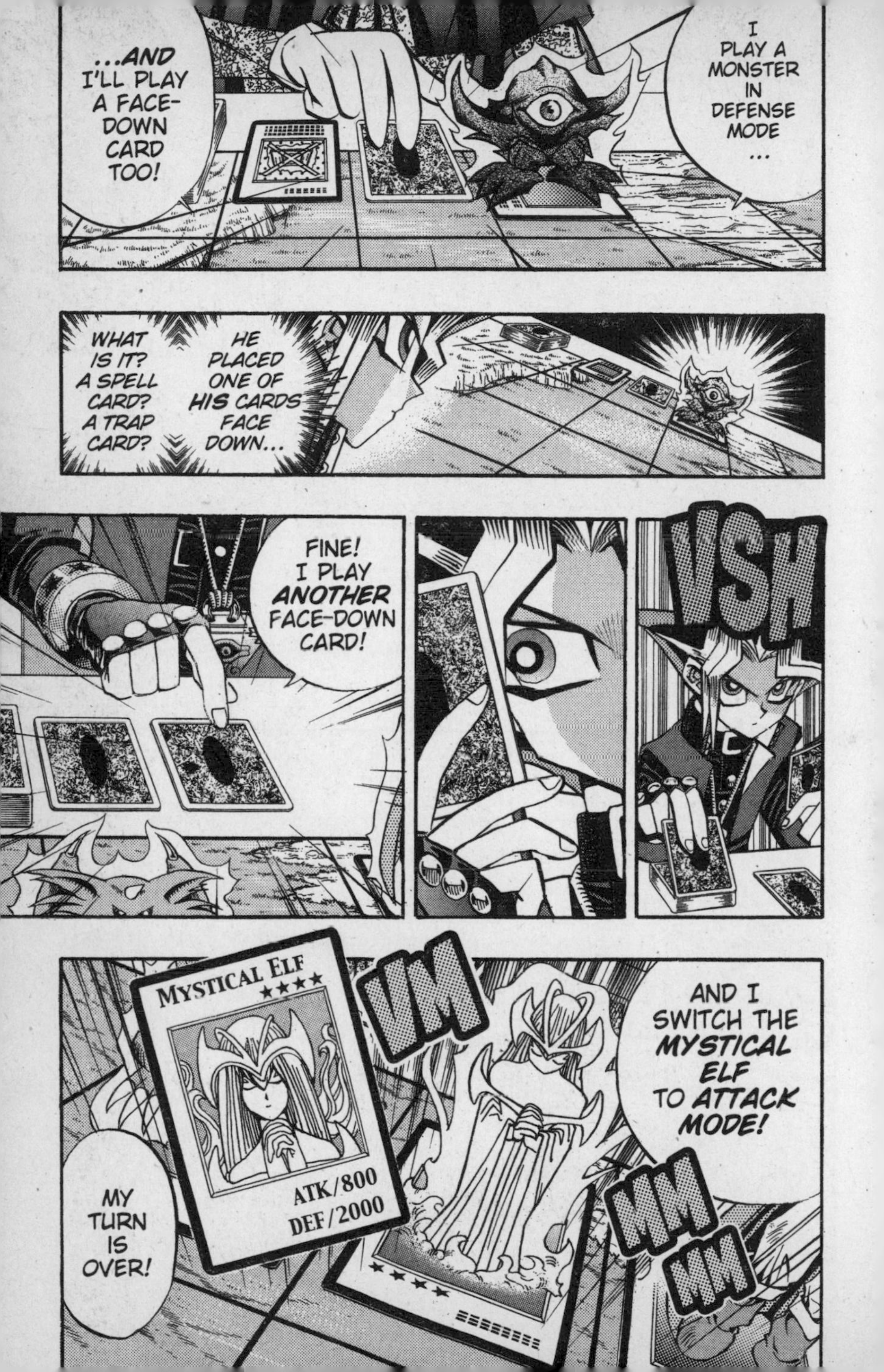
I PLAY A MONSTER IN DEFENSE MODE ...
...AND I'LL PLAY A FACE-DOWN CARD TOO!
HE PLACED ONE OF HIS CARDS FACE DOWN...
WHAT IS IT? A SPELL CARD? A TRAP CARD?
VSH
FINE! I PLAY ANOTHER FACE-DOWN CARD!
AND I SWITCH THE MYSTICAL ELF TO ATTACK MODE!
VM
MYSTICAL ELF
ATK/800
DEF/2000
MM MM
MY TURN IS OVER!

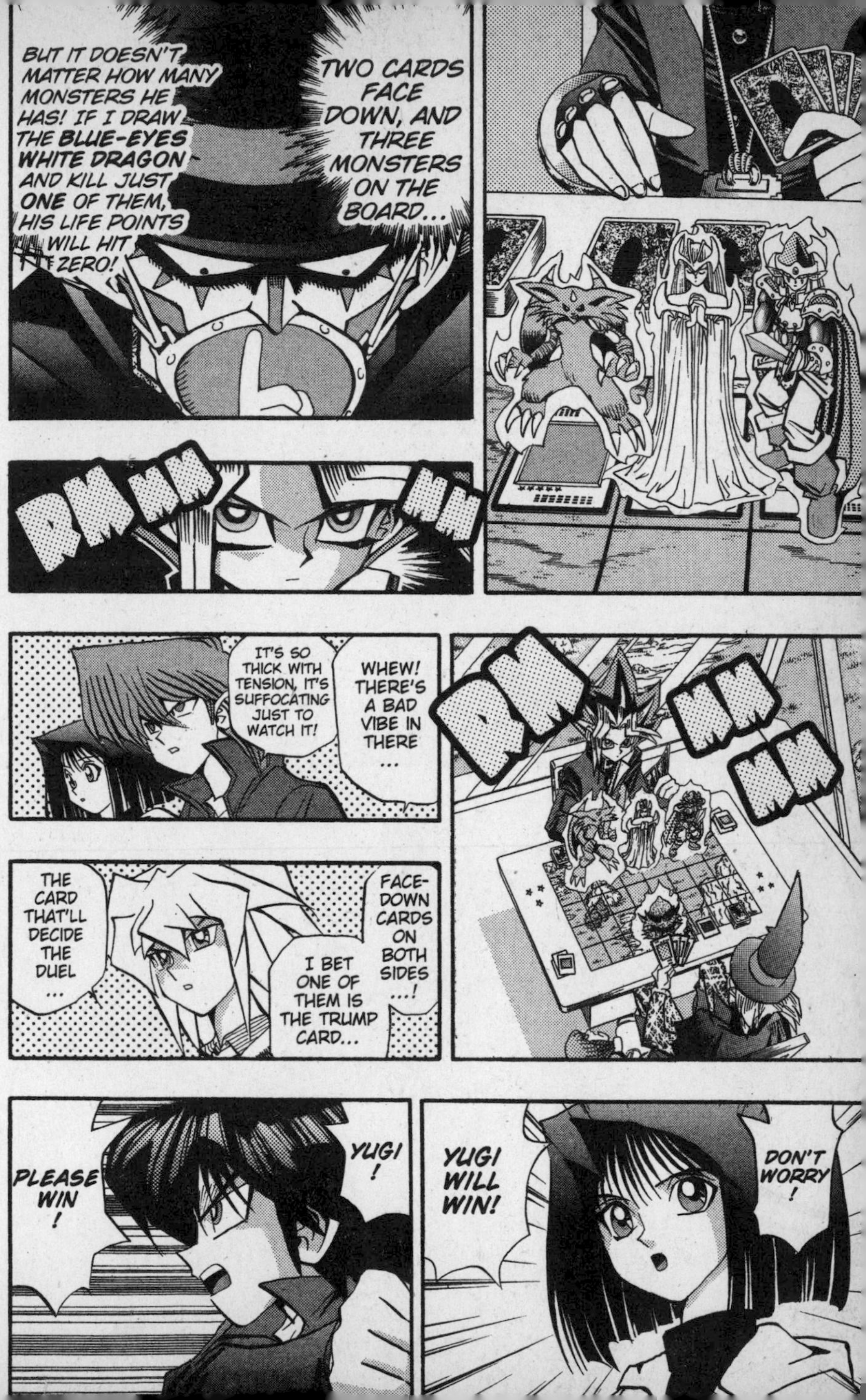
TWO CARDS FACE DOWN, AND THREE MONSTERS ON THE BOARD...
BUT IT DOESN'T MATTER HOW MANY MONSTERS HE HAS! IF I DRAW THE BLUE-EYES WHITE DRAGON AND KILL JUST ONE OF THEM, HIS LIFE POINTS WILL HIT ZERO!
WHEW! THERE'S A BAD VIBE IN THERE...
IT'S SO THICK WITH TENSION, IT'S SUFFOCATING JUST TO WATCH IT!
FACE-DOWN CARDS ON BOTH SIDES...!
I BET ONE OF THEM IS THE TRUMP CARD...
THE CARD THAT'LL DECIDE THE DUEL...
DON'T WORRY!
YUGI WILL WIN!
YUGI!
PLEASE WIN!

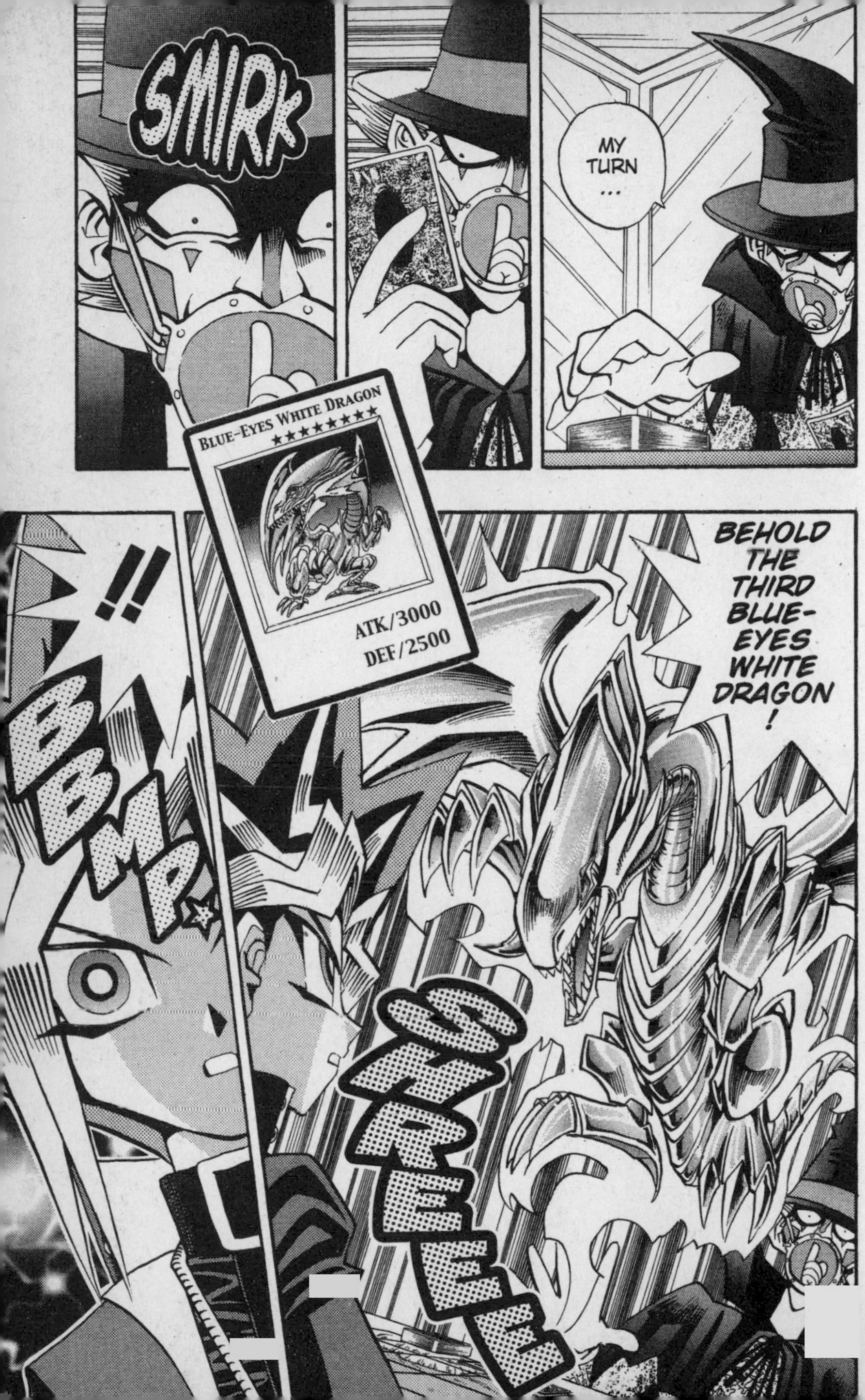
MY TURN ...
SMIRK
BEHOLD THE THIRD BLUE-EYES WHITE DRAGON!
BLUE-EYES WHITE DRAGON
ATK/3000
DEF/2500
SHREEE
!!
BBMP

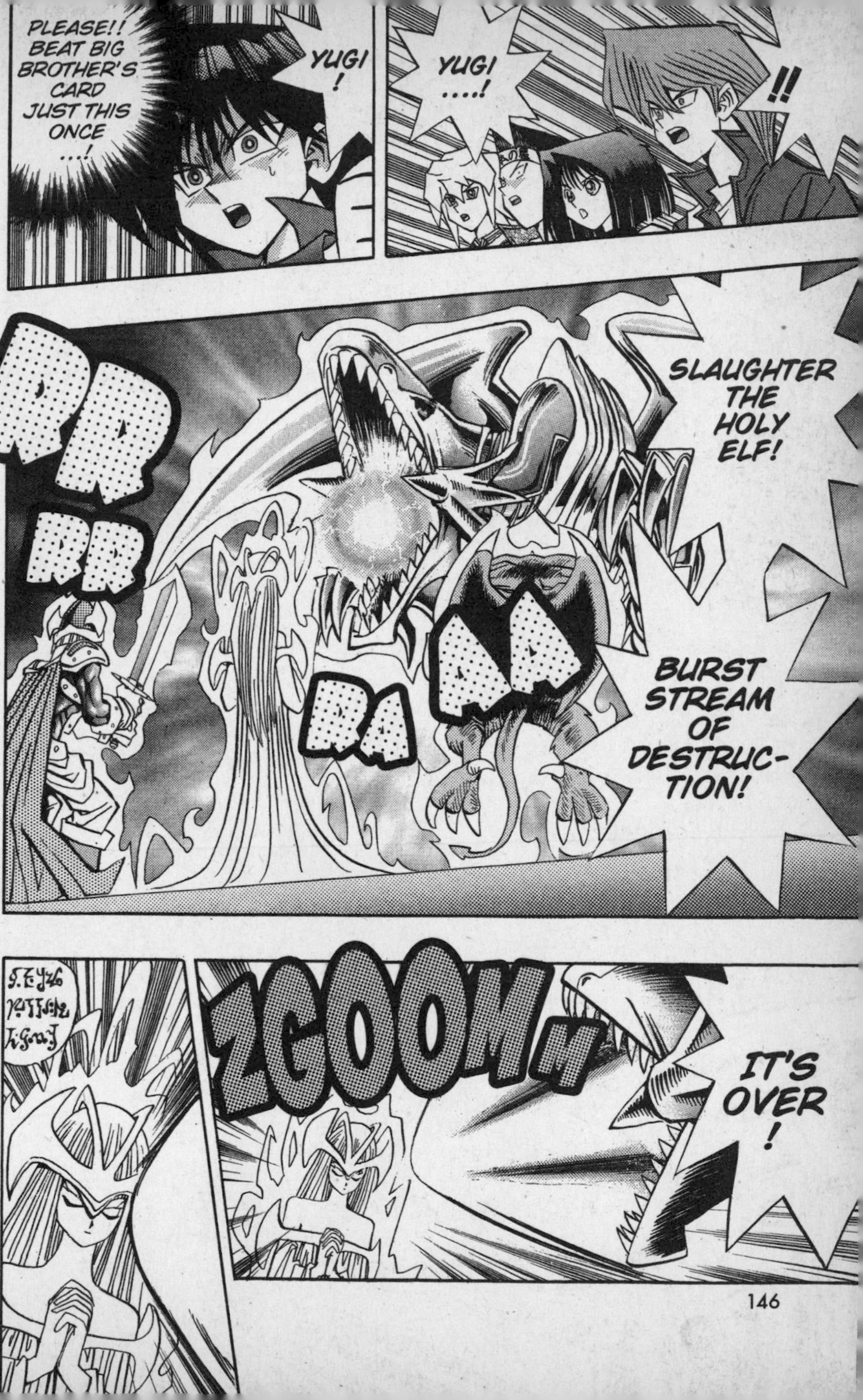

!!
YUGI ....!
YUGI!
PLEASE!! BEAT BIG BROTHER'S CARD JUST THIS ONCE ...!
SLAUGHTER THE HOLY ELF!
BURST STREAM OF DESTRUCTION!
RRRR
DA DA
IT'S OVER!
ZGOOM

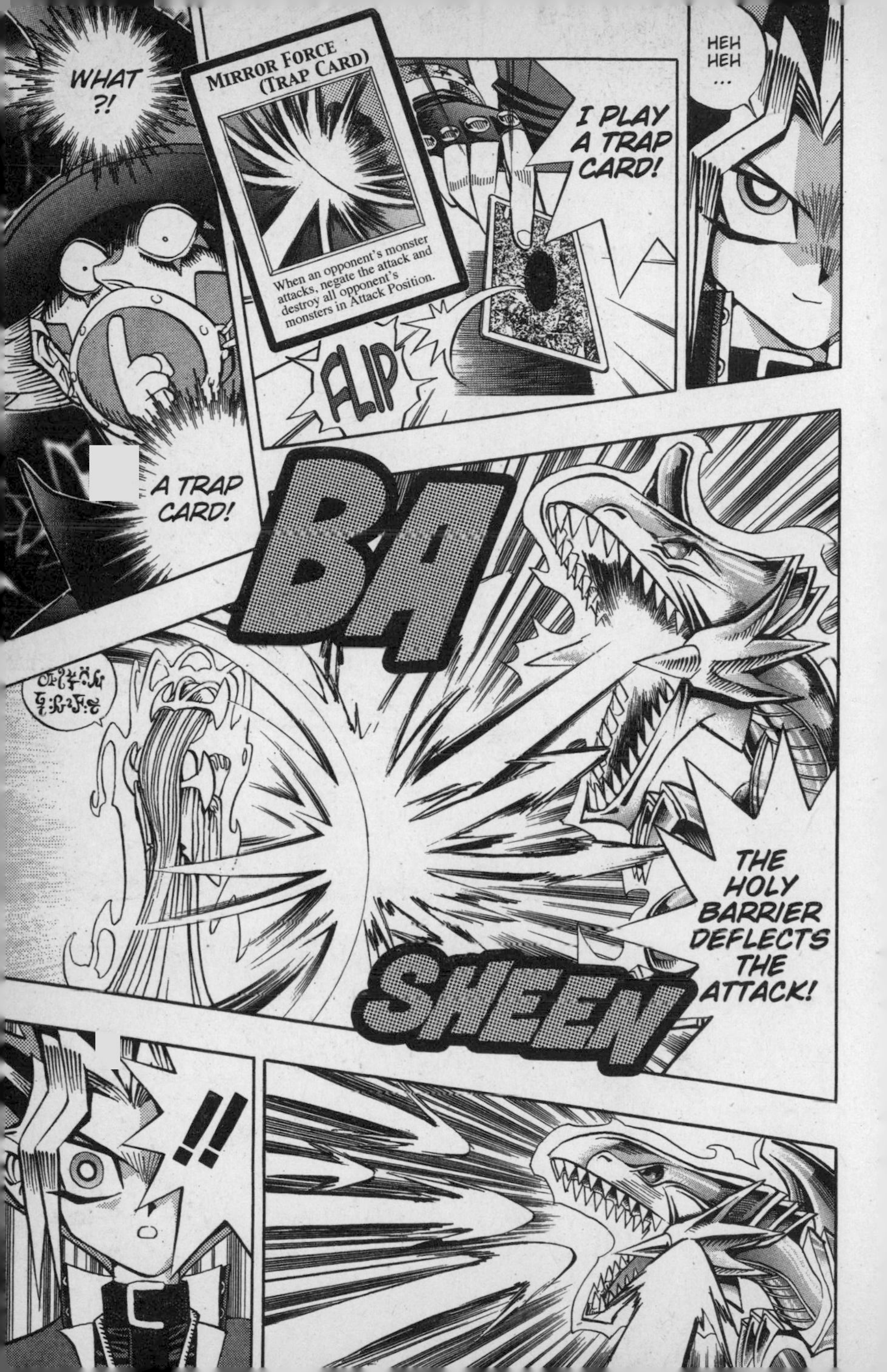
HEH HEH ...
I PLAY A TRAP CARD!
MIRROR FORCE (TRAP CARD)
When an opponent's monster attacks, negate the attack and destroy all opponent's monsters in Attack Position.
FLIP
WHAT ?!
A TRAP CARD!
BA
THE HOLY BARRIER DEFLECTS THE ATTACK!
SHEEN
!!

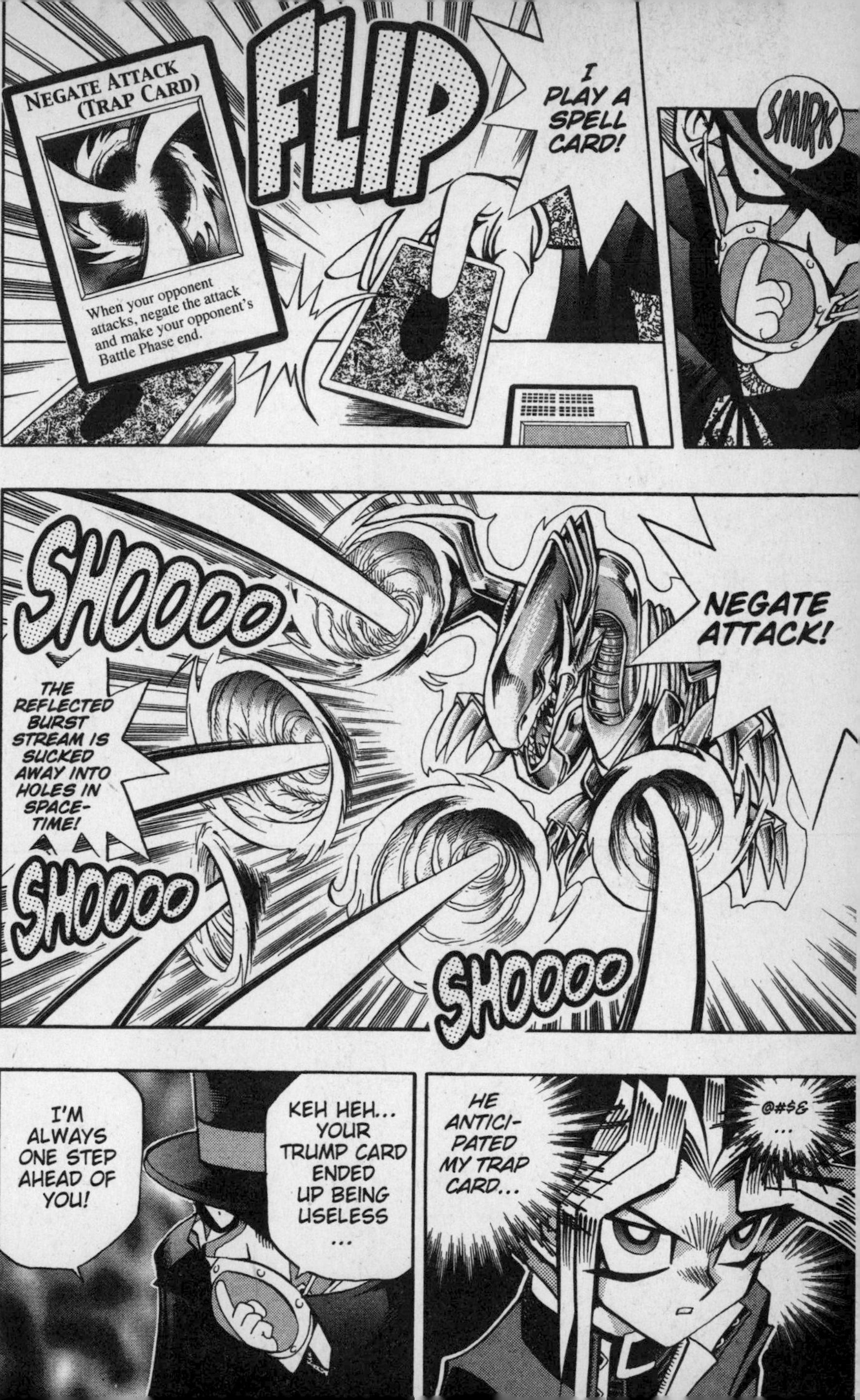
SMIRK
I PLAY A SPELL CARD!
FLIP
NEGATE ATTACK (TRAP CARD)
When your opponent attacks, negate the attack and make your opponent's Battle Phase end.
NEGATE ATTACK!
SHOOOOO
THE REFLECTED BURST STREAM IS SUCKED AWAY INTO HOLES IN SPACE-TIME!
SHOOOOO
SHOOOOO
@#$&...
HE ANTICIPATED MY TRAP CARD...
KEH HEH... YOUR TRUMP CARD ENDED UP BEING USELESS...
I'M ALWAYS ONE STEP AHEAD OF YOU!

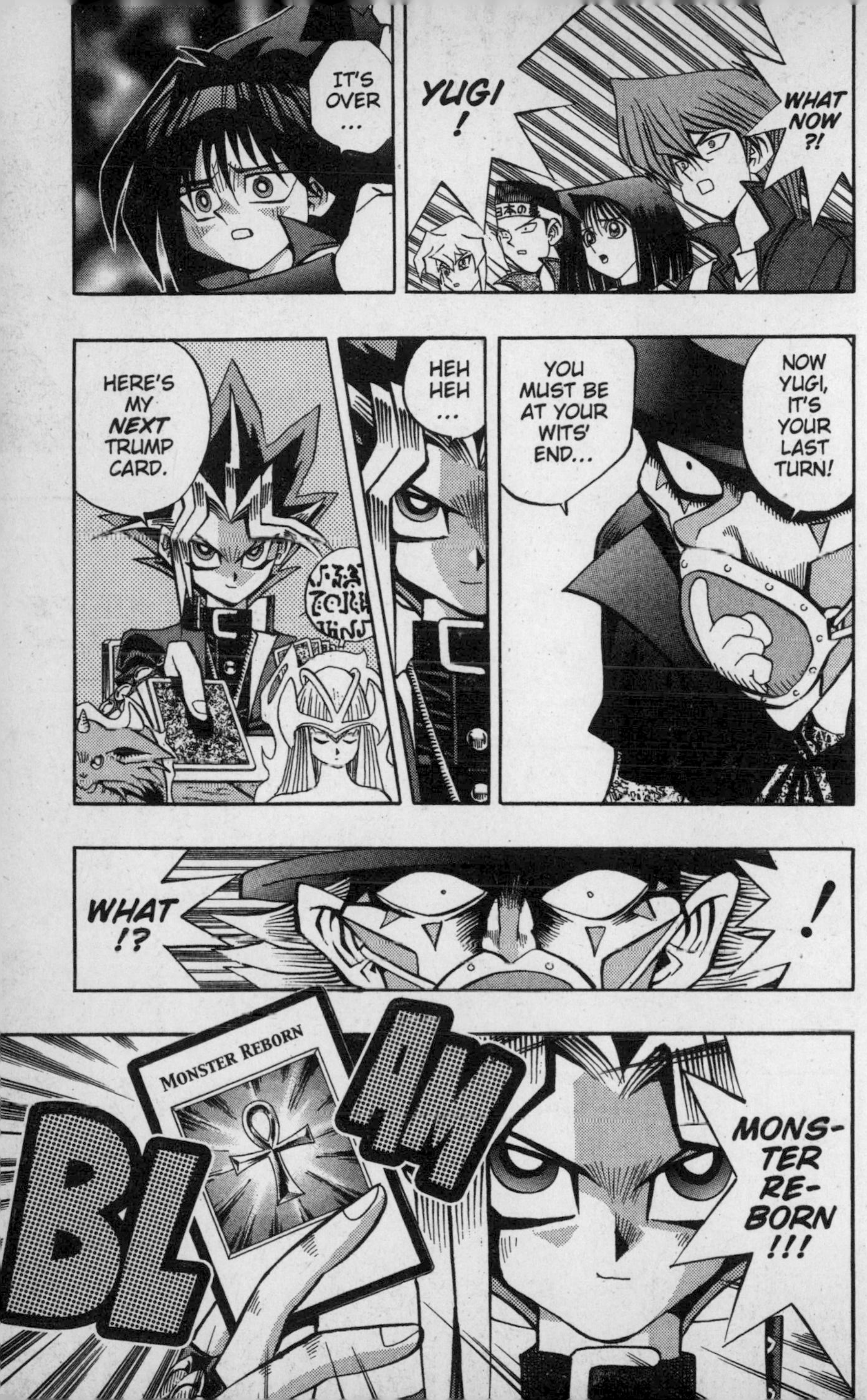
WHAT NOW?!
YUGI!
IT'S OVER...
NOW YUGI, IT'S YOUR LAST TURN!
YOU MUST BE AT YOUR WITS' END...
HEH HEH...
HERE'S MY NEXT TRUMP CARD.
!
WHAT!?
MONSTER-REBORN!!!
BLAM
MONSTER REBORN

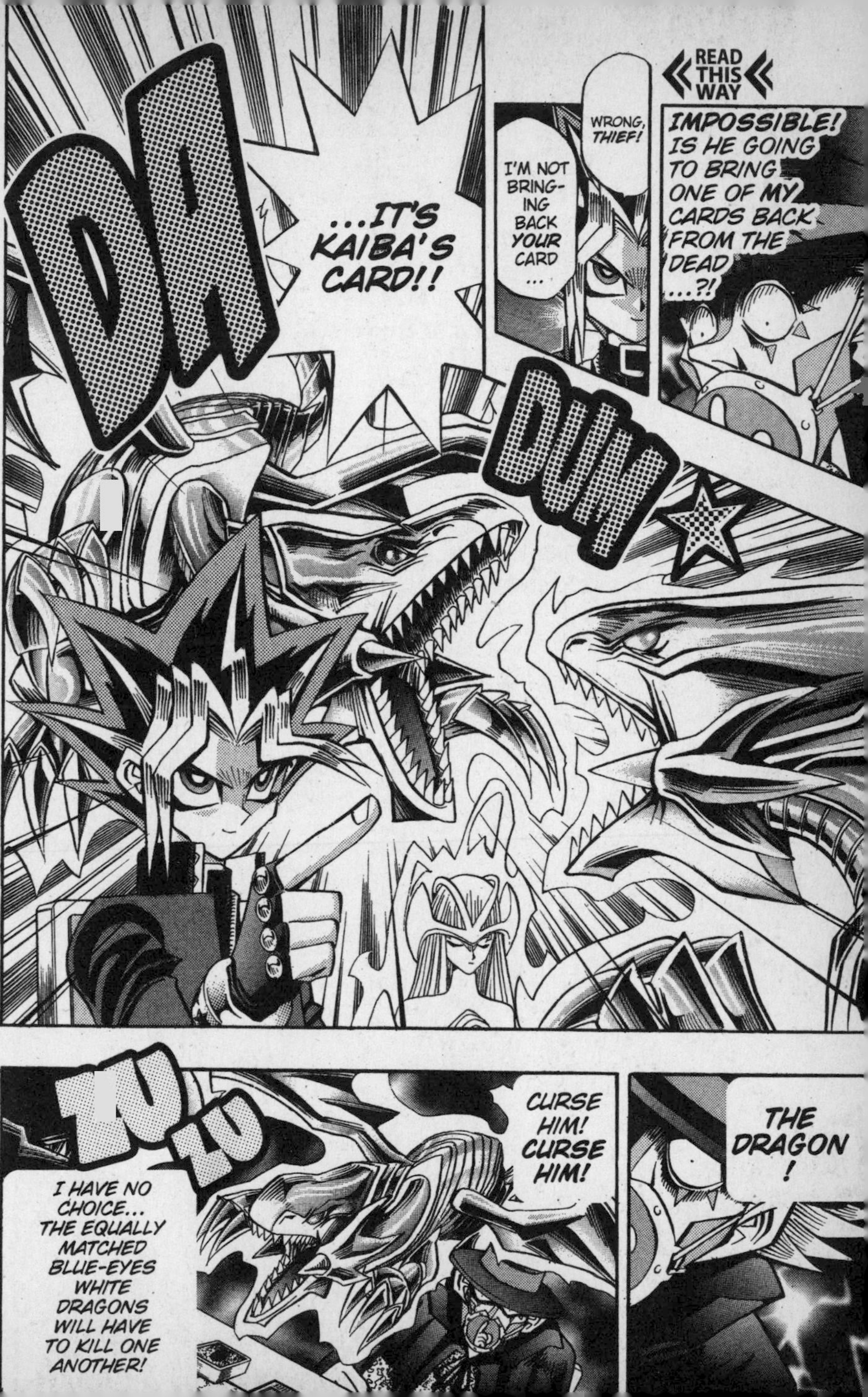
READ THIS WAY
IMPOSSIBLE! IS HE GOING TO BRING ONE OF MY CARDS BACK FROM THE DEAD ...?!
WRONG, THIEF!
I'M NOT BRINGING BACK YOUR CARD ...
...IT'S KAIBA'S CARD!!
DA
DUN
THE DRAGON!
CURSE HIM! CURSE HIM!
I HAVE NO CHOICE... THE EQUALLY MATCHED BLUE-EYES WHITE DRAGONS WILL HAVE TO KILL ONE ANOTHER!

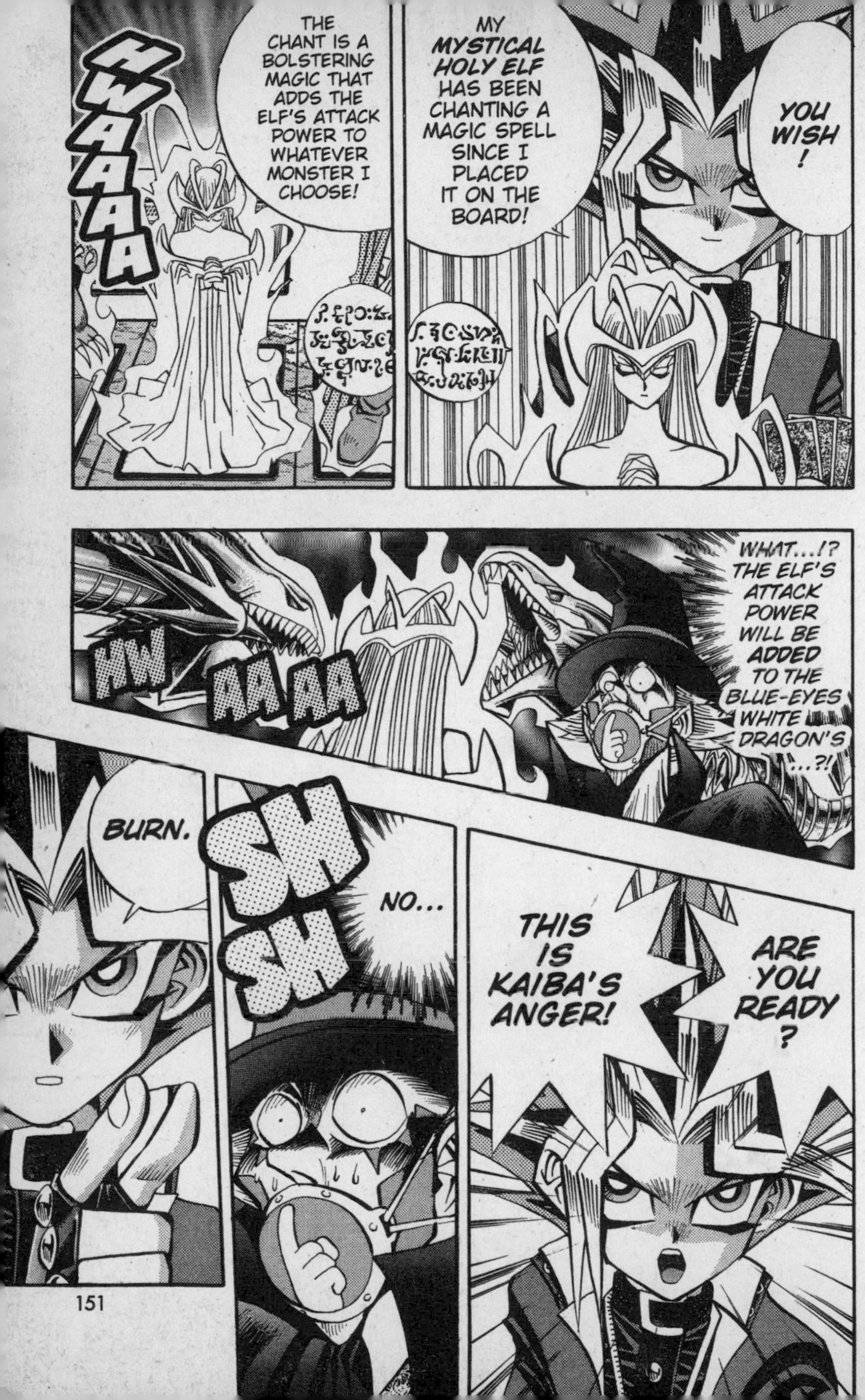
YOU WISH!
MY MYSTICAL HOLY ELF HAS BEEN CHANTING A MAGIC SPELL SINCE I PLACED IT ON THE BOARD!
THE CHANT IS A BOLSTERING MAGIC THAT ADDS THE ELF'S ATTACK POWER TO WHATEVER MONSTER I CHOOSE!
HWAAAAAA
WHAT...!? THE ELF'S ATTACK POWER WILL BE ADDED TO THE BLUE-EYES WHITE DRAGON'S ...?!
HWAAAA
ARE YOU READY?
THIS IS KAIBA'S ANGER!
NO...
SHSH
BURN.

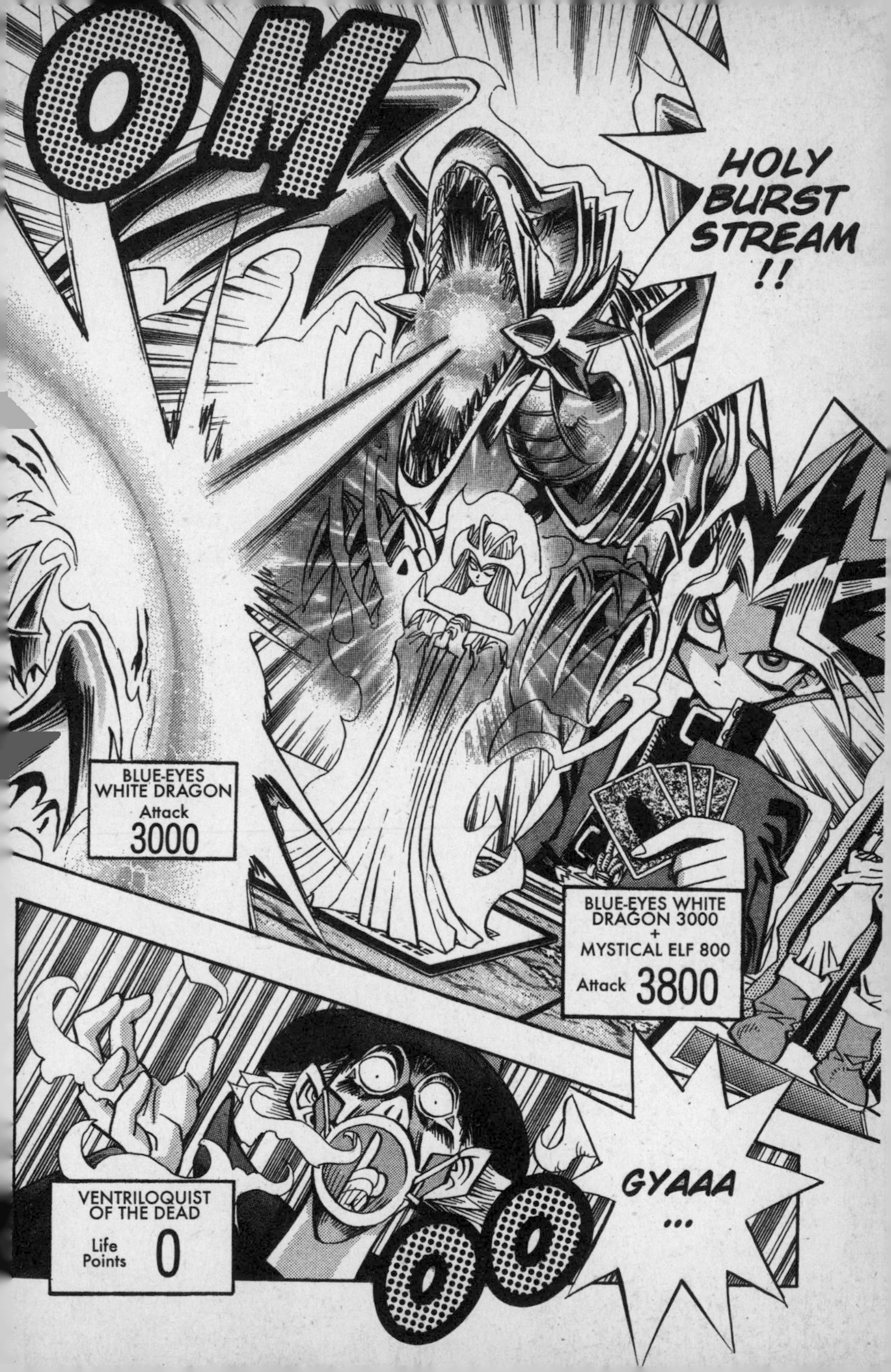
HOLY BURST STREAM !!
OM
BLUE-EYES WHITE DRAGON 3000 + MYSTICAL ELF 800 Attack 3800
BLUE-EYES WHITE DRAGON Attack 3000
GYAAA ...
OOO
VENTRILOQUIST OF THE DEAD Life Points 0

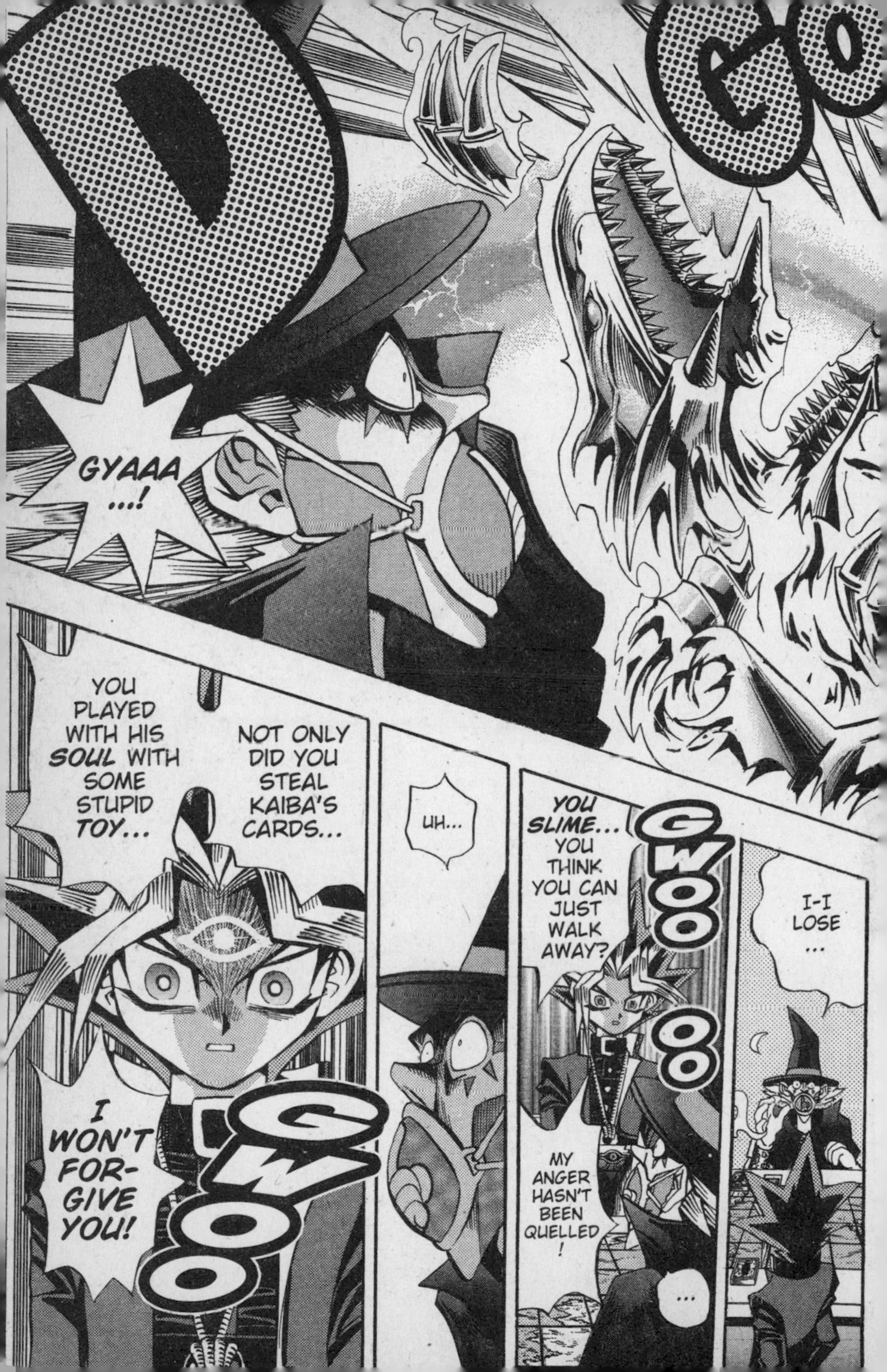
GYAAA ...!
I-I LOSE ...
...
YOU SLIME... YOU THINK YOU CAN JUST WALK AWAY?
GWOOOO
MY ANGER HASN'T BEEN QUELLED!
UH...
NOT ONLY DID YOU STEAL KAIBA'S CARDS...
YOU PLAYED WITH HIS SOUL WITH SOME STUPID TOY...
I WON'T FOR-GIVE YOU!
GWOOO

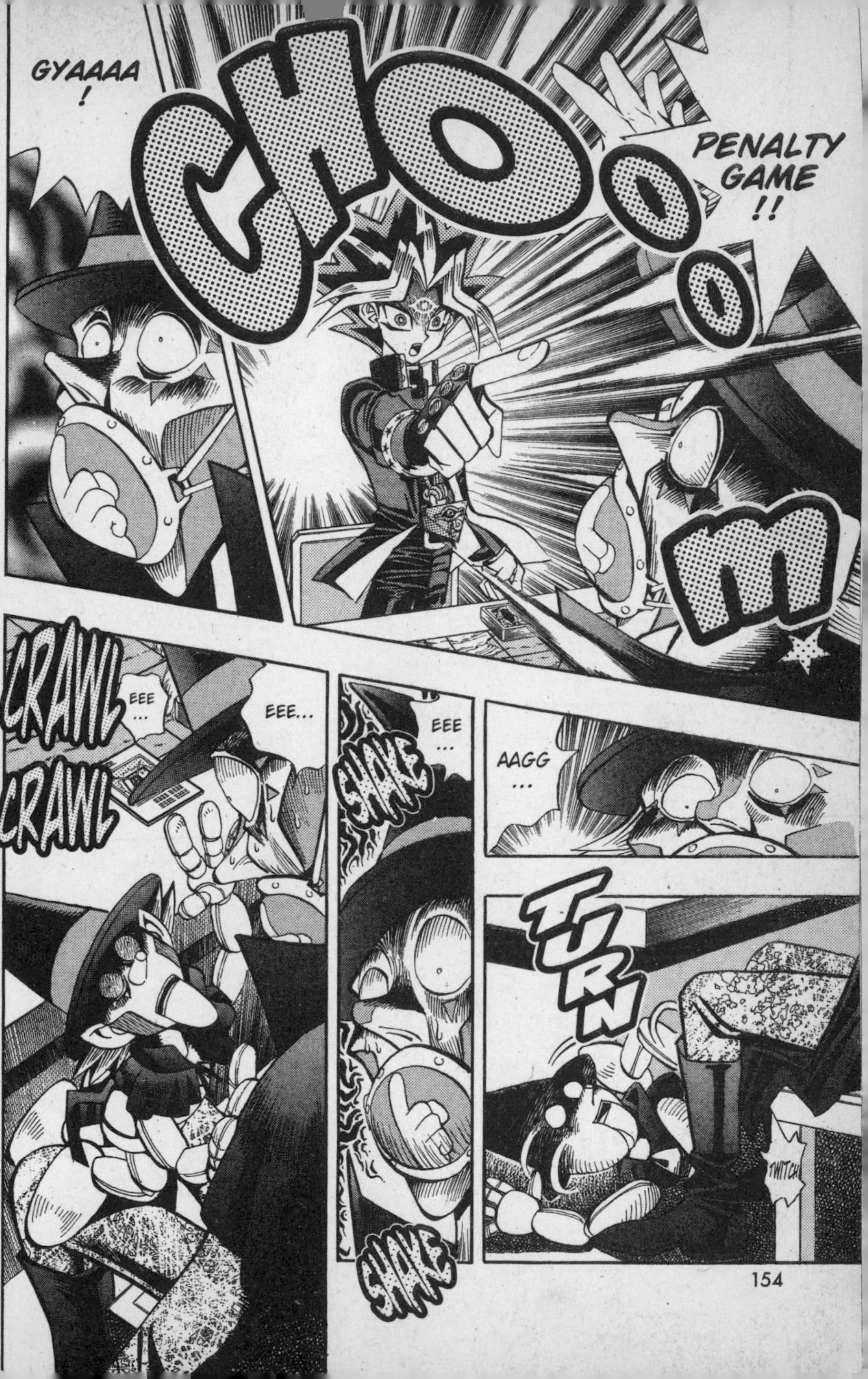
PENALTY GAME !!
CHOOOOM
GYAAAA !
AAGG ...
TURN
TWITCH
EEE ...
SHAKE
SHAKE
CRAWL CRAWL
EEE ...
EEE...

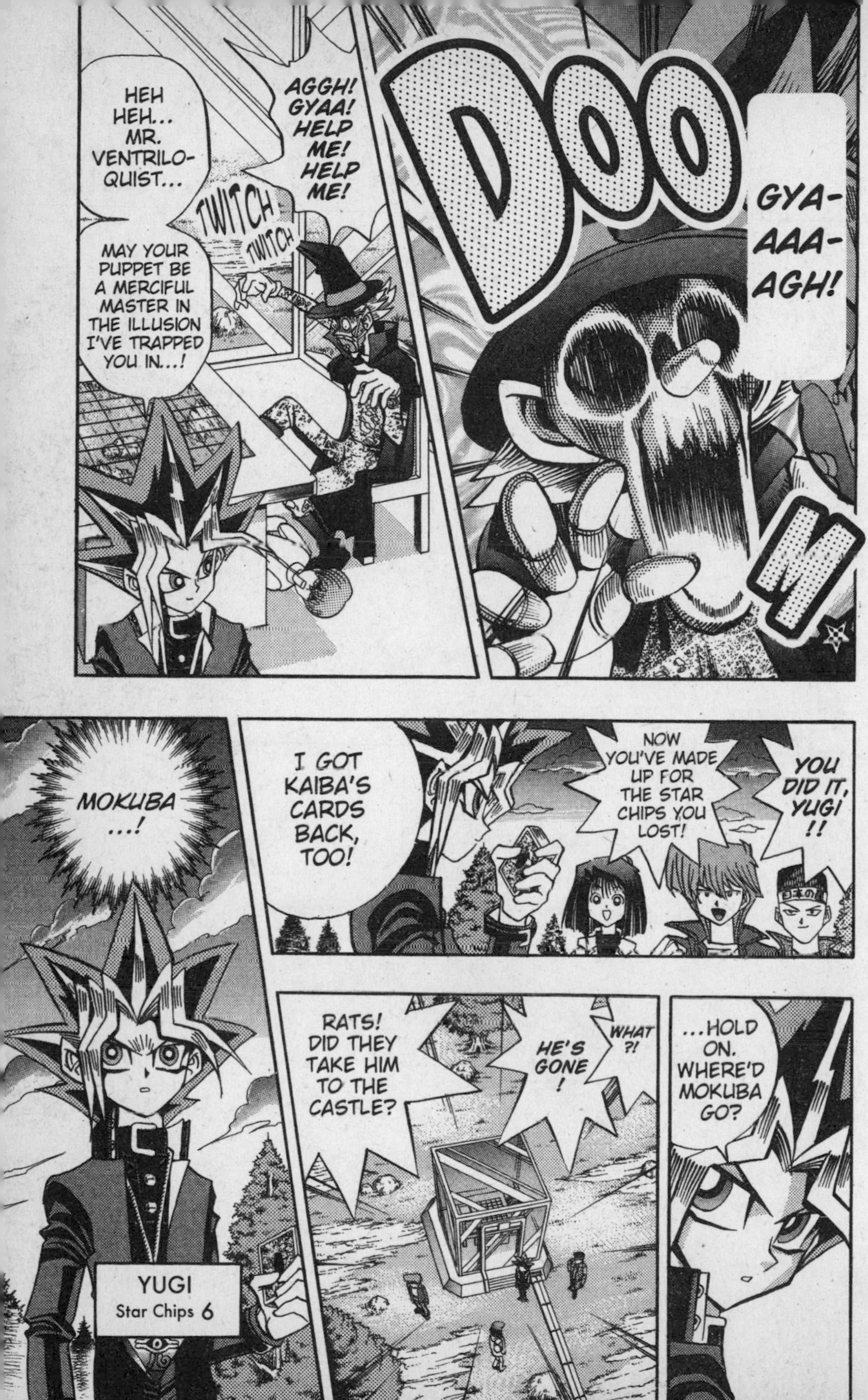
DOOM
GYA-AAA-AGH!
AGGH! GYAA! HELP ME! HELP ME!
HEH HEH... MR. VENTRILO-QUIST...
TWITCH TWITCH
MAY YOUR PUPPET BE A MERCIFUL MASTER IN THE ILLUSION I'VE TRAPPED YOU IN...!
YOU DID IT, YUGI!!
NOW YOU'VE MADE UP FOR THE STAR CHIPS YOU LOST!
I GOT KAIBA'S CARDS BACK, TOO!
...HOLD ON. WHERE'D MOKUBA GO?
WHAT?!
HE'S GONE!
RATS! DID THEY TAKE HIM TO THE CASTLE?
MOKUBA...!
YUGI
Star Chips 6

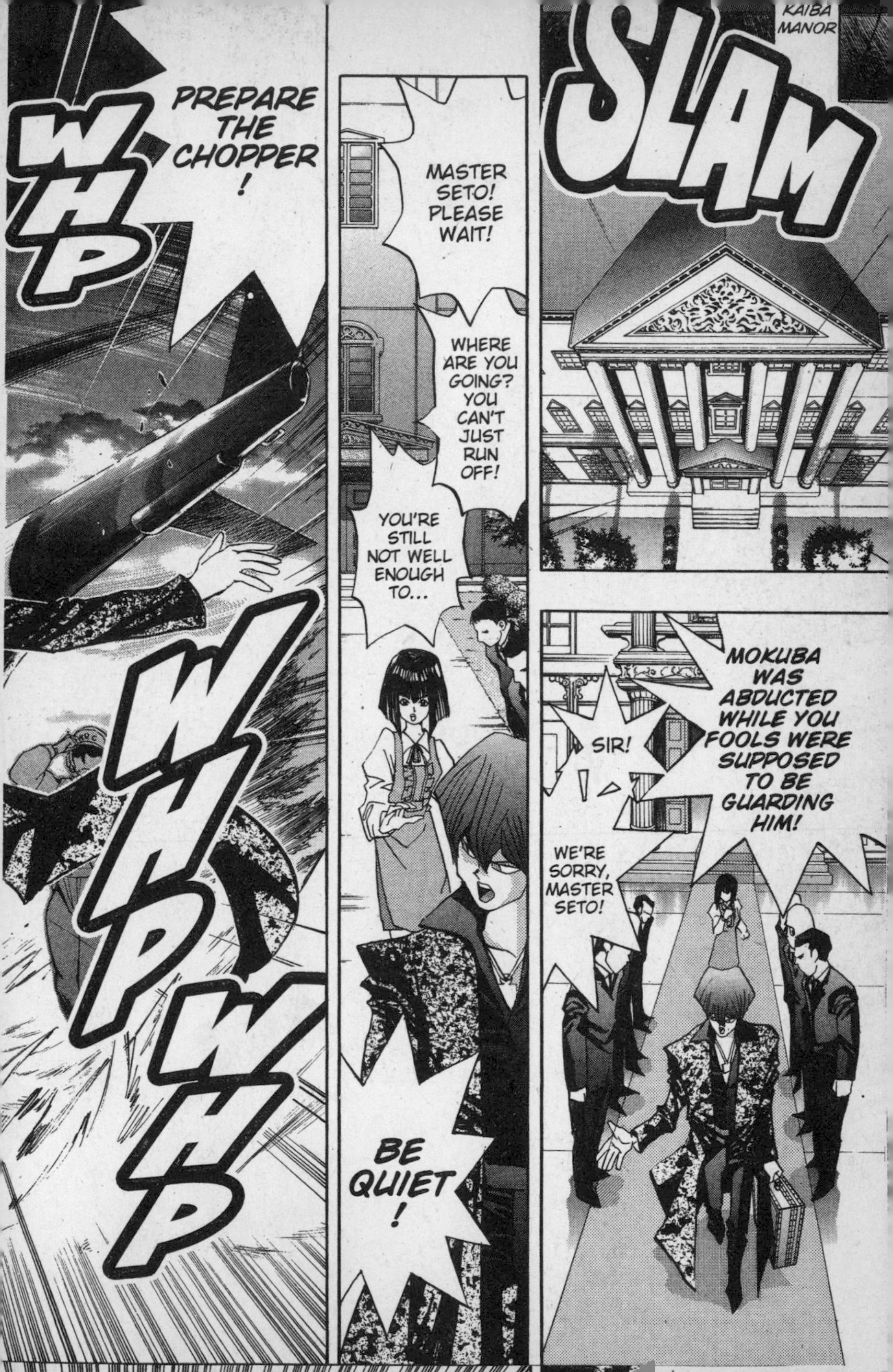
KAIBA MANOR
SLAM
MOKUBA WAS ABDUCTED WHILE YOU FOOLS WERE SUPPOSED TO BE GUARDING HIM!
SIR!
!
WE'RE SORRY, MASTER SETO!
MASTER SETO! PLEASE WAIT!
WHERE ARE YOU GOING? YOU CAN'T JUST RUN OFF!
YOU'RE STILL NOT WELL ENOUGH TO...
BE QUIET!
WHP
PREPARE THE CHOPPER!
WHPWHP

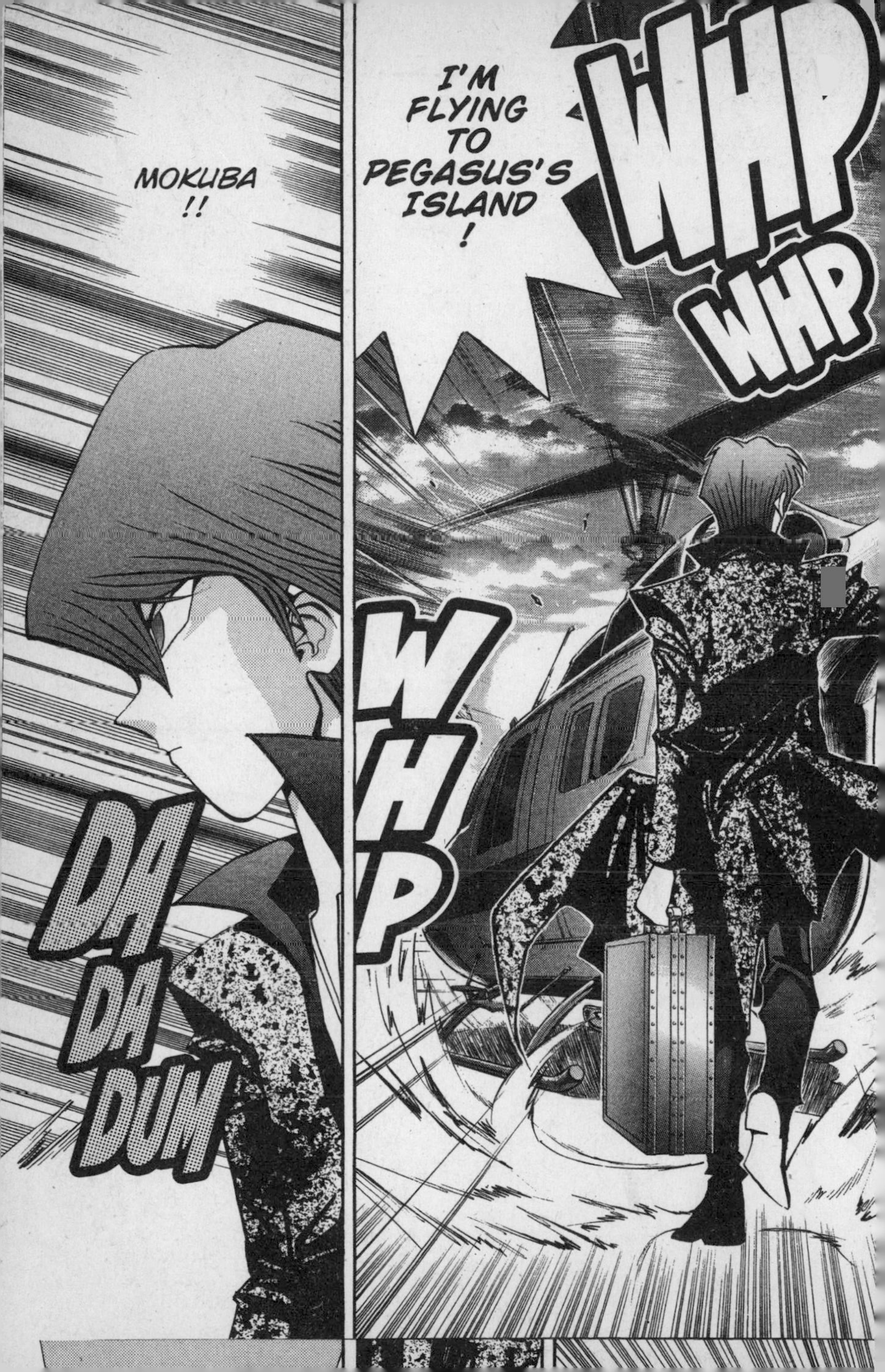
WHP WHP
I'M FLYING TO PEGASUS'S ISLAND!
WHP
MOKUBA!!
DA DA DUM

Duel 18: On My Own

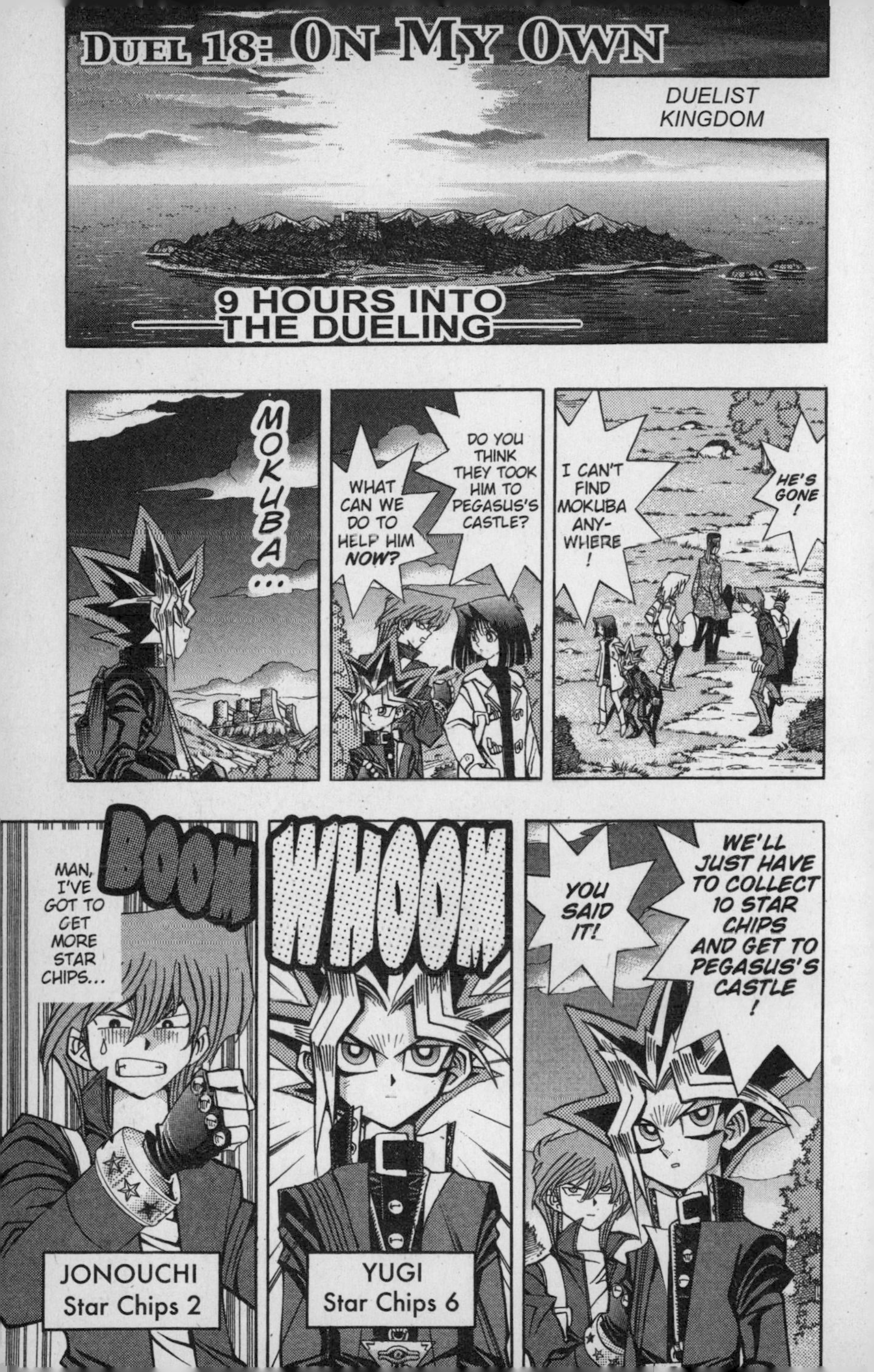
Duel 18: On My Own
DUELIST KINGDOM
9 HOURS INTO THE DUELING
HE'S GONE!
I CAN'T FIND MOKUBA ANYWHERE!
DO YOU THINK THEY TOOK HIM TO PEGASUS'S CASTLE?
WHAT CAN WE DO TO HELP HIM NOW?
MOKUBA...
WE'LL JUST HAVE TO COLLECT 10 STAR CHIPS AND GET TO PEGASUS'S CASTLE!
YOU SAID IT!
WHOOM
YUGI
Star Chips 6
BOOM
MAN, I'VE GOT TO GET MORE STAR CHIPS...
JONOUCHI
Star Chips 2

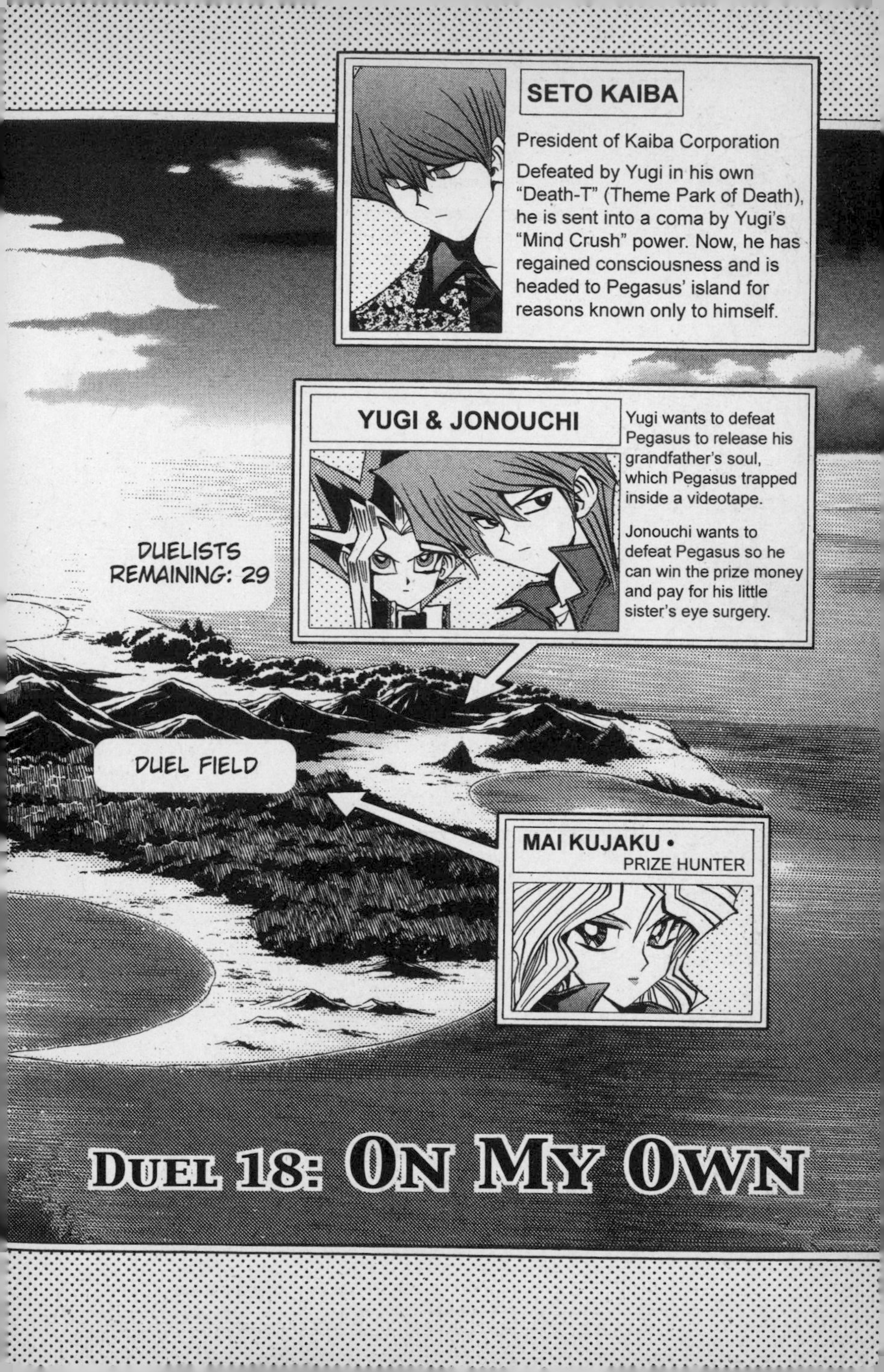
SETO KAIBA
President of Kaiba Corporation
Defeated by Yugi in his own "Death-T" (Theme Park of Death), he is sent into a coma by Yugi's "Mind Crush" power. Now, he has regained consciousness and is headed to Pegasus' island for reasons known only to himself.
YUGI & JONOUCHI
Yugi wants to defeat Pegasus to release his grandfather's soul, which Pegasus trapped inside a videotape.
Jonouchi wants to defeat Pegasus so he can win the prize money and pay for his little sister's eye surgery.
DUELISTS REMAINING: 29
MAI KUJAKU • PRIZE HUNTER
DUEL FIELD
DUEL 18: ON MY OWN

PEGASUS J. CRAWFORD

Nationality: American • Age: 24

Genius game designer and President of I² (Industrial Illusions), the colossal game company which sells the collectible card game "Duel Monsters." Under the pretext of a "Duel Monsters" tournament, he invited Yugi to his island to defeat him. Like Yugi, he possesses a Millennium Item, the mysterious Millennium Eye.

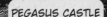

PEGASUS CASTLE

MOKUBA KAIBA

In his stomach is the key to a safe containing important documents regarding the sale of KaibaCorp. He is currently confined in Pegasus' castle.

KAIBA CORPORATION "BIG FIVE"

The secret executive group of KaibaCorp. They plan to fire Seto Kaiba and sell the corporation to Pegasus...on the condition that Pegasus beats Yugi.

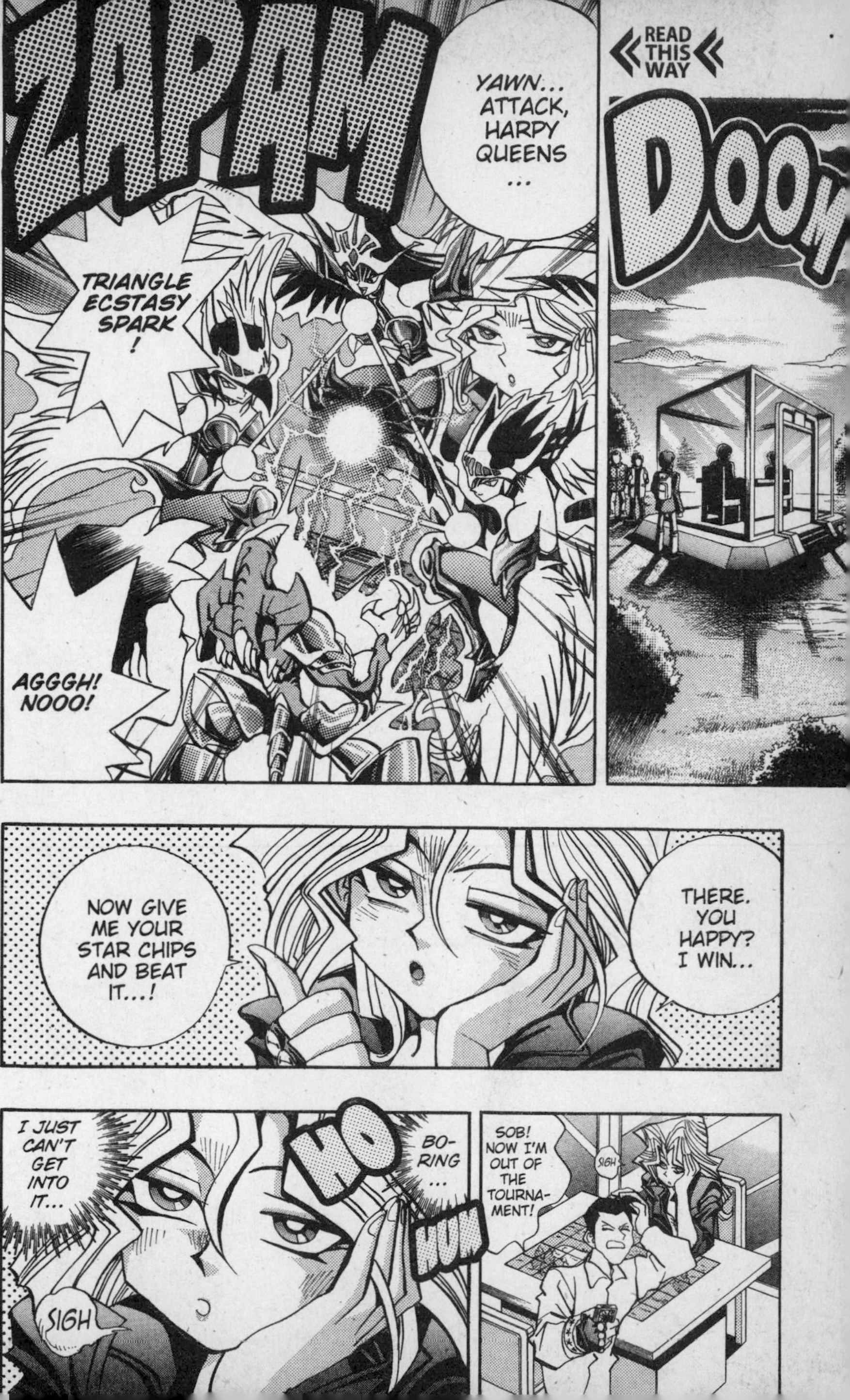
READ THIS WAY
DOO
YAWN... ATTACK, HARPY QUEENS ...
ZAPAM
TRIANGLE ECSTASY SPARK !
AGGGH! NOOO!
THERE. YOU HAPPY? I WIN...
NOW GIVE ME YOUR STAR CHIPS AND BEAT IT...!
SOB! NOW I'M OUT OF THE TOURNAMENT!
SIGH
BO-RING ...
HO HUM
I JUST CAN'T GET INTO IT...
SIGH

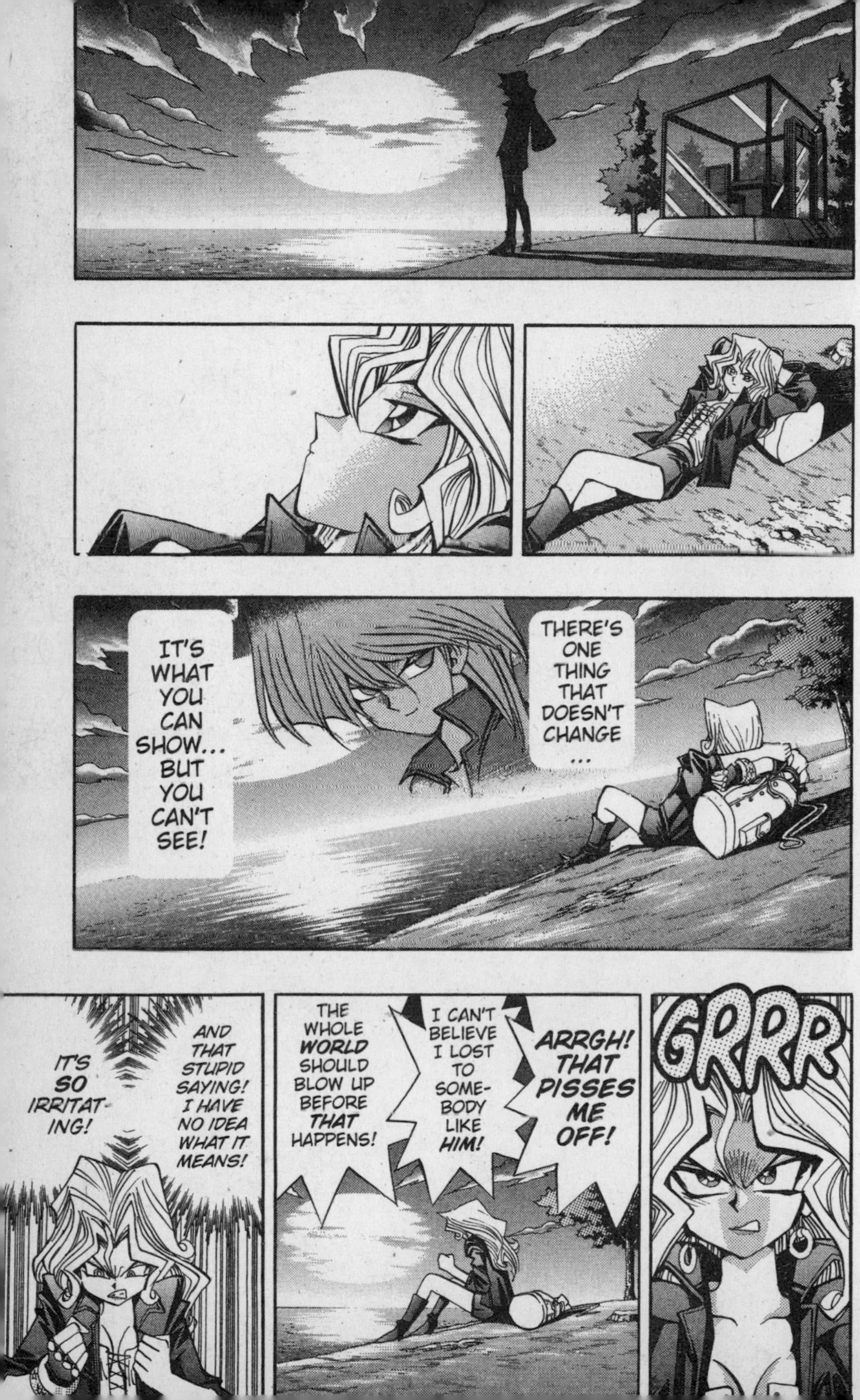
THERE'S ONE THING THAT DOESN'T CHANGE...
IT'S WHAT YOU CAN SHOW... BUT YOU CAN'T SEE!
GRRR
ARRGH! THAT PISSES ME OFF!
I CAN'T BELIEVE I LOST TO SOME-BODY LIKE HIM!
THE WHOLE WORLD SHOULD BLOW UP BEFORE THAT HAPPENS!
AND THAT STUPID SAYING! I HAVE NO IDEA WHAT IT MEANS!
IT'S SO IRRITAT-ING!

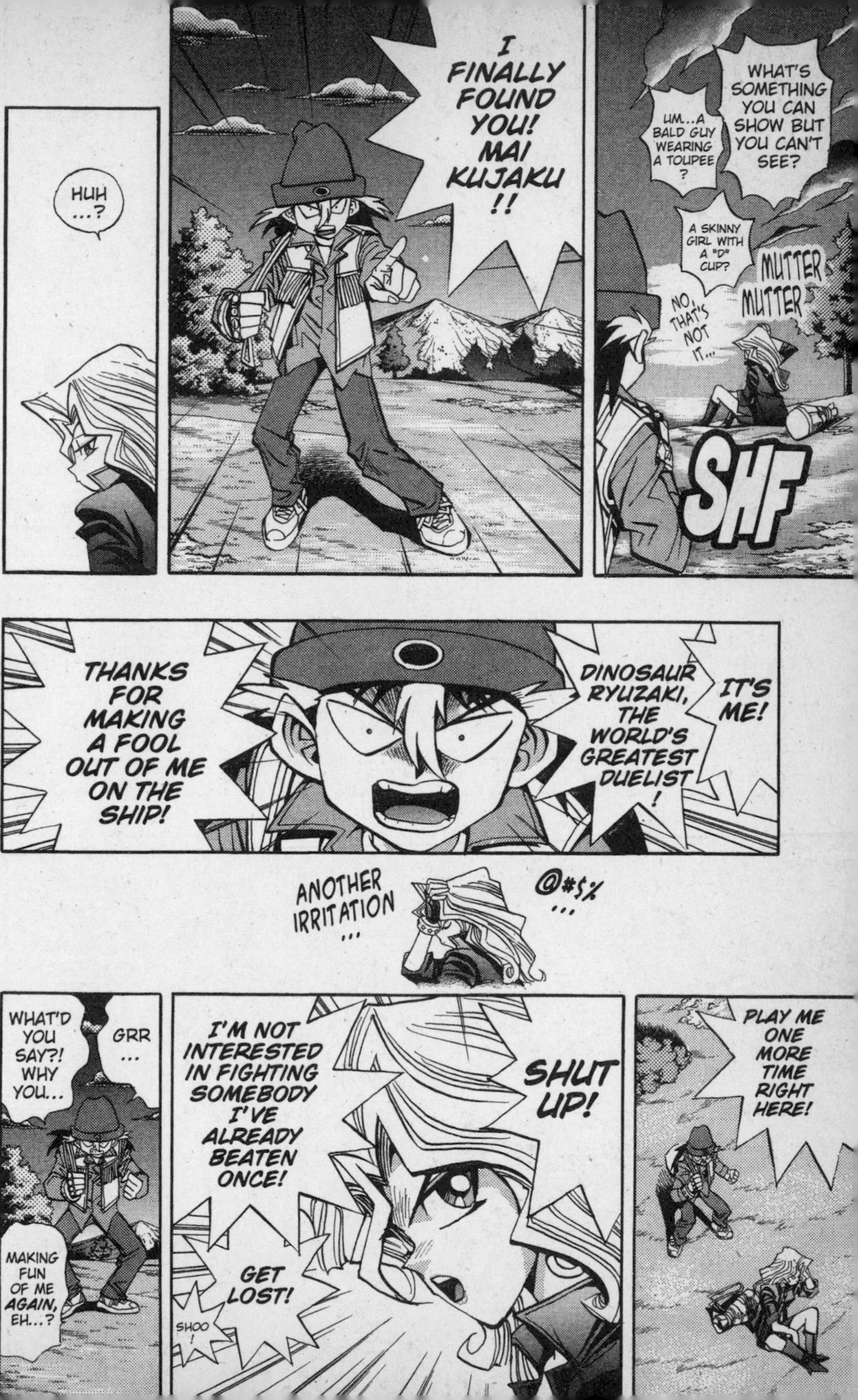
WHAT'S SOMETHING YOU CAN SHOW BUT YOU CAN'T SEE?
UM...A BALD GUY WEARING A TOUPEE?
A SKINNY GIRL WITH A "D" CUP?
MUTTER MUTTER
NO, THAT'S NOT IT...
SHF
I FINALLY FOUND YOU! MAI KUJAKU!!
HUH...?
IT'S ME!
DINOSAUR RYUZAKI, THE WORLD'S GREATEST DUELIST!
THANKS FOR MAKING A FOOL OUT OF ME ON THE SHIP!
@#$%...
ANOTHER IRRITATION...
PLAY ME ONE MORE TIME RIGHT HERE!
SHUT UP!
I'M NOT INTERESTED IN FIGHTING SOMEBODY I'VE ALREADY BEATEN ONCE!
GET LOST!
SHOO!
GRR...
WHAT'D YOU SAY?! WHY YOU...
MAKING FUN OF ME AGAIN, EH...?

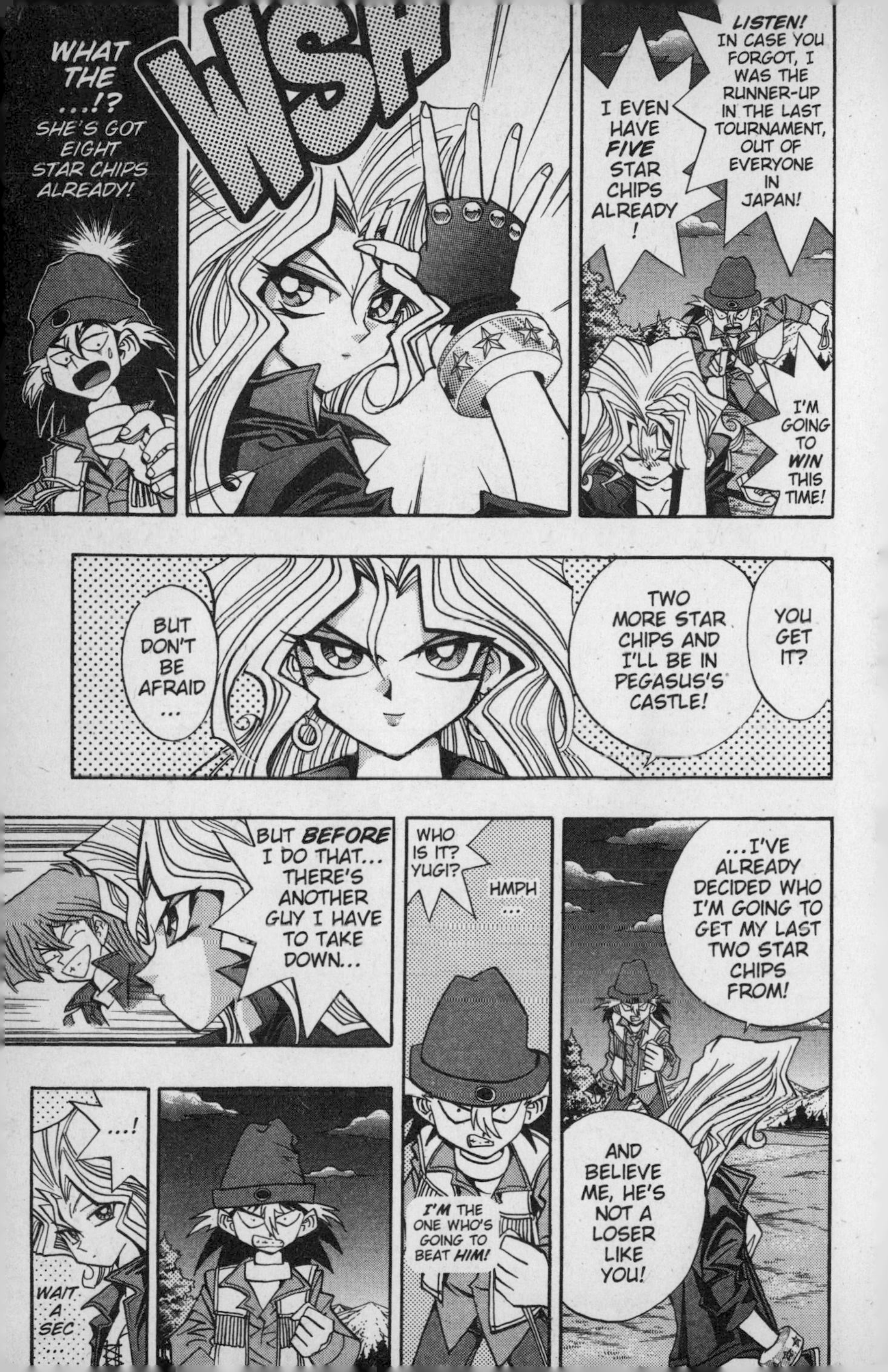

LISTEN! IN CASE YOU FORGOT, I WAS THE RUNNER-UP IN THE LAST TOURNAMENT, OUT OF EVERYONE IN JAPAN!
I EVEN HAVE FIVE STAR CHIPS ALREADY!
I'M GOING TO WIN THIS TIME!
WISH
WHAT THE ...!?
SHE'S GOT EIGHT STAR CHIPS ALREADY!
YOU GET IT?
TWO MORE STAR CHIPS AND I'LL BE IN PEGASUS'S CASTLE!
BUT DON'T BE AFRAID ...
...I'VE ALREADY DECIDED WHO I'M GOING TO GET MY LAST TWO STAR CHIPS FROM!
AND BELIEVE ME, HE'S NOT A LOSER LIKE YOU!
WHO IS IT? YUGI?
HMPH ...
I'M THE ONE WHO'S GOING TO BEAT HIM!
BUT BEFORE I DO THAT... THERE'S ANOTHER GUY I HAVE TO TAKE DOWN...
...!
WAIT A SEC ...

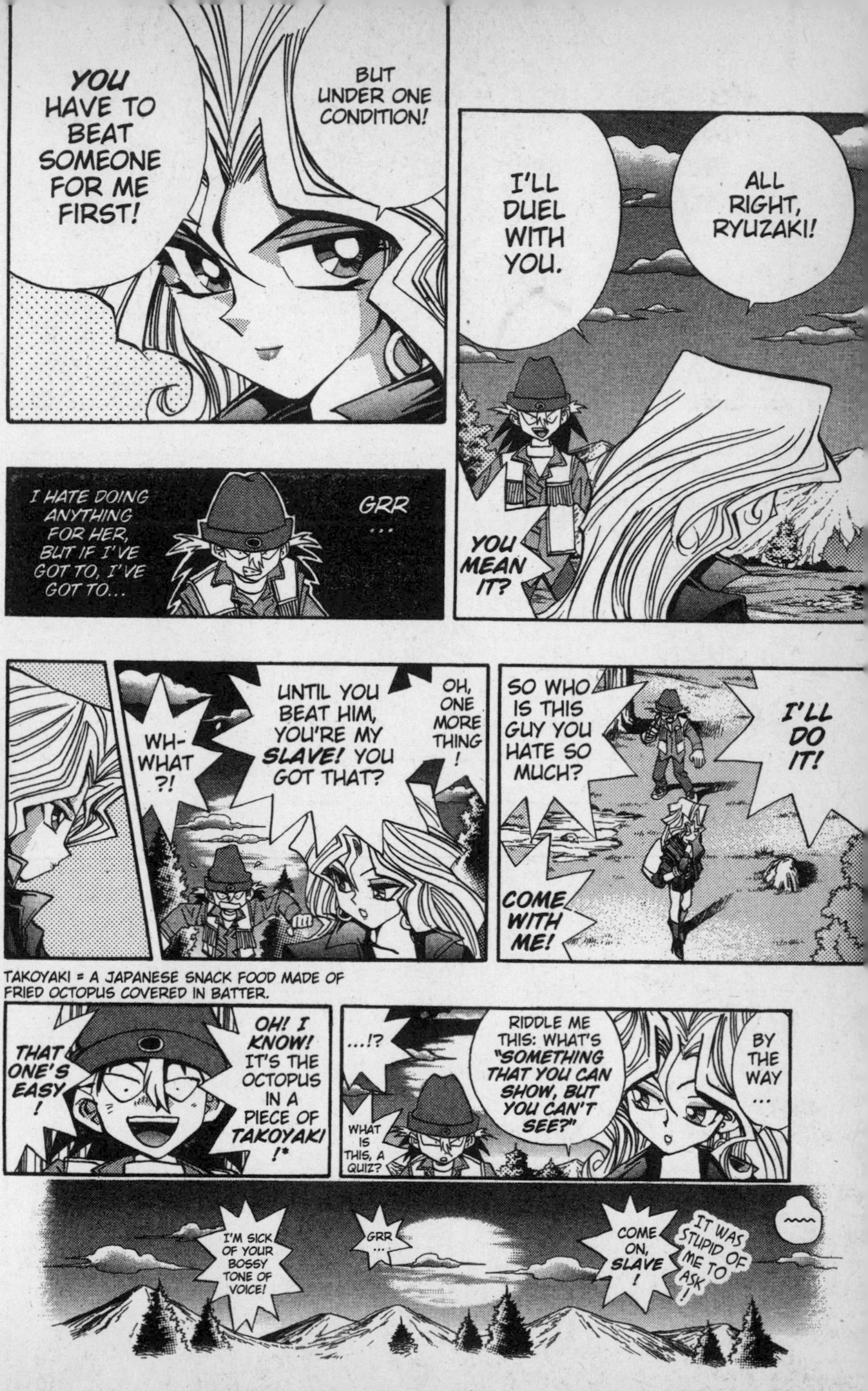
ALL RIGHT, RYUZAKI!
I'LL DUEL WITH YOU.
YOU MEAN IT?
BUT UNDER ONE CONDITION!
YOU HAVE TO BEAT SOMEONE FOR ME FIRST!
GRR...
I HATE DOING ANYTHING FOR HER, BUT IF I'VE GOT TO, I'VE GOT TO...
I'LL DO IT!
SO WHO IS THIS GUY YOU HATE SO MUCH?
COME WITH ME!
OH, ONE MORE THING!
UNTIL YOU BEAT HIM, YOU'RE MY SLAVE! YOU GOT THAT?
WH-WHAT?!
BY THE WAY...
RIDDLE ME THIS: WHAT'S "SOMETHING THAT YOU CAN SHOW, BUT YOU CAN'T SEE?"
...!?
WHAT IS THIS, A QUIZ?
OH! I KNOW! IT'S THE OCTOPUS IN A PIECE OF TAKOYAKI!*
THAT ONE'S EASY!
~~~
IT WAS STUPID OF ME TO ASK!
COME ON, SLAVE!
GRR...
I'M SICK OF YOUR BOSSY TONE OF VOICE!

TAKOYAKI = A JAPANESE SNACK FOOD MADE OF FRIED OCTOPUS COVERED IN BATTER.
~~~

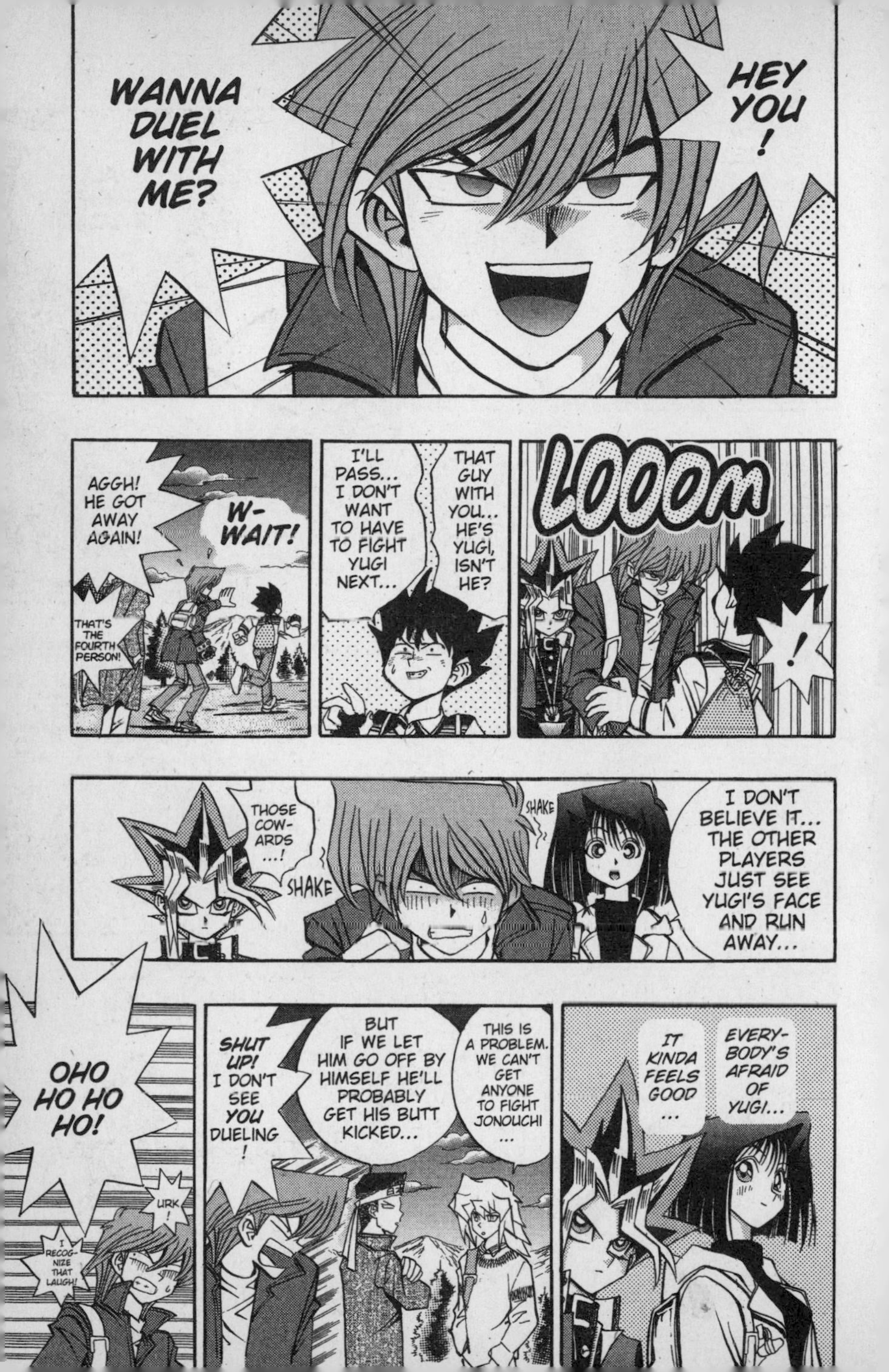
HEY YOU!
WANNA DUEL WITH ME?
LOOOM
!
THAT GUY WITH YOU... HE'S YUGI, ISN'T HE?
I'LL PASS... I DON'T WANT TO HAVE TO FIGHT YUGI NEXT...
W-WAIT!
AGGH! HE GOT AWAY AGAIN!
THAT'S THE FOURTH PERSON!
I DON'T BELIEVE IT... THE OTHER PLAYERS JUST SEE YUGI'S FACE AND RUN AWAY...
SHAKE
SHAKE
THOSE COWARDS...!
EVERYBODY'S AFRAID OF YUGI...
IT KINDA FEELS GOOD...
THIS IS A PROBLEM. WE CAN'T GET ANYONE TO FIGHT JONOUCHI...
BUT IF WE LET HIM GO OFF BY HIMSELF HE'LL PROBABLY GET HIS BUTT KICKED...
SHUT UP! I DON'T SEE YOU DUELING!
OHO HO HO HO!
URK!
I RECOGNIZE THAT LAUGH!

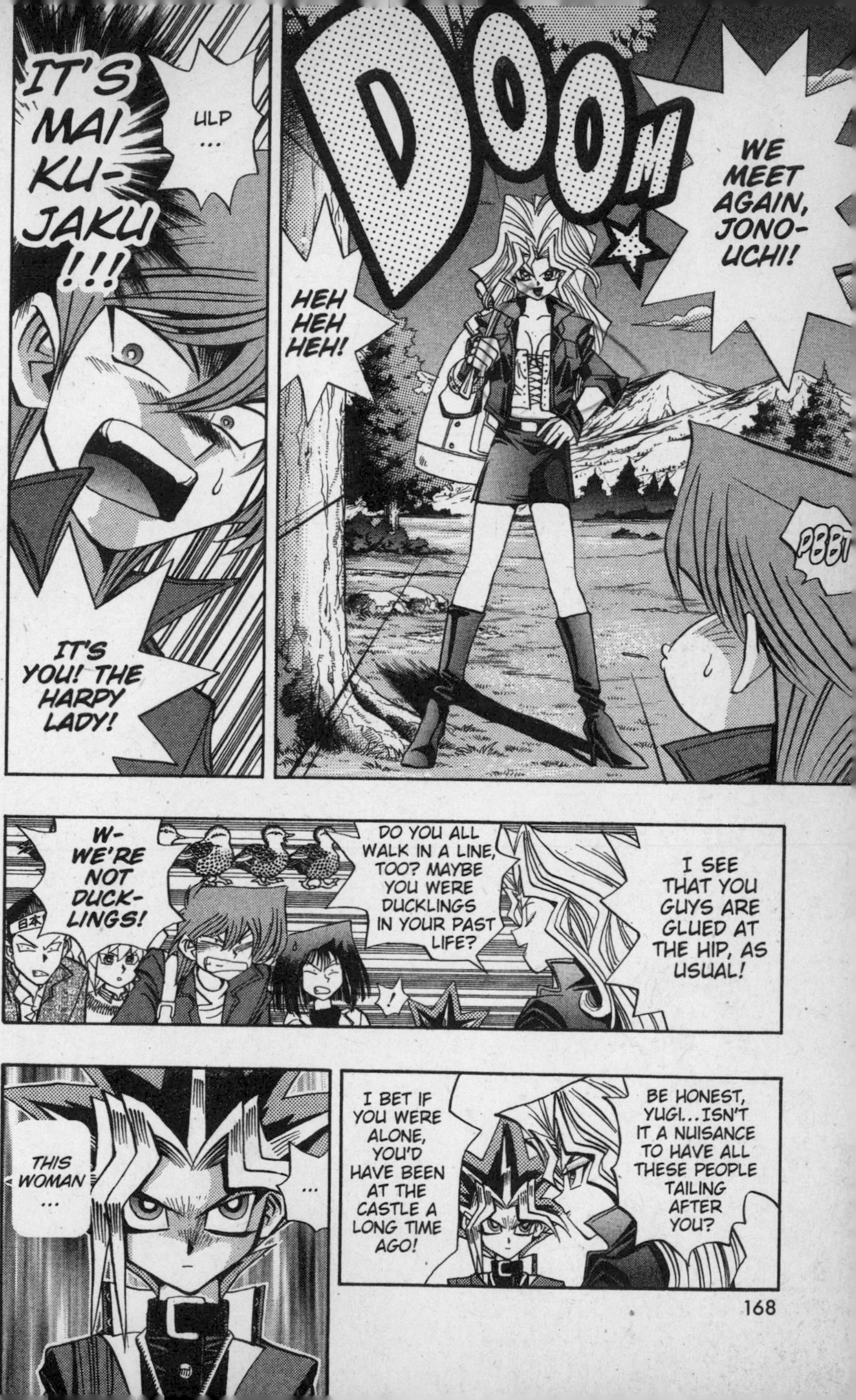
DOOOM
WE MEET AGAIN, JONO-UCHI!
HEH HEH HEH!
PBBT
IT'S MAI KU-JAKU!!!
ULP ...
IT'S YOU! THE HARPY LADY!
I SEE THAT YOU GUYS ARE GLUED AT THE HIP, AS USUAL!
DO YOU ALL WALK IN A LINE, TOO? MAYBE YOU WERE DUCKLINGS IN YOUR PAST LIFE?
!
W-WE'RE NOT DUCK-LINGS!
日本
BE HONEST, YUGI...ISN'T IT A NUISANCE TO HAVE ALL THESE PEOPLE TAILING AFTER YOU?
I BET IF YOU WERE ALONE, YOU'D HAVE BEEN AT THE CASTLE A LONG TIME AGO!
...
THIS WOMAN ...

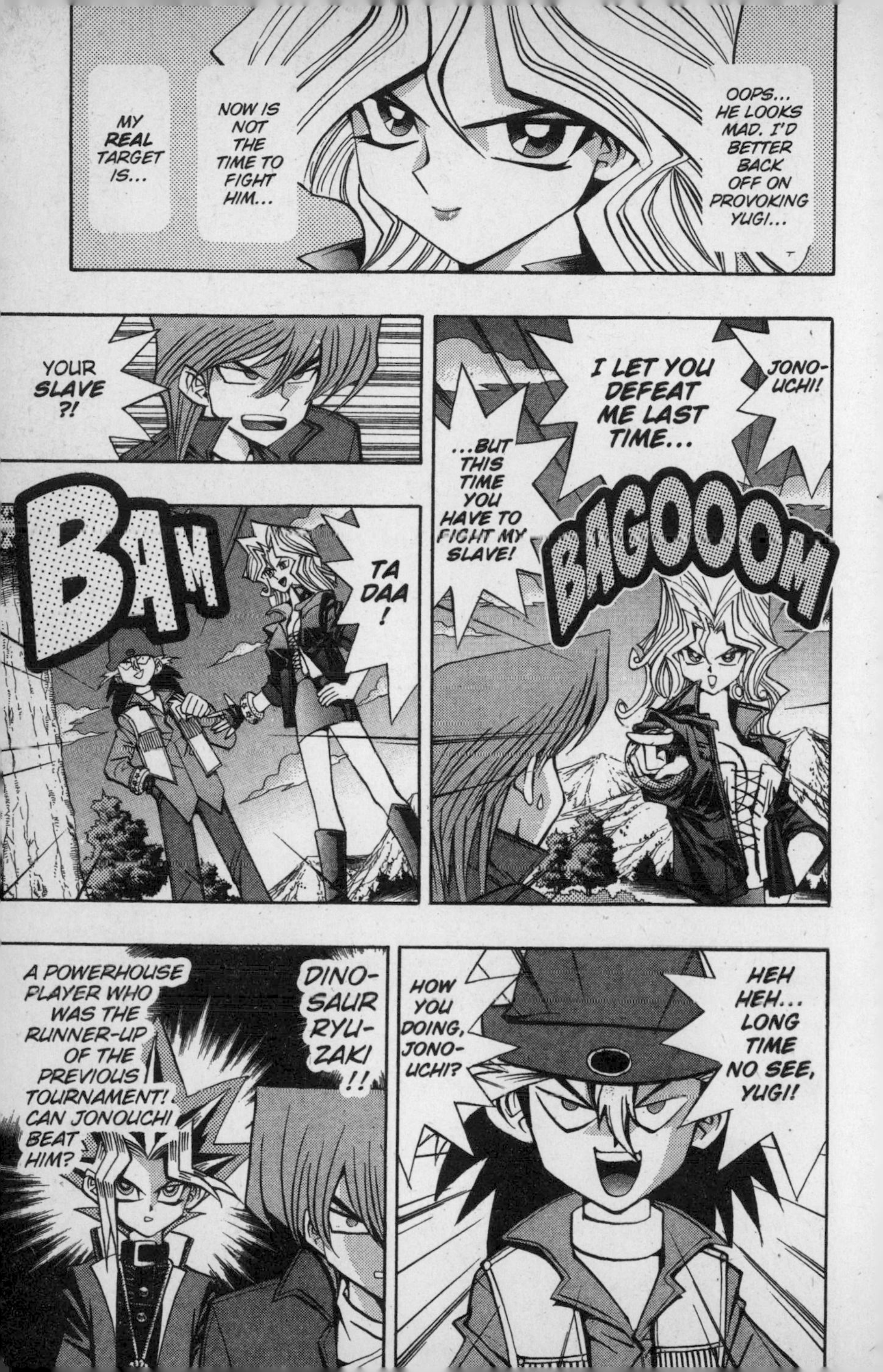
OOPS... HE LOOKS MAD. I'D BETTER BACK OFF ON PROVOKING YUGI...
NOW IS NOT THE TIME TO FIGHT HIM...
MY REAL TARGET IS...
JONO-UCHI!
I LET YOU DEFEAT ME LAST TIME...
...BUT THIS TIME YOU HAVE TO FIGHT MY SLAVE!
BAGOOOOM
YOUR SLAVE?!
TA DAA!
BAM
HEH HEH... LONG TIME NO SEE, YUGI!
HOW YOU DOING, JONOUCHI?
DINO-SAUR RYU-ZAKI!!
A POWERHOUSE PLAYER WHO WAS THE RUNNER-UP OF THE PREVIOUS TOURNAMENT! CAN JONOUCHI BEAT HIM?

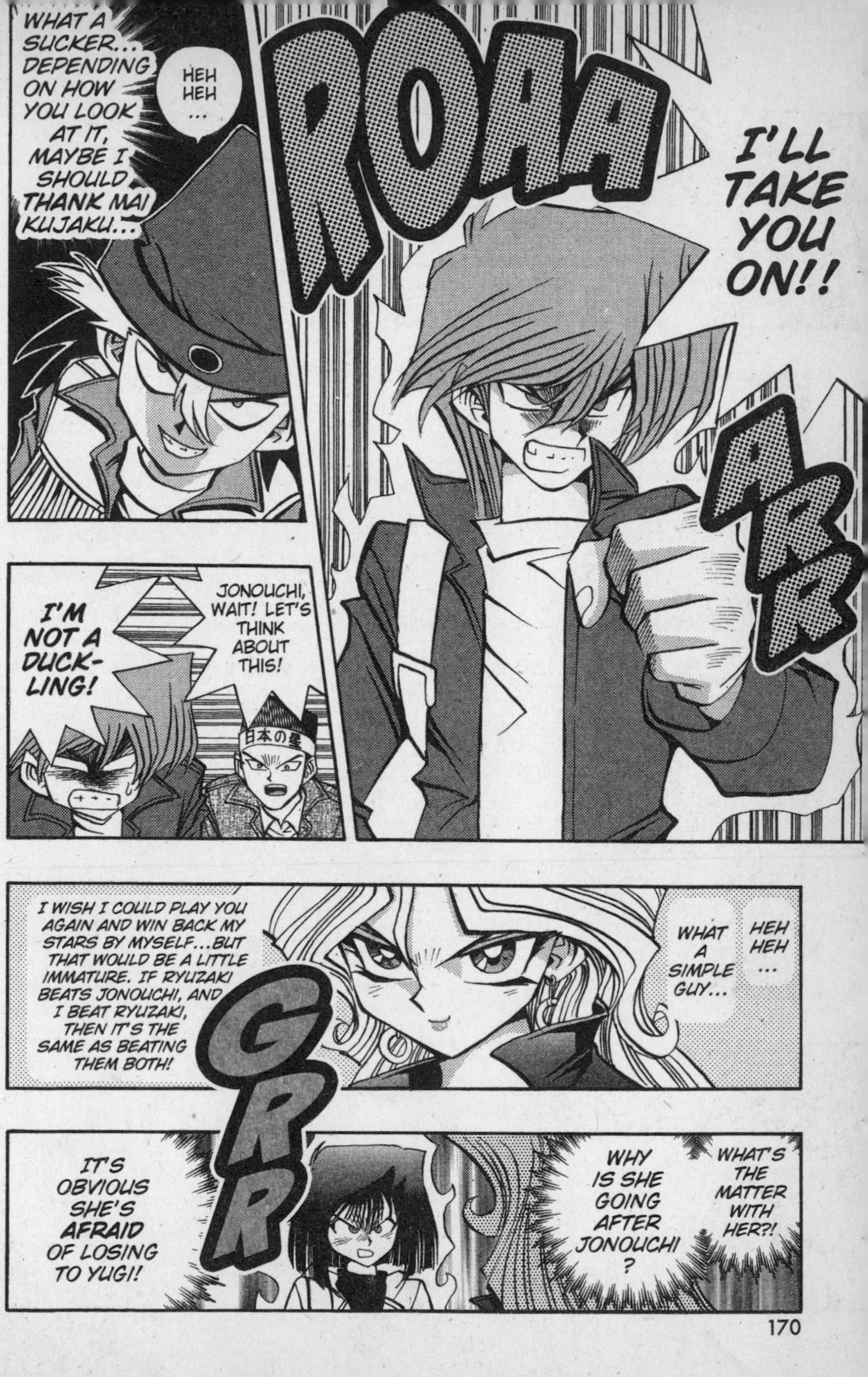
ROAA
I'LL TAKE YOU ON!!
ARR
HEH HEH ...
WHAT A SUCKER... DEPENDING ON HOW YOU LOOK AT IT, MAYBE I SHOULD THANK MAI KUJAKU...
JONOUCHI, WAIT! LET'S THINK ABOUT THIS!
日本の星
I'M NOT A DUCK-LING!
HEH HEH ...
WHAT A SIMPLE GUY...
I WISH I COULD PLAY YOU AGAIN AND WIN BACK MY STARS BY MYSELF...BUT THAT WOULD BE A LITTLE IMMATURE. IF RYUZAKI BEATS JONOUCHI, AND I BEAT RYUZAKI, THEN IT'S THE SAME AS BEATING THEM BOTH!
GRR
WHAT'S THE MATTER WITH HER?!
WHY IS SHE GOING AFTER JONOUCHI ?
IT'S OBVIOUS SHE'S AFRAID OF LOSING TO YUGI!

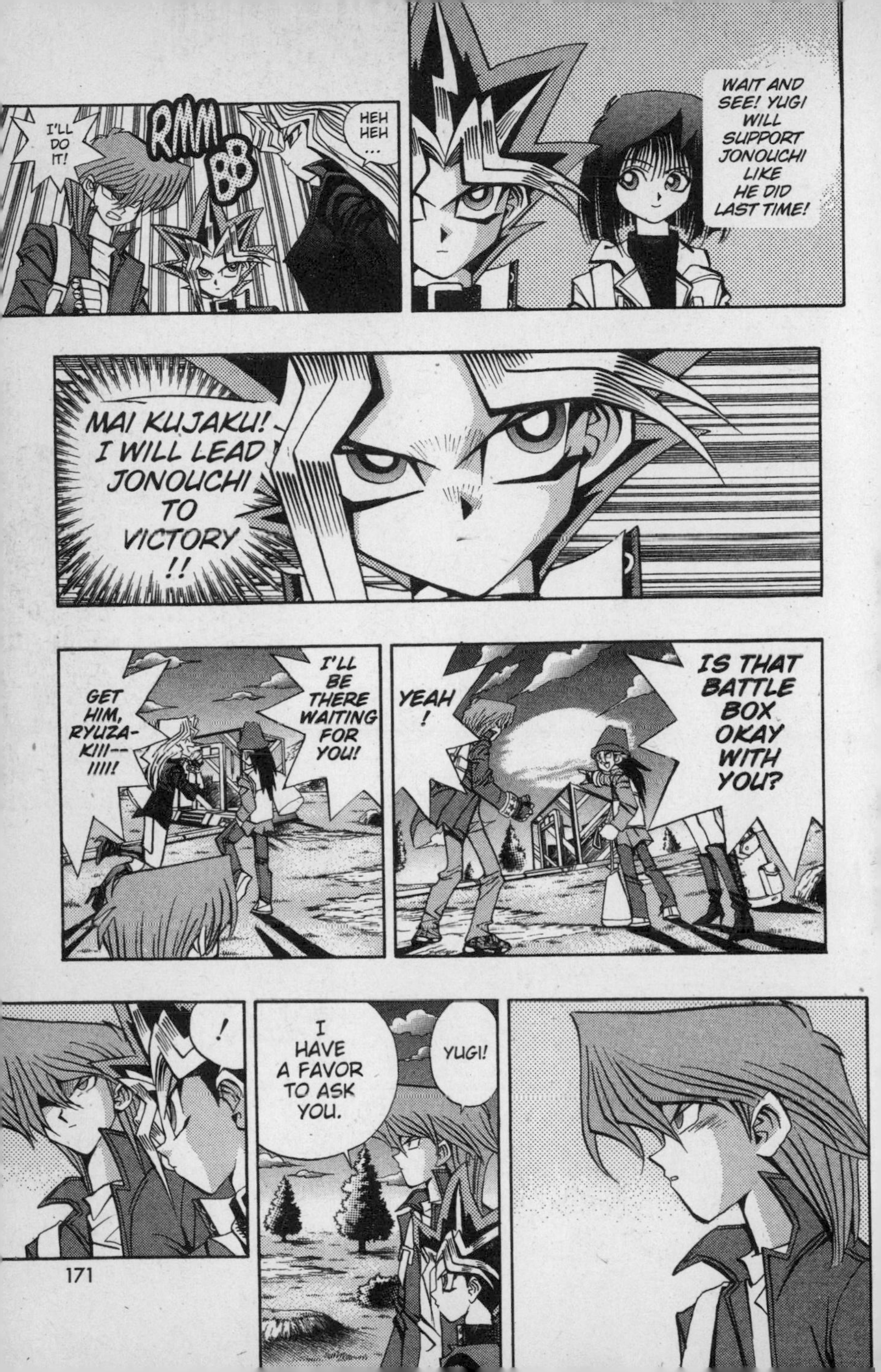
WAIT AND SEE! YUGI WILL SUPPORT JONOUCHI LIKE HE DID LAST TIME!
HEH HEH ...
RMM BB
I'LL DO IT!
MAI KUJAKU! I WILL LEAD JONOUCHI TO VICTORY !!
IS THAT BATTLE BOX OKAY WITH YOU?
YEAH!
I'LL BE THERE WAITING FOR YOU!
GET HIM, RYUZA-KIII-- !!!!!
YUGI!
I HAVE A FAVOR TO ASK YOU.
!

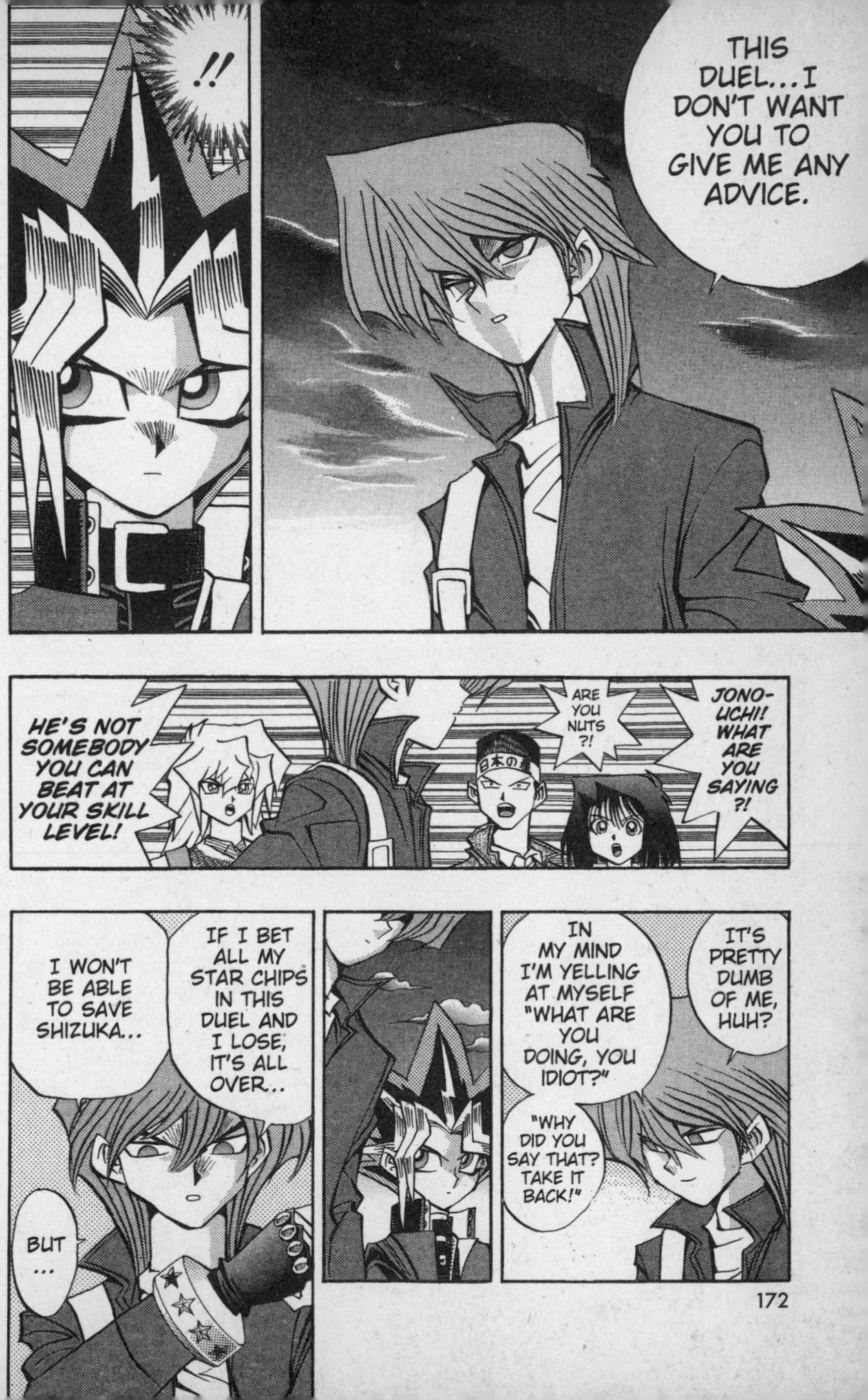
THIS DUEL...I DON'T WANT YOU TO GIVE ME ANY ADVICE.
!!
JONO-UCHI! WHAT ARE YOU SAYING?!
ARE YOU NUTS?!
HE'S NOT SOMEBODY YOU CAN BEAT AT YOUR SKILL LEVEL!
IT'S PRETTY DUMB OF ME, HUH?
IN MY MIND I'M YELLING AT MYSELF "WHAT ARE YOU DOING, YOU IDIOT?"
"WHY DID YOU SAY THAT? TAKE IT BACK!"
IF I BET ALL MY STAR CHIPS IN THIS DUEL AND I LOSE, IT'S ALL OVER...
I WON'T BE ABLE TO SAVE SHIZUKA...
BUT...

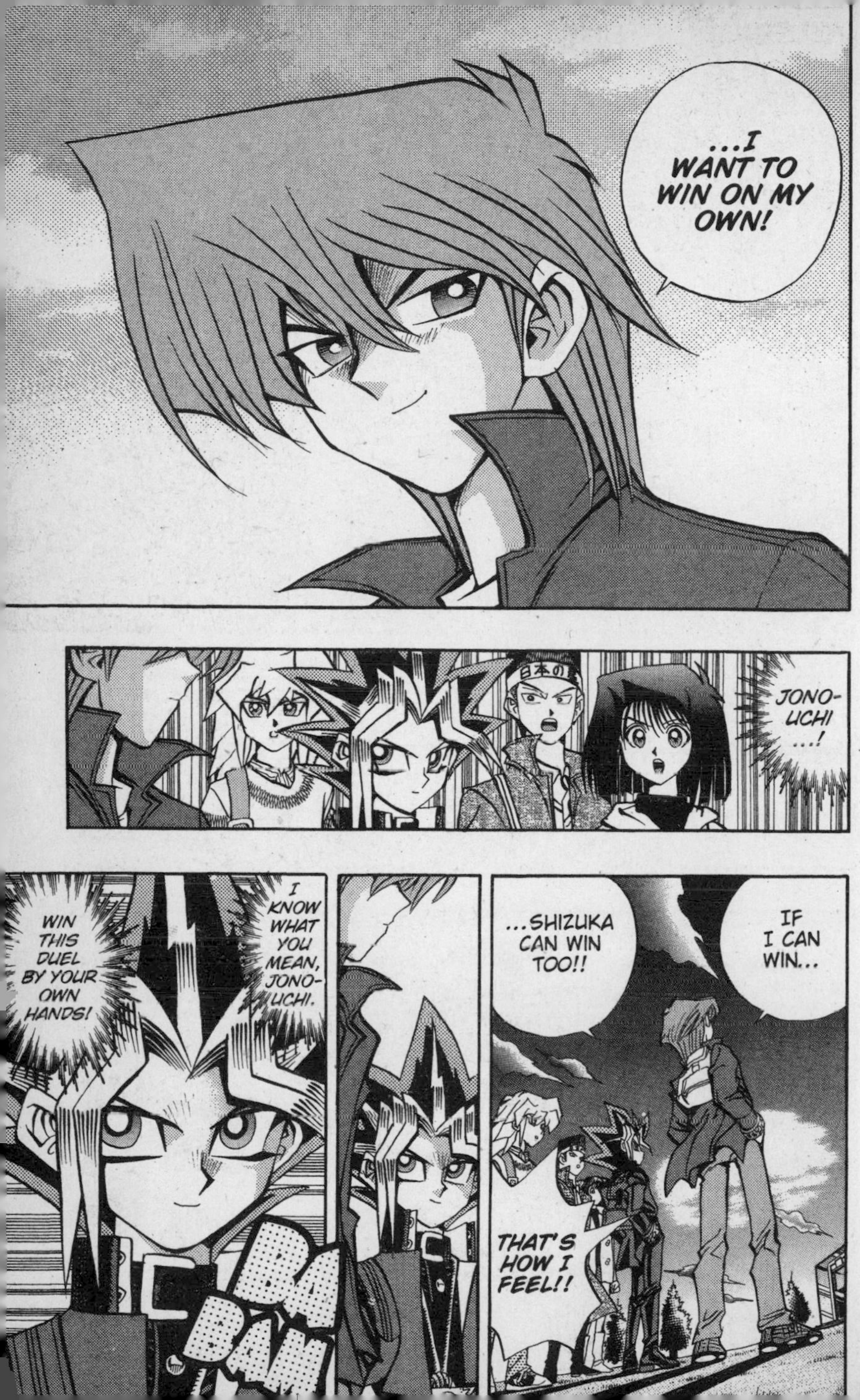
...I WANT TO WIN ON MY OWN!
JONO-UCHI ...!
IF I CAN WIN...
...SHIZUKA CAN WIN TOO!!
THAT'S HOW I FEEL!!
I KNOW WHAT YOU MEAN, JONO-UCHI.
WIN THIS DUEL BY YOUR OWN HANDS!
BA BAM

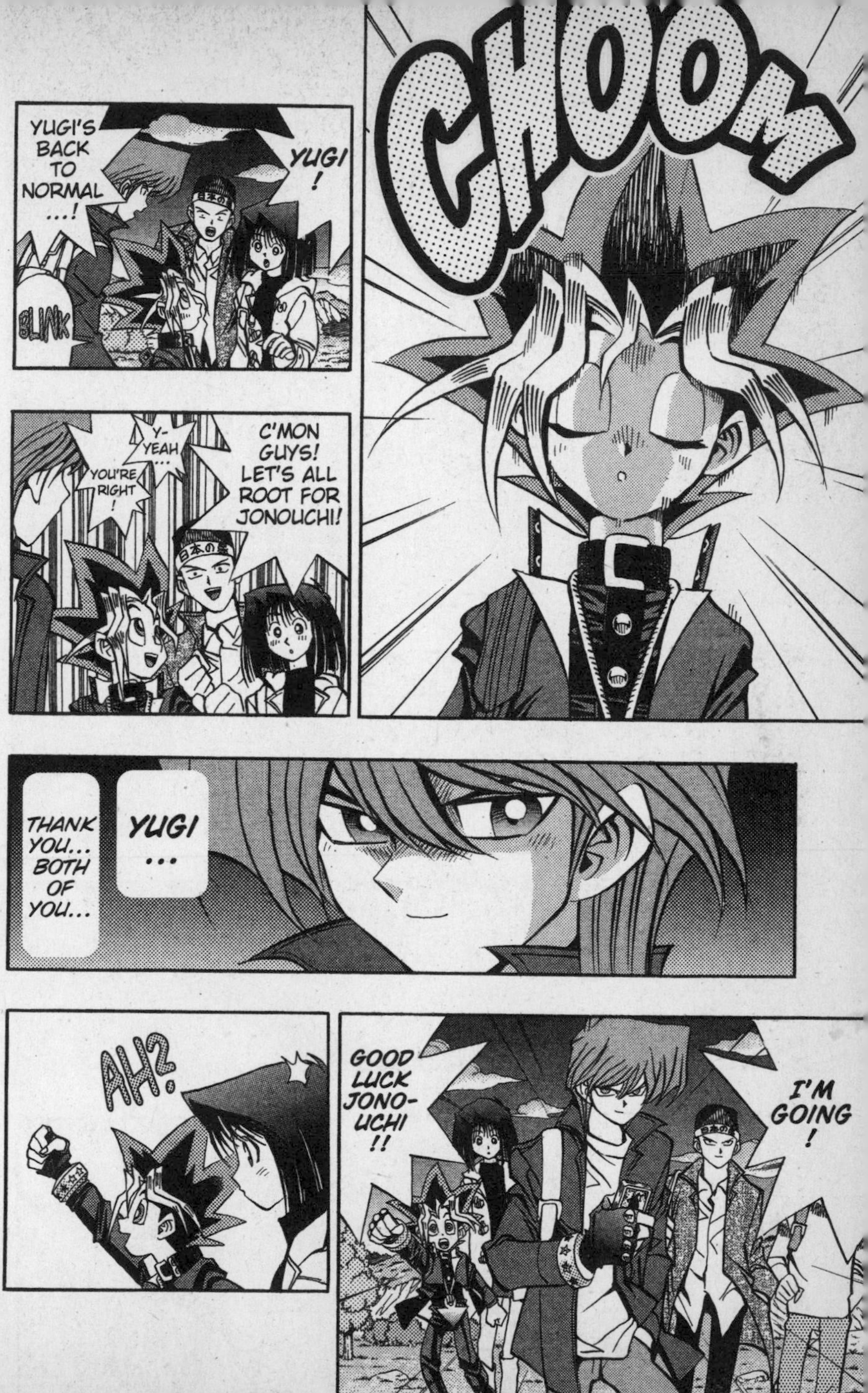
CHOOM
YUGI!
YUGI'S BACK TO NORMAL...!
BLINK
C'MON GUYS! LET'S ALL ROOT FOR JONOUCHI!
Y-YEAH...
YOU'RE RIGHT!
YUGI...
THANK YOU... BOTH OF YOU...
I'M GOING!
GOOD LUCK JONO-UCHI!!
AH?

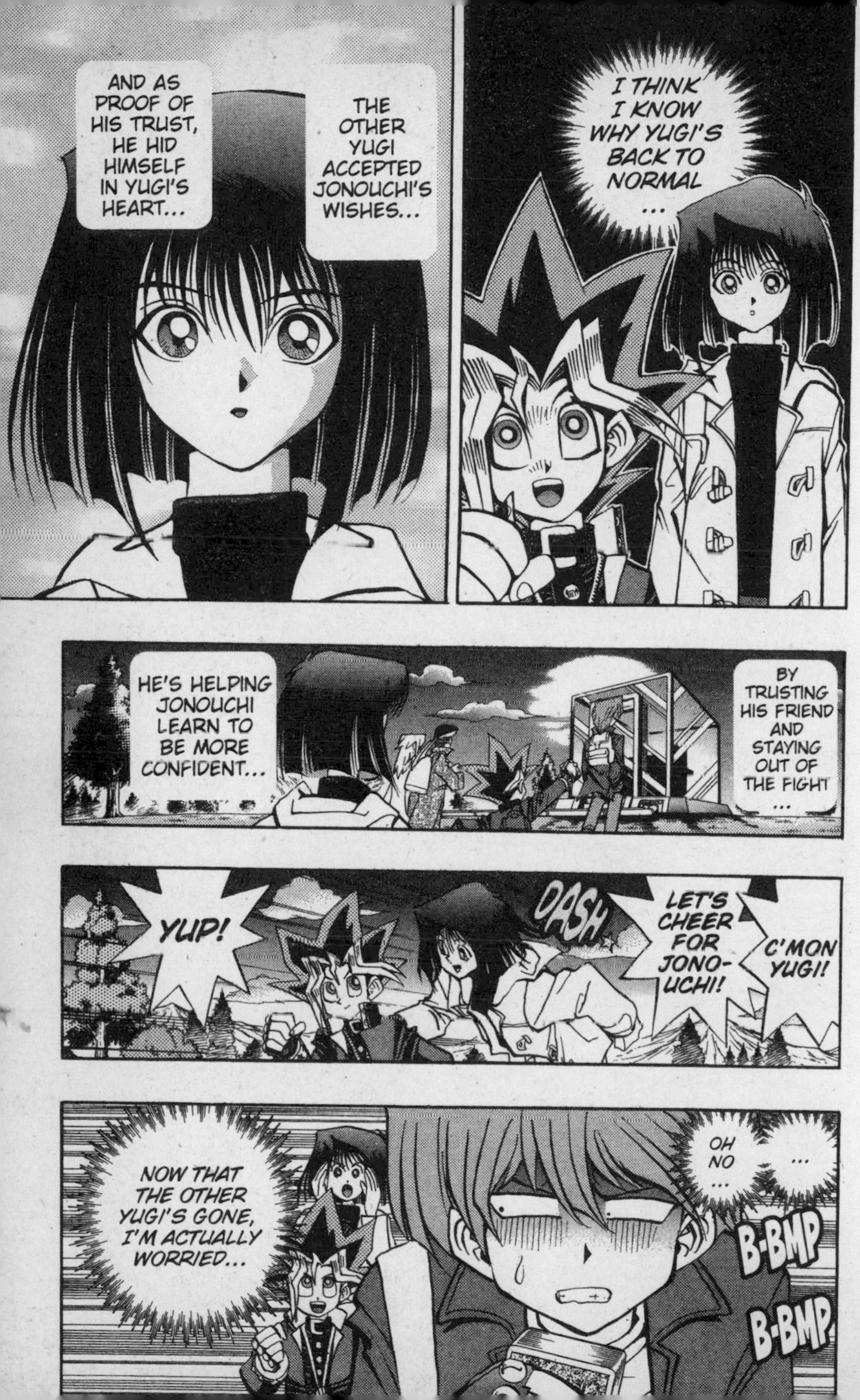
I THINK I KNOW WHY YUGI'S BACK TO NORMAL ...
THE OTHER YUGI ACCEPTED JONOUCHI'S WISHES...
AND AS PROOF OF HIS TRUST, HE HID HIMSELF IN YUGI'S HEART...
BY TRUSTING HIS FRIEND AND STAYING OUT OF THE FIGHT ...
HE'S HELPING JONOUCHI LEARN TO BE MORE CONFIDENT...
C'MON YUGI!
LET'S CHEER FOR JONO-UCHI!
DASH
YUP!
...
OH NO ...
B-BMP
B-BMP
NOW THAT THE OTHER YUGI'S GONE, I'M ACTUALLY WORRIED...

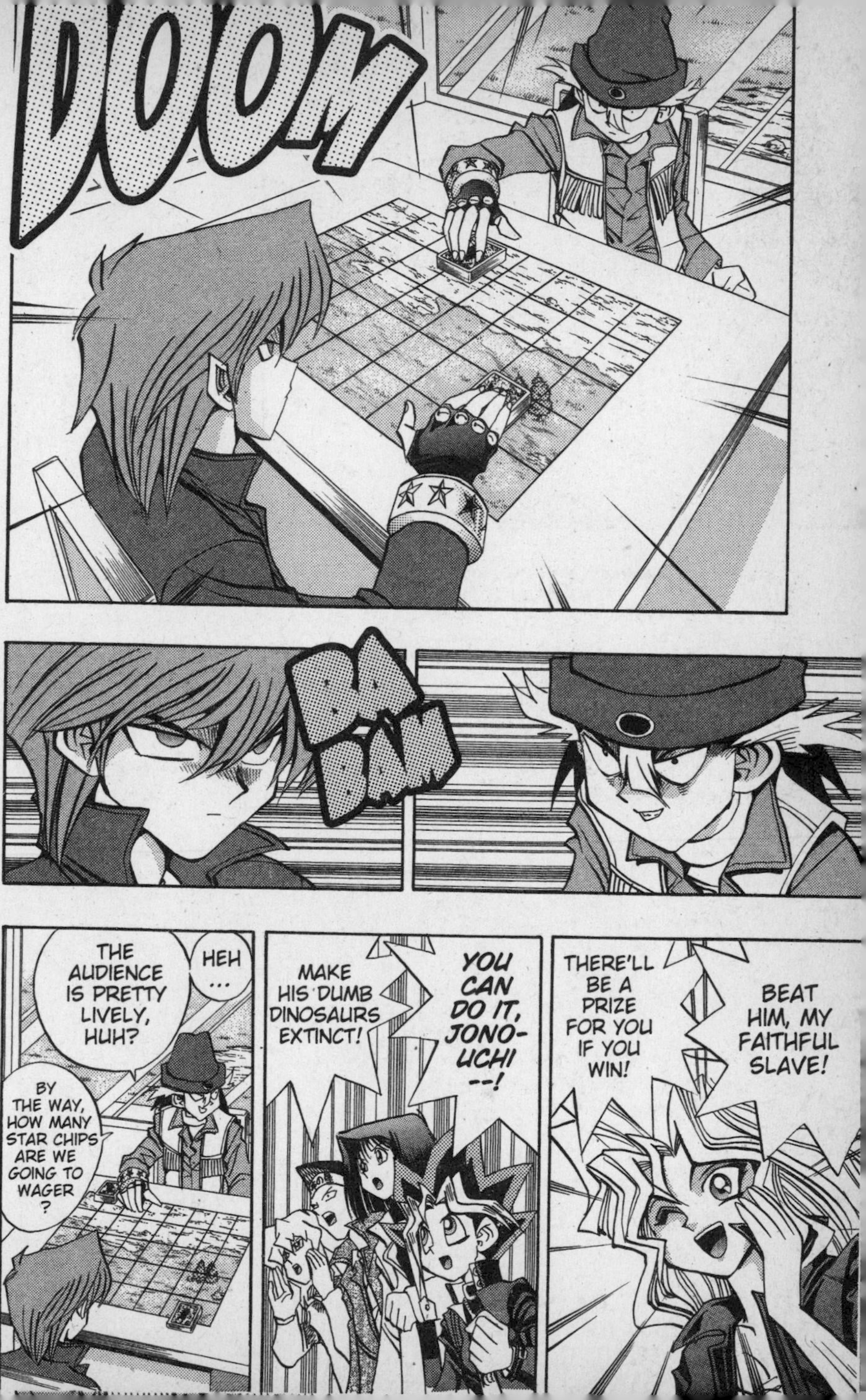
DOOM
BEAT HIM, MY FAITHFUL SLAVE!
THERE'LL BE A PRIZE FOR YOU IF YOU WIN!
YOU CAN DO IT, JONOUCHI--!
MAKE HIS DUMB DINOSAURS EXTINCT!
HEH...
THE AUDIENCE IS PRETTY LIVELY, HUH?
BY THE WAY, HOW MANY STAR CHIPS ARE WE GOING TO WAGER?

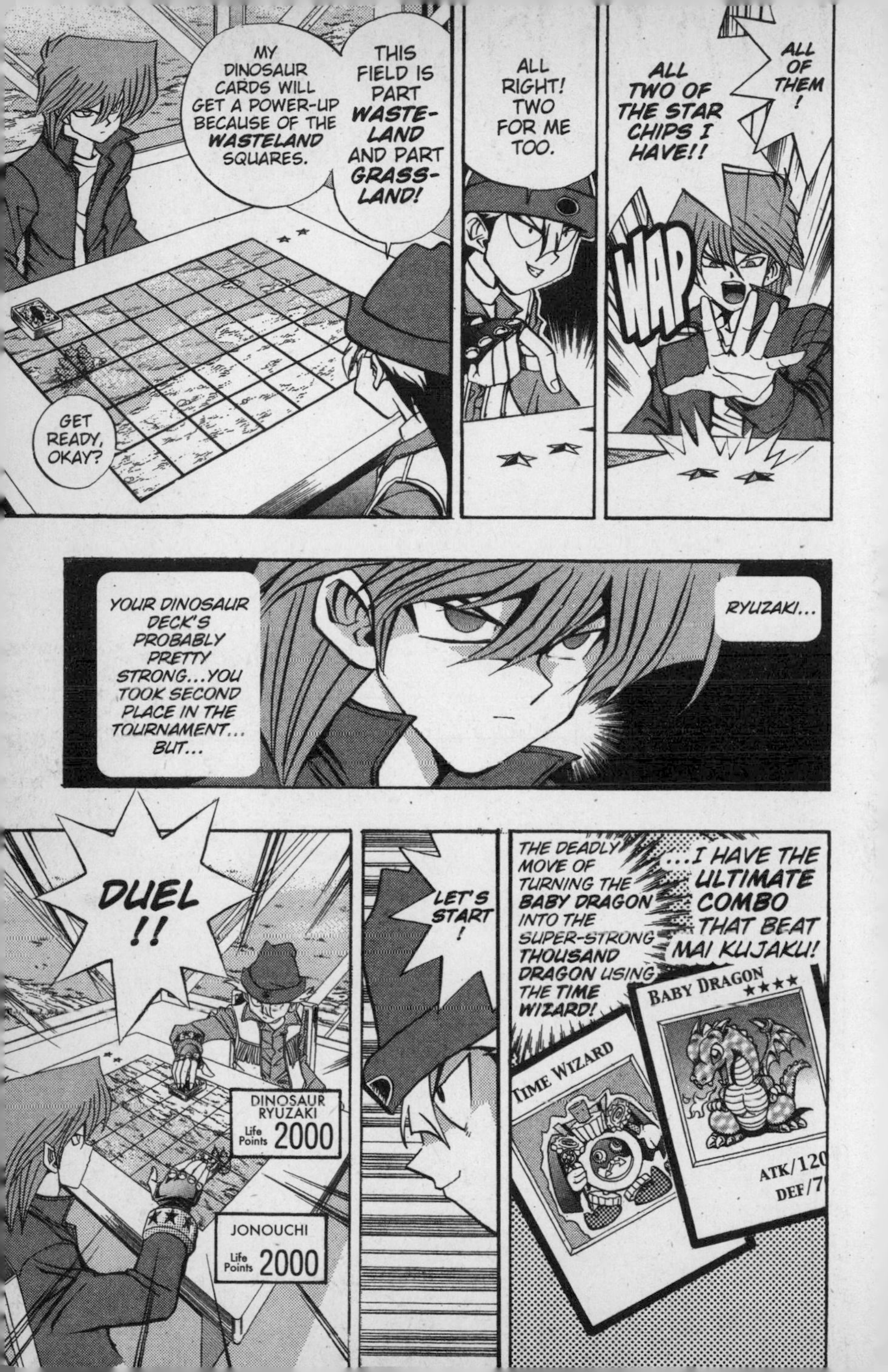
ALL OF THEM!
ALL TWO OF THE STAR CHIPS I HAVE!!
WAP
ALL RIGHT! TWO FOR ME TOO.
THIS FIELD IS PART WASTELAND AND PART GRASSLAND!
MY DINOSAUR CARDS WILL GET A POWER-UP BECAUSE OF THE WASTELAND SQUARES.
GET READY, OKAY?
RYUZAKI...
YOUR DINOSAUR DECK'S PROBABLY PRETTY STRONG...YOU TOOK SECOND PLACE IN THE TOURNAMENT... BUT...
...I HAVE THE ULTIMATE COMBO THAT BEAT MAI KUJAKU!
THE DEADLY MOVE OF TURNING THE BABY DRAGON INTO THE SUPER-STRONG THOUSAND DRAGON USING THE TIME WIZARD!
BABY DRAGON
ATK/120
DEF/7
TIME WIZARD
LET'S START!
DUEL!!
DINOSAUR RYUZAKI
Life Points 2000
JONOUCHI
Life Points 2000

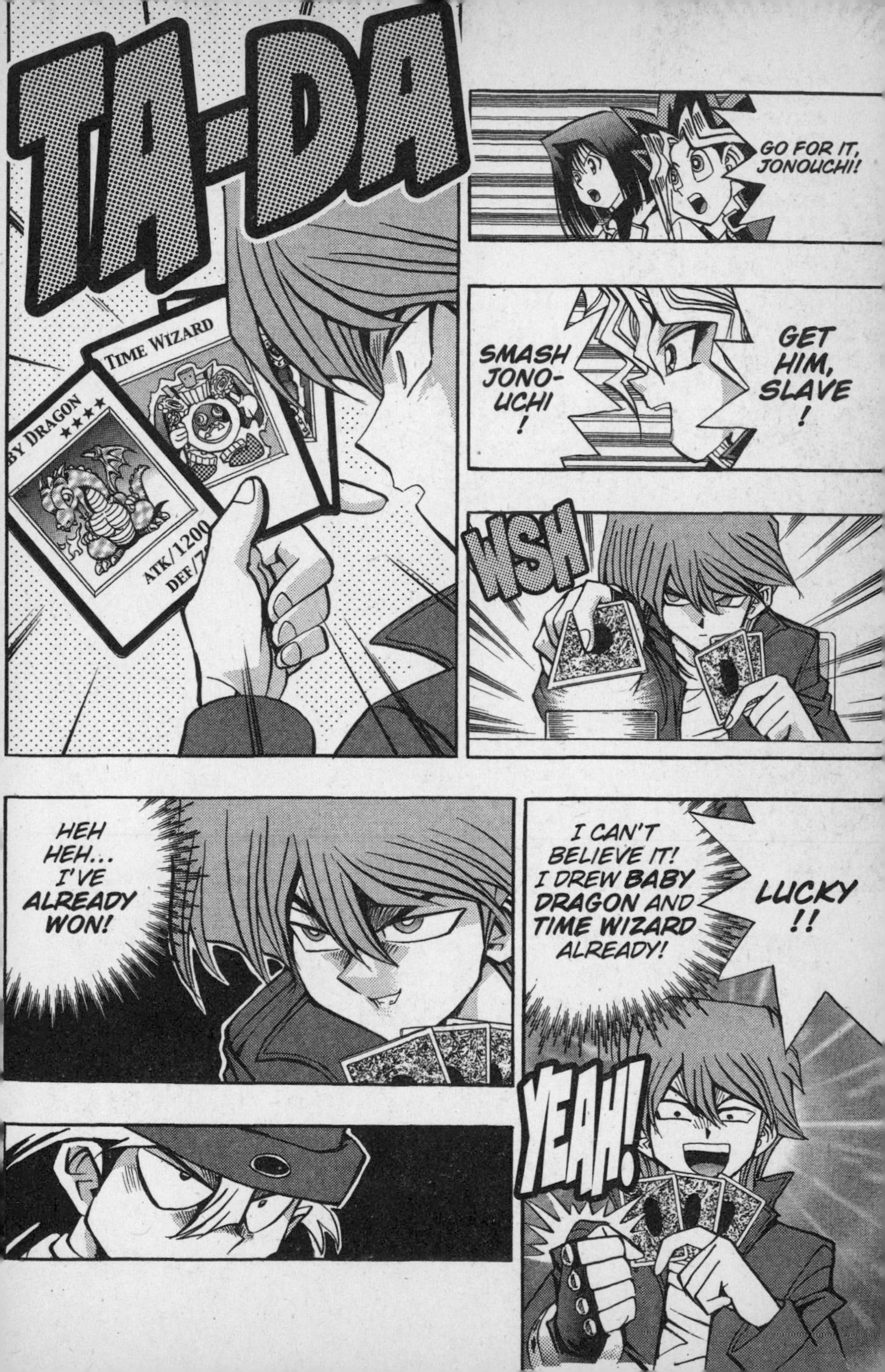
GO FOR IT, JONOUCHI!
GET HIM, SLAVE!
SMASH JONOUCHI!
WSH
TA-DA
TIME WIZARD
ATK/1200
LUCKY!!
I CAN'T BELIEVE IT! I DREW BABY DRAGON AND TIME WIZARD ALREADY!
YEAH!
HEH HEH... I'VE ALREADY WON!

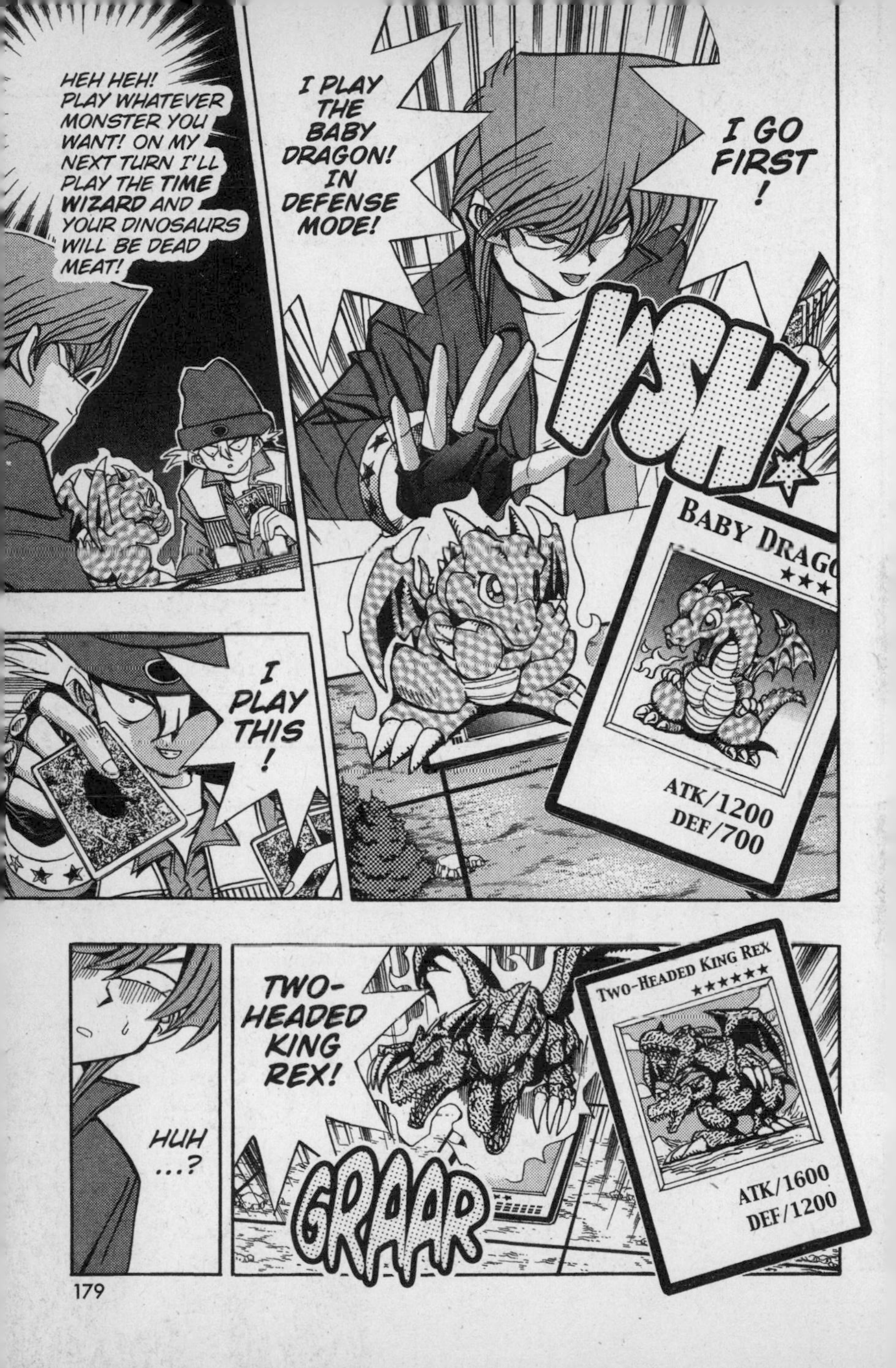
I GO FIRST!
I PLAY THE BABY DRAGON! IN DEFENSE MODE!
VSH
BABY DRAGO
★★★
ATK/1200
DEF/700
HEH HEH! PLAY WHATEVER MONSTER YOU WANT! ON MY NEXT TURN I'LL PLAY THE TIME WIZARD AND YOUR DINOSAURS WILL BE DEAD MEAT!
I PLAY THIS!
TWO-HEADED KING REX!
TWO-HEADED KING REX
★★★★★
ATK/1600
DEF/1200
GRAAR
HUH ...?

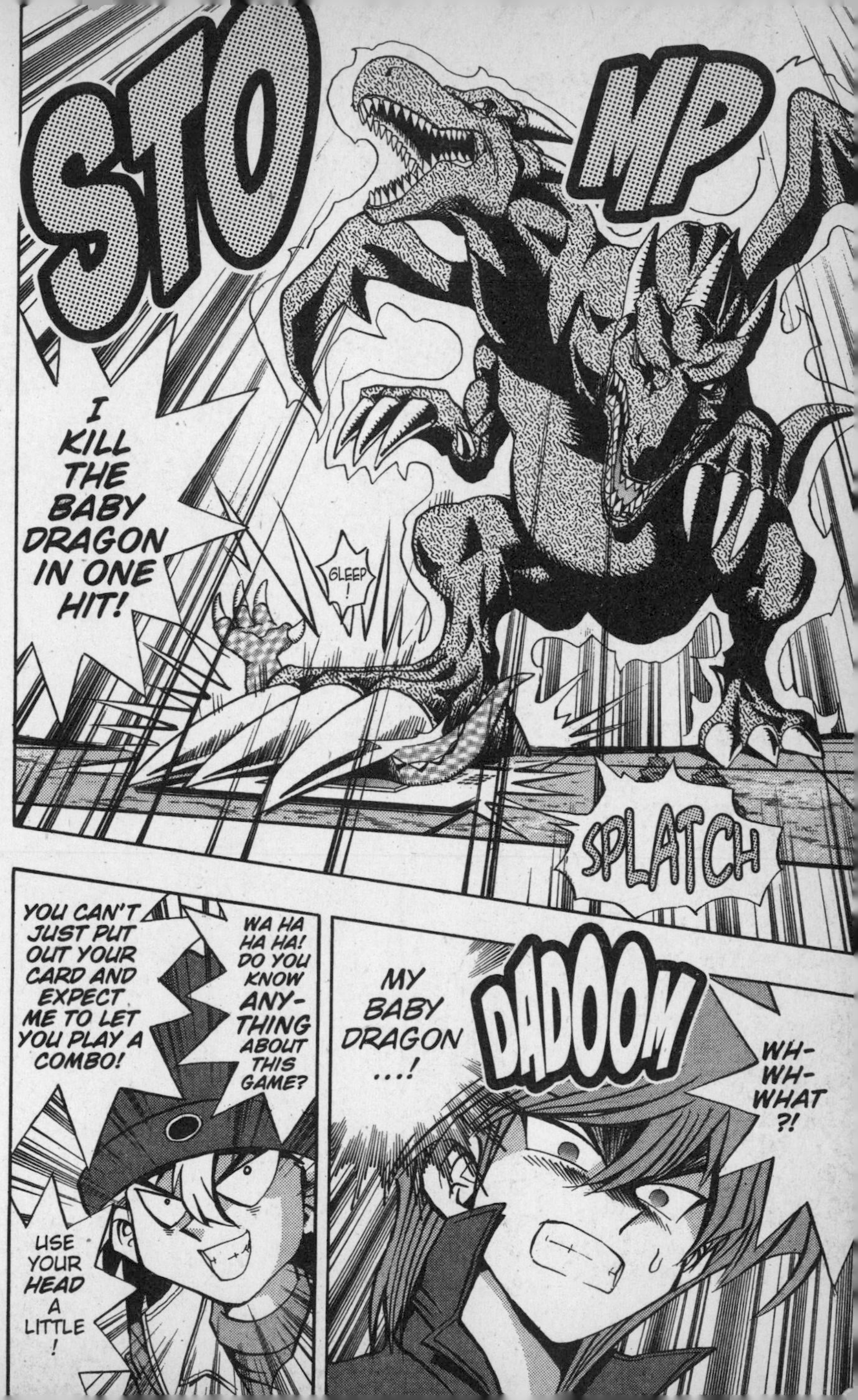
STOMP
I KILL THE BABY DRAGON IN ONE HIT!
GLEEP!
SPLATCH
DADOOM
WH-WH-WHAT?!
MY BABY DRAGON ...!
WA HA HA HA! DO YOU KNOW ANYTHING ABOUT THIS GAME?
YOU CAN'T JUST PUT OUT YOUR CARD AND EXPECT ME TO LET YOU PLAY A COMBO!
USE YOUR HEAD A LITTLE!

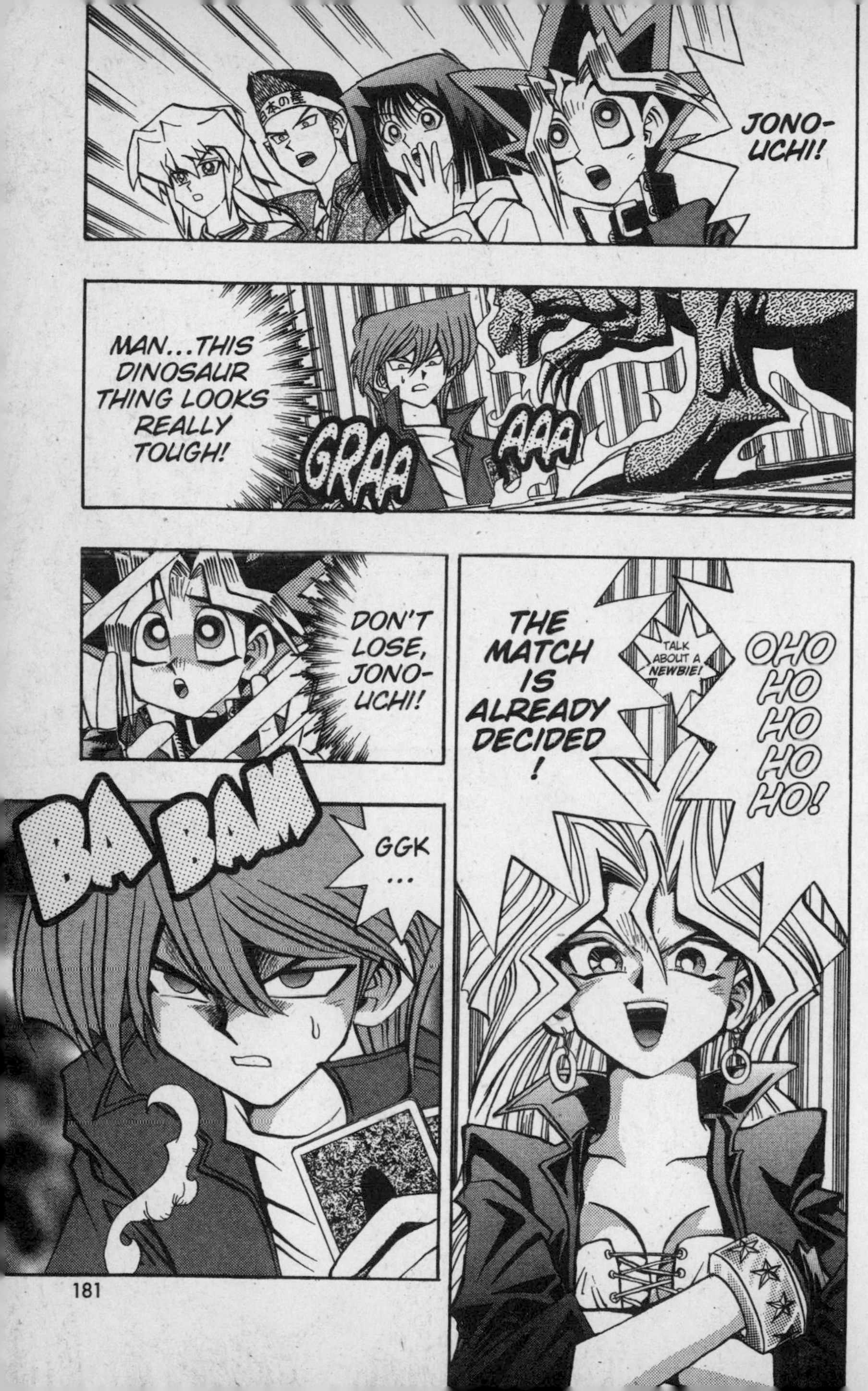
JONO-UCHI!
MAN...THIS DINOSAUR THING LOOKS REALLY TOUGH!
GRAA AAA
OHO HO HO HO HO!
TALK ABOUT A NEWBIE!
THE MATCH IS ALREADY DECIDED!
DON'T LOSE, JONO-UCHI!
BA BAM
GGK ...

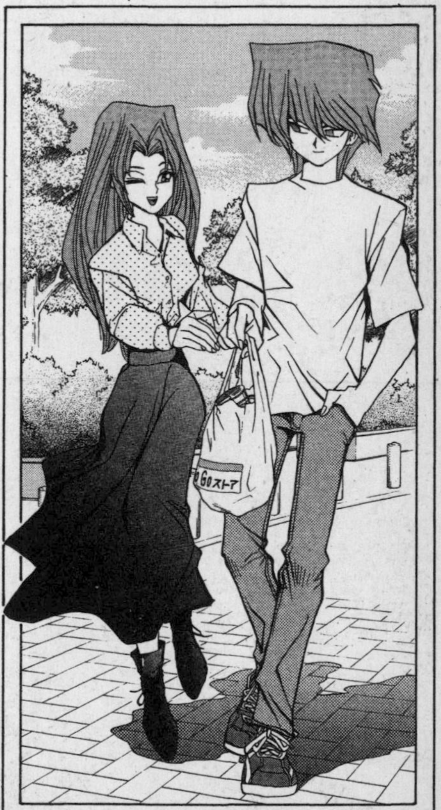
GoGoストア

Duel 19: I Won't Lose!

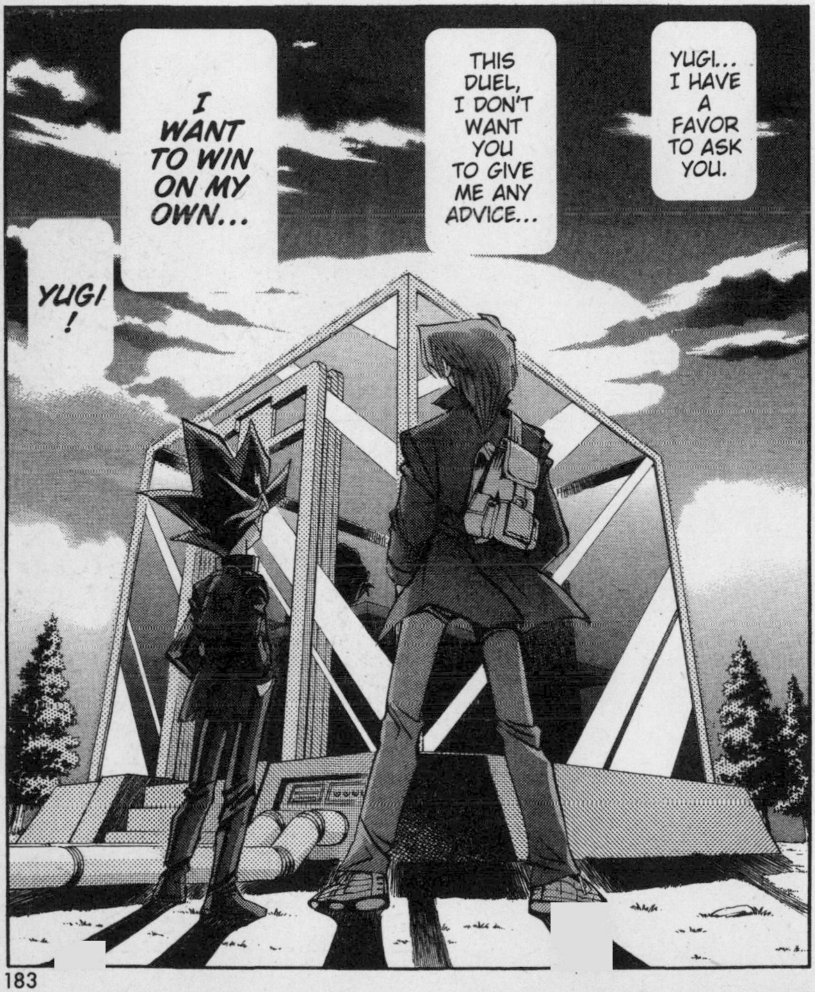
YUGI... I HAVE A FAVOR TO ASK YOU.
THIS DUEL, I DON'T WANT YOU TO GIVE ME ANY ADVICE...
I WANT TO WIN ON MY OWN...
YUGI!

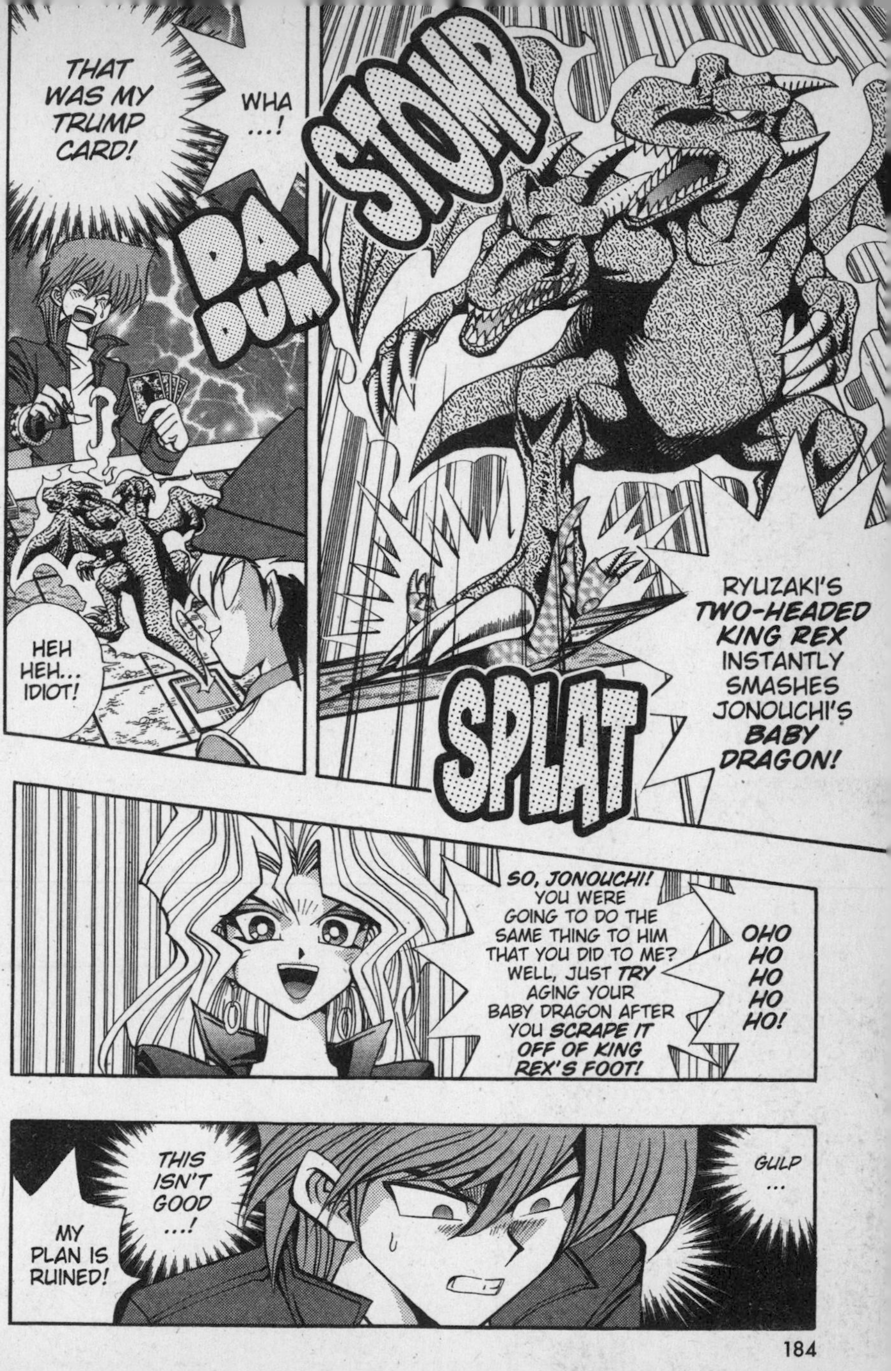
STOMP
DA DUN
SPLAT
RYUZAKI'S TWO-HEADED KING REX INSTANTLY SMASHES JONOUCHI'S BABY DRAGON!
WHA ...!
THAT WAS MY TRUMP CARD!
HEH HEH... IDIOT!
OHO HO HO HO HO!
SO, JONOUCHI! YOU WERE GOING TO DO THE SAME THING TO HIM THAT YOU DID TO ME? WELL, JUST TRY AGING YOUR BABY DRAGON AFTER YOU SCRAPE IT OFF OF KING REX'S FOOT!
GULP ...
THIS ISN'T GOOD ...!
MY PLAN IS RUINED!

READ THIS WAY

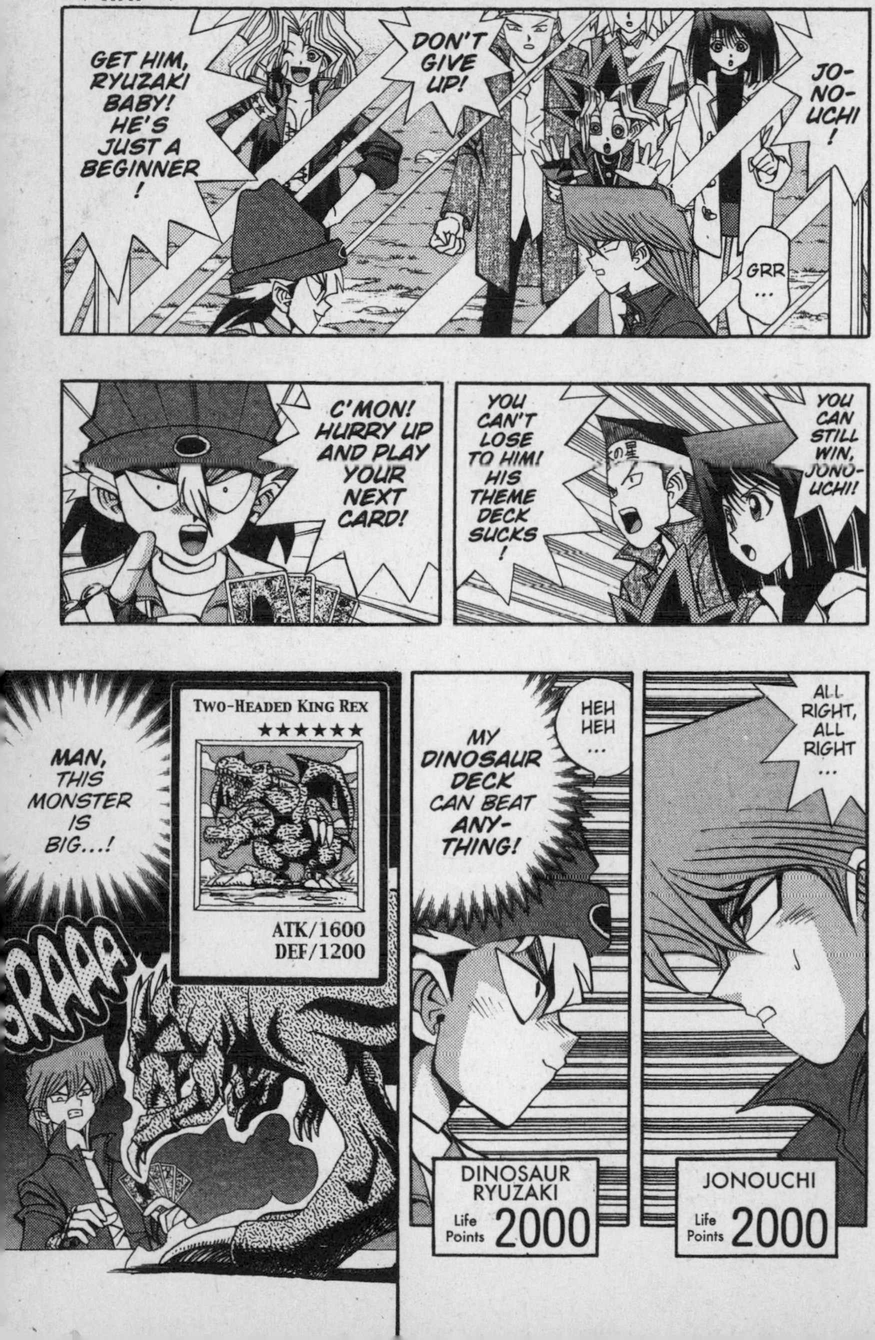
JO-NO-UCHI!
DON'T GIVE UP!
GET HIM, RYUZAKI BABY! HE'S JUST A BEGINNER!
GRR...
YOU CAN STILL WIN, JONOUCHI!
YOU CAN'T LOSE TO HIM! HIS THEME DECK SUCKS!
C'MON! HURRY UP AND PLAY YOUR NEXT CARD!
ALL RIGHT, ALL RIGHT...
JONOUCHI
Life Points 2000
HEH HEH...
MY DINOSAUR DECK CAN BEAT ANYTHING!
DINOSAUR RYUZAKI
Life Points 2000
TWO-HEADED KING REX
ATK/1600
DEF/1200
MAN, THIS MONSTER IS BIG...!

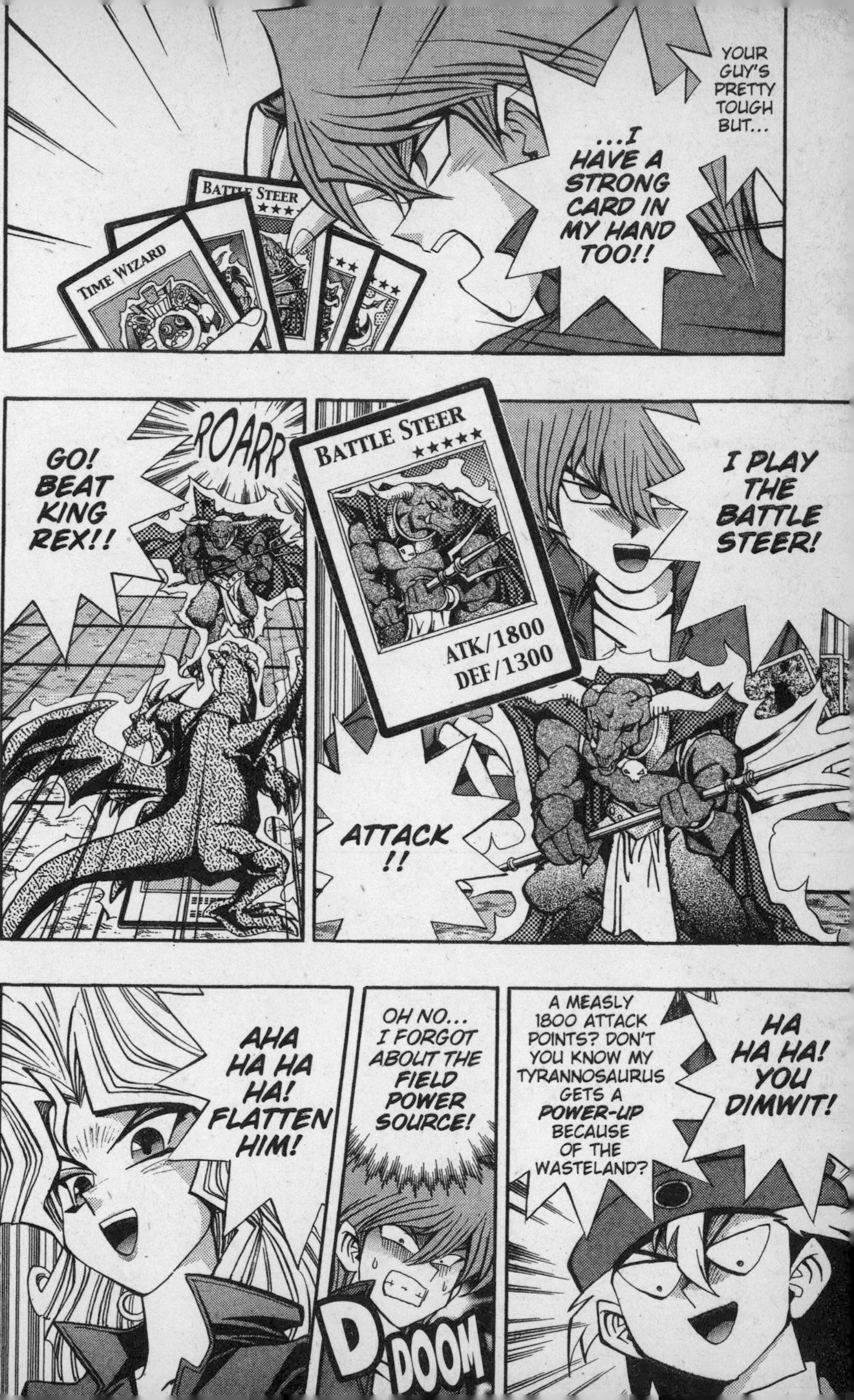
YOUR GUY'S PRETTY TOUGH BUT...
...I HAVE A STRONG CARD IN MY HAND TOO!!
BATTLE STEER
TIME WIZARD
I PLAY THE BATTLE STEER!
BATTLE STEER
ATK/1800
DEF/1300
ATTACK!!
ROARR
GO! BEAT KING REX!!
HA HA HA! YOU DIMWIT!
A MEASLY 1800 ATTACK POINTS? DON'T YOU KNOW MY TYRANNOSAURUS GETS A POWER-UP BECAUSE OF THE WASTELAND?
OH NO... I FORGOT ABOUT THE FIELD POWER SOURCE!
D DOOM
AHA HA HA HA! FLATTEN HIM!

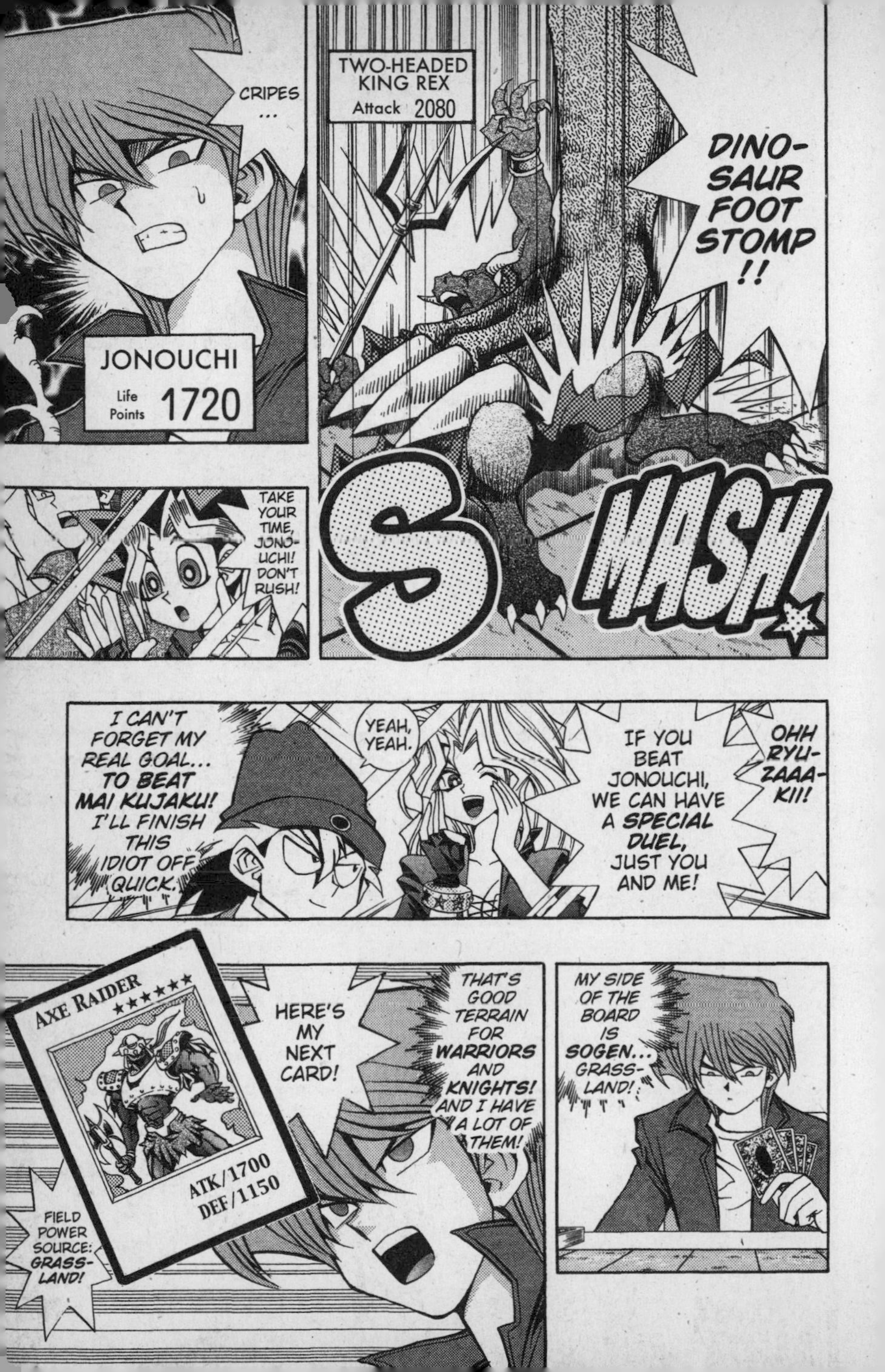
TWO-HEADED KING REX
Attack 2080
DINOSAUR FOOT STOMP!!
SMASH
CRIPES...
JONOUCHI
Life Points 1720
TAKE YOUR TIME, JONOUCHI! DON'T RUSH!
OHH RYUZAAAKII!
IF YOU BEAT JONOUCHI, WE CAN HAVE A SPECIAL DUEL, JUST YOU AND ME!
YEAH, YEAH.
I CAN'T FORGET MY REAL GOAL... TO BEAT MAI KUJAKU! I'LL FINISH THIS IDIOT OFF QUICK.
MY SIDE OF THE BOARD IS SOGEN... GRASSLAND!
THAT'S GOOD TERRAIN FOR WARRIORS AND KNIGHTS! AND I HAVE A LOT OF THEM!
HERE'S MY NEXT CARD!
AXE RAIDER
ATK/1700
DEF/1150
FIELD POWER SOURCE: GRASSLAND!

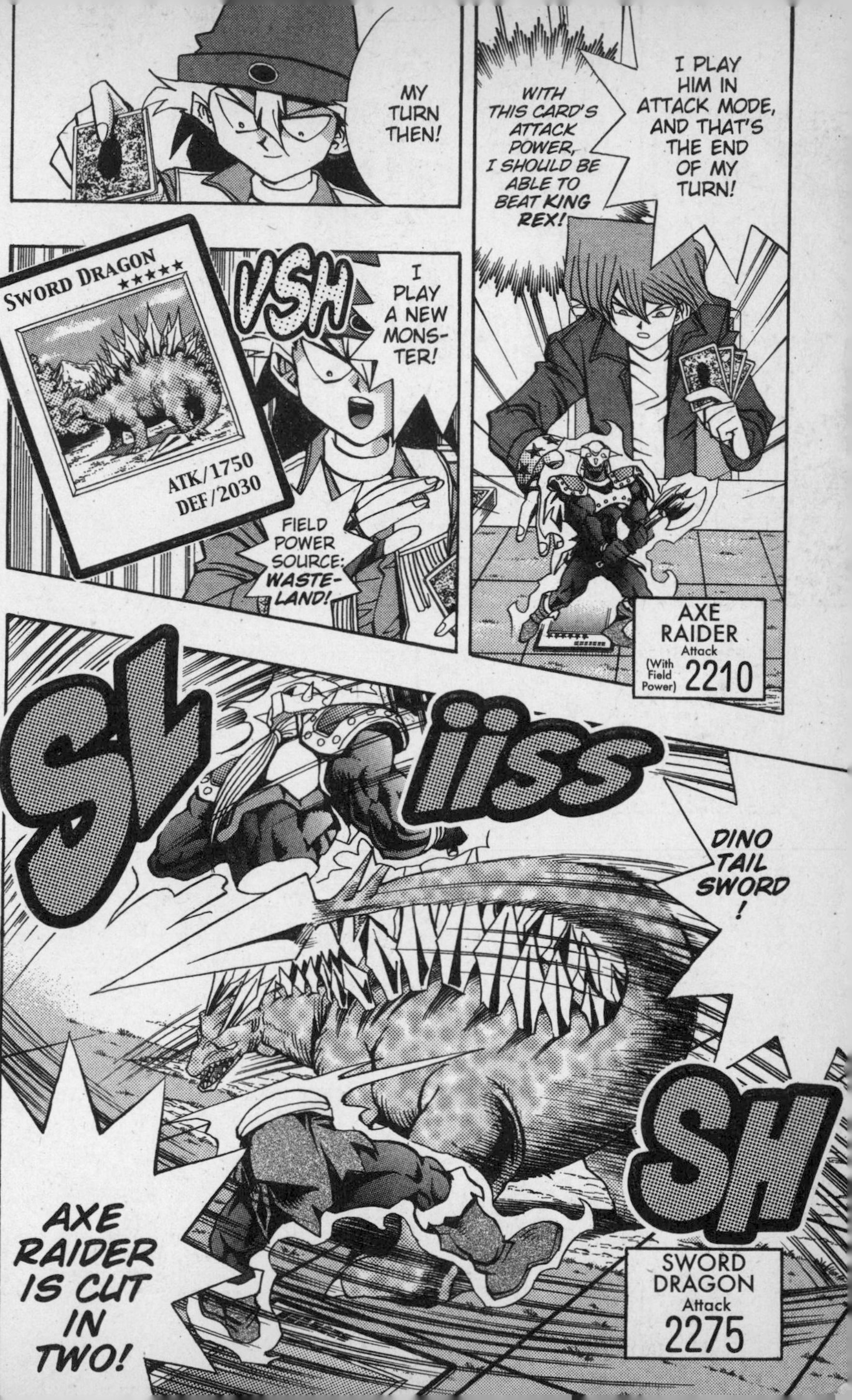
I PLAY HIM IN ATTACK MODE, AND THAT'S THE END OF MY TURN!
WITH THIS CARD'S ATTACK POWER, I SHOULD BE ABLE TO BEAT KING REX!
AXE RAIDER Attack (With Field Power) 2210
MY TURN THEN!
I PLAY A NEW MONSTER!
VSH
SWORD DRAGON
ATK/1750
DEF/2030
FIELD POWER SOURCE: WASTELAND!
Sh iiss
DINO TAIL SWORD!
SH
SWORD DRAGON Attack 2275
AXE RAIDER IS CUT IN TWO!

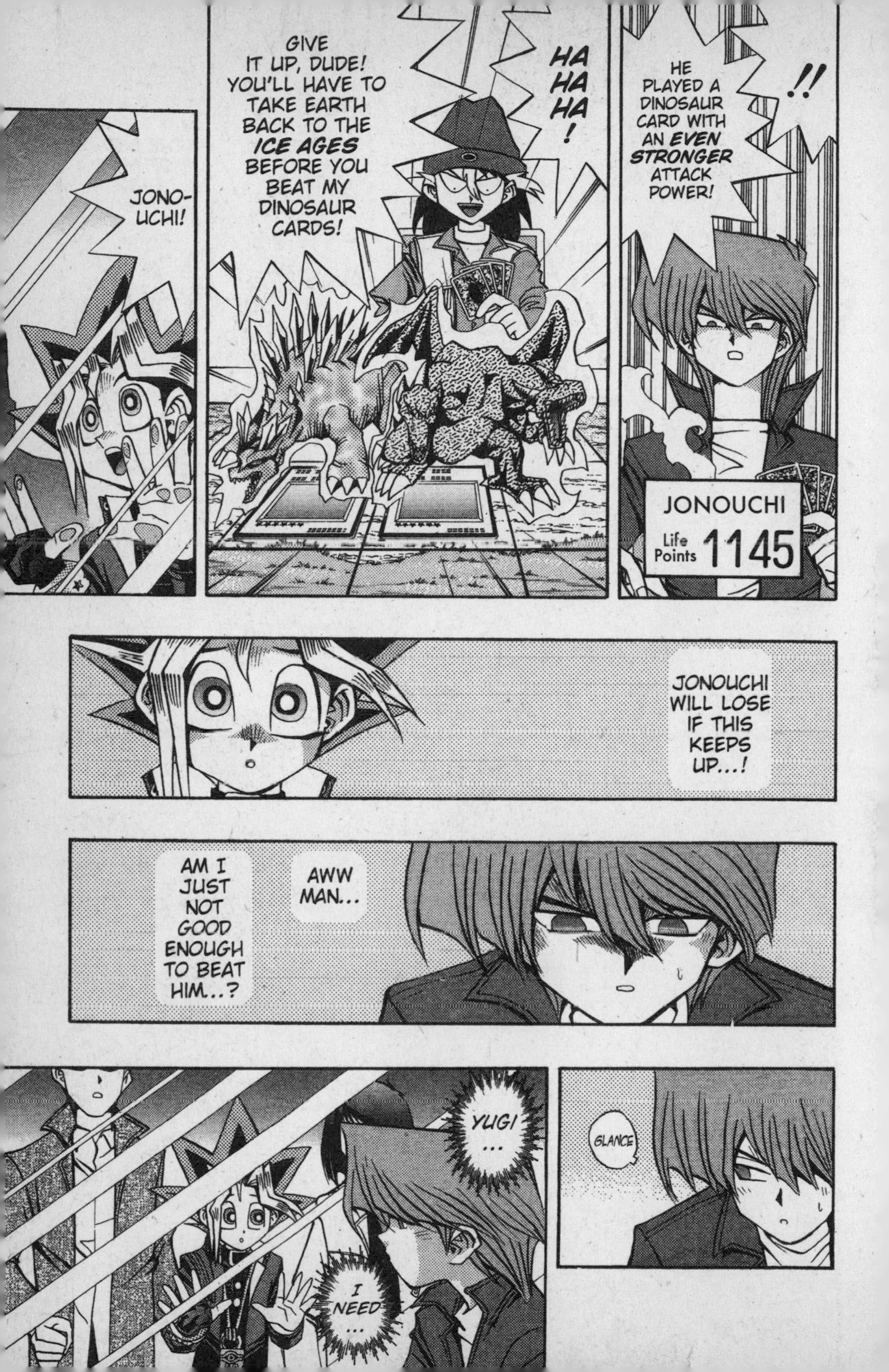
!!
HE PLAYED A DINOSAUR CARD WITH AN EVEN STRONGER ATTACK POWER!
JONOUCHI
Life Points 1145
HA HA HA!
GIVE IT UP, DUDE! YOU'LL HAVE TO TAKE EARTH BACK TO THE ICE AGES BEFORE YOU BEAT MY DINOSAUR CARDS!
JONO-UCHI!
JONOUCHI WILL LOSE IF THIS KEEPS UP...!
AWW MAN...
AM I JUST NOT GOOD ENOUGH TO BEAT HIM...?
GLANCE
YUGI ...
I NEED ...

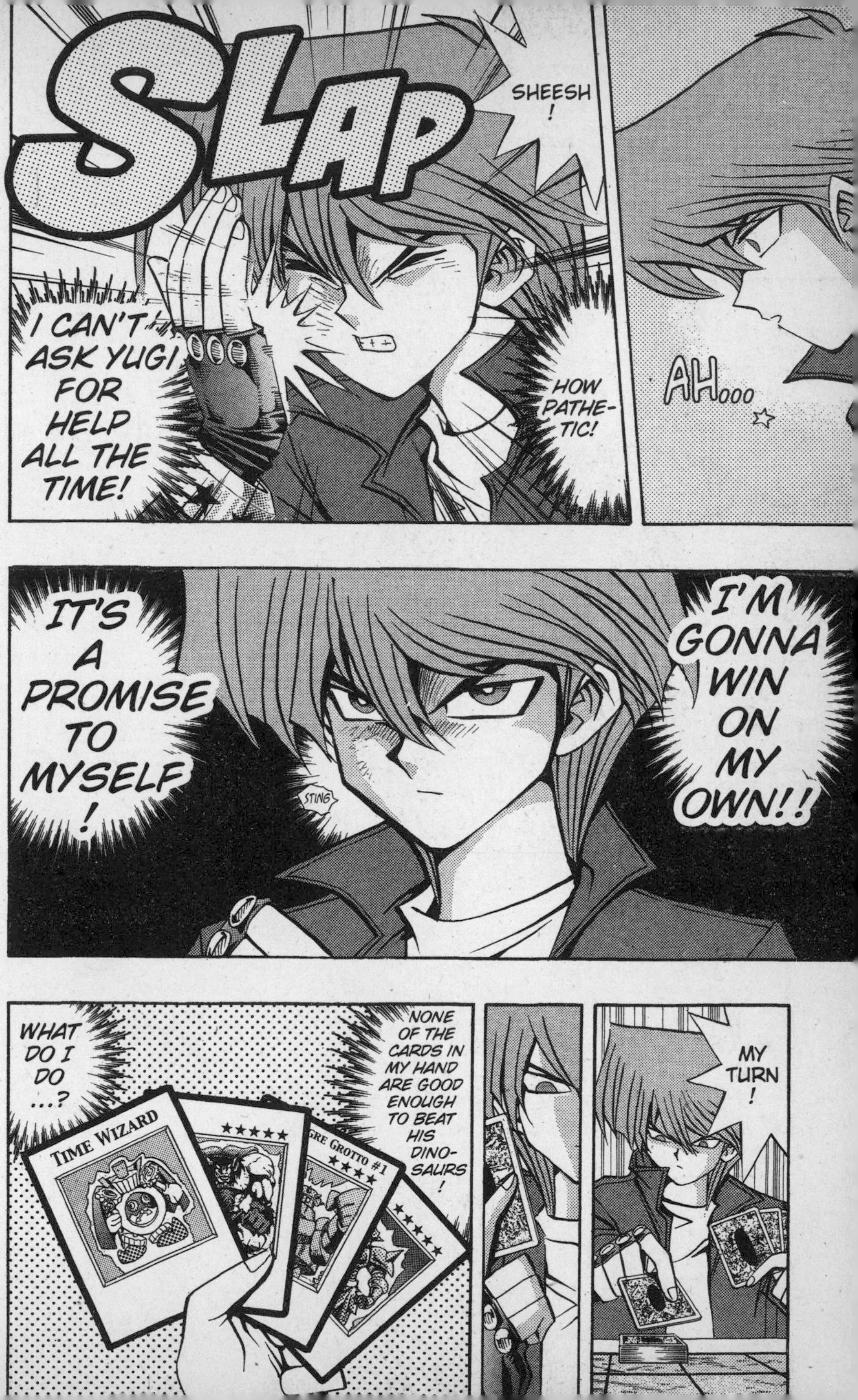
AHooo
SLAP
SHEESH!
HOW PATHETIC!
I CAN'T ASK YUGI FOR HELP ALL THE TIME!
I'M GONNA WIN ON MY OWN!!
STING
IT'S A PROMISE TO MYSELF!
MY TURN!
NONE OF THE CARDS IN MY HAND ARE GOOD ENOUGH TO BEAT HIS DINOSAURS!
WHAT DO I DO ...?
TIME WIZARD
GRE GROTTO #1

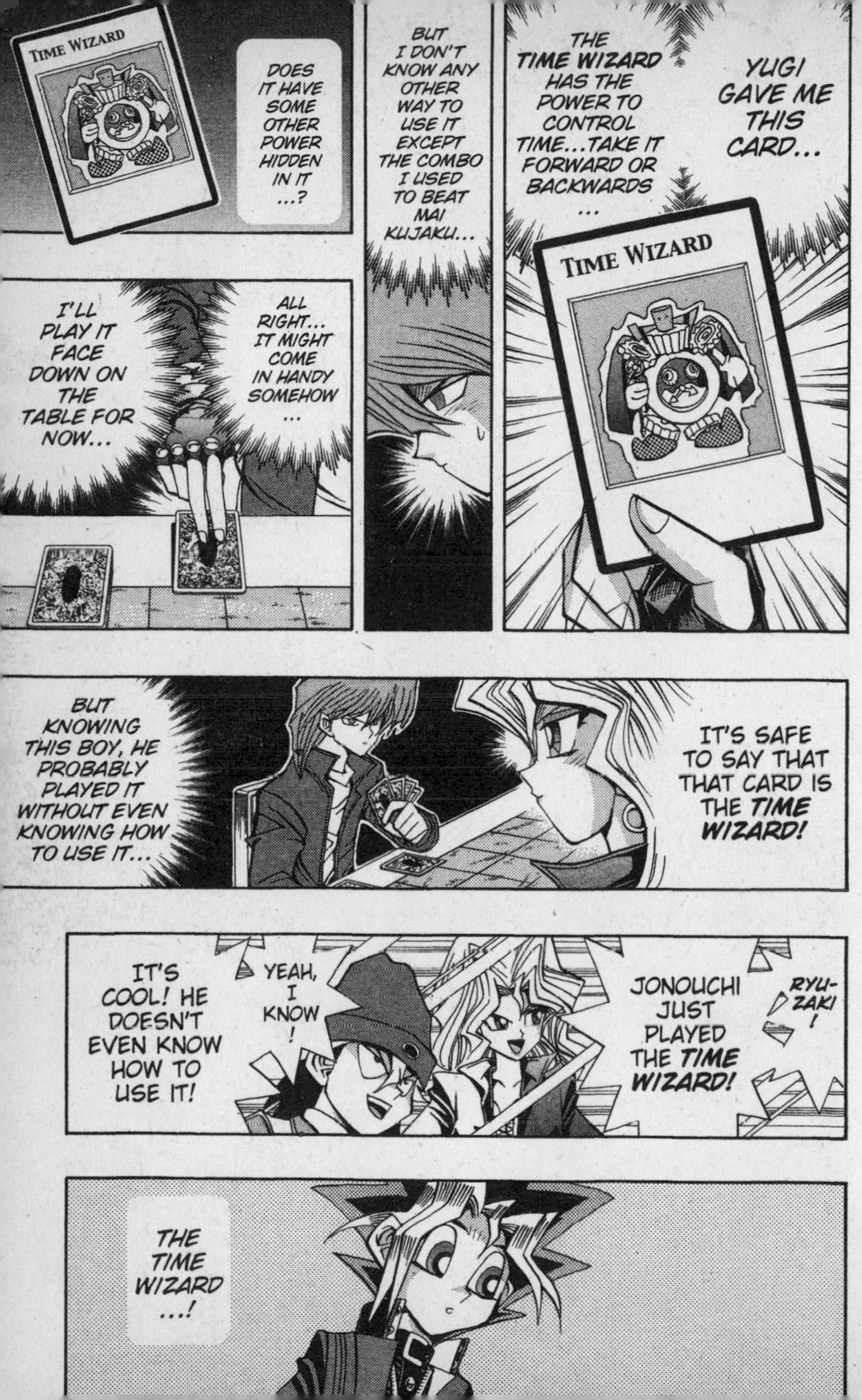

TIME WIZARD
YUGI GAVE ME THIS CARD...
THE TIME WIZARD HAS THE POWER TO CONTROL TIME...TAKE IT FORWARD OR BACKWARDS ...
BUT I DON'T KNOW ANY OTHER WAY TO USE IT EXCEPT THE COMBO I USED TO BEAT MAI KUJAKU...
TIME WIZARD
DOES IT HAVE SOME OTHER POWER HIDDEN IN IT ...?
ALL RIGHT... IT MIGHT COME IN HANDY SOMEHOW ...
I'LL PLAY IT FACE DOWN ON THE TABLE FOR NOW...
IT'S SAFE TO SAY THAT THAT CARD IS THE TIME WIZARD!
BUT KNOWING THIS BOY, HE PROBABLY PLAYED IT WITHOUT EVEN KNOWING HOW TO USE IT...
RYU-ZAKI!
JONOUCHI JUST PLAYED THE TIME WIZARD!
YEAH, I KNOW!
IT'S COOL! HE DOESN'T EVEN KNOW HOW TO USE IT!
THE TIME WIZARD ...!

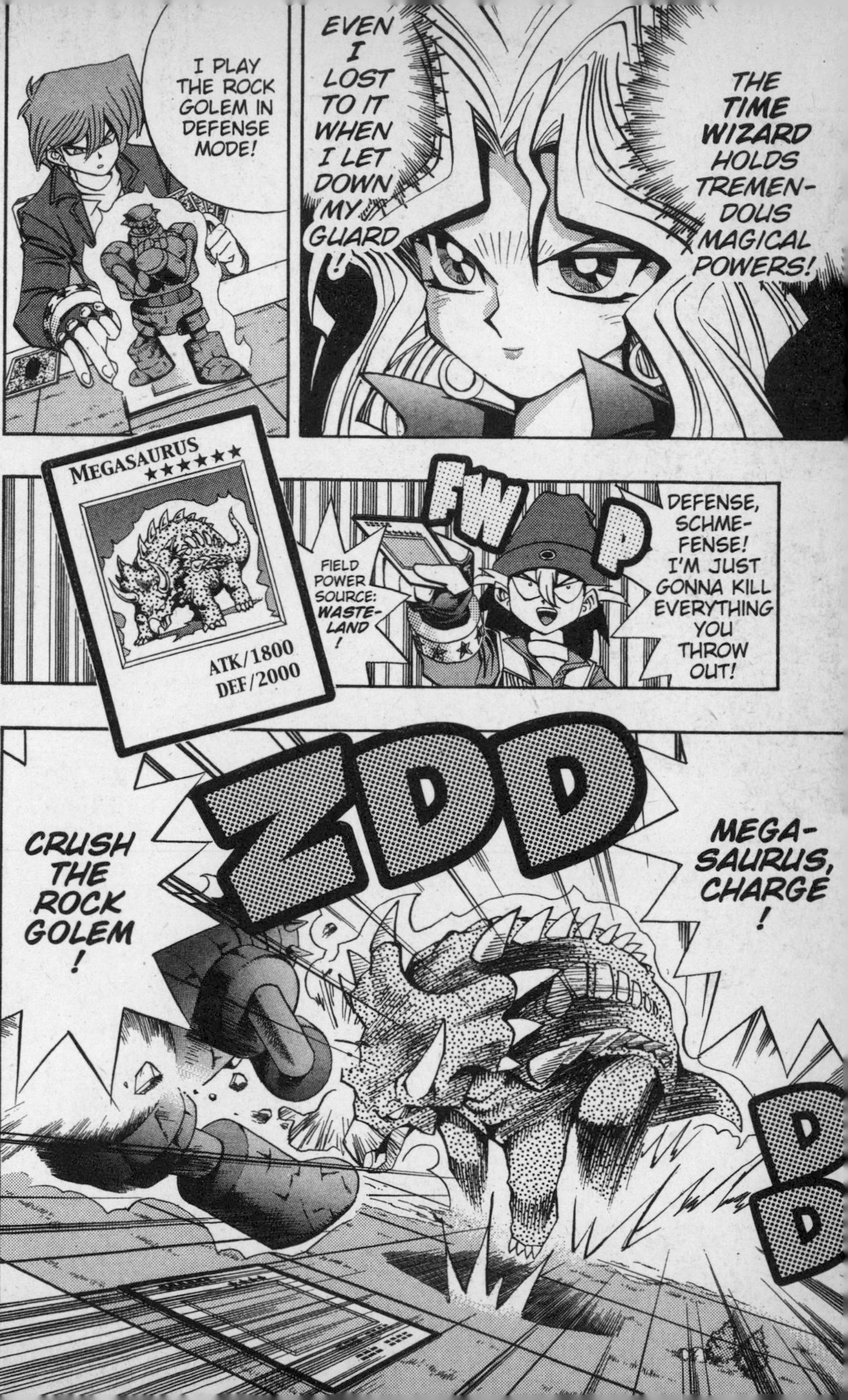
THE TIME WIZARD HOLDS TREMEN-DOUS MAGICAL POWERS!
EVEN I LOST TO IT WHEN I LET DOWN MY GUARD!
I PLAY THE ROCK GOLEM IN DEFENSE MODE!
DEFENSE, SCHME-FENSE! I'M JUST GONNA KILL EVERYTHING YOU THROW OUT!
FWP
FIELD POWER SOURCE: WASTE-LAND!
MEGASAURUS ★★★★★★
ATK/1800
DEF/2000
MEGA-SAURUS, CHARGE!
ZDD
DD
CRUSH THE ROCK GOLEM!

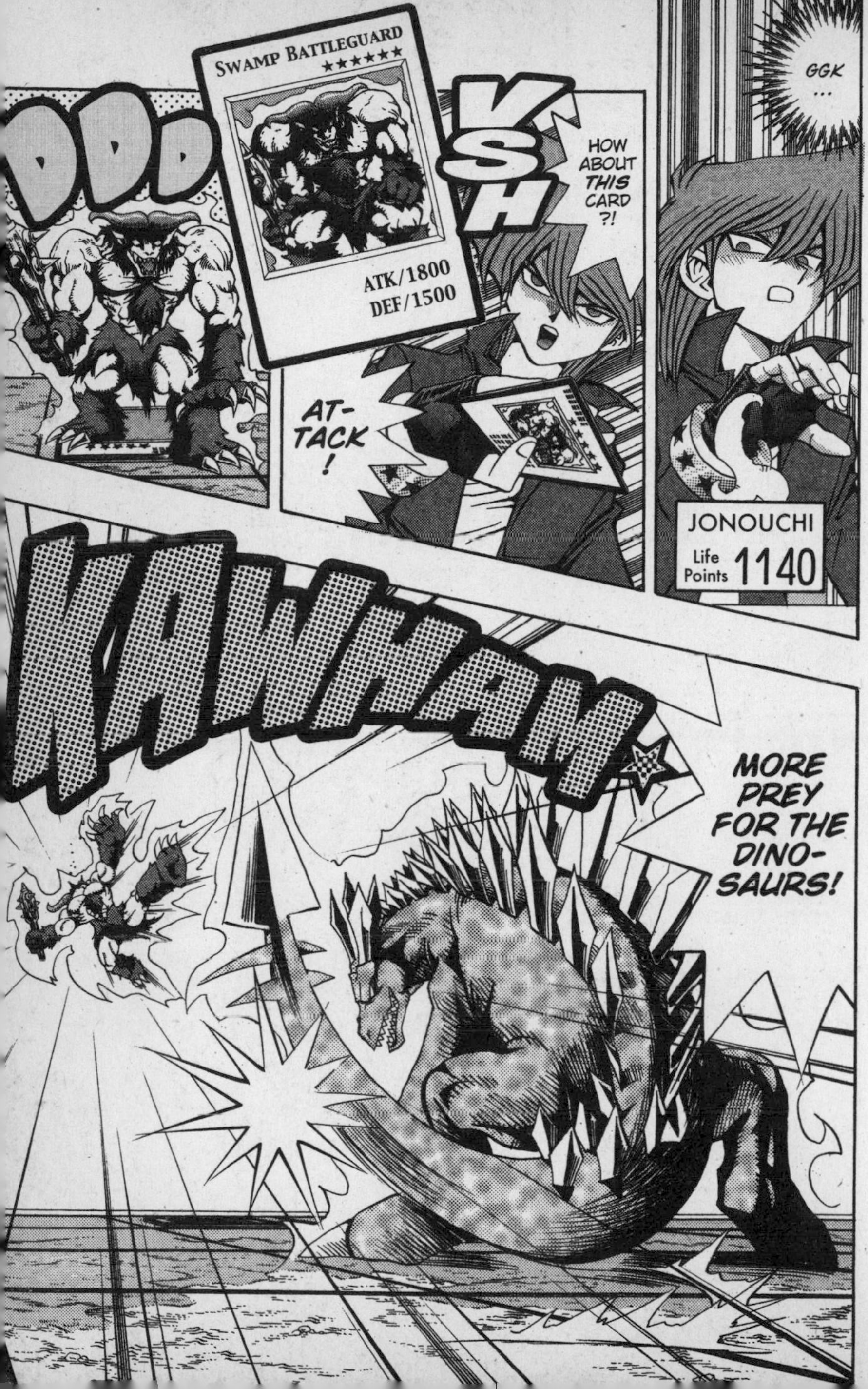
GGK ...
JONOUCHI
Life Points 1140
HOW ABOUT THIS CARD ?!
KSH
AT-TACK!
SWAMP BATTLEGUARD
ATK/1800
DEF/1500
MORE PREY FOR THE DINOSAURS!
KAWHAM

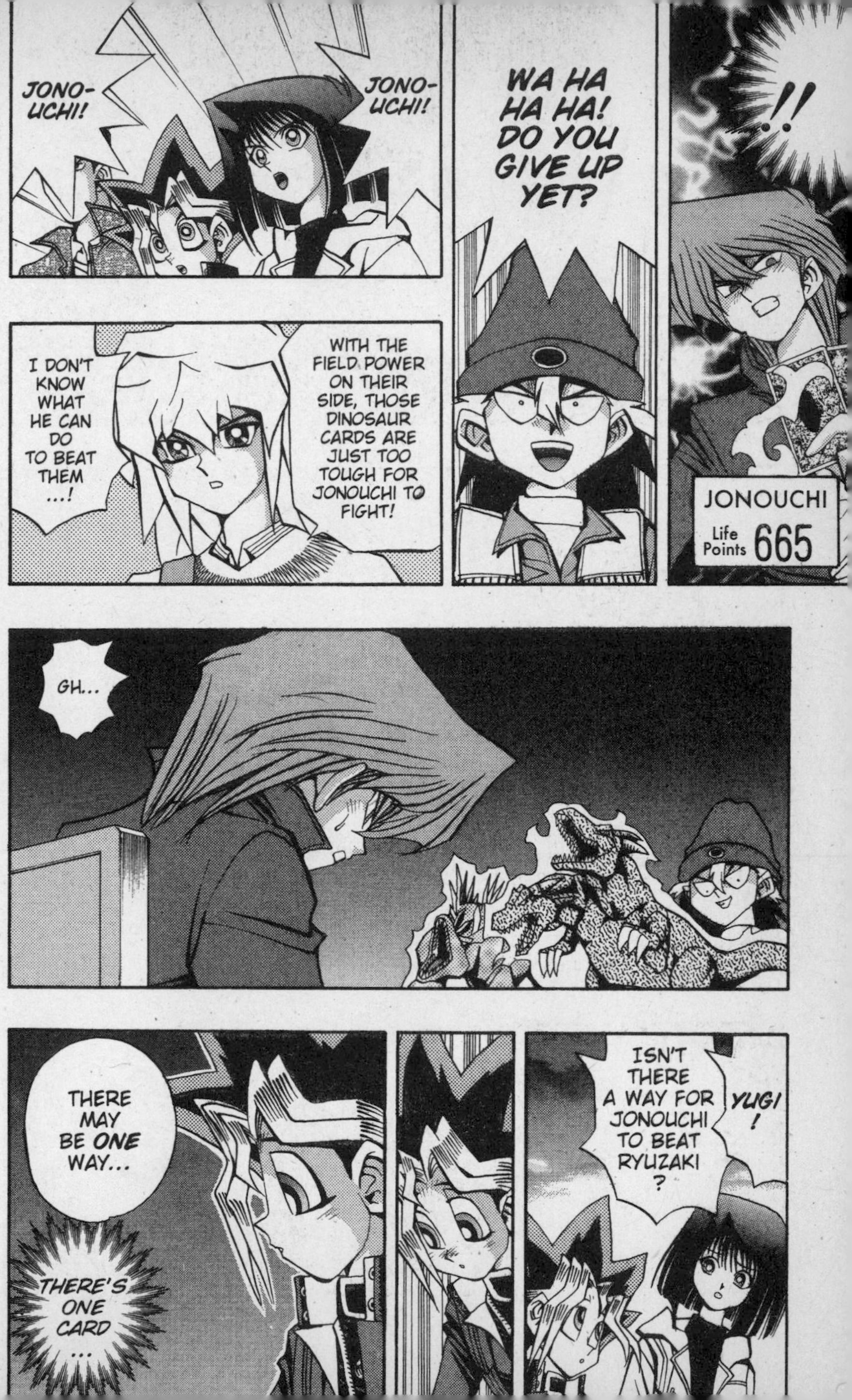
!!
JONOUCHI Life Points 665
WA HA HA HA! DO YOU GIVE UP YET?
JONO-UCHI!
JONO-UCHI!
WITH THE FIELD POWER ON THEIR SIDE, THOSE DINOSAUR CARDS ARE JUST TOO TOUGH FOR JONOUCHI TO FIGHT!
I DON'T KNOW WHAT HE CAN DO TO BEAT THEM ...!
GH...
YUGI!
ISN'T THERE A WAY FOR JONOUCHI TO BEAT RYUZAKI?
THERE MAY BE ONE WAY...
THERE'S ONE CARD ...

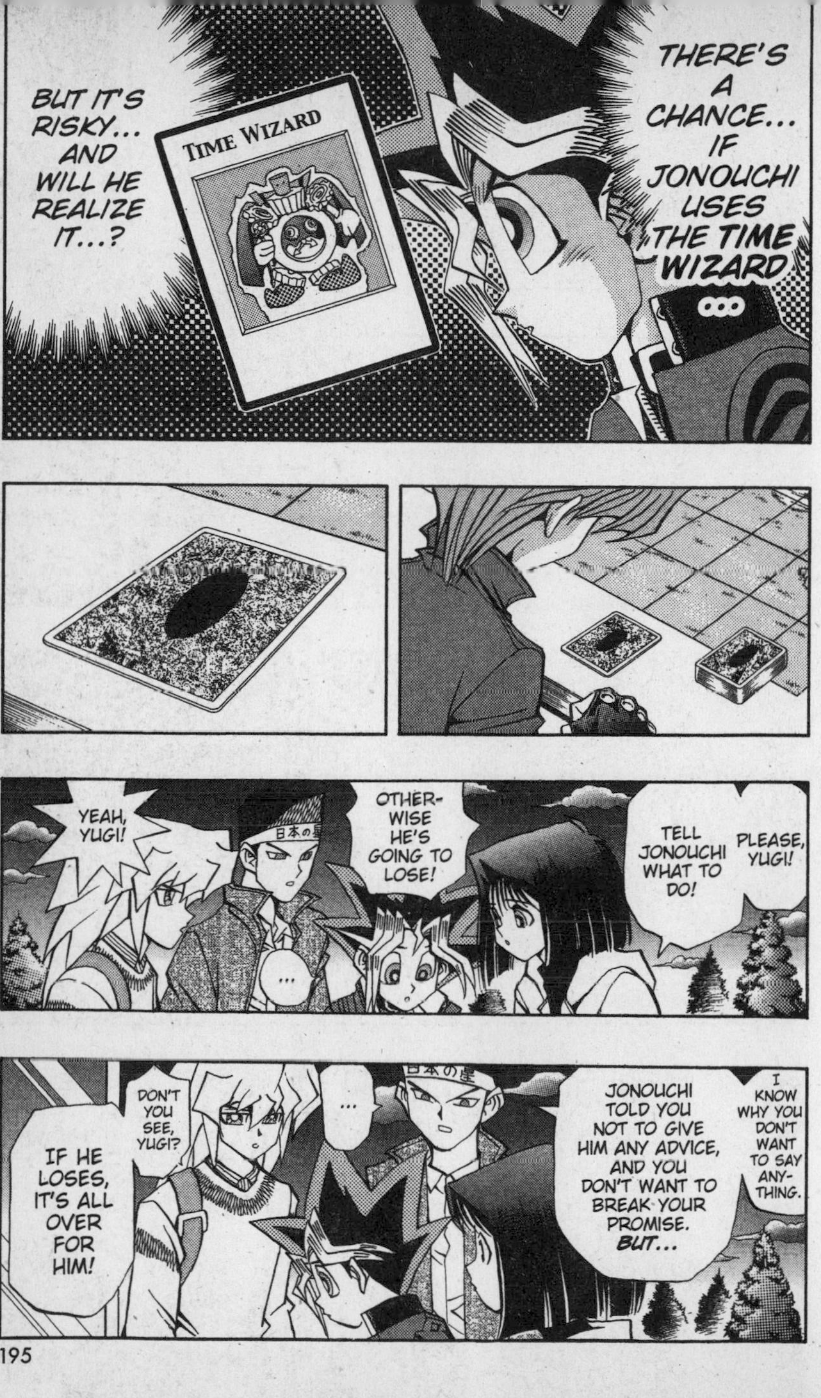
THERE'S A CHANCE... IF JONOUCHI USES THE TIME WIZARD...
TIME WIZARD
BUT IT'S RISKY... AND WILL HE REALIZE IT...?
PLEASE, YUGI!
TELL JONOUCHI WHAT TO DO!
OTHERWISE HE'S GOING TO LOSE!
日本の星
YEAH, YUGI!
...
I KNOW WHY YOU DON'T WANT TO SAY ANYTHING.
JONOUCHI TOLD YOU NOT TO GIVE HIM ANY ADVICE, AND YOU DON'T WANT TO BREAK YOUR PROMISE. BUT...
日本の星
...
DON'T YOU SEE, YUGI?
IF HE LOSES, IT'S ALL OVER FOR HIM!

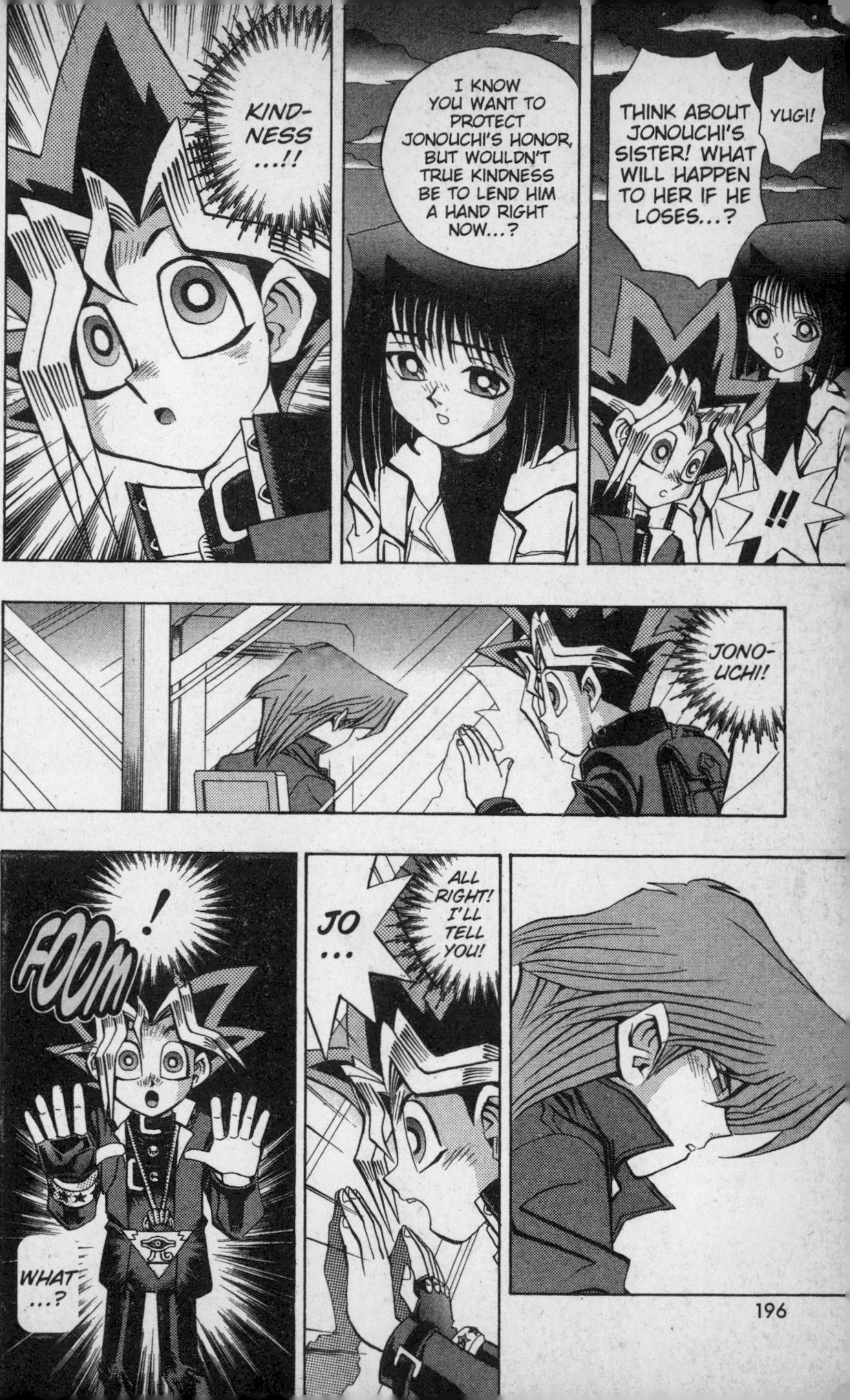
YUGI!
THINK ABOUT JONOUCHI'S SISTER! WHAT WILL HAPPEN TO HER IF HE LOSES...?
!!
I KNOW YOU WANT TO PROTECT JONOUCHI'S HONOR, BUT WOULDN'T TRUE KINDNESS BE TO LEND HIM A HAND RIGHT NOW...?
KINDNESS ...!!
JONOUCHI!
ALL RIGHT! I'LL TELL YOU!
JO ...
!
FOOM
WHAT ...?

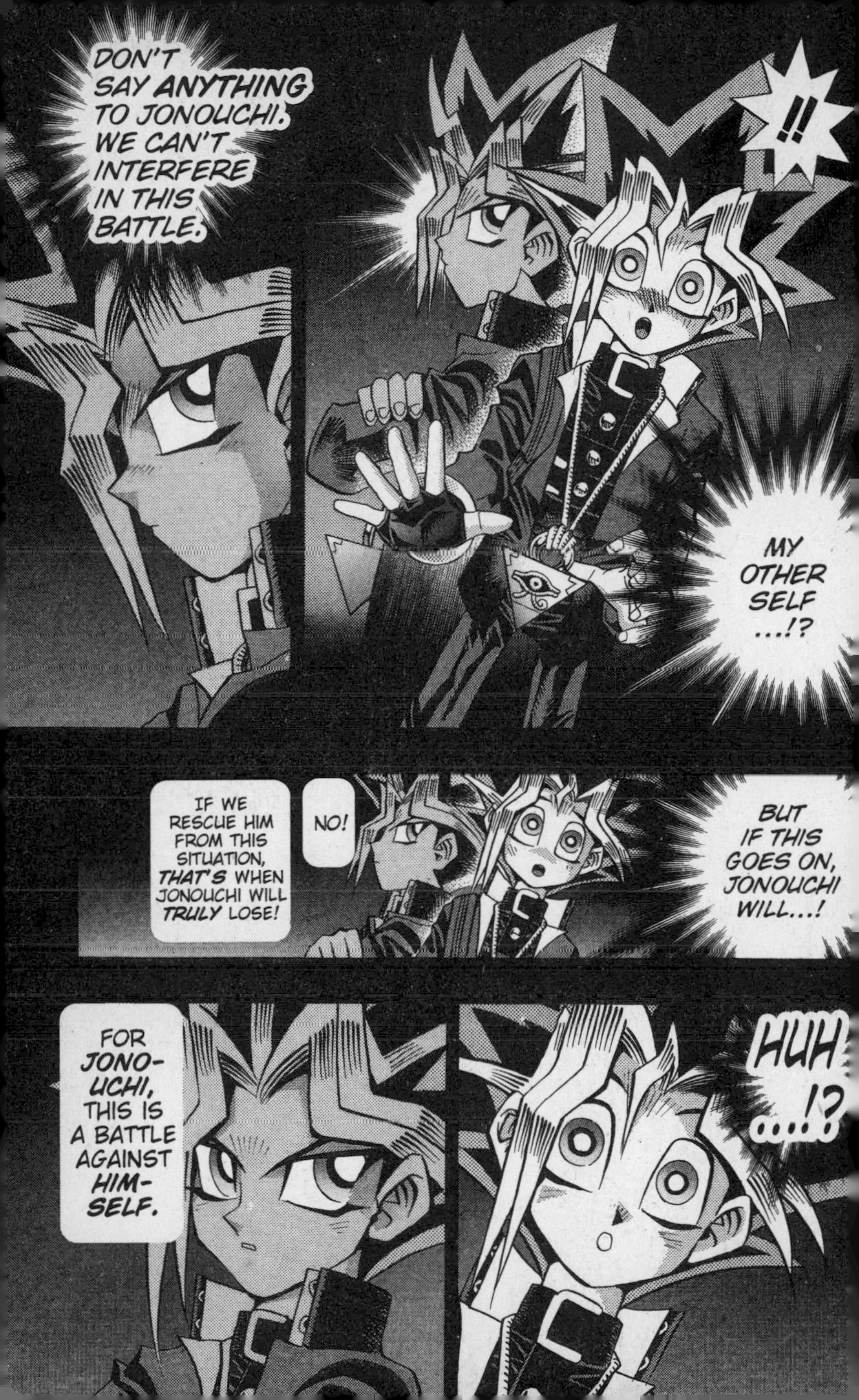
!!
MY OTHER SELF ...!?
DON'T SAY ANYTHING TO JONOUCHI. WE CAN'T INTERFERE IN THIS BATTLE.
BUT IF THIS GOES ON, JONOUCHI WILL...!
NO!
IF WE RESCUE HIM FROM THIS SITUATION, THAT'S WHEN JONOUCHI WILL TRULY LOSE!
HUH ...!?
FOR JONO-UCHI, THIS IS A BATTLE AGAINST HIM-SELF.

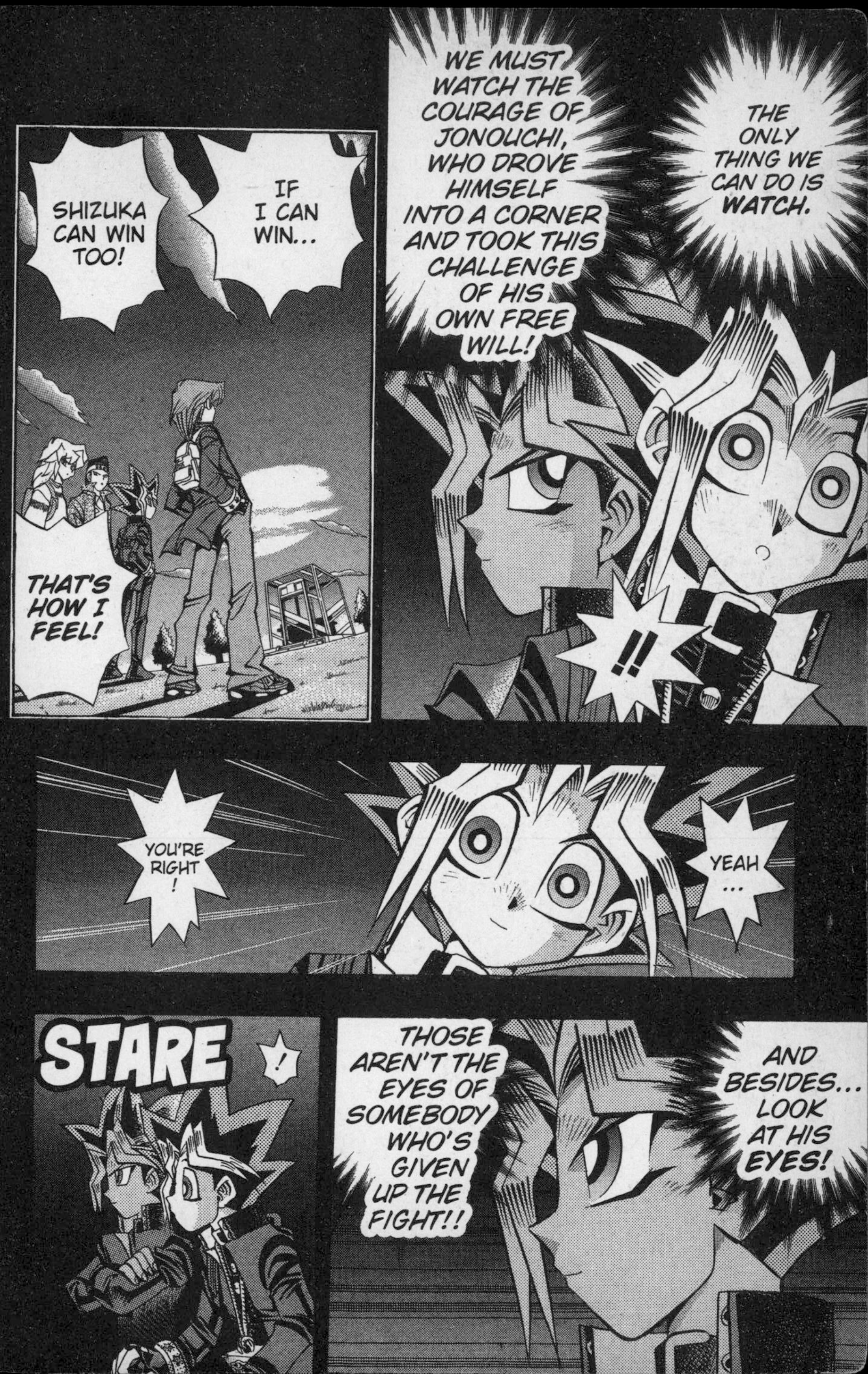
THE ONLY THING WE CAN DO IS WATCH.
WE MUST WATCH THE COURAGE OF JONOUCHI, WHO DROVE HIMSELF INTO A CORNER AND TOOK THIS CHALLENGE OF HIS OWN FREE WILL!
!!
IF I CAN WIN...
SHIZUKA CAN WIN TOO!
THAT'S HOW I FEEL!
YEAH...
YOU'RE RIGHT!
AND BESIDES... LOOK AT HIS EYES!
THOSE AREN'T THE EYES OF SOMEBODY WHO'S GIVEN UP THE FIGHT!!
STARE
!

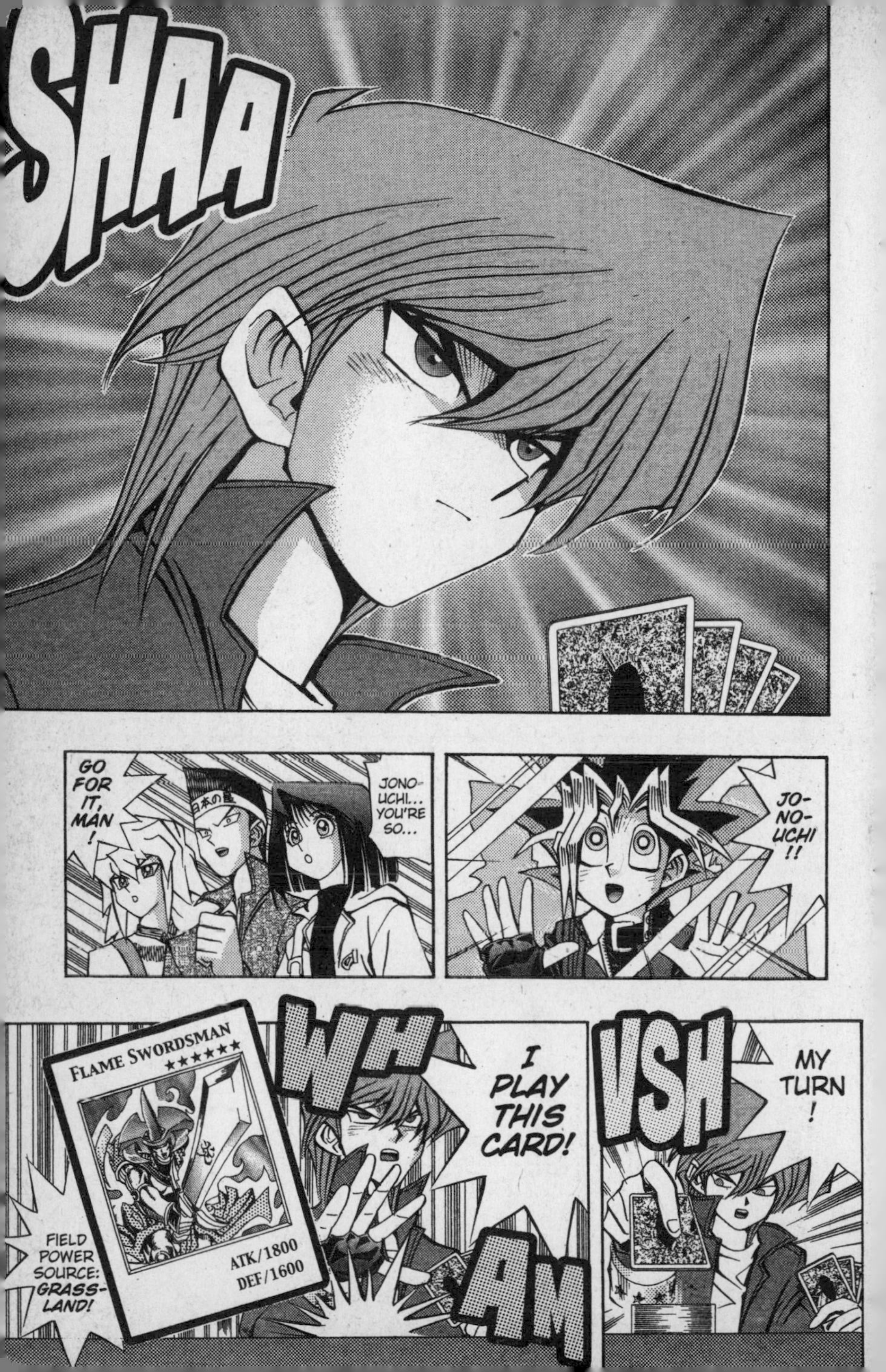
SHAA
JO-NO-UCHI!!
JONO-UCHI... YOU'RE SO...
GO FOR IT, MAN!
VSH
MY TURN!
WH
I PLAY THIS CARD!
AM
FLAME SWORDSMAN
★★★★★★
ATK/1800
DEF/1600
FIELD POWER SOURCE: GRASSLAND!

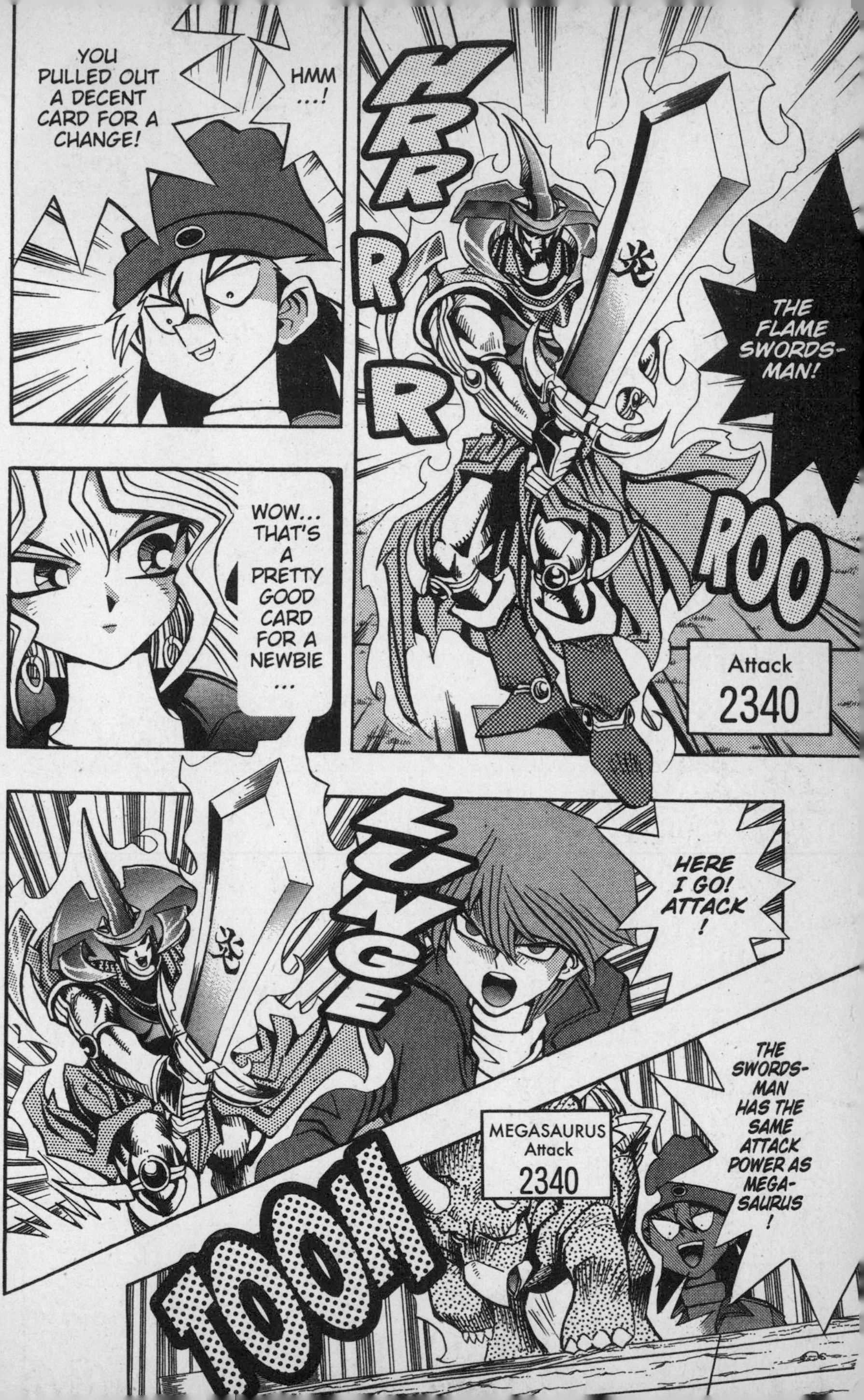
HRRR
THE FLAME SWORDSMAN!
ROO
Attack 2340
HMM ...!
YOU PULLED OUT A DECENT CARD FOR A CHANGE!
WOW... THAT'S A PRETTY GOOD CARD FOR A NEWBIE ...
HERE I GO! ATTACK!
LUNGE
THE SWORDSMAN HAS THE SAME ATTACK POWER AS MEGASAURUS!
MEGASAURUS Attack 2340
TOOOM

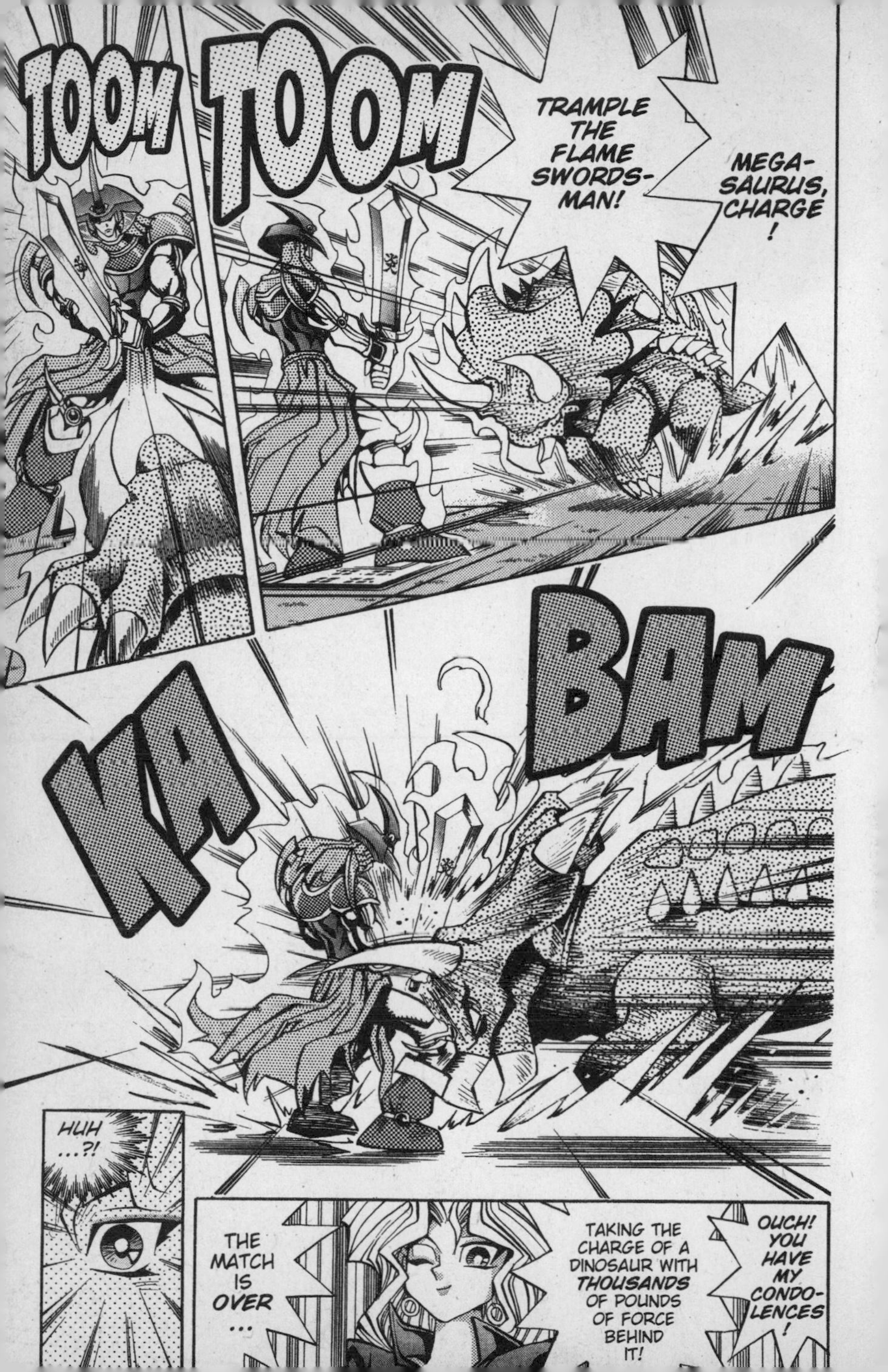
MEGA-SAURUS, CHARGE!
TRAMPLE THE FLAME SWORDS-MAN!
TOOM
TOOM
BAM
KA
OUCH! YOU HAVE MY CONDO-LENCES!
TAKING THE CHARGE OF A DINOSAUR WITH THOUSANDS OF POUNDS OF FORCE BEHIND IT!
THE MATCH IS OVER...
HUH ...?!

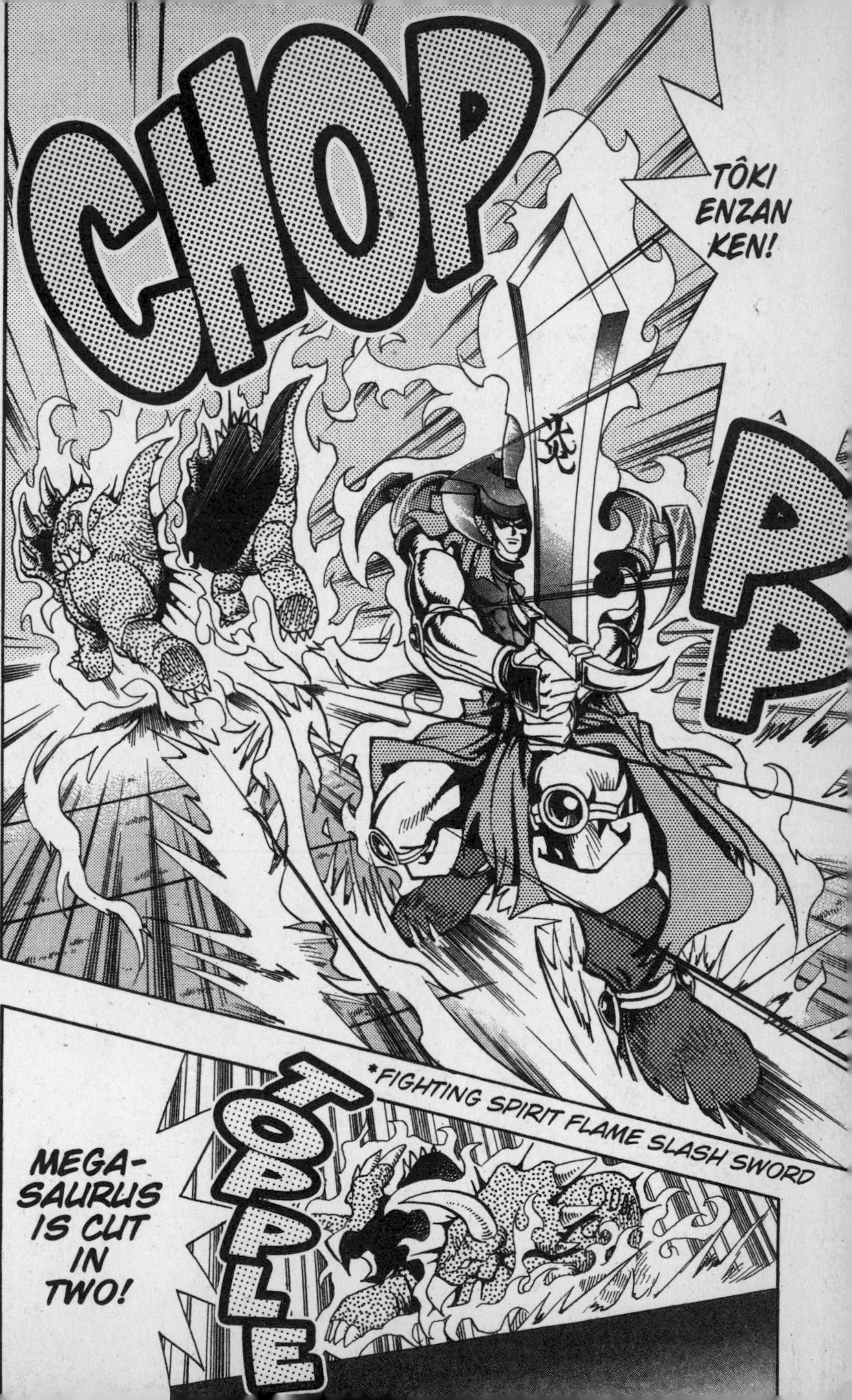
CHOP
TÔKI ENZAN KEN!
*FIGHTING SPIRIT FLAME SLASH SWORD
TOPPLE
MEGA-SAURUS IS CUT IN TWO!

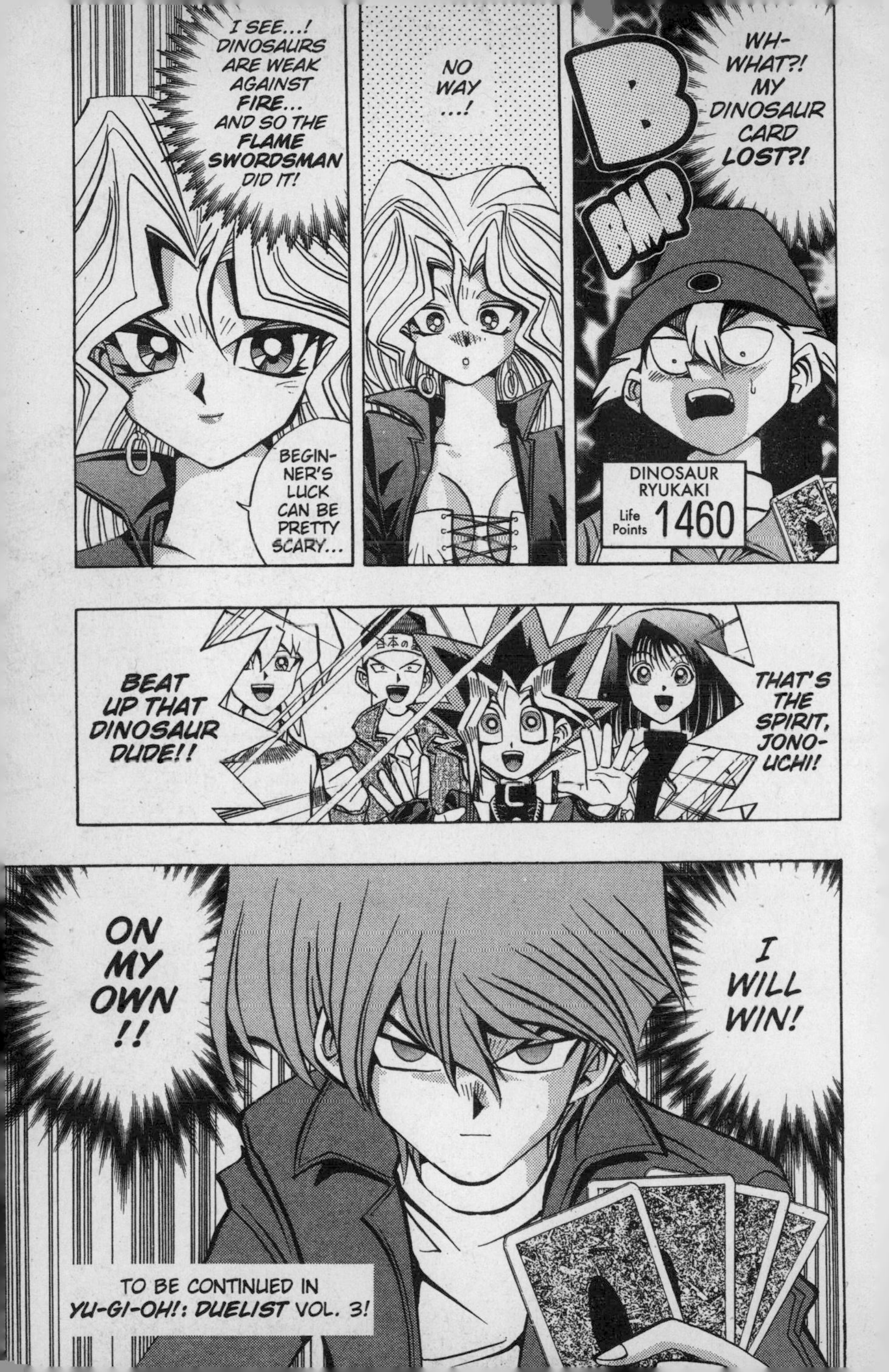

B
BMP
WH-WHAT?! MY DINOSAUR CARD LOST?!
DINOSAUR RYUKAKI
Life Points 1460
NO WAY ...!
I SEE...! DINOSAURS ARE WEAK AGAINST FIRE... AND SO THE FLAME SWORDSMAN DID IT!
BEGIN-NER'S LUCK CAN BE PRETTY SCARY...
THAT'S THE SPIRIT, JONO-UCHI!
BEAT UP THAT DINOSAUR DUDE!!
I WILL WIN!
ON MY OWN!!
TO BE CONTINUED IN YU-GI-OH!: DUELIST VOL. 3!

BONUS!

Battle Trump Game

○ THIS IS A STRATEGIC BATTLE GAME FOR TWO PLAYERS USING REGULAR PLAYING CARDS! (BASICALLY, IT'S CARD CHESS.) THE PLAYERS TAKE TURNS MOVING THEIR CARDS AND FIGHTING. TO WIN, YOU MUST TRAP YOUR OPPONENT'S JOKER. LEARN THE RULES AND PLAY IT WITH YOUR FRIENDS!

WHAT YOU NEED:

○ A DECK OF ORDINARY PLAYING CARDS
○ A BIG PIECE OF PAPER WITH A 5X5 GRID DRAWN ON IT (SEE THE NEXT PAGE) (OPTIONAL)
○ NINE COINS

PREPARATIONS BEFORE PLAYING

○ FOR THIS GAME, YOU ONLY NEED THE 2S, 3S, 4S, 5S, ACES AND TWO JOKERS. REMOVE ALL THE OTHER CARDS FROM THE DECK. IF YOUR DECK OF CARDS DOESN'T HAVE JOKERS, USE TWO KINGS INSTEAD.

○ PREPARE A 5X5 GRID (SEE BELOW). THE SQUARES OF THE GRID SHOULD BE BIG ENOUGH TO FIT CARDS IN THEM. YOU DON'T HAVE TO DRAW THE GRID AS LONG AS IT'S CLEAR WHERE THE SQUARES ARE.

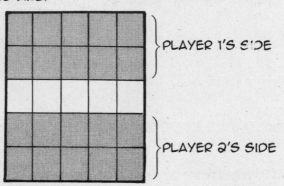

} PLAYER 1'S SIDE

} PLAYER 2'S SIDE

HOW TO PLAY

○ EACH PLAYER PLACES ONE JOKER CARD, FACE UP, ANYWHERE ON THEIR SIDE. (THE JOKER IS LIKE THE KING IN CHESS.)

○ SHUFFLE THE OTHER 20 CARDS (ACES, 2S, 3S, 4S AND 5S) AND PLACE THEM IN A SINGLE STACK.

○ EACH PLAYER DRAWS 8 CARDS FROM THE STACK, TAKING TURNS. HOWEVER, EVEN AFTER YOU DRAW THEM, *YOU CAN'T LOOK AT YOUR OWN CARDS!*

○ PLAYERS PLACE THE 8 CARDS FACE DOWN ON THEIR OWN SIDES, TAKING TURNS. YOU CAN'T PUT MORE THAN ONE CARD ON THE SAME SPACE.

○ PLACE A COIN ON EACH OF PLAYER 1'S CARDS (SO YOU CAN TELL THEM APART FROM PLAYER 2'S CARDS).

○ USE ROCK-PAPER-SCISSORS TO DECIDE WHO GOES FIRST.

○ WHEN THE GAME STARTS, THE PLAYERS TAKE TURNS. ON YOUR TURN, YOU MUST DO **ONE** OF THE FOLLOWING (NOT BOTH!):

● FLIP OVER ONE OF YOUR OWN FACE-DOWN CARDS SO IT'S FACE-UP.
● MOVE ONE OF THE FACE-UP CARDS. EACH CARD MOVES DIFFERENTLY BASED ON ITS NUMBER (ACE, 2, 3, 4, ETC.), AND FIGHTS DIFFERENTLY BASED ON ITS SUIT (HEARTS, DIAMONDS, ETC.). IF YOU MOVE INTO A SPACE WITH THE OTHER PLAYER'S CARD, YOU MUST STOP AND FIGHT THEM.

=============== *MOVEMENT AND BATTLE* ===============

CARD MOVEMENT

JOKER / A	CAN MOVE **ONE SPACE** IN ANY DIRECTION
2	CAN MOVE **UP TO TWO SPACES** LEFT, RIGHT, UP OR DOWN
3	CAN MOVE **UP TO THREE SPACES** DIAGONALLY
4	CAN MOVE **UP TO FOUR SPACES** LEFT, RIGHT, UP OR DOWN
5	CAN MOVE **UP TO FIVE SPACES** DIAGONALLY

CARD BATTLE

WIN ♡ WIN
♣ TIE | TIE ♠
TIE | TIE
WIN ◇ WIN

♡ ······ ELEMENT OF FIRE
♠ ······ ELEMENT OF WOOD
◇ ······ ELEMENT OF EARTH
♣ ······ ELEMENT OF WATER

WHEN TWO CARDS FIGHT, THE WINNER IS DETERMINED BY THE SUIT (HEARTS, DIAMONDS, ETC.). USE THIS CHART TO SEE WHO WINS.

♡ ···BEATS ♠ LOSES TO ♣

♠ ···BEATS ◇ LOSES TO ♡

◇ ···BEATS ♣ LOSES TO ♠

♣ ···BEATS ♡ LOSES TO ◇

JOKER ···♡ · ♠ · ◇ · ♣ LOSE TO ANY CARD. JOKERS CAN ONLY ATTACK THE ENEMY JOKER.

	♡	♠	◇	♣
♡	BOTH CARDS DIE	HEART BEATS SPADE	TIE	CLUB BEATS HEART
♠	HEART BEATS SPADE	BOTH CARDS DIE	SPADE BEATS DIAMOND	TIE
◇	TIE	SPADE BEATS DIAMOND	BOTH DIE	DIAMOND BEATS CLUB
♣	CLUB BEATS HEART	TIE	DIAMOND BEATS CLUB	BOTH DIE

BATTLE SYSTEM

○ MOVE YOUR CARDS ACCORDING TO THEIR NUMBER (SEE PAGE 206). YOU CAN JUMP OVER YOUR OWN CARDS WHILE MOVING, BUT YOU CAN'T STOP ON THE SAME SPACE WITH THEM. YOU CAN'T JUMP OVER YOUR OPPONENT'S CARDS! *IF YOU MOVE ONTO YOUR OPPONENT'S CARDS, YOU MUST STOP AND FIGHT THEM.*

○ IF YOU MOVE ONTO AN OPPONENT'S CARD WHICH IS FACE DOWN, FLIP IT FACE UP BEFORE YOU FIGHT. (THE CARD STAYS FACE UP AFTER THE BATTLE.)

○ THERE ARE THREE OUTCOMES OF BATTLE:

- *ONE CARD BEATS THE OTHER CARD.* REMOVE THE LOSING CARD FROM PLAY. THE WINNER DOESN'T GET TO TAKE IT. IF THE WINNING CARD MOVED ONTO THE LOSING CARD'S SPACE, THE WINNING CARD MUST STOP AND THE WINNING PLAYER'S TURN ENDS.

- *BOTH CARDS DIE.* IF BOTH CARDS HAVE THE SAME SUIT, BOTH CARDS ARE REMOVED FROM PLAY.

- *TIE.* BATTLES BETWEEN CERTAIN CARDS (LIKE HEARTS VERSUS DIAMONDS) RESULT IN A TIE. IN THIS CASE, THE PLAYER WHO STARTED THE BATTLE MUST MOVE THEIR CARD BACK TO ITS ORIGINAL POSITION AT THE START OF THE TURN. THAT PLAYER'S TURN ENDS.

WINNING THE GAME

○ TO WIN, YOU MUST ATTACK THE OTHER PLAYER'S JOKER, OR TRAP THEM SO THAT THEY CAN'T MOVE. (JOKERS CAN'T ATTACK OTHER CARDS, EXCEPT FOR ENEMY JOKERS.)

○ IF TWO JOKERS FIGHT EACH OTHER, THE ONE WHO INITIATED THE ATTACK WINS THE GAME.

THE RULES MIGHT SEEM COMPLICATED AT FIRST, BUT IT'S EASY ONCE YOU START PLAYING!!

MASTER OF THE CARDS

The "Duel Monsters" card game first appeared in volume two of the original **Yu-Gi-Oh!** graphic novel series, but it's in **Yu-Gi-Oh!: Duelist** (originally printed in Japan as volumes 8-31 of **Yu-Gi-Oh!**) that it gets really important. As many fans know, some of the card names are different between the English and Japanese versions. In case you play the game, or you're interested in playing, here's a rundown of the cards in this graphic novel. Some cards only appear in the **Yu-Gi-Oh!** video games, not in the actual collectible card game.

FIRST APPEARANCE IN THIS VOLUME	JAPANESE CARD NAME	ENGLISH CARD NAME
p.7	*Harpie Lady*	Harpy Lady
p.7	*Tiger Axe*	Tiger Axe
p. 9	*Mamono no Kariudo* (Demon Hunter)	Kojikocy
p.10	*Dengeki Muchi* (Electric Shock Whip)	Electro-Whip
p.11	Cyber Bondage	Cyber Bondage (NOTE: Not a real game card. Called "Cyber Shield" in the video games.)

GIANT SOLDIER OF STONE

[ROCK]

ATK/1300 DEF/2000

JELLYFISH

[AQUA]

ATK/1200 DEF/1500

STOP DEFENSE

[MAGIC CARD]

FIRST APPEARANCE IN THIS VOLUME	JAPANESE CARD NAME	ENGLISH CARD NAME
p.18	Baby Dragon	Baby Dragon
p.19	*Mangekyô: Karei naru Bunshin* (Kaleidoscope: Splendid Doppelganger)	Elegant Egotist
p.20	*Garoozis*	Garoozis
p.22	*Toki no Majutsushi* (Magician of Time)	Time Wizard
p.25	Thousand Dragon (NOTE: Japanese kanji reads: Thousand-year Dragon)	Thousand Dragon
p.44	Devil Kraken	Devil Kraken (NOTE: Not a real game card. Called "Fiend Kraken" in the video games.)
p.44	Imp	Imp (NOTE: Not a real game card. Called "Horned Imp" in the anime.)
p.51	Gremlin	Feral Imp

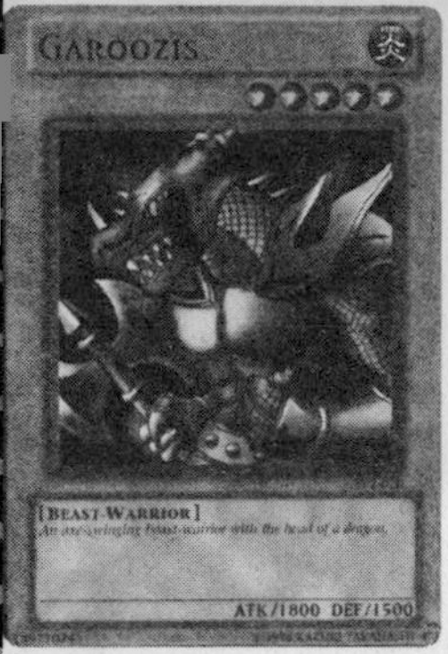
Garoozis
[Beast-Warrior]
ATK/1800 DEF/1500
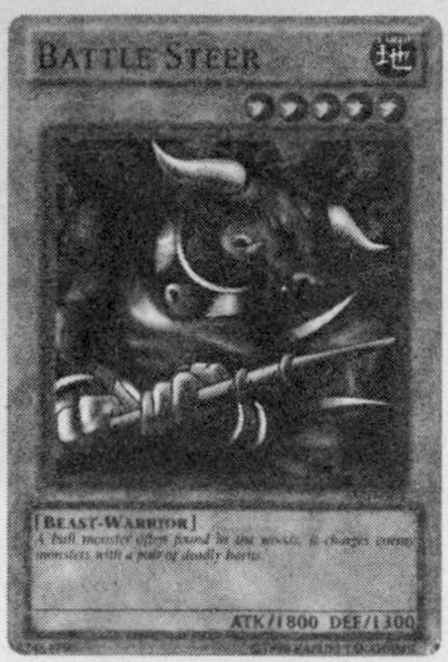
Battle Steer
[Beast-Warrior]
ATK/1800 DEF/1300
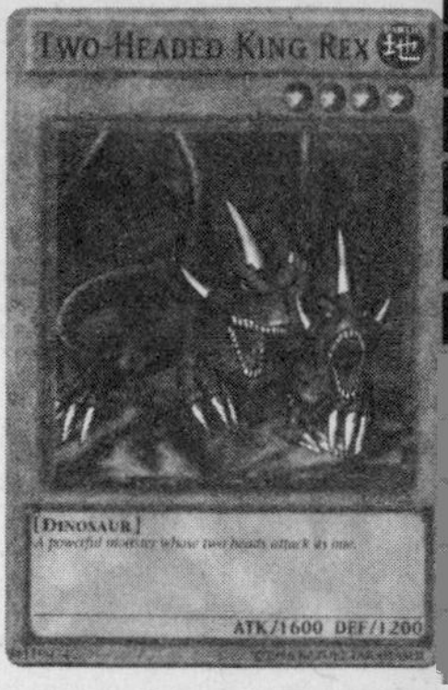
Two-Headed King Rex
[Dinosaur]
ATK/1600 DEF/1200

FIRST APPEARANCE IN THIS VOLUME	JAPANESE CARD NAME	ENGLISH CARD NAME
p.52	*Kurage Jellyfish* (Sea Moon Jellyfish)	Jellyfish
p.53	*Ikkakujû no Horn* (Unicorn's Horn)	Horn of the Unicorn
p.57	*Silver Fang*	Silver Fang
p.57	*Mashô no Tsuki* (Mystical Moon)	Mystical Moon
p.58	Leviathan (NOTE: Japanese text reads: Sea Dragon God)	Leviathan (NOTE: Not a real game card. Called "Kairyu-shin" (Sea Dragon God) in the video games.)
p.63	*Ganseki no Kyohei* (Giant Soldier of Stone)	Giant Soldier of Stone
p.63	Megalodon	Megalodon (NOTE: Not a real game card.)
p.68	*Curse of Dragon*	Curse of Dragon

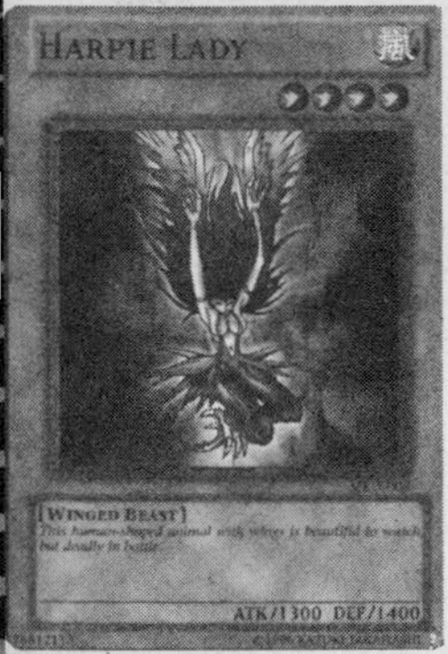
HARPIE LADY
[WINGED BEAST]
ATK/1300 DEF/1400

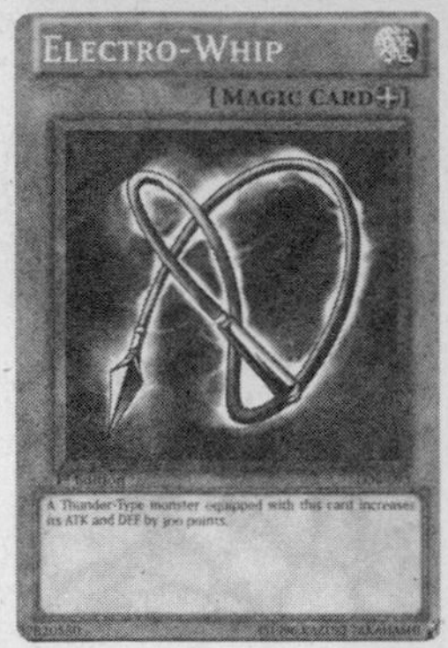
ELECTRO-WHIP
[MAGIC CARD]

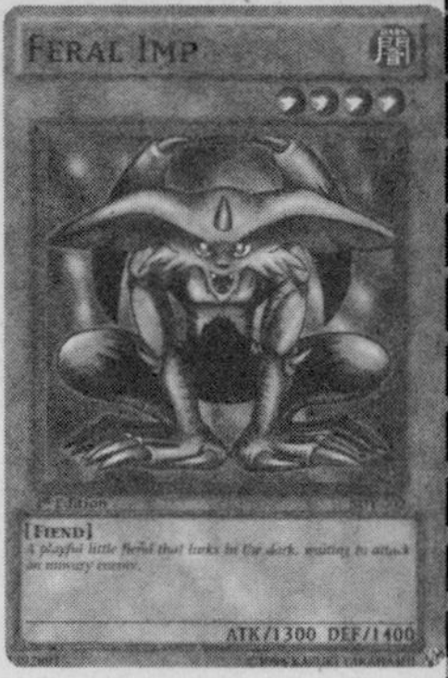
FERAL IMP
[FIEND]
ATK/1300 DEF/1400

FIRST APPEARANCE IN THIS VOLUME	JAPANESE CARD NAME	ENGLISH CARD NAME
p.85	*Hitokui Shokubutsu* (Man-Eating Plant)	Man Eater (NOTE: Art looks different in the real card game.)
p.86	*Toride o Mamoru Yokuryû* (Fortress-Protecting Winged Dragon)	Winged Dragon, Guardian of the Fortress
p.86	Crocodilus	Crocodilus
p.87	*Elf no Senshi* (Elf Soldier)	Celtic Guardian
p.108	Minotaurus	Battle Ox
p.109	Black Magician	Dark Magician
p.110	Blue-Eyes White Dragon	Blue-Eyes White Dragon
p.120	*Shubi Fûji* (Defense Seal)	Stop Defense

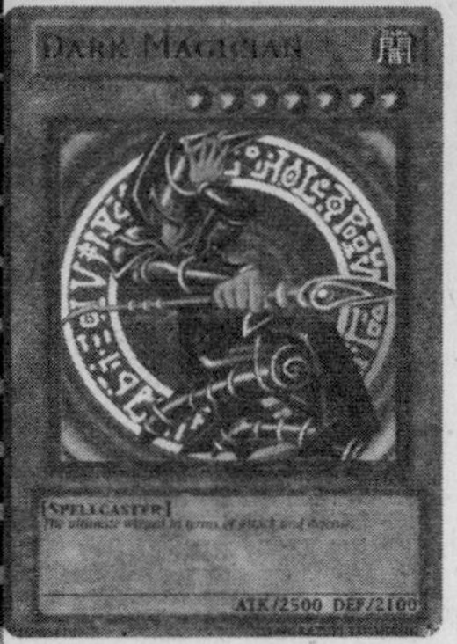
Dark Magician
[Spellcaster]
ATK/2500 DEF/2100
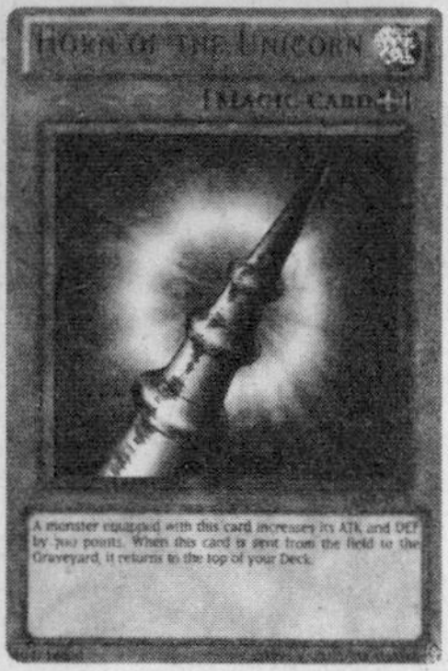
Horn of the Unicorn
[Magic Card]
When this card is sent from the field to the Graveyard, it returns to the top of your Deck.
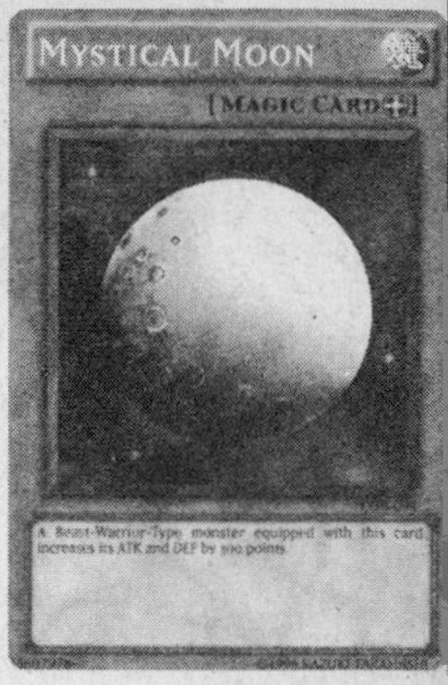
Mystical Moon
[Magic Card]

FIRST APPEARANCE IN THIS VOLUME	JAPANESE CARD NAME	ENGLISH CARD NAME
p.124	Magical Silk Hat	Magical Hats
p.128	*Rokubôsei no Jubaku* (Binding Curse of the Hexagram)	Spellbinding Circle
p.141	Grappler	Grappler (NOTE: Not a real game card. Called "Grappler" in the video games.)
p.143	Holy Elf	Mystical Elf
p.147	*Sei naru Barrier Mirror Force* (Holy Barrier Mirror Force)	Mirror Force
p.148	*Kôgeki no Muryokuka* (Nullificiation of Attack)	Negate Attack
p.149	*Shisha Sosei* (Resurrection of the Dead)	Monster Reborn
p.179	*Nitô o Motsu King Rex* (Two-Headed King Rex)	Two-Headed King Rex

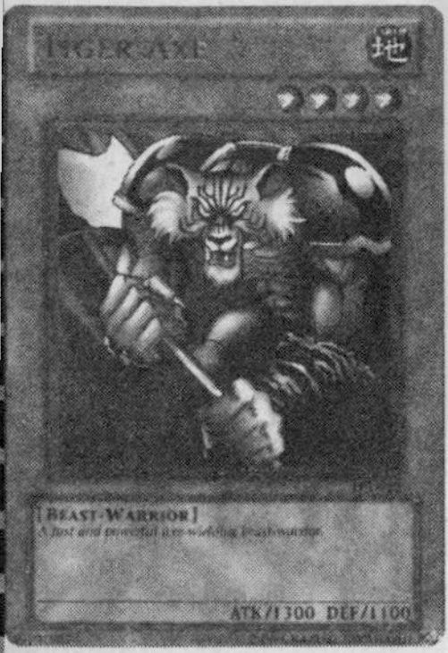
Tiger Axe
地
[Beast-Warrior]
ATK/1300 DEF/1100
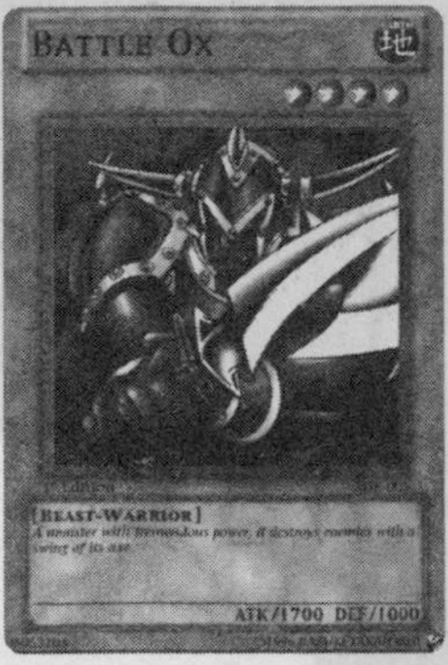
Battle Ox
地
[Beast-Warrior]
ATK/1700 DEF/1000
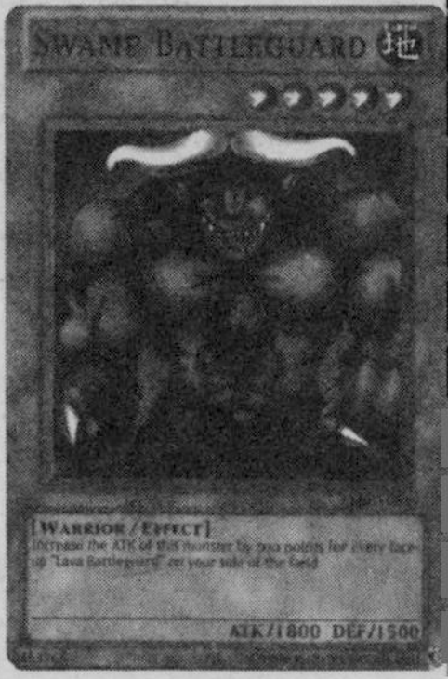
Swamp Battleguard
地
[Warrior / Effect]
ATK/1800 DEF/1500

FIRST APPEARANCE IN THIS VOLUME	JAPANESE CARD NAME	ENGLISH CARD NAME
p.186	*Gyû Majin* (Ox Demon)	Battle Steer
p.187	Axe Raider	Axe Raider
p.188	Sword Dragon	Sword Dragon (NOTE: Not a real game card. Called "Sword Arm of Dragon" in the video games.)
p.190	*Gankutsu Majin Ogre Rock* (Grotto/Cave Golem/Djinn Ogre Rock)	Rock Ogre Grotto #1
p.192	*Megazaura*	Megasaurus (NOTE: Not a real game card. Called "Megazowler" in the video games.)
p.193	*Barbarian 2-Go* (Barbarian #2)	Swamp Battleguard
p.199	*Honô no Kenshi* (Swordsman of Flames)	Flame Swordsman

IN THE NEXT VOLUME...

The Flame Swordsman has turned the fight in Jonouchi's favor...but is it enough to beat Dinosaur Ryuzaki? Then, the diabolical Player Killer of Darkness, Pegasus's second gaming assassin, challenges Yugi to a duel in the dark! But across the ocean in Japan, an even greater gaming force has been awakened. Kaiba, Yugi's No. 1 rival, is back. Back to reclaim his fortune...back to get revenge on Pegasus...and back to defeat Yugi and his friends!

COMING APRIL 2005!

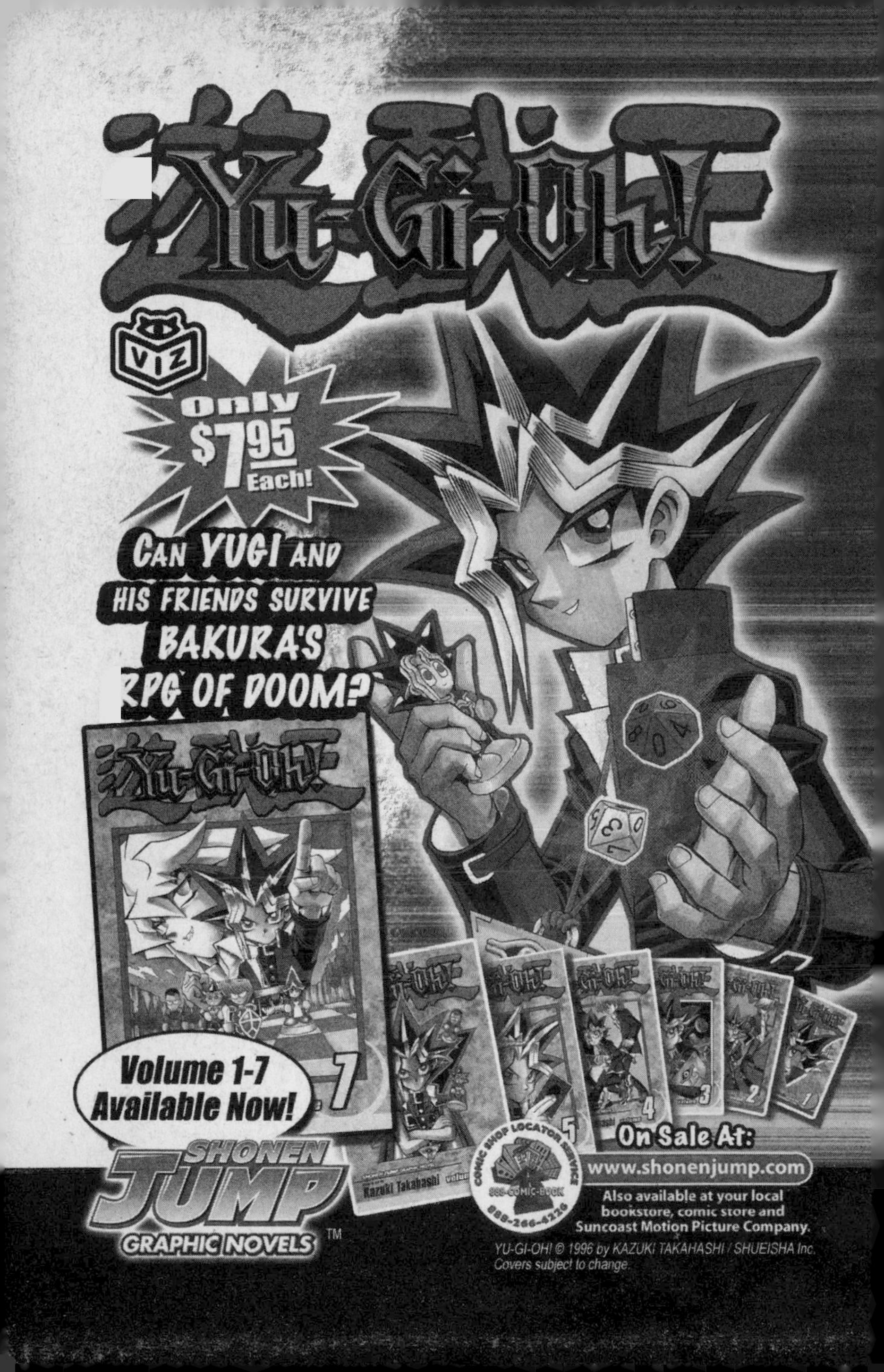

YU-GI-OH!
VIZ
Only $7.95 Each!
CAN YUGI AND HIS FRIENDS SURVIVE BAKURA'S RPG OF DOOM?
Volume 1-7 Available Now!
SHONEN JUMP GRAPHIC NOVELS TM
On Sale At:
www.shonenjump.com
Also available at your local bookstore, comic store and Suncoast Motion Picture Company.
COMIC SHOP LOCATOR SERVICE
888-COMIC-BOOK
888-266-4226
YU-GI-OH! © 1996 by KAZUKI TAKAHASHI / SHUEISHA Inc.
Covers subject to change.

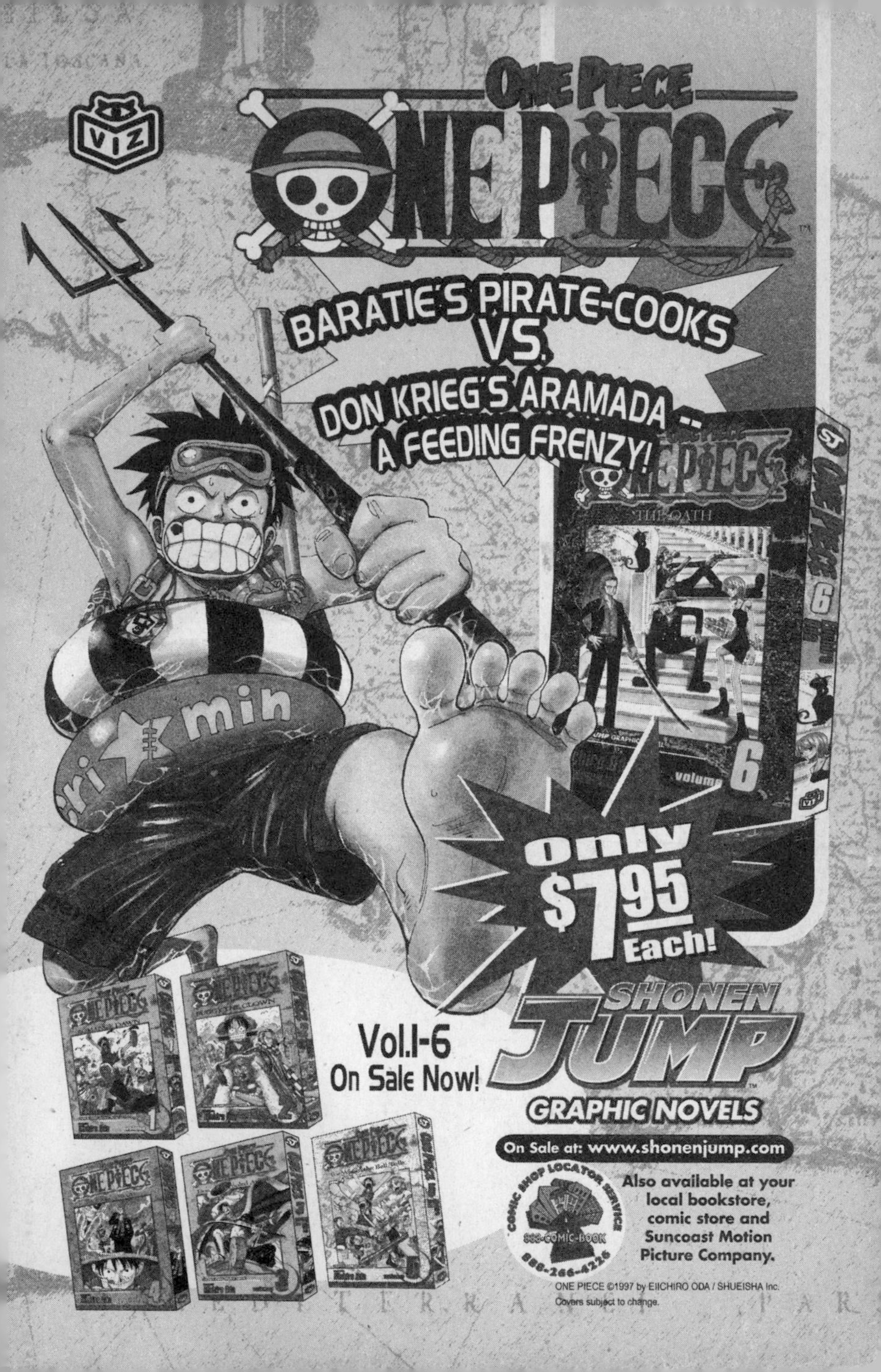
VIZ
ONE PIECE
ONE PIECE
BARATIE'S PIRATE-COOKS
VS.
DON KRIEG'S ARAMADA --
A FEEDING FRENZY!
ONE PIECE
THE OATH
volume 6
Only
$7.95
Each!
SHONEN
JUMP
GRAPHIC NOVELS
Vol.1-6
On Sale Now!
On Sale at: www.shonenjump.com
COMIC SHOP LOCATOR SERVICE
888-COMIC-BOOK
888-266-4226
Also available at your
local bookstore,
comic store and
Suncoast Motion
Picture Company.
ONE PIECE ©1997 by EIICHIRO ODA / SHUEISHA Inc.
Covers subject to change.